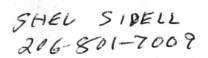

THE GREAT BOOK OF
SEATTLE SPORTS LISTS

THE GREAT BOOK OF SEATTLE SPORTS LISTS

By Mike Gastineau,
Steve Rudman, and Art Thiel

RUNNING PRESS
PHILADELPHIA · LONDON

Dedicated to my friends and family, who have
always encouraged me to follow my dreams.
And to Renee for everything.
—Mike Gastineau

To Julia.
—Art Thiel

To Ed, Karen, and Anna.
—Steve Rudman

9 8 7 6 5 4 3 2
Digit on the right indicates the number of this printing

Library of Congress Control Number: 2008926967
ISBN 978-0-7624-3522-7

Cover and Interior Designed by Matthew Goodman
Cover photograph by Michael A. Urban
Edited by Greg Jones

Running Press Book Publishers
2300 Chestnut Street
Philadelphia, PA 19103-4371

Visit us on the web!
www.runningpress.com

Contents

Acknowledgements

The authors would like to thank the many athletes, coaches, celebrities, media colleagues and friends who generously contributed their time and expertise to this project. The authors would also like to offer special thanks to *Seattle Post-Intelligencer* publisher Roger Oglesby, managing editor David McCumber, sports editor Nick Rousso and the P-I's outstanding library duo of Lytton Smith and Marsha Milroy. The authors would further like to thank Elizabeth Wales for her wise counsel.

In addition to the dozens of coaches, athletes, athletic administrators and long-time Seattle sports fans we relied upon to provide assistance, we are especially grateful for the great variety of source material provided in the following newspapers, books and web sites:

Newspapers: *Seattle Post-Intelligencer, Seattle Times, Tacoma News Tribune, Everett Herald, Wenatchee World, Spokane Spokesman Review*; Books: *Out Of Left Field* (Art Thiel), *100 Years of Husky Football* (Steve Rudman and Karen Chaves), *The Glory of Washington* (Jim Daves and W. Thomas Porter), *Bow Down To Washington* (Dick Rockne), *Torchy!* (Torchy Torrance), *Tales From The Seattle Mariners Dugout* (Kirby Arnold); *The Good, The Bad & The Ugly* (Chris Cluff), *Steve Raible's Tales From The Seahawks Sidelines* (Mike Sando), *Sonny Sixkiller's Huskies Sideline* (Bob Condotta), *Tales From the Seattle SuperSonics* (Slick Watts and Frank Hughes), *Playgrounds To The Pros* (Caroline Gallacci, Marc H. Blau and Doug McArthur), *Rain Check: Baseball In The Pacific Northwest* (edited by Mark Armour); Web Sites: http://www.historylink.org, http://www.seattlehockey.net, http://www.washingtonsportshalloffame.com, http://www.pclbaseball.com, http://www.baseballreference.com and http://www.retrosheet.com.

Funny thing about sports history: Fans and media claim to cherish the feats and people of the past, yet don't recall much of them.

Now they can—as long as followers of sports in Seattle and throughout the state of Washington buy this book, instead of indulging an idle thumb-through at the bookstore.

This book is the first comprehensive account of the Seattle sports market's legacy of achievements, failures, traditions, scandals, controversies, ironies and hilarities. Written in the ever-popular form of lists, this tour through our moss-draped deeds reveals a breadth and depth that belie Seattle's relatively late entry into the world of big-time American sports.

Local sports fans are often a little defensive when national pundits mock the paucity of team sports championships from the upper-left corner of the fruited plain. So what? We're getting there. Meantime, try finding a commercial airliner or logging on to your computer without our help, wise guys. And no salmon for you.

Fact is, once gathered in a single spot, deeds performed by athletes with state roots is impressive:

Kentucky Derby, Indianapolis 500, Daytona 500, Masters golf—all have champions from the state. Before World War II, our athletes embarrassed Hitler in the Fatherland. In the Cold War days, our athletes stunned the Soviet sports machine by land and sea. Medalists abound from Olympic Games, summer and winter. It was a Seattle man who was the first American atop Mt. Everest, and it was a Seattle outfit that was the first American team atop hockey's Stanley Cup.

The flip side is in heavy supply as well—the flops, missteps, blunders and colossal screw-ups that keep teams and athletes humble and give sports fans heartburn. Since one of sports' fundamental truths is that the scoreboard doesn't lie, we couldn't, either. If a team, athlete, coach or executive stepped on an upturned rake in a big way, the bruise is visible here.

Besides a salute to a plentiful sports legacy, what sets this tome apart are contributions from the history-makers themselves.

More than 40 current and former athletes and coaches, as well as local celebrities and media figures, responded to our request for their thoughts on sports subjects they know well.

From Pearl Jam and Sir Mix-A-Lot to Marv Harshman, Kasey Kahne and Sue Bird, a diverse sports community of participants and fans offered lists filled with humor, wryness, insight, passion and unpredictability. For the first time, readers will learn what astonishing things referees told Seahawks coach Mike Holmgren about bad calls; what Ichiro really thinks about Americans in general and players in particular; how George Karl and Gary Payton once "celebrated" a Christmas by angrily throwing things at each other; what it was like when Chip Hanauer flew his hydroplane upside down and Dave Niehaus drank with Casey Stengel until 5 a.m. Then there's the best Seattle sports parties ever thrown, courtesy of restaurateur Mick McHugh. Nor would a study of local sports culture be complete without a demonstration of the Huskies' contempt for the Cougars, and the Cougars' contempt for the Huskies.

The book concludes with a ranking of the 100 best athletes in state history. The great ones who didn't make the list reinforce the notion of how fortunate we've been to enjoy for more than a century the exploits of a superb collection of athletes, teams and feats that have enriched our lives and civic history.

—Mike Gastineau, Steve Rudman, Art Thiel
September 2008

As much as this book contains the best and worst of Seattle and Washington state's lore of ball and strikes, first downs and touchdowns, fantastic finishes and dull thuds, the events were shaped by influences far beyond the moments they happened. War, peace, fire, gold rushes, accidental encounters and improbable decisions created impacts beyond the daily headline of each. The following chronological list offers an original account of key points in the region's history that rippled through the sports culture to create permanent change.

25. Great Seattle Fire, 1889. In the aftermath of the June 6 inferno that consumed most of downtown Seattle, the city's political leaders placed a series of ads in eastern newspapers offering "honest work" to able-bodied young men willing to head west and help rebuild the city. Among the hundreds who came was William Goodwin, a former rugby player and rower at Yale. Goodwin taught University of Washington students how to play rugby, organized a team and proposed a match between UW students and other graduates of eastern colleges (Harvard, Yale and Brown) who had also headed west to help rebuild Seattle. On September 8, 1889, during preparations for the match, Goodwin's single scull arrived from the east, enabling him to introduce Washington students to rowing. Three months later, on Thanksgiving Day, the rugby match took place in a park located near the end of the Madison Street cable car line, marking the launch of what would become Husky football.

24. Klondike Gold Rush, 1898. Among the thousands lured to Seattle en route to the Klondike gold fields was Daniel E. Dugdale, a Peoria, IL, native. But instead of continuing on to the Yukon to prospect, Dugdale remained in the Queen City to speculate in real estate. Dugdale's dabblings not only made him wealthy, it forever altered the city's athletic landscape. A former major league catcher with the Kansas City Cowboys (1886) and Washington Senators (1894), Dugdale became Seattle's first sporting entrepreneur. He built two of city's earliest baseball fields (Yesler Way Park at 12th Avenue and Yesler Way, and Dugdale Park on a site that would one day become Sicks' Stadium) and organized many of its first professional teams, including the Klondikers, Rainmakers, Clamdiggers, Chinooks and Siwashes. Dugdale also helped found the Pacific Northwest League and later became owner of the Pacific Coast League's Seattle Giants, a forerunner of the Seattle Rainiers.

23. Hiram Conibear meets Bill Speidel, 1906. A Chicago native, Conibear held two jobs in 1906. He served as athletic trainer at the University of Chicago and performed similar duties for the Chicago White Sox. While working at the university, Conibear was introduced to Speidel, a second-year medical student who had captained and quarterbacked the 1903 UW football team. Speidel was so impressed with Conibear that he contacted UW athletic manager Lorin Grinstead and talked him into offering Conibear the job of UW athletic trainer, then talked Conibear into moving to Seattle. Shortly after Conibear arrived at the UW, Grinstead talked Conibear, who admitted he "didn't know one end of a boat from the other," into becoming Washington's crew coach. Conibear then persuaded George Pocock to abandon his boat-building business in Vancouver, BC, and set up shop on the Washington campus. Conibear coached Washington into national rowing prominence and Pocock built a fleet of shells that were used all over the world, and in several Olympic Games. Speidel later returned to Seattle and conducted his medical practice at Providence Hospital. His son, Bill Jr., became a prominent author and founder of the popular Seattle Underground Tour.

22. World War I armistice, 1918. Roscoe "Torchy" Torrance, a volunteer in the Student Army Training Corps, was scheduled to leave for artillery school at Fort Sill, OK, at the end of October 1918. But days before his departure, World War I ended when Turkey, followed by Austria-Hungary, capitulated and an armistice was declared. Instead of going off to fight in Europe, Torrance continued his studies at UW. The armistice enabled Torrance to become UW student body president, play baseball, serve as athletic property manager, and raise funds to build Husky Stadium. Hooked on the do-good, Torrance went on to help found the "101 Club" (it funded Helene Madison's 1932 Olympic trip); help Joe Gottstein launch Longacres Race Track; acquire the land for Emil Sick that became Sicks' Stadium; sign Fred Hutchinson to a pro baseball contract; help recruit football legend Hugh McElhenny to UW; help develop Seafair; and run the Washington March of Dimes campaign for two decades.

21. Darwin Meisnest's fundraisers, 1919. On November 10, 1919, during the first assembly of the school year, UW graduate student Darwin Meisnest opined that if Washington hoped to compete with California and Stanford, it needed a bigger and better football stadium and proposed that he spearhead a drive to build one. Twelve months later, on November 27, 1920, 30,000-seat Husky Stadium opened for business. Six years later, the Washington Pavilion (later Hec Edmundson Pavilion) opened for business after a fund-raising drive spearheaded by Meisnest, who had been appointed graduate manager (effectively the athletic director). Meisnest left UW in 1927 to become one of the four original trustees of the new Washington Athletic Club. It took Meisnest only a year to gain the controlling stock in the WAC, which he operated for more than a decade.

20. Stock market crash, 1929. Not long after the Washington Legislature banned gambling in January 1909, The Meadows, the state's first thoroughbred racing venue, went out of business. Starting in 1922, Joseph Gottstein and business associate William Edris embarked on a campaign to revive the sport. They got nowhere until the stock market crashed on October 28–29, 1929, triggering the Great Depression, which severely impacted the state's ability to generate revenue. With support from future senator Warren G. Magnuson, then a state representative, Gottstein and Edris enlisted another state representative, Joseph B. Roberts, to introduce House Bill 59, a measure that would legalize pari-mutuel wagering on horse races and guarantee that a five percent tax on the gross handle (total money wagered) would end up in the state's coffers. State lawmakers found the deal too appealing to pass up. The bill sailed through the House on February 20, 1933, passed the Senate three days later and was signed into law on March 19, 1933 by Gov. Clarence Martin. Gottstein wasted no time reviving the sport of kings. He founded the Washington Jockey Club three months later (June 20, 1933), took a 10-year lease on a 107-acre dairy farm near the Renton Junction, and hired architect B. Marcus Priteca to design a race track. Longacres opened 28 days after Priteca submitted his design.

19. Serial arsonist Robert Driscoll, 1935. Driscoll played an odd but significant role in shaping local sports history. In 1935, after his capture by police, Driscoll confessed that he had gone on an arson spree three years earlier (1932) during which he torched 115 different structures, including Dugdale Park, home of the Pacific Coast League's Seattle Indians. The fire not only destroyed the ballpark and three Rainier Valley homes near it, it forced the Indians to move their games to less-than-desirable Civic Stadium at Fifth Ave. N. and Harrison Street, which became the club's home for the next six years. When Emil Sick purchased the club in 1938 and renamed it the Rainiers, he determined Civic Stadium to be inadequate for his club and sought a location for a new ballpark. He settled on the corner of Rainier Ave. S. and S. Mc-Clellan Street, which happened to be a vacant lot thanks to Driscoll's torching of Dugdale Park. Sick's namesake creation, Sicks' Stadium, served as home to the Triple A Rainiers (and Angels) for more than 30 years. Without Driscoll's book of matches, no Sicks' Stadium. Without Sicks' Stadium, the American League would not have been able to expand to Seattle in 1969.

18. Harvey Cassill's big ideas, 1946. A one-time insurance salesman, Cassill came to UW as its new athletic director in 1946 intent on putting the school on the sporting map. He instituted UW's first home-and-home series with Notre Dame (1948-49), oversaw the construction of a 15,000-seat south-side addition to Husky Stadium (1950), convinced the NCAA to bring its men's national championships in track and field (1951) and basketball (1952) to Seattle and was instrumental in the formation of the Washington Advertising Association. The financial resources of the downtown booster group made it possible for UW to recruit on a national scale, but its excesses landed UW on NCAA probation for two years, forcing Cassill's resignation.

17. Ted Jones' APBA Gold Cup victory, 1950. The Seattle native designed and drove the Slo-Mo-Shun IV, the first prop-riding unlimited hydroplane, to victory in all three heats of the 1950 Gold Cup in Detroit, a triumph that carried with it far more than prize money and a trophy. The sport's rules at the time dictated that the Gold Cup race location be determined by the yacht club of the winning boat. Jones and the Slo-Mo-Shun IV represented the Seattle Yacht Club, which elected to defend the Cup in 1951 on Lake Washington. Jones' Gold Cup victory launched the hydroplane tradition that is the marquee event of Seafair, Seattle's annual summer celebration.

16. UW slush fund scandal, 1956. Several dominoes toppled after the NCAA slapped a two-year probation on UW athletics for condoning a secret fund to pay the school's football players. UW fired coach John Cherberg and forced athletic director Harvey Cassill's resignation. With all teams banned from NCAA postseason competition, the men's rowing team accepted an invitation to a 1958 race in Moscow against the Trud Club. The crew upset the Soviets in one of the greatest achievements in UW sports history, one that would not have occurred if UW hadn't been on probation. When Cassill departed, he was replaced by 31-year-old George Briggs, who tried to replace Cherberg with the highest-profile coach he could find, offering the job to Duffy Daugherty of Michigan State, Bear Bryant of Texas A&M and Bud Wilkinson of Oklahoma. All three turned him down, but Wilkinson suggested Darrell Royal, his former assistant and head coach at Mississippi State. So Briggs hired Royal, who lasted one year before departing for Texas. But during the interview process, Bryant told Briggs and UW booster Torchy Torrance that he had an assistant who would "make a great coach for somebody someday." That assistant was 29-year-old Jim Owens, whose 18 years at Washington not only elevated the football program in a way that no other coach ever had, but changed the balance of power between the Big 10 and Pac-10 conferences with Rose Bowl victories in 1960–61.

15. World's Fair, 1962. When far-off Seattle put on the World's Fair, 10 million people came and stories about the city appeared on the front page of the *New York Times* and cover of *LIFE* magazine. In order to display acres of exhibits, fair organizers went on a building spree, constructing, among other things, a venue to hold "The World of Tomorrow," an exhibit aimed at providing a glimpse of what the future might hold (nobody envisioned Benoit Benjamin and Jim McIlvaine). Six years after the "temporary" building went up, the Washington Coliseum (subsequently renamed the Seattle Coliseum) became the key asset in Seattle landing an NBA franchise. The building not only gave the city a modern venue for basketball and minor league hockey, it enabled Seattle to host hundreds of sports, music and ice events over the ensuing four decades that would not have taken place without it.

14. Sam Schulman and Gene Klein, 1966. The Los Angeles businessmen were partners in National General Corporation, an insurance and entertainment company whose subsidiary, Evergreen Theaters, distributed movies to Seattle theaters. They also both loved sports. The pair first collaborated in mid-1966 to purchase the American Football League's San Diego Chargers for $10 million, for which Klein became the front man. Later that year, they paid a $1.75 million expansion fee (borrowed money) for an NBA franchise that became the Seattle SuperSonics, Schulman serving as the front man. Schulman and Klein not only introduced Seattle to major league professional sports, they hired Dick Vertlieb, a 36-year-old investment securities representative, to help run the franchise. Vertlieb later became an advisor to the Nordstrom family when it sought an NFL franchise for Seattle, as well as the first CEO of the Seattle Mariners.

13. Passage of Forward Thrust, 1968. During a speech to the Rotary Club of Seattle on November 4, 1965, bond lawyer Jim Ellis called upon regional leaders to consider funding $815 million worth of capital improvements that included rapid transit, new parks, fire stations, swimming pools, a modern zoo and aquarium, low-income housing, rapid transit, Lake Washington clean-up and a domed stadium. In all, Ellis' "Forward Thrust" package included 12 major projects, of which seven eventually came to fruition. By agreeing to fund the King County Domed Stadium, voters enabled Seattle to obtain a Major League Baseball franchise (Mariners), a National Football League franchise (Seahawks) and attract more than 73 million fans to the facility over the next 24 years to watch thousands of events, including three NCAA Final Fours, a Pro Bowl, an NBA All-Star Game and an MLB All-Star Game.

12. Seattle's suit against the American League, 1970. After the Seattle Pilots were plucked out of bankruptcy court by Milwaukee car salesman Bud Selig and moved to Milwaukee, state attorney general Slade Gorton, on behalf of local governments, sued the American League for breach of contract, asking for $32 million in damages. The suit dragged on until 1976, when Seattle attorney (and future federal judge) William Dwyer argued so persuasively on behalf of the city that the American League offered to give Seattle a new baseball franchise in return for dropping the suit. The Seattle Mariners came into existence a year later.

11. Joe Kearney's judgment calls, 1971, 1974. Kearney spent only seven years as UW athletic director (1969–76), but made two decisions that had a profound effect on the history of Seattle sports. In 1971, after Tex Winter resigned as the school's basketball coach, Kearney picked Washington State's Marv Harshman as Winter's replacement from a field of candidates that included Central Washington's Dean Nicholson, Ohio State's Fred Taylor, Illinois State's Will Robinson and Grambling's Fred Hobdy. Harshman stayed on for 14 years, leading the Huskies to four 20-win seasons, two Pac-10 titles (1984–85) and five postseason appearances, including three trips to the NCAA Tournament. In December 1974, after football coach Jim Owens resigned, Kearney went through a succession of candidates to replace him, including Mike White of California, Douglas Porter of Howard University and Darryl Rogers of San Jose State. Kearney selected the last man he interviewed, Kent State's little-known Don James, who, over the ensuing 18 years (1975–92), became the greatest coach in Seattle sports history.

10. Huskies' Sun Bowl loss, 1986. Washington had enjoyed a successful 10-year run under coach Don James, winning two Rose Bowls and an Orange Bowl. But a crushing loss to Alabama in El Paso on Christmas Day, 1986, had a profound impact of James' thinking. The defeat, in which James watched Bobby Humphrey, Cornelius Bennett and the Crimson Tide destroy the Huskies with flat-out speed, convinced him that he needed to change the type of athlete he recruited. The Huskies needed to get faster and quicker. Without the change, Washington would never have acquired the athletes it needed to win the 1991 co-national championship.

9. Roger Jongewaard's persuasion, 1987. Because he was attempting to rid himself of the Mariners and acquire the San Diego Padres, and also because he was leery of drafting high school players, Mariners owner George Argyros did not want use the No. 1 overall pick in the 1987 June free agent draft on can't-miss prospect Ken Griffey Jr. Argyros preferred a less expensive and, in his view, a safer alternative, Cal State Fullerton right-hander Mike Harkey. Fortunately for the Mariners, Jongewaard, the club's director of scouting, convinced Argyros that the Mariners had to take Griffey. They did, signing him for $169,000. Griffey not only became the greatest player in the history of the franchise, he became the player most responsible for saving baseball in Seattle.

8. Nordstroms sell the Seahawks, 1988. The $80 million sale put the franchise into the clueless clutches of California real estate developer Ken Behring, who inherited a waiting list of 30,000 prospective season ticket buyers and alienated every last one of them, and several thousand more to boot. His purchase cost Seattle an opportunity to host the 1992 Super Bowl (NFL owners were prepared to award the game to Seattle because of the Nordstrom family, but wanted nothing to do with Behring), and his failed attempt to move the Seahawks to Los Angeles (and their profound mediocrity under his stewardship) killed interest in the team for years upon its return.

7. Slade Gorton's interventions, 1991, 1996. When Mariners owner Jeff Smulyan wanted to escape his Kingdome lease and move the club to Florida, Gorton used his clout as a U.S. senator to persuade Hiroshi Yamauchi, founder of Nintendo of Japan, to partner with several Seattle businessmen and purchase the franchise. Without Gorton's intervention, the team likely would have left town. In 1996, Gorton intervened again when the King County Council balked at swiftly approving bonds needed to pay for the construction of Safeco Field. Gorton brokered a lease arrangement that satisfied club owners and launched the construction of the new ballpark, which opened to rave reviews in 1999 and made the Mariners one of the most successful business operations in sports.

6. UW hires Barbara Hedges, 1991. Hired as the anti-Mike Lude, her predecessor as athletic director, Hedges came from USC under orders from UW president Bill Gerberding to get the department into compliance with Title IX federal law mandating gender equality, as well as upgrading non-revenue sports. She implemented a $90 million fundraising effort and created new and improved athletic facilities. She also pushed for higher academic standards for athletes. What Hedges didn't do was pay enough attention to the school's cash cow, football, and the doings of her department underlings. Football coach Rick Neuheisel ran afoul of NCAA rules multiple times and was caught in a betting-pool scandal that led to his firing in 2003. A subsequent department investigation discovered the compliance director was out of compliance with NCAA rules and that a renegade team doctor was drugging the softball team. Citing "glitches," Hedges resigned in 2004. The once-dominant football program collapsed into one of its worst periods, failing to make a bowl for six years through 2008.

5. Billy Joe Hobert scandal, 1992. When UW quarterback Hobert accepted an illegal $50,000 loan from an Idaho businessman, he set off a chain of events that led to a two-year NCAA probation, the resignation of icon coach Don James, a long-term deterioration of the football program and a significant loss of the program's fan base. After Billy Joe took the dough, nothing was ever as good as it was.

4. Woody Woodward hires Lou Piniella, 1993. The Mariners' general manager during the club's renaissance, Woodward was often castigated for poor deal making, talent judgments and work habits. But it was his friendship with one-time Yankees hero Lou Piniella that proved pivotal in drawing the well-regarded manager to a moribund franchise that was the slowest expansion team in modern American sports history to reach a winning record (15 seasons). Piniella was told by many in baseball that the game would never work in Seattle, but new ownership and the force of

Piniella's personality helped break the losing culture that had swallowed the team. The first playoff team in 1995 built momentum for a new publicly funded stadium, and the 2001 season of 116 wins shoved the Mariners into national prominence.

3. Kingdome tiles fall, 1994. When four wood acoustic tiles, damaged by leaks, tumbled from the Kingdome ceiling two hours before a Mariners game in July, it set off a chain of events no one could have forecast. The ceiling failure doomed the Dome, ending Seattle's involvement with the NCAA tourney's Final Four. It also forced the Mariners into an American League record 20-game road trip, which the principals involved agreed created a team-wide bonding that, a year later, helped the Mariners' six-week charge to the AL West title. The Kingdome's physical vulnerability also prompted the Seahawks to attempt to flee to Los Angeles. After the NFL stopped the move and helped force a sale, new owner Paul Allen demanded and received a new publicly funded stadium like the Mariners. Twenty-four years after its creation, the Dome was imploded, but not before spawning two sport-specific stadiums that anchored major league football and baseball in Seattle.

2. Testaverde's non-touchdown, 1998. On December 6, 1998 at the Meadowlands, the Seahawks stopped quarterback Vinny Testaverde of the New York Jets about a half-yard shy of a touchdown. Head linesman Earnie Frantz signaled TD, and referee Phil Luckett, without benefit of instant replay, let the call stand. Because of the play, the Seahawks lost and missed the postseason by one game. The Seahawks fired head coach Dennis Erickson and replaced him with Mike Holmgren, who would take the Seahawks to the postseason six times in his first ten years, including a Super Bowl appearance following the 2005 season. Testaverde's non-touchdown also resulted in the NFL adopting instant replay.

1. Gary Payton's training-camp boycott, 2002. At the time, it seemed the typical holdout—a superstar wanted an extension and a raise, and his Sonics employers balked. But Payton's holdout began the disillusionment of owner Howard Schultz, who previously was convinced his success with Starbucks coffee would translate into NBA championships after he and a group of Seattle wealthies bought the team in 2000. Schultz discovered Payton—whom he found to be unpardonably selfish—and alcoholic forward Vin Baker were impervious to his charms. At the same time, the economic limitations of KeyArena, despite the fact that it had been upgraded seven years earlier to applause from locals as well as NBA commissioner David Stern, became burdensome when Schultz could get no traction with politicians and fans for another publicly funded upgrade. When mediocre basketball results were added to the mix, Schultz leaped at the chance in 2006 to make a profit on a sale and get out of the NBA. The $350 million price Schultz fetched from Clay Bennett of Oklahoma City made Schultz and his investor group whole, but it ultimately led to the Sonics' move—following a week-long trial and a $45 million settlement with the City of Seattle—to Oklahoma City on July 2, 2008, thus ending the franchise's 41-year stint in the Emerald City. If only Payton had reported to training camp on time.

Depending on your age and sports passions, you will remember where you were and what you were doing when you experienced one or more of these moments.

10. Cougars celebrate in the Dawghouse, November 22, 1997. For long-pained Washington State football fans, no day was ever better. The Cougars qualified for the Rose Bowl for the first time in 67 years by beating Washington 41–35. Best of all, they did it at Husky Stadium, where they also shook bouquets of roses in the faces of University of Washington fans. Their former and most famous quarterback, Jack Thompson, spoke for generations of Cougars when he stated, "We've been playing the underdog for so many years. This is the culmination of a lot of dreams."

9. End of two eras: Longacres, September 21, 1992; Kingdome, March 26, 2000. The final race at the 59-year-old thoroughbred track went off without commentary so the 23,258 patrons could simply listen to the pounding of the horses' hooves. Hundreds of fans poured onto the track to gather dirt as a souvenir while others wandered aimlessly around the Longacres infield, wishing it weren't. The Kingdome was only 24 when it died, imploded by the ravenous demands for money from the pro sports franchises it housed, and the inability of King County to maintain it properly. It perished $40 million in debt, still being paid by the taxes collected for Qwest Field.

8. Pilots move to Milwaukee, April 1, 1970; Seahawks move to Los Angeles, February 3, 1996; Sonics move to Oklahoma City OK'ed, April 17, 2008. All three franchises have been vulnerable to predation. The Pilots left and were replaced; the Seahawks move was thwarted, and the Sonics move was given the green light on April 17, 2008. The Pilots had no chance, playing in a 30-year-old minor league park for an under-funded ownership group, but a successful lawsuit brought the Mariners in 1977 as compensation. The Seahawks were owned by Ken Behring, a man as loathed by the NFL as he was by Seahawks fans, who was turned back from LA and forced to sell. The Sonics move to Oklahoma City was approved by NBA owners, but faced multiple lawsuits. Why is everything so hard here?

7. Trading "Babe Ruth," February 10, 2000. The inevitable swap, forced by Ken Griffey Jr., himself, was accompanied by the realization that Seattle had seen the best and brightest of a generation—398 home runs, 10 All-Star appearances, incredible feats in center field—and might not see someone like him again. As team president Chuck Armstrong put it to thunderstruck Mariners fans, "We just traded Babe Ruth."

6. Two come-from-behind wins in one day, September 19, 1995. During a six-week stretch in which improbable rallies seemed an everyday occurrence, the pair on September 19 wound up among the most memorable in Seattle sports history. The first, a 5–4 triumph over the Rangers fueled by an unlikely two-run run pinch homer by Doug Strange, rocked the Kingdome and brought the Mariners to within one game of tying the Angels for the AL West lead. Just as the game concluded, the local 11 p.m. TV news reported that a vote to build a new ballpark for the Mariners, which had zero chance two months earlier, seemed to be passing. Although the stadium bill eventually lost by about 1,000 votes, the momentum for a new ballpark was sufficient for the Legislature to approve new taxes that created Safeco Field.

5. Seahawks reach the Super Bowl, January 22, 2006. After the Seahawks beat Carolina for the NFC championship, thousands of face-painted fans swept from Qwest Field to celebrate throughout Pioneer Square the Seahawks' first trip to the Super Bowl. The Seahawks hadn't done squat in the playoffs in 21 years, and suddenly they were in the biggest game in American sports.

4. The parade for Queen Helene, August 26, 1932. After returning to Seattle from the Olympics in Los Angeles, where she won three gold medals in swimming, Seattle threw 19-year-old Helene Madison the largest ticker-tape parade for an individual athlete in state history. More than 200,000 people—Seattle's population was 350,000—lined Second Avenue.

3. International man of mystery saves the Mariners, January 13, 1992. The announcement was so big, delivered in front of a humongous throng of reporters and cameras at the Madison Hotel, that it made the front page of *The New York Times* and was the top story on the *CBS Evening News.* A man few had heard of, Hiroshi Yamauchi, CEO of Nintendo of Japan, led a consortium of smaller Seattle investors to purchase the Mariners, the worst franchise in baseball, for $100 million. Jeff Smulyan and his fellow AL owners were upset that they were thwarted in moving the club to Tampa, where a domed stadium sat empty. Despite months of resistance to the Japanese-led ownership, political and baseball pressure finally brought about sale approval.

2. Don James resigns in protest, August 22, 1993. When the long-time coach abruptly announced 12 days before the season that he would no longer lead a UW football program that he had elevated to unparalleled heights, the news rocked Husky Nation. Upset with sanctions imposed by the Pac-10 after an investigation into recruiting rules violations, James fell on his sword. The best modern era of UW football ended with a thud that still echoes.

1. Seattle celebrates the Sonics, June 4, 1979. Three days after they won the NBA championship, Seattle threw a downtown parade for the Sonics and the city's first modern pro championship. The unofficial public holiday, which drew more than 300,000 fans, came off with little violence and few arrests as coach Lenny Wilkens and players waved from cars and were hailed at a civic presentation. The 300,000 that attended that rally would have found it inconceivable that the Sonics would no longer exist three decades later.

For no reason other than randomness, some sports years click. Many more clank, especially around here. Here are three good ones from a small field, and three bad ones from a large field.

BEST

3. 1997

Mariners went 90–72 and won the AL West.

Sonics went 57–25 and reached the Western Conference semifinals.

Huskies went 8–4 and defeated Michigan State in the Aloha Bowl.

UW basketball team won 20 and played in the National Invitational Tournament.

2. 1936

University of Washington eight-man crew captured the Olympic gold medal in Berlin.

Also at the Olympics, UW swimmer Jack Medica won a gold and two silver medals, and UW star Ralph Bishop won a gold medal as part of the USA basketball team.

UW basketball team had a 17-game winning streak and finished 25–7 (there was no NCAA tournament) and fell one game shy of qualifying for the Olympic Games.

UW football team went 7–2–1 and qualified for the Rose Bowl for the first time since 1925.

Seattle hosted its first world championship boxing match and a local fighter, Freddie Steele, won it.

1. 1984

Seahawks posted their best record at 12–4 and won the AFC West.

UW football team went 11–1 and defeated Oklahoma in the Orange Bowl to finish No. 2 in the country.

UW basketball team went 24–7 and played in the NCAA tournament.

Although the Mariners went 75–88, they unveiled a pair of notable rookies, Alvin Davis (Rookie of the Year) and Mark Langston (runner-up for Rookie of the Year).

At the Olympic Games in Los Angeles, Washington athletes won 14 gold, six silver and two bronze medals.

Seattle hosted the NCAA Final Four for the first time since 1952.

WORST
3. 1992

Seahawks went 2–14 with one of the worst offenses in NFL history (140 points).

Mariners went 64–98 and finished seventh (and last) in the AL West, 32 games behind.

Sonics went 47–35, but were ousted 4–1 by Utah in the Western Conference semifinals.

UW basketball team finished 12–17.

UW football team went 9–3 but lost to Michigan in the Rose Bowl.

2. 1969

The Washington football team went 1–9, outscored 304–116 (lone win was a 1–8 WSU team in the Apple Cup).

Pilots went 64–98 and then moved to Milwaukee, becoming the Brewers.

Sonics finished 30–52, next-to-last in the Western Division.

The Totems of the Western Hockey League finished fourth with a 33–30–11 mark, the last time the franchise had a winning record.

Racial turmoil plagued the Washington football program.

1. 2008

The UW basketball team went 16-17 and failed to make the NCAA Tournament.

UW fielded an 0-12 football team, the worst in its 119-year football history.

Washington State went 2-11 and allowed a PAC-10-record 570 points.

A sporting institution for 41 years, the Sonics went 20–62 in their final season in Seattle and then moved to Oklahoma City, becoming the Thunder.

Mike Holmgren, the most successful coach in Seahawks history, resigned.

The Mariners, projected to contend in the AL West, instead finished 61–101 and failed to make the postseason for the seventh consecutive season.

Yeah, this list is a little thin. What of it? We still have Mount Rainier, and try to get fresh Dungeness crab in Boston. Yeah, we're defensive about not winning many big-time championships. See if we ever let you use Microsoft software again.

11. Washington football, 1910. The Huskies didn't win their first national opinion-poll championship in 1959 (Helms Foundation) or in 1991 (coaches poll), but way back in 1910 when the Libby Foundation, a recognized selector that voted on national champions through the 1950s, tabbed Gil Dobie's team. Washington went 6–0 against Lincoln High School, Puget Sound, Whitman, Idaho, Washington State and Oregon State, outscoring the bunch 150–8.

10. Pay 'N Pak softball, 1986. The Seattle fast pitch team had an amazing run in the 1980s, winning national championships in 1980, 1982, 1985, 1986 and 1987, but no year topped 1986. That year, Pay 'N Pak, led by pitching ace Jimmy Moore, became the first team to win three major titles in one year: the International Softball Congress world tournament, the Olympic Sports Festival gold medal, and the American Softball Association's national tournament (Pay 'N Pak's record in the 1980s: 873–187, .824).

9. Seattle Metropolitans, 1917. After the Montreal Canadiens defeated the Mets 8–4 in Game 1 in the best-of-five series at the Seattle Ice Arena, Seattle ripped off three consecutive victories—6–1, 4–1, 9–1—to become the first American-based team to capture the Stanley Cup. Bernie Morris tallied 14 of Seattle's 23 goals in the series and future Hockey Hall of Fame goalie Hap Holmes recorded a 2.90 goals-against average.

8. Kirkland Little League, 1982. Not many people gave the Kirkland National All-Stars a chance to win the Little League World Series in Williamsport, PA. The favorite, Taiwan, had won five consecutive titles, 10 of the previous 13, and had never been defeated in the championship game. But Taiwan had no answer for Cody Webster, a five-foot-six, 170-pound 12-year-old with a 70 mph fastball and a very big bat. Webster, who fanned 13 batters in Kirkland's 5–3 opening victory over Sarasota, FL, threw a two-hitter at Taiwan and struck out 12, including the last three batters in the sixth and final inning. Webster also belted a 280-foot home run, the longest in LLWS history, as Kirkland won 6–0.

7. Seattle Storm basketball, 2004. The Storm captured the city's first pro championship since 1979 on October 12 when Lauren Jackson, Sue Bird and playoff Most Valuable Player Betty Lennox collectively led Seattle to a 2–1 WNBA championship-series victory over the Connecticut Sun. The final two games, played at KeyArena, each attracted a throng of more than 17,000 fans.

6. UW Women's Cross Country, 2008. The UW runners capped a perfect season by winning the NCAA championship with 79 points, beating runner-up Oregon with ease.

5. Washington volleyball, 2005. Not only did coach Jim McLaughlin's Huskies, making their 10th postseason appearance, defeat Nebraska 30–26, 30–25 and 30–26 at San Antonio's Alamadome to win the NCAA championship, they became just the second program in history to sweep through the tournament by winning all six of their postseason matches in three games.

4. Washington women's crew, 1997. Between 1981 and 2001, UW captured 11 Intercollegiate Rowing Association or NCAA rowing championships, none more emphatically than the varsity eight boat's victory in 1997 at Lake Natoma, near Sacramento. Two factors made it a landmark triumph: It marked the university's first national championship in any NCAA-sanctioned sport, and UW's six-second margin of victory over Massachusetts and Princeton was its largest in any of the 11 championship races.

3. Washington football, 1991. Three UW teams (1959, 1960, 1984) before the 1991 edition came within one victory of pulling off an undefeated season. The 1991 team not only did it, it did it emphatically, flattening 12 opponents, including Michigan in the Rose Bowl, by a combined score of 461–101. The Huskies scored 40 or more points seven times and 50 or more four times. In the season's final polls, the Huskies were named national champions by the coaches (they finished No. 2 to Miami in the *Associated Press* poll).

2. Washington men's crew, 1936. On August 14, UW's eight-oar rowing scull, coached by Al Ulbrickson and containing Robert Moch (coxswain), Roger Morris (bow), Charles Day (No. 2 seat), Gordon Adam (No. 3 seat), John White (No. 4 seat), Jim McMillin (No. 5 seat), George Hunt (No. 6 seat), Joe Rantz (No. 7 seat) and Don Hume (stroke), slashed through the 2,000-meter Lake Grunau course in 6:25.4 to win the Olympic gold medal in Berlin with Adolph Hitler watching from a boathouse balcony. This marked the first international triumph by a team from Seattle. "I know it didn't make Hitler very happy," Morris told the *Post-Intelligencer's* Dan Raley years later, "But we weren't there to make him happy."

1. Seattle SuperSonics, 1979. Although the Sonics had lost starting center Marvin Webster in free agency to the New York Knicks, they started the season 7–0 and won 20 of their first 26 en route to a 52–30 finish. Once in the playoffs, the Sonics beat the Lakers, Suns and Bullets, capturing 12 of 17 postseason games, including a 97–93 win over Washington on June 1 that made celebrities out of Dennis Johnson, John Johnson, Gus Williams, Jack Sikma, Lonnie Shelton and Paul Silas—and provoked a downtown victory parade that drew 300,000 people.

No person in Seattle has served more cocktails to more sports fans than Mick McHugh. Owner of several restaurants and bars in his Seattle days, he is best known as the genial proprietor of legendary Pioneer Square bistro F.X. McRory's, which opened across the street from the Kingdome in November 1977. It continues today serving sports fans heading to Qwest Field and Safeco Field.

5. Seahawks beat the Patriots, December 18, 1983.
A special win needed a special celebration. The win put the Seahawks in the NFL playoffs for the first time. A Patriots fan helped fuel the celebration. This guy came up to me and said, "I'm from Boston. My name is John O'Brien. This win was big for the Seahawks. This calls for a round on the house and I'd like to do that." I said, "OK, let me tell the bartenders." He said, "No, not drinks. I think we should give everyone a round . . .of oysters. Everyone gets a half-dozen." I said, "Oh my God! I've got to talk to my shucker and see if I have enough." I went to the shucker and we shucked oysters for an hour and a half. It was a huge deal. A $1,600 tab, plus tip.

4. Spencer Haywood returns to Seattle, January 7, 1976.
In October 1975, the Sonics traded the town's only superstar, Spencer Haywood, to the New York Knicks. It was a very emotional trade for the city. So the Knicks came to Seattle for the first time with Spencer and the Coliseum was packed. The Sonics won a close game and everyone flooded back over to Jake's (McHugh at the time owned Jake O'Shaughnessy's, walking distance from the Seattle Center and the Coliseum). Up to the bar came Sonics owner Sam Schulman. He had his GM, Zollie Volchok, behind him and they're both about 30 years older than anyone in the place. Sam worked his way to the bar and says, "I'd like to buy a round for the house." I got on the microphone and said, "Mr. Schulman is here and he'd like to buy you a drink." A huge cheer went up. Sam loved it. He loved mixing with the fans. Everyone ordered doubles. We had a pretty good tab. I gave it to him. He handed it to Zollie and said, "Pay the man."

3. Seahawks owner makes good on a promise, November 8, 1981.
Elmer Nordstrom was the son of John W. Nordstrom, who founded the first Nordstrom store in downtown Seattle after the Klondike gold rush. He and his family were the original owners of the Seahawks. Elmer's wife, Kitty, was a second cousin of my mother, Alice. We were up at Hood Canal at their house one summer and my mom said, "Elmer, did you see where Sam Schulman bought a round for the house at Mickey's restaurant? How about you buying a round for the house at F.X. McRory's?" Elmer said if the Seahawks ever beat the Steelers, he'd do it. As luck would have it, they beat the Steelers the next year at the Kingdome. After the game, who came toddling over but Elmer and Kitty Nordstrom. He was 76, not the kind of guy who's coming in here after a game. They were both dressed to the nines. We didn't have a stage for them to stand on, so I ran out into the alley and got a couple plastic milk crates and there they were: Elmer and his wife standing behind the bar announcing to the crowd that they were buying a round.

2. Seahawks win the NFC Championship, January 22, 2006. Best day, business-wise, in F. X. McRory's history. From 8 a.m. to 10 p.m. we were packed. Pre-game, in-game, post-game. Everyone was eating the good stuff and drinking the good stuff. Mike Gastineau helped me serve champagne to the crowd during the post-game celebration. Maybe he was a little too revved up because he referred to me on the microphone as "Mick McRory."

1. M's win game, and an election (almost), September 18–19, 1995. The Mariners were in the middle of the miraculous run to their first AL West title at the same time an election was going to decide whether to publicly fund a new ballpark. (Even though election-night results showed the ballot measure winning, it eventually lost by about 1,000 votes, leaving the state Legislature to create new taxes for what became Safeco Field). KJR wanted to broadcast 24 hours to encourage the voters. No one had ever done a 24-hour party before. So I had to call the liquor board to get approval because we were supposed to be closed from 2 to 6 a.m. The liquor board wanted to know how many people would be there from 2 to 6. I said, "Probably the on-air guy, an engineer, and the janitors." But we ended up with quite a crowd. It was a huge deal, huge. That night, Seattle grew up. We pushed Seattle onto the stage of big-time sports. It was nuts in here. I got cigars out of the cigar case and handed them out. There were people lined up out the door to get in.

In the desert of team championships in big-time Northwest sports, the locals have come close numerous times, and second often. Agonizingly close. Painfully close. Mortifyingly close. For want of a shot here, a hit there, a fair call by the refs, the region could be belly-button deep in ticker tape. Alas, no. Here's the list of coulda-shoulda-woulda.

10. 1977 Sounders, 14–12; 1982 Sounders, 18–14. Twice a middling regular season turned spectacular in the playoffs for the North American Soccer League Sounders. Behind a great defense that gave up only two goals in five postseason games, the Sounders reached Soccer Bowl 1977 in Portland against the heralded New York Cosmos. But Pelé and Georgio Chinaglia proved too much; the Cosmos won 2–1. A title rematch in 1982 in San Diego had the same result, Chinaglia scoring the game's only goal for the NASL title.

9. 1983 Seahawks, 9–7. Reaching the NFL playoffs for the first time in the franchise's eight-year history, the Seahawks opened the postseason by crushing Denver 31–7 as Dave Krieg tossed three TD passes. The Seahawks then scored one of the biggest upsets in NFL postseason history when they traveled to Miami and knocked off the defending AFC champion Dolphins 27–20 in the Orange Bowl. But in the AFC title game, the Los Angeles Raiders denied the Seahawks a trip to the Super Bowl by jumping out to a 27–0 lead and cruising to a convincing 31–14 win in Los Angeles.

8. 1996 Sonics, 64–18. Good as the Gary Payton–Shawn Kemp tandem was, the Sonics were overshadowed by the 72–10 Chicago Bulls, who welcomed back Michael Jordan after a two-year "retirement" with one of the great seasons in NBA history. The Sonics split the season series, and looked strong in the run-up. But the Bulls dashed any bravado quickly, racing to a 3–0 series lead. Seattle won Games 4 and 5 at home, sending the series back to Chicago, but the Bulls opened up a 17-point lead in the third quarter and cruised to an 87–75 victory and the NBA title.

7. 1959 UW football, 10–1; 1960, 10–1. The renaissance of Huskies football under coach Jim Owens began with back-to-back single-loss seasons, just missing what passes for national championships in college. On October 17, 1959, the Huskies lost at home to seventh-ranked Southern California 22–15, a defeat that dropped UW from No. 18 in the national polls to out of the rankings. The Huskies rallied to finish eighth, but could climb no higher since final polls then were conducted before the bowl season. Washington routed Wisconsin 44–8 in the Rose Bowl. In 1960, the perfect season was ruined by a 15–14 home loss to Navy. UW was sixth in the final Associated Press poll, then beat national champ Minnesota 17–7 in the Rose Bowl. The Helms Foundation, then a recognized selector, awarded Washington its mythical title, but national recognition was otherwise elusive.

6. 1958 Seattle U. basketball, 23–6. Behind star forward Elgin Baylor, the Chieftains reached the NCAA championship game opposite Adolph Rupp's Kentucky Wildcats. The Chieftains led by three at the half and 60–58 with seven minutes remaining, but Kentucky, with Vern Hatton scoring 30 points, blew ahead and won 84–72. Baylor scored 25 points for Seattle U. but was 9 for 32.

5. 1978 SuperSonics, 47–35. With the homecourt advantage, the unlikely Sonics were three-point favorites to beat the Washington Bullets in Game 7 and win the NBA title despite a 117–82 road pummeling in Game 6. A tight contest throughout, the Bullets sealed a 105–99 victory when center Wes Unseld hit two free throws with 12 seconds to play.

4. 1984 Huskies, 11–1. For a showdown at Southern Cal November 10, the Huskies were 9–0 and ranked No. 1. A 16–7 loss to the Trojans not only cost the Huskies a possible national championship and a berth in the Rose Bowl, it sent them for the first time to the Orange Bowl. Even though they beat heavily favored and second-ranked Oklahoma 28–17, the Huskies finished second in the final AP poll to undefeated BYU.

3. 1994 Sonics, 63–19. Pacific Division champs, top-seeded in the West and a title favorite, the Sonics won the first two opening-round games against the lowly Nuggets, then proceeded to collapse twice in Denver and once at home, losing Game 5 in OT. It was the first time in NBA history an eighth seed beat a top seed, an epic humiliation.

2. 2005 Seahawks, 13–3. Seattle had multiple opportunities to defeat the Pittsburgh Steelers in Super Bowl XL, but a series of dubious officiating calls and numerous misplays (especially dropped passes and broken coverages) of their own relegated the Seahawks to 21–10 losers in their first appearance in the national holiday.

1. 2001 Mariners, 116–46. No major league team ever won more regular-season games without winning the World Series than these guys. But after their record-breaking regular season, as well as the horrors of 9/11, it was never the same. In the Division Series, they barely squeezed past Cleveland 3–2. In the ALCS against what was suddenly the nation's team, New York, the Mariners hit just .211 and lost 4–1.

Eight Things that Made the 1979 Sonics World Champions :: Fred Brown

Drafted out of Iowa after averaging 28 points per game in 1971, Downtown Freddy Brown became as synonymous as anyone with the history of the Super Sonics. He spent his entire career in a Seattle jersey and his number 32 was retired in 1986. He captained the 1979 Sonics, who hold the unique distinction of being the only NBA champions to not have a single player in the Basketball Hall of Fame.

8. In 1979, "We Are Family" Applied to More than Just the Pirates.
First of all, I think we cared about each other and were interested in each other on and off the floor. We were family-oriented. That took time for us to grow into—striving for teamwork above individual. And we would not allow any player to get down on himself. We did not allow negative stuff that was written or said to get in the way.

7. Hard Work on Defense and in Setting Picks Was Rewarded. We understood everyone wanted to be an offensive guy; there's not a player out there who doesn't want to be an offensive star. We made a point of trying to reward guys who were more defensive-oriented with offensive opportunities. We were a great passing team and we rewarded guys for hard work. J.J. (John Johnson) was the setup guy and everything ran through him. He was a stellar defensive player and a great passer.

6. The Toughness of Paul Silas and Lonnie Shelton. Paul would knock you down and then pick you up and smile like he didn't mean to do it. Lonnie would just knock you down and dare you to get back up. Paul worked to get guys space on the offensive end. He drove guys like Maurice Lucas, Elvin Hayes and Truck Robinson crazy. They wanted to kill him because they knew his antics and tactics and they didn't think too kindly of him. Paul knew how to take advantage of his skills. His offensive rebounds were high because he missed so many shots.

5. Remember, Everyone Has a Mother. We went to Phoenix to play the Suns in Game 6 of the Western Conference Finals down 3–2. It was Mother's Day. The thing that got our goats was they handed out flowers to all the moms and Paul Westphal (Suns captain) made a comment about winning the game for all the Suns' moms. We took it as a challenge. It was OUR Mother's Day as well. No way were we coming out of there without a win. Phoenix was outstanding. What I remember most is we were able to collectively take them out of their comfort zone with our defense. We made several tough defensive plays. Lonnie did an outstanding job on Truck Robinson, D.J. (Dennis Johnson) did a great job on Westphal, and Jack Sikma was great on Alvan Adams.

4. Timing Was Everything on Defense. We didn't double-team anyone straight up. We'd wait for them to dribble the ball once and then swarm them and force them to go where we wanted. We were really good at knowing which way to funnel players, especially the other teams' stars. We pushed them to where we wanted them to go and then took advantage of them trying to pass out of those situations. We were good at taking a guy's vision away.

31

3. It Was Still the Flex Before It Was the Triangle . . . and the Sonics Ran It Well. We were great as a team at the two-man game and we could use any two guys in the combination. We learned that from the best because no one was better at playing the two-man game than Lenny Wilkens. I remember playing with Lenny and watching him run pick and rolls with everyone...Don Smith and Don Kojis and Spencer Haywood.

2. The Coach. Lenny was the classic player's coach. He'd only been out of the league a couple years and he really understood the players. He set the tone that if we were going to win we had to get along. If you couldn't do that you weren't on the team. He had one huge immeasurable thing, too. He was a calming effect on us. He was always so controlled. Seeing him get mad was a scary thing because he didn't do it often. One thing that set him off was complacency. A couple times we'd start to forget about our team concept and he would loudly put us back on the right track. But usually he was completely controlled when talking to us. He was a huge inspiration for us in terms of credentials and knowledge.

1. No Hall Of Famers. We were ultimate team players. You wouldn't expect to see a Hall of Famer. With that said, when you look at D.J.'s career in Phoenix and in Boston you can make a strong argument that he should be in the Hall of Fame. But in terms of the rest of us, we might have been the best to ever win the NBA title in terms of pure teamwork. We needed to perform on our level to be successful, striving for teamwork above individual.

What Made the 2001 Mariners So Good
:: Jamie Moyer

Quietly, Jamie Moyer became the winningest pitcher in Mariners history, racking up 145 wins between 1996 and 2006. He was 20–6 in 2001 when the M's won an American League-record 116 games.

5. Offense was relentless, whatever the task. We were fundamentally sound; runners were moved via bunt, or hit and run, or hit behind the runner, or a fly ball to score a run. Not only did we have the ability, we had the type of guys willing to do it.

4. Defense was outstanding. (The M's not only led the AL in fielding, they made 33 fewer errors than the average AL team.) Defense comes from dedication, but you have to stay focused. That may have come from so many guys having great offensive years. When a guy has good offensive stats, there's a potential carryover into the field. Our starting pitching helped too, because we all had good years and worked quickly.

3. Bullpen was consistent and willing to work. If you had to pitch two or three innings, or pitch for two or three consecutive days, it was not a problem. Their attitude was "we can do this."

2. Starting pitching was healthy, experienced and competitive. We were competitive in two ways. Among ourselves: You wanted to keep up your responsibility. You didn't want to be the guy sloughing off. Against the opponent: Guys prepared well and brought a lot of confidence to the team. That kept everyone in the game. There's a lot to be said for how a pitcher can help his team.

1. Manager and coaching staff were committed to whatever it took. Lou Piniella had a passion for winning. He also cared about his players. You felt that. It was genuine. He looked you in the eye and talked to you like a human being. If he saw you working hard, he was going to go to the wall for you. When you saw him take losses as hard as he did…he was your manager, but it often felt as if he was another teammate. Ultimately, the 2001 Mariners were experts at preparation, winning, camaraderie, confidence and accountability—all was contagious.

A derided second-round pick, Lofa Tatupu of USC became the anchor of the Seahawks' 2005 defense at middle linebacker, and made the Pro Bowl in his rookie year. He only got better over the next three seasons, but the 2005 Hawks that made the team's first Super Bowl appearance remain special. Here's why he thinks it happened.

10. Heart. Often dubbed the underdog in many games, we kept proving so-called "experts" wrong, reeling off a record streak of 11 consecutive victories.

9. Maniacs on special teams. Blocking four field goals…nothing was a sure thing. A kickoff team that pursued the ball like wild dogs, just punishing ball carriers.

8. Dominating D-line. Fast and incredibly strong, they held up blockers for three (allegedly) undersized linebackers to make plays. Finished No. 5 in rush defense.

7. Opportunistic defense. Recorded many turnovers (16 interceptions and 11 fumbles) resulting in many points for our offense.

6. Number 37. Shaun Alexander was virtually unstoppable en route to capturing the NFL MVP award.

5. Quarterback. Pro Bowl pick Matt Hasselbeck orchestrated numerous lopsided victories, despite 10 games in which he did not have his two starting receivers.

4. Offensive line. Boasting three Pro Bowlers in the starting five, they paved lanes for Alexander and protected Hassel's back. The heart was 13-year veteran fullback Mack Strong, who blew up linebackers for Alexander, and made the Pro Bowl as well.

3. Defensive front seven. Relentless in getting after the QB, we finished No. 1 in sacks.

2. No. 1 offense in the NFL. Defenses struggled to keep pace with this high-tempo attack.

1. Fans at Qwest. Teams changed their game plans based on the noise. The Giants in particular had a rough day (11 false start penalties), as did the Panthers in the NFC championship. Teams were intimidated by the noise.

Sorrow. Woe. Heaving sobs. Mass wailing. Oh, come on—it's only a bad sports season. Every town has 'em. But why so many here?

12. 1994 UW basketball, 5–22. The Huskies, led by new head coach Bob Bender, played a schedule ranked fourth toughest in the nation (faced seven ranked teams) and did it without any returning starters. They started out 0–5, had a nine-game losing streak in the middle of the season and a five-game losing streak to end it. The remarkable thing was not the 22 defeats—the most in school history—but that the Huskies somehow managed to defeat No. 12 Arizona on February 5.

11. 1972–73 Sonics, 26–56. Even with Spencer Haywood averaging 29.2 points and 12.9 rebounds, the Sonics still finished with the fewest wins in franchise history until the 2007–08 mess. Coach Tom Nissalke (13–32) so alienated his players that a story circulated for years that the Sonics tanked a game at Philadelphia in January to hasten Nissalke's firing.

10. 2004 UW football, 1–10. Picked to finish seventh in the conference race, the Huskies not only failed to meet expectations, they were unbearably bad, finishing with the worst record in 115 years of Washington football. The Huskies featured the nation's worst offense, couldn't stop anybody, and were so uninteresting that they played in a half-empty stadium most of the season.

9. 1992 Seahawks, 2–14. After Tom Flores replaced Chuck Knox as head coach, he let quarterback Dave Krieg go into free agency so that No. 1 picks Dan McGwire and Kelly Stouffer could battle it out for the starting job. Stouffer won, but lasted only four games before suffering a shoulder injury. McGwire went down after one game with a hip injury. That left the team in the hands of Stan Gelbaugh, who lost all eight of his starts. The Seahawks scored a league-low 140 points as Gelbaugh, Stouffer and McGwire combined to complete just 48.3 percent of their passes while throwing 23 interceptions. The remarkable thing was that DE Cortez Kennedy became the first player from a two-win team named the NFL's Defensive Player of the Year.

8. 1983 Mariners, 63–102. The ugliest of all Mariners teams scored 100 fewer runs than any club in the majors and featured three pitchers with at least 15 losses. In a misguided attempt at pizzazz, the M's placed a tugboat beyond the center field wall, christening it the "USS Mariner." The tug fired off a cannon after every infrequent home run, and a companion tug was supposed to ferry in relievers from the bullpen, although many of them refused to ride. In addition to playing dismal baseball, the M's alienated fans by trading popular second baseman Julio Cruz to Chicago for Tony Bernazard, then fired manager Rene Lachemann, replacing him with Del Crandall. On the same day Lachemann was axed, the Mariners also released Gaylord Perry and shortstop Todd Cruz, moves that collectively became known as the "Saturday Night Massacre."

35

7. 1978 Mariners, 56–104. The second edition of the Mariners, which attracted approximately one customer to every 10 seats in the Kingdome, was less competitive than the 1977 expansion team. It led the majors in times shut out (15), lost 36 games by five or more runs, was outscored by 220 runs and finished last in the American League in ERA (5.21). The five starting pitchers, Paul Mitchell, Glenn Abbott, Rick Honeycutt, Jim Colborn and Dick Pole, went 8–14, 7–15, 5–11, 3–10 and 4–11, respectively.

6. 1971–72 Seattle Totems, 12–53–7. The Totems usually contended in the Western Hockey League, but had the worst season in their history, finishing with 17 fewer victories than the next-worst team. The Totems scored 175 goals, lowest in league history, and allowed an astounding 331. Goaltender Jack Norris had a 5–28–5 record and allowed 4.14 goals per game. Bob Sneddon had a 3–13–2 record and allowed 5.31. The Totems' 53 defeats were the most in a single season in WHL history.

5. 2007–08 Sonics, 20–62. A deliberately planned emasculation by owner Clay Bennett, the worst season in the Sonics' 41 years was a casualty of the fight to move the franchise to Oklahoma City. Bennett bought the team from Seattleite Howard Schultz with four years left on the KeyArena lease, and made the Sonics non-competitive by unloading top talent and acquiring draft picks and salary cap space that would benefit the team after it left Seattle. The Sonics lucked into the No. 2 pick in the draft lottery and took Kevin Durant of Texas, who became Rookie of the Year. But he was about the lone highlight in a disastrous season—the Sonics gave up 168 points in one game, and scored only 66 in another—under retread coach P.J. Carlesimo.

4. 1969 UW football, 1–9. The only redeeming feature of the season occurred in the final game when an awful Washington defeated even worse Washington State 30—21. The Huskies opened by spending 10 days in Michigan where they lost to Michigan State 27—11 and Michigan 47—7. That was the good news. On October 30, coach Jim Owens suspended four African-Americans for what he described as a lack of commitment to the team. That prompted the eight other African-Americans on the team to refuse to travel to Los Angeles to play against UCLA, leading to a 57–14 defeat, one of the worst in school history. The Huskies allowed 40 or more points four times and were outscored 304–116.

3. 1969 Pilots, 64–98. Their best hitter (minimum 400 at-bats), Don Mincher, hit .246. Their best pitcher, Gene Brabender, went 13–14 with a 4.36 ERA. Joe Schultz's expansion Pilots not only allowed the most runs in the majors (799), they suffered 26 losses by five or more runs. The Pilots had no television deal with any local broadcasting station, and went bankrupt after one season. Their pitiable year of existence likely would have vanished without a trace had not pitcher Jim Bouton immortalized the Pilots in *Ball Four*.

2. 2008 UW Football, 0-12. No team in 119 years of Husky football disgraced itself more than the '08 Dawgs. These Huskies not only became the first school history to fail to win a game, they became the first team in Pac-10 history to go 0-12. They allowed a school-record 463 points, scored just 159 and got beat weekly by an average of 38.6 to 13.2. It was even worse than statistics suggest. Against Oregon State, the Huskies got flagged for delay of game–on the first scrimmage play. Against Washington State, the Huskies committed a personal foul–on the opening kickoff. Who commits a personal foul on the opening kickoff? Washington played such buffoon football that it could not even beat a hapless 2-11 Washington State team that allowed 60 points in a game four different times, and 570 points for tyhe season, second most in NCAA history. By the time the Huskies lost to the Cougars in the Apple Cup, Tyrone Willingham had been cashiered as head coach

1. 2008 Mariners, 61–101. The expectation was that the Mariners would challenge the Angels in the AL West. The reality was that they degenerated into a virtually unwatchable mess (bloated ERAs by the starters, inept hitting with runners in scoring position, dysfunctional locker room) that got GM Bill Bavasi and manager John McLaren cashiered before the All-Star break. For the last three months of the season the only intrigue surrounding the pitching-poor, free-swinging, aimless, clueless and leaderless Mariners was whether they would become the first team in major league history with a $100 million payroll (actually $120 million) to lose 100 games. They not only did, finishing 61–101, but they even managed to botch the No. 1 pick in the 2009 June free-agent draft by sweeping Oakland in the final series of the year, thereby handing the No. 1 pick to the Washington Nationals.

Considering the greatness that didn't make this list—George Wilson 1925, Don Heinrich 1952, Al Worley 1968, Sonny Sixkiller 1970, Greg Lewis 1990, Randy Johnson 1997, Ken Griffey Jr. 1998, to name just a few—this may have been the hardest list in the book. Many athletes have put up stupendous years; only these 25 survived.

25. Adam Morrison, Gonzaga basketball, 2005–06. A consensus *Associated Press* All-America and West Coast Conference Player of the Year, Morrison led the nation in scoring at 28.1 points per game. He was NABC Co-Player of the Year, Oscar Robertson Trophy Co-Player of the Year and a finalist for the Naismith Award.

24. Lauren Jackson, Storm, 2007. Jackson became Seattle's first professional athlete to win two league Most Valuable Player awards (also 2003) after leading the WNBA in scoring (28.3) and rebounding (9.7). Jackson, who received 42 first-place votes and 473 points, was also the WNBA's Defensive Player of the Year.

23. Gary Payton, Sonics, 1995–96. In addition to winning the NBA's Defensive Player of the Year award, the only Sonics player to do so, Payton averaged 19.8 points, 7.7 assists and a career-high 2.9 steals as Seattle won a team-record 64 games and reached the NBA Finals for just the second time in franchise history.

22. Hugh McElhenny, UW football, 1950. McElhenny became the first running back in University of Washington football history to surpass 1,000 rushing yards in a season (1,107 in just 10 games) and scored 12 touchdowns, including a modern school record of five in the Apple Cup against Washington State.

21. Ryan Leaf, WSU football, 1997. Leaf put together the best season by a Washington State quarterback in school annals. He threw for 3,637 yards and 33 touchdowns, was named the Pac-10's Offensive Player of the Year, and led the Cougars to their first Rose Bowl appearance in 67 years.

20. Fred Hutchinson, Rainiers, 1938. The pitcher from Franklin High became an instant local celebrity when he compiled a 25–7 record with a 2.48 ERA and 29 complete games, while also batting .313. Hutchinson, named Pacific Coast League Player of the Year and Minor League Player of the Year by *The Sporting News*, helped Seattle draw a league-leading 437,161 fans, 16,354 of whom jammed Sicks' Stadium on August 12, 1938. On that day, his 19th birthday, Hutch earned his 19th win, 3–2 over the San Francisco Seals.

19. Marques Tuiasosopo, UW football, 2000. No UW quarterback was more responsible for his team's success than Tuiasosopo in 2000 (Huskies trailed in eight of their 11 wins, only to have Tuiasosopo rally them to victories). He threw for 2,284 yards and 15 TDs and rushed for 469 yards and seven touchdowns in leading Washington to its first Rose Bowl since 1992. Against Purdue in Pasadena, in an MVP performance, he completed 16 of 22 passes for 138 yards and a TD and ran 15 times for 75 yards and a TD as the Huskies won 34–24.

18. Rueben Mayes, WSU football, 1984 and 1985. Washington State's bruising running back became the second player in Pac-10 history, following USC's Charles White in 1978–79, to be named the league's top offensive player in consecutive years. In his final season in the Palouse, he gained 1,236 yards and scored 10 touchdowns. The year before as a junior, he won the award after rushing for 1,637 yards and 11 touchdowns.

17. Roger Davies, Sounders, 1980. It was the best soccer of the day in America, and the Sounders' English striker was the best of the best. He edged the New York Cosmos' more celebrated Giorgio Chinaglia for the Most Valuable Player award by scoring 25 goals and 61 points (scored four times against Rochester on May 31) in leading Seattle to a 25–7 record, the best mark in the league. It marked the apex moment for pro soccer in Seattle.

16. Brandon Roy, UW basketball, 2005–06. Washington's first, first-team All-America selection since Bob Houbregs in 1953, Roy was Pac-10 Player of the Year and a finalist for the Wooden, Naismith and Oscar Robertson awards after averaging 20.2 points, 5.6 rebounds, 4.1 assists and 1.4 steals and leading the Huskies to a 26–7 record and an NCAA tourney berth that reached the Sweet Sixteen.

15. Warren Moon, UW football, 1977. The UW's key figure in igniting the Don James era, senior quarterback Moon helped take the Huskies to a 10–2 record after a 1–2 start. Winning the Pac-10 title meant the first Rose Bowl for Washington since 1964. In a 27–20 defeat of Michigan in Pasadena, Moon ran for two TDs and threw a 28-yard TD pass to Spider Gaines. He was both Pac-10 co-Player of the Year and Rose Bowl MVP.

14. Corey Dillon, UW football, 1996. Dillon produced the greatest single season ever by a University of Washington running back when he amassed 1,555 yards and 22 regular-season touchdowns. In the first quarter of a late-season game against San Jose State, Dillon rushed for 222 yards and three touchdowns and caught an 83-yard touchdown pass, setting an NCAA record for rushing yards (222) and all-purpose yards (305) in one quarter.

13. Edgar Martinez, Mariners, 1995. Martinez not only won his second American League batting title with a career-high .356 average, he led the league in on-base percentage (.479) and doubles (52) and finished third in slugging (.628) as the Mariners advanced to postseason play for the first time in franchise history. His team-record 33 RBIs in August helped the Mariners roar back from a 13½ game deficit and win the AL West.

12. Cortez Kennedy, Seahawks, 1992. After a season in which he produced 14 sacks and accounted for 28 tackles for loss, Kennedy became the consensus choice as NFL Defensive Player of the Year. Kennedy also became only the third player in history to win the *Associated Press* Defensive Player of the Year award on a team with a losing record (2–14), joining Lawrence Taylor of the 1982 New York Giants and Reggie White of the 1987 Philadelphia Eagles.

11. Bob Houbregs, UW basketball, 1953. A second-team All-America in 1952 as a junior, Houbregs was so good as a senior in 1953 that the UW retired his jersey immediately after that season. He was named NCAA Player of the Year, a first-team All-America and helped lead the UW to the Final Four for the first and only time in school history.

10. Spencer Haywood, Sonics, 1973. Haywood scored a franchise-record 2,251 points (29.2 average), third best in the NBA, and pulled down 12.9 rebounds per game, also a team record. Named to start in the All-Star Game, Haywood was also selected to the All-NBA First Team for the second time in his career.

9. Elgin Baylor, Seattle U. basketball, 1957–58. Baylor produced ungodly numbers in the 1956–57 and 1957–58 seasons. As a sophomore, he averaged 30.5 points and 20.5 rebounds. As a junior (his last year) he averaged 31.5 points and 19.3 rebounds and led the Chieftains to the NCAA title game opposite Kentucky.

8. Steve Emtman, UW football, 1991. The defensive lineman had such a dominant season—60 tackles, 19.5 for loss, 6.5 sacks, Outland Trophy, Lombardi Award—that he became the No. 1 overall pick in the 1992 NFL Draft and earned induction into the College Football Foundation Hall of Fame in 2006.

7. Randy Johnson, Mariners, 1995. The Big Unit went 18–2 with an American League-leading 2.48 ERA and an AL-best 294 strikeouts, a performance that netted Johnson the Cy Young Award, making him the only Seattle pitcher to win one. Johnson also led the AL in winning percentage (.900), K's per nine innings pitched (12.35) and batting average against (.201).

6. Alex Rodriguez, Mariners, 1996. At age 20, Rodriguez enjoyed one of the greatest seasons in Mariners history by hitting an American League-high .358 with 36 home runs, 54 doubles, 123 RBIs, an on-base percentage of .414 and a slugging percentage of .631. Had Jim Street of the *Seattle Post-Intelligencer* and Bob Finnigan of the *Seattle Times* cast their MVP votes for Rodriguez instead of teammate Ken Griffey Jr., Rodriguez would have won the MVP award instead of Juan Gonzalez of Texas.

5. Shaun Alexander, Seahawks, 2005. Alexander set an NFL record (since broken) with 28 touchdowns and amassed 1,880 rushing yards as the Seahawks finished 13–3. His 168 points were the second most in a single season in NFL history behind Paul Hornung's 176 in 1960. With four touchdowns against Arizona (September 25) and Houston (October 16), Alexander, named NFL MVP, joined Jim Taylor (1962) as the only players to rush for four touchdowns twice in a game in one season.

4. Kenny Easley, Seahawks, 1984. Seattle's strong safety figured so prominently in the game plans of every opponent that he not only wound up in the Pro Bowl for the third time, he was a unanimous choice as NFL Defensive Player of the Year. Easley, the first safety to win the award since Dick Anderson of the Miami Dolphins in 1973, intercepted a league-high 10 passes, returning two for touchdowns, as the Seahawks finished 12–4.

3. Ichiro Suzuki, Mariners, 2001 and 2004. Named the American League Most Valuable Player and the Rookie of the Year in 2001, Ichiro won the batting title, a Gold Glove, a Silver Slugger award and received more All-Star votes than any player in the majors. Three years later, he won another batting title by hitting .372 and set the major league record with 262 hits.

2. Phil Mahre, U.S. ski team, 1982. The Yakima skier won three consecutive World Cup overall titles from 1981 through 1983, but his best year was 1982 when he recorded eight victories, 20 podium finishes and scored 309 total points, overwhelming Sweden's Ingemar Stenmark, who had 211. In addition to winning the World Cup overall title, Mahre also won event titles in the slalom and giant slalom.

1. Ken Griffey Jr., Mariners, 1997. The best season by the best athlete in Seattle history, Griffey was just the ninth player in American League history to win the American League Most Valuable Player award unanimously. Griffey hit 56 home runs and led the league in runs (125), total bases (393), RBIs (147) and extra-base hits (93) and was the best center fielder in the game.

As with the best seasons, the sweep of futility was also broad and deep, this list failing to find room for Casey Paus 2004, Jeff Weaver 2007, Frank Oleynick 1975–76, Mike Schooler 1992. But scan this baby, and you won't be begging for more.

11. Richie Sexson, Mariners, 2007. Sexson spent most of the season threatening to finish below the Mendoza Line (.200), finally screeching to a stop at .205. Of more significance, Sexson, paid $14 million for his power, had a slugging percentage of .399. Ichiro, the team's leadoff hitter and master of the infield dribbler, checked in at .431. When Sexson continued to make like Magoo at the plate in 2008 (.218 batting average in 74 games), the Mariners released him, eating his salary.

10. Stan Gelbaugh, Seahawks, 1992. Gelbaugh quarterbacked the worst team in Seahawks history, a 2–14 calamity that scored only 140 points (worst in modern NFL history) and allowed 312, for a differential of -172. Gelbaugh completed just 47.5 percent of his passes, threw six touchdowns against 11 interceptions and had a passer rating of 52.5.

9. Jeff Fassero, Mariners, 1999. Fassero allowed 12 earned runs in his first 10 innings of the season and posted one of the most miserable years by a starting pitcher in Mariners history. He gave up at least five earned runs in 12 of his 24 starts and left town (via a trade to Texas at midseason) with a 4–14 record and a 7.38 ERA.

8. Rick Mirer, Seahawks, 1995. The ex-Notre Dame quarterback guaranteed his exit from Seattle by throwing for five touchdowns and 12 interceptions in nine starts, while compiling a passer rating of 56.6.

7. Jeff Cirillo, Mariners, 2003. Cirillo's season went south so fast that he actually spent part of it in the Arizona Instructional League. He suffered a nightmarish year at the plate, hitting a career-low .205 in 87 games. He appeared in just two of Seattle's final 35 games and became one of the biggest free-agent busts in franchise history.

6. Jim McDaniels, Sonics, 1972–73. Once a star in the American Basketball Association, McDaniels flopped after joining the Sonics in 1971–72. His one full season was his worst, as the 7-footer averaged 5.5 points and 5.1 rebounds while hitting 39.9 percent of his shots.

5. Mario Mendoza, Mariners, 1979. The Mariners shortstop had 373 at-bats in 148 games, posted a .216 on-base percentage, a .249 slugging percentage and made 401 outs, launching the legend of the Mendoza Line by hitting .198.

4. Bobby Ayala, Mariners, 1998. One of the most-booed players in Mariners history, Ayala pitched himself out of a job in Seattle by compiling a 1–10 record, nine blown saves and a 7.29 ERA in 62 appearances. "Let's face it," manager Lou Piniella told the *Seattle Post-Intelligencer* when the club traded Ayala to the Expos, "Bobby just wasn't very good."

3. Jim McIlvaine, Sonics, 1997–98. McIlvaine may have made less of an impact on the court than any 7–1, 240-pound center in NBA history. He averaged 3.2 points and 3.3 rebounds while making only 45 percent of his shots in 78 games, including 72 starts. For that meager effort, McIlvaine received $3.6 million.

2. Mike Parrott, Mariners, 1980. Parrott started and won Seattle's Opening Day game, then dropped 16 consecutive decisions, a major league record, to finish 1–16. He had a 7.28 ERA and opponents hit .356 against him, turning the average opposing batter into Ty Cobb.

1. Ray Oyler, Pilots, 1969. Only five players in major league history had a minimum of 250 at-bats in a season and posted a lower batting average than Oyler's .165—Bill Bergen (.139 in 1909), Fritz Buelow (.141 in 1904), Les Moss (.157 in 1947), Bergen (.159 in 1906), Bill Sullivan (.162 in 1909) and Greg Vaughn (.163 in 2002). So plate challenged was Oyler that Seattle fans, feeling him in need of support, organized the "Ray Oyler Fan Club." Neither the fan club nor Oyler could stop the franchise from annulling its relationship with Seattle after one season.

The first year has been a good one for many pros in Seattle. Sustaining it was a little tougher for some, but there's nothing like an exciting new kid on the block to electrify a moribund team.

10. Mark Langston, Mariners, 1984. Langston would have won the Rookie of the Year award had it not been for teammate Alvin Davis. Langston won 17 games (3.40 ERA) and led the AL in strikeouts with 204, becoming the fourth rookie to lead the league in whiffs. His 17 wins were the most by a MLB left-hander since Gary Peters won 19 for the Chicago White Sox in 1963.

9. Rick Mirer, Seahawks, 1993. Seahawks fans may not recall it, but Mirer was a stud his rookie year. The No. 2 pick in the draft behind Washington State's Drew Bledsoe, the ex-Notre Damer signed a five-year, $15 million contract and then set rookie records for attempts (486), completions (274) and yards (2,833), and became the third rookie quarterback since 1970 to start all of his team's games. To the Seahawks' dismay, Mirer never again came close to duplicating that performance, and was gone by 1997.

8. Kevin Durant, Sonics, 2007–08. The Sonics' most trumpeted draft choice ever (national player of the year as a freshman at Texas), the 19-year-old forward-guard became the best offensive first-year player in franchise history and the league's Rookie of the Year. He averaged 20.3 points and finished his first campaign with a 42-point, 13-rebound performance at Golden State. Durant was often the lone option on a team whose roster was deliberately torn down to help the franchise relocate to Oklahoma City.

7. Lofa Tatupu, Seahawks, 2005. Selected in the second round of the 2005 draft (45th overall), the stubby ex-USC Trojan stepped in as Seattle's starting middle linebacker and immediately made fans wonder why the Seahawks—or any club—hadn't taken him in the first round. He led the Seahawks in tackles with 104 (85 solo), including a career-high 13 against the New York Giants and a team-high nine in Super Bowl XL. He had four sacks and three interceptions, returning one 38 yards for a touchdown in a Monday night game at Philadelphia. When Tatupu made the Pro Bowl, he became the first Seahawks rookie defender so honored.

6. Jack Sikma, Sonics, 1977–78. A mystery pick out of NAIA Illinois Wesleyan when the Sonics made him the eighth overall choice in the draft, the 6–11 Sikma quickly became a force on a front line that included 7–1 Marvin Webster and 6–7 John Johnson. He averaged 10.7 points and 8.3 rebounds during the regular season then significantly stepped up his play in the postseason. In 22 playoff games, Sikma averaged 14.9 points and 11.7 rebounds as the Sonics reached the Finals for the first time in franchise history.

5. Curt Warner, Seahawks, 1983. The Seahawks hadn't had a winning season in four years when they moved up in the draft and made Warner the No. 3 overall pick behind John Elway and Eric Dickerson. Warner quickly delivered a 60-yard run on his first pro carry at Kansas City. He led the AFC in rushing yards with 1,449, had six 100-yard games (high of 207), scored 13 TDs and produced 1,774 yards from scrimmage to rank fourth in the NFL. Named AFC Offensive Rookie of the Year and voted to the Pro Bowl, Warner's performance helped the Seahawks to reach their first conference championship game.

4. Alvin Davis, Mariners, 1984. Scheduled to spend the year at AAA Salt Lake City, Davis received a summons from the Mariners four days into the regular season. In his first start on April 11, he hit a home run off Boston's Dennis Eckersley. He wound up in the All-Star Game, hit .284 with 27 home runs and 116 RBIs (most by an AL rookie since Al Rosen in 1950) and set an MLB rookie record by drawing 16 intentional walks. Davis received 25 of 28 first-place votes in Rookie of the Year balloting, beating, among others, teammate Mark Langston, Boston's Roger Clemens and Minnesota's Kirby Puckett.

3. Kazuhiro Sasaki, Mariners, 2000. A major leaguer for the first time at 32, the Japanese import single-handedly put an end to a horrid string of Gasoline Alley bullpens that plagued the Mariners in the late 1990s. His 37 saves were a major league record for a rookie (his .919 save percentage led the AL), and broke by four the previous Seattle club record (33, Jose Mesa, 1999). In Rookie of the Year balloting, Sasaki received 17 of 28 first-place votes to edge Oakland's Barry Zito, becoming the first closer to win the award in more than a decade.

2. Bob Rule, Sonics, 1967–68. Rule ranks as the most cost-effective draft choice in Sonics history. Seattle selected the six-foot-nine, 220-pound Colorado State lefty center in the second round of the 1967 draft (19th overall), paid him a salary of $22,000, then reaped an 18.1-point, 9.5-rebound windfall. Among Sonics rookies, only Kevin Durant scored more points, and only Pete Cross (1970–71) averaged more rebounds. Just one month into a season in which he was named to the all-rookie team, he put up a career-high 47 points against the Lakers, and had 46 at Cincinnati March 13.

1. Ichiro Suzuki, Mariners, 2001. Yes, we know he was 27 and, like Kazuhiro Sasaki, already a star in another country when he came to the Mariners. But he was still a rookie by MLB standards, and he also broke through a cultural prejudice that said Japanese position players weren't good enough to make it in America. Here are the first words manager Lou Piniella uttered about Ichiro during that first spring training: "I'd be satisfied if he hits .280." Seven months later, he had 242 hits, most in the majors since 1930, and won the batting title with a .350 average. Ichiro not only made the American League All-Star team, he became the first rookie to start since Tony Oliva in 1964—and he led in votes.

In the modern sports era of specialization, the multi-sport elite athlete has become nearly a dinosaur. But before their legends become fossilized, here's a salute to the 10 best in the state.

10. Sammy White, basketball, baseball. An All-Northern Division basketball forward at the UW in 1948 and 1949 who helped lead the Huskies to their first NCAA Tournament berth, White was also the leading hitter on the UW baseball team in 1947 and 1948. After graduation, he played for the Seattle Rainiers from 1949 to 1951, then spent nine years in the major leagues as a catcher with the Boston Red Sox (1951–59). He wound up his career with Milwaukee (1961) and Philadelphia (1962). On June 18, 1943, White became the only player in major league history to score three runs in an inning.

9. Sterling Hinds, football, track. As a youth hockey player, the Toronto native rose to the junior B level, one step below the professional ranks. Recruited to Washington on a football scholarship, Hinds won three letters as a tailback between 1981–83 and also played a prominent role on the UW track team. He ran the second-fastest 100 meters (10.27) in school history, the second-fastest 200 (20.61), and ran the second leg on UW's 1983 400-meter relay team that finished second in the NCAA track championships. Representing Canada in the 1984 Olympics, he earned a bronze medal in the 400 relay.

8. Ray Frankowski, football, wrestling, fencing. Frankowski gained his greatest athletic fame as a two-time consensus All-America football guard at the UW under coach Jimmy Phelan, and later as a pro with the Green Bay Packers and Los Angeles Dons (All-American Football Conference.) Frankowski also won the 1940 Pacific Coast Conference Northern Division heavyweight wrestling championship and was a member of the UW fencing team.

7. Spider Gaines, football, track. A big-play wide receiver who caught seven touchdown passes of 50 yards or longer during his UW football career (1975–78), Gaines also starred in track. As a high school athlete, he won the 1975 California high hurdles title (13.3). In 1976, he won the Pac-8 hurdles title, advanced to the finals of the U.S. Olympic trials, became a two-time All-America and set the UW 110-meter hurdles record at 13:57. Gaines' biggest track moment occurred in 1977 when he won the hurdles race in the annual USA-USSR outdoor dual meet.

6. Nate Robinson, football, basketball, track. After setting a state hurdles record for the Rainier Beach High track team, the 5–8 Robinson became a freshman starter at cornerback for the 2002 Washington football team. Switching full time to basketball following his freshman season, Robinson developed into a third-team *Associated Press* All-America and led the Huskies to the round of 16 in the 2005 NCAA Tournament. A first-round draft choice by the New York Knicks, Robinson won the NBA Slam Dunk Contest at the 2006 All-Star Weekend.

5. Reggie Rogers, football, basketball. A member of two Pac-10 champion basketball teams at Washington (1984 and 1985), The Sacramento product also played in three bowl games (1985 Orange, 1985 Freedom, 1986 Sun) for the Huskies footballers. As a senior in 1986, he was selected a first-team All-America and won the Morris Trophy as the Pac-10's top defensive lineman. The Detroit Lions made him the seventh overall pick in the 1986 draft.

4. Herman Brix, football, track. A Tacoma native, Brix played tackle for three years under Enoch Bagshaw (1923–25) when the Washington Huskies appeared in their first two Rose Bowls. He also won a silver medal in the shot put in the 1928 Olympics, and held both indoor and outdoor world records after the Games while competing for the Los Angeles Track Club. Brix broke his shoulder filming the 1931 football movie *Touchdown*, thwarting his entry into the 1932 Los Angeles Olympics, but hastening an acting career in which Brix appeared in more than 100 films under the name Bruce Bennett.

3. Mark Hendrickson, basketball, baseball. A three-sport standout in basketball, baseball and tennis at Mount Vernon High, Hendrickson pitched and played basketball at Washington State University, where he was twice named first-team All-Pac-10 in basketball. After he was selected in the second round of the 1996 NBA draft by Philadelphia, the six-foot-nine Hendrickson played four years with the 76ers, Kings and Nets before switching to baseball. A left-hander, Hendrickson won 43 games for the Blue Jays, Devil Rays and Dodgers between 2002–07.

2. Johnny and Eddie O'Brien, basketball, baseball. All-America basketball players at Seattle University in the early 1950s, the New Jersey-bred O'Brien twins later formed the double-play combination for the MLB Pittsburgh Pirates. Johnny, first player in NCAA basketball history to score 1,000 points in a season (1953), had a six-year major league career while Eddie played five seasons.

1. Gene Conley, basketball, baseball. A Washington State All-America in basketball and baseball, the Richland native pitched for 11 years (1952–63) in the major leagues with the Braves, Phillies and Red Sox, winning 91 games, and also played for six years (1952–64) with the Boston Celtics. Conley won a World Series ring with the 1957 Milwaukee Braves, three NBA championship rings with the Celtics (1959–62), and was the winning pitcher in the 1955 MLB All-Star Game.

In contrast to scheduled events, the major sports leagues don't know who will play what and when for championships. Here are 10 events that depended on previous outcomes to create a Seattle entry into a big-time title contest.

10. Two National Hockey League Stanley Cup Finals, Seattle Ice Arena, March 17–26, 1917; March 19–30, 1919. Believe it or not, a Seattle

team's name is etched onto Lord Stanley's most spectacular stemware. During the War to End All Wars, the Seattle Metropolitans won the Pacific Coast Hockey Association title with a 16–8 record, drawing the Montreal Canadiens in a five-match finals. The Mets dropped the first but swept the next three 6–1, 4–1 and 9–1 as Bernie Morris scored 14 of Seattle's 23 series goals. Hap Holmes, a Hall of Fame goaltender, posted a 2.9 goals-against average. Two years later, a rematch of the teams ended in a 2–2–1 tie when the Spanish flu pandemic rendered many Canadiens players helpless. The Canadiens offered to forfeit, but Mets manager Pete Muldoon refused.

9. Gold Cup unlimited hydroplane race, Lake Washington, August 4, 1951. The first big motor sports championship in Washington was won by Slo-Mo-

Shun V, driven by Lou Fageol and owned by legendary Seattle hydroplane figure Stan Sayres. It marked the first time since 1904 that the sport's premier event was held west of the Mississippi River. The win ushered in an era of roostertail glory unsurpassed in the sport's long history in Seattle. The annual Seafair race, which drew hundreds of thousands to the lake shoreline each August, joined University of Washington football as the only big-time sports in town. Slo-Mo-Shun's win was the first of eight Seattle Gold Cups in the next nine summers.

8. MLB American League Championship Series, Safeco Field, October 10–17, 2000. A surprising three-game sweep of the Chicago White Sox in the Di-

vision Series set up well the 91-win Mariners, playing without the traded Ken Griffey Jr. for the first time in a decade, for a series against the 87-win Yankees. It started favorably, with ace right-hander Freddy Garcia gaining a shutout win in New York in the opener. But the Yankees won the next three by a combined score of 20–3. Another stout effort by Garcia won Game 5. But in Game 6, the Mariners blew a 4–0 lead to lose the game 9–7 and the series 4–2. It was the last game as a Mariner for star shortstop Alex Rodriguez. No one could tell then that the losses foreshadowed seasonal greatness in 2001.

7. MLB American League Championship Series, Kingdome, October 10–17, 1995. After winning so dramatically over the Yankees in the Division Series,

the Mariners were spent. But even fresh legs may not have helped against the Cleveland Indians, who won 100 of 144 games in a strike-shortened season and took it to the locals 4–2. The Mariners, who came from 13 games down in late August, then had to win a one-game playoff before drawing the Yankees in the postseason, hit .184 against Cleveland pitching, including 2 for 23 for DH Edgar Martinez. But while the players were flailing valiantly, state legislators were putting together a series of taxes that helped build a new stadium with a retractable roof that saved the franchise from being sold out of town.

6. NBA Finals, Coliseum, May 20–June 1, 1979. Seattle's lone major sports championship wound up a rout, with the Sonics whipping Washington 4–1 in a rematch of the 1978 finals. But because the NBA was in its pre-Bird/Magic/Air doldrums, the star-light Sonics didn't register much with the sports nation. In fact, the series was aired by CBS on taped delay at 11:30 p.m. in most parts of the country. But in Seattle, the news couldn't have been bigger. The region's first major pro team in 1967 was feted by a downtown tickertape parade that was said to have drawn more than 300,000 party-goers. Coach Lenny Wilkens and team stalwarts Jack Sikma, Dennis Johnson, Gus Williams, Lonnie Shelton, Fred Brown, John Johnson and Paul Silas became fixtures in the Seattle sports pantheon.

5. MLB American League Championship Series, Safeco Field, October 17–22, 2001. Led by amazing rookie Ichiro Suzuki, the first Japanese position player to make the majors, the Mariners, without Ken Griffey Jr., Randy Johnson and Alex Rodriguez, astonished baseball with an absurd 116 wins that equaled the best single season in history. As manager Lou Piniella would say years later, "I still don't know how we did that." However, the Mariners' best chance to make a World Series came to naught. As with the rest of the world, the club was changed by the tragic events of 9/11. Lost mojo was apparent in the Division Series against a 91-win Cleveland team. The Mariners barely won 3–2, thanks largely to a brilliant four-hitter in Game 5 from Jamie Moyer. Then came an ALCS rematch with the Yankees, who were, for once, America's Team. Losing the first two games at Safeco, the Mariners bounced back 14–3 in Game 3, but were overpowered by Roger Clemens and Andy Pettitte in the final two games for a 4–1 series loss. The quiet denouement of a remarkable season was hardly a matter for a grieving nation.

4. NBA Finals, Coliseum, May 21–June 7, 1978. It may seem odd to rank higher the title series the Sonics lost rather than the one the Sonics won, but the first match between the Bullets and Sonics was the first modern major pro sports championship event for Seattle, and far more preposterous than the 1979 rematch. The Sonics began the season 5–17, fired coach Bob Hopkins and replaced him with former player Lenny Wilkens, whose emphasis on defense helped produce a 42–18 run to the playoffs. The Sonics in the playoffs beat the Lakers, the Trail Blazers and the Nuggets. Against the Bullets, the Sonics ran out of steam, losing a 3–2 series lead and the title when the Bullets prevailed 105–99 in Game 7 at the Coliseum.

3. NFL National Conference Championship game, Qwest Field, January 22, 2006. After 28 years of soaring, sweeping mediocrity, the Seahawks had a breakthrough season in 2005 that would reach the Super Bowl. But since the Roman numerals will never be contested in chilly Seattle, hosting a conference title game is as close to pro football nirvana as a single home game will get. After a 13–3 regular season in which RB Shaun Alexander was named MVP, the Seahawks drew a bye, then beat Washington 20–10 for their first playoff win in 21 seasons. They drew Carolina for the NFC title match, but it wasn't much of a match. The Seahawks led 20–7 at the half and cruised to a 34–14 win. Then they moved on to the Super Bowl in Detroit against the Pittsburgh Steelers, a game that, in deference to the sensibilities of children and the infirm, shall not be discussed here.

2. MLB Division Series, Kingdome, October 3–8, 1995. How can a division series rate ahead of three ALCS? Four reasons: Thanks to the introduction of the wild card, it was the first division series in history; it was the first playoff action since the disastrous 1994–95 strike that wiped out a World Series; it marked the return to postseason play by the sport's most legendary team, the Yankees, after a 14-year absence; and it was the Mariners' first appearance in the postseason after 18 years of futility. So what should happen but the greatest division series in history? After losing the first two games in New York, the Mariners returned to the Kingdome to take the next two to set up an epic Game 5. Both Game 3 starters came on to pitch in the 11th inning, whereupon Edgar Martinez doubled home Ken Griffey Jr. with the biggest run, biggest win and biggest yippee-yahoo in Mariners history. Now tell the hair on the back of your neck to stand down.

1. NBA Finals, Key Arena, June 5–16, 1996. Never did a more uproarious sports circus come to town than the title series that featured the 72-win Chicago Bulls of Michael Jordan, Scottie Pippen, Dennis Rodman and coach Phil Jackson against the 64-win Sonics of Gary Payton, Shawn Kemp and coach George Karl. Among the Bulls' five championship teams, this may have been the best. The Sonics, drained by a brutal seven-game series in the Western finals against Utah and missing defensive stopper Nate McMillan, dropped the first two games before returning to Seattle. Game 3 was the series' only blowout, a 22-point Seattle defeat. The Bulls slipped into cruise control and were upended twice, forcing the series back to Chicago. The Bulls took the series in Game 6 with an 87–75 win. The Sonics never reached so much as a conference final again.

Steve Kelley's sports columns in the *Seattle Times* have been winning awards since the 1980s. Sports readers presume the longest-tenured columnist in the Northwest has seen it all. But no.

I was walking the hallways at an elementary school where I do some teaching. One of my fifth-grade students, Solana, came running up to tell me about her Halloween costume. "You'll never guess who I'm going to be," she said. "I'm going to be a mini-Mr. Kelley." I mentioned the impossibility of her mission, but she promised she could do it. A week later, she greeted me with a long face and I asked her how her costume was coming. "I can't do it," she said. "I'm just having too much trouble getting all the wrinkles in."

I'm old, and the only advantage I can see in my 60th year is that, as sports fan and sportswriter, I was lucky to have witnessed many great moments and almost all of the great modern athletes. I've seen every great baseball player from Willie Mays to, um, does Barry Bonds still count? From Sandy Koufax to, um, does Roger Clemens still count? I was in Convention Hall in Philadelphia to see epic battles between Boston's Bill Russell and Philadelphia's Wilt Chamberlain. I've seen Jerry West, Elgin Baylor, Walt Frazier, all the way up through Julius Erving, Kareem Abdul-Jabbar, Bill Walton, Magic Johnson, Larry Bird, Michael Jordan, Kobe Bryant and LeBron James.

I've seen Lawrence Taylor turn linebacker into an offensive position. I've seen Joe Montana-to-Jerry Rice. Brett Favre cavorted in Lambeau snow as I sat in awe in the press box. I've witnessed Dan Marino's hair-trigger release and seen John Elway's high heat. I'm lucky. I've covered eight Olympics, and more Super Bowls, Rose Bowls and even Seattle Bowls than I can count. I saw one generation of World Series games in Yankee Stadium with Mickey Mantle in centerfield, and another with Bernie Williams. I saw Muhammad Ali fight at Madison Square Garden. And I saw Sugar Ray Leonard and Mike Tyson in their primes.

Being 60 allowed me to see John McEnroe, Bjorn Borg, Jimmy Connors, Chris Evert and Martina Navratilova at the U.S. Open. I walked Amen Corner when Jack Nicklaus made his last Masters charge. I've seen Tiger Woods and Phil Mickelson win at Augusta.

Yet there are events I still want to see.

5. A British Open at St. Andrews. It has to be St. Andrews. It has to be cold, wet, windy and bitterly uncomfortable. Tiger Woods has to be challenged by some hometown favorite, the next Lee Westwood or Colin Montgomerie, and I've got to be inside the ropes.

4. Wimbledon. I've seen the Sistine Chapel and the statue of David. I stared into Mona Lisa's eyes. But watching Roger Federer or a healthy Serena Williams at Centre Court at Wimbledon, would dwarf those other sights. I imagine there is a reverence at Wimbledon toward the game and the athletes that is rare in modern sports.

3. An FC Barcelona football game at Camp Nou Stadium (preferably against Real Madrid). Sitting with 120,000 soccer fans, who live for these games with more passion than Duke basketball fans, or Red Wings hockey fans, or Packers football fans, would be, for me, a religious experience. Plan B: Wembley for one of England's World Cup or European Cup qualifiers.

2. Indianapolis 500. Long ago NASCAR passed open-wheel as the great American racing spectacle, but I'm old school. The snarly competitiveness of A.J. Foyt. The glamour of Mario Andretti. The guts of Jackie Stewart. The Indy 500 has always been a can't-miss television event for me. Those moments before the race, when the drivers are sitting in their cars and the cameras close in on the faces of the drivers are riveting. There is something about looking into their eyes and understanding that they're about to spend the afternoon risking their lives wheel-to-wheel at more than 200 miles an hour that is thrilling. I'd love to feel that drama in person.

1. A game at Notre Dame. I can't believe I haven't done this. I had a chance a few years ago to see USC play in South Bend in that game where USC quarterback Matt Leinart willed himself into the end zone to win in the final seconds. I kick myself for kicking away the chance. The Notre Dame campus on a football Saturday has to be magic. It's a must-see before I'm prune-wrinkled beyond recognition.

Unlike some bigger, older markets, the state has had relatively few scheduled big-time national championship events on the calendar. Which doesn't mean there haven't been some memorable moments.

10. U.S. Figure Skating Championships, Tacoma Dome, February 4–8, 1987.

For someplace so far north, winter sports have had a modest profile. That started changing with the big names in Tacoma. Although he missed a first-ever quadruple jump, Brian Boitano won his third consecutive men's title. Jill Trenary hit four triple jumps in the long program and won the women's gold over defending U.S. and world champion Debi Thomas. Jill Watson and Peter Oppegard became the first team in 52 years to regain a pairs title when they defeated defending champions Gillian Wachsman and Todd Waggoner.

9. NCAA Track and Field Championships, University of Washington, June 17–19, 1971.

Some little-known athletes started becoming legends at the event. Villanova's Marty Liquori ran the first sub-four-minute mile in Seattle track history (3:57.6), Sid Sink of Bowling Green clocked the second-fastest steeplechase by an American (8:30.9), Oregon's Steve Prefontaine won the three-mile (13:20.1), and UCLA scored 52 points to win the team title. Cary Feldman of the UW won the javelin with a throw of 259–9.

8. PGA championship, Manito Golf and Country Club, Spokane, August 14–20, 1944.

In what was considered then the most spectacular upset in the history of the tournament, 28-year-old Bob Hamilton, an Evansville, Ind., club pro, defeated 10–1 favorite Byron Nelson 1-up over 36 holes in the match-play final. Nelson entered the final having played the tournament's first 196 holes of medal play in 30-under par. But he three-putted the ninth, 16th and 29th holes of match play. The week-long event drew 154,893 fans, breaking the previous record of 125,345 set in Los Angeles.

7. Two NCAA men's basketball Final Fours: University of Washington, March 26, 1949 and March 26, 1952.

Before shorts went long and March went mad, the college basketball championships were played in college gyms without TV and Dick Vitale, and with serious competition from the National Invitation Tournament. The UW's Hec Edmundson Pavilion hosted a pair that featured a couple of coaching legends. In 1949, Kentucky, coached by Adolph Rupp, held Oklahoma A&M without a field goal for more than 13 minutes and won 46–36. Alex Groza was MVP. Three years later, another Hall of Fame coach, Phog Allen, won his only NCAA title when Kansas, led by Clyde Lovellette's 33 points, routed St. John's 80–63.

6. NBA All-Star Game, February 8, 1987, Kingdome. When Houston's Ralph Sampson sustained a knee injury the week before the game, Seattle's Tom Chambers was added to the West squad. He scored a game-high 34 points, including four in overtime, to lead the West to a 154–149 victory over the East. Chambers won the MVP award. In his final All-Star game, Philadelphia's Julius Erving scored 22 points and Houston's Hakeem Olajuwon became the first player to foul out of an All-Star Game since Rick Barry in 1978.

5. PGA Championship, Sahalee Country Club, August 13–16, 1998. Absent a regular tour stop since the 1960s, Seattle finally made the pro golf radar with a Grand Slam event at the heavily treed course in suburban Redmond. Vijay Singh fired rounds of 70–66–67–68 for a 271 to defeat Steve Stricker by two strokes. Tiger Woods was a non-factor, and Seattle native Fred Couples finished nine strokes off the lead (280).

4. Goodwill Games, July 20–Aug. 5, 1990, Husky Stadium, Federal Way Aquatics Center, Coliseum, et al. An event invented by starry-eyed cable-TV mogul Ted Turner, who sought world peace through sports, found its first American home in Seattle after the inaugural in Moscow in 1986. The Soviet Union won the most medals in the 21-sport, 186-event program, capturing 188 overall, including 66 gold. The U.S. was second with 161 medals, including 60 gold. American swimmer Mike Barrowman trimmed 1.36 seconds off his world record in the 200 breaststroke, clocking 2:11.53. Also in swimming, Matt Biondi won four golds and a silver, and Janet Evans captured three golds and two silvers. In track and field, Leroy Burrell defeated Carl Lewis in the 100, but Lewis won the long jump with a leap of 27–6 ½. Jackie Joyner-Kersee won the heptathlon.

3. MLB All-Star Game, Safeco Field, July 10, 2001. The first All-Star game in Seattle since 1979 could not have been more Seattle-centric. Amid a spectacular season that produced a record-tying 116 wins, the Mariners had a record eight All-Star selections—Ichiro Suzuki, Bret Boone, John Olerud, Edgar Martinez, Mike Cameron, Freddy Garcia, Jeff Nelson and Kazuhiro Sasaki—as well as manager Lou Piniella. Ichiro opened the bottom of the first with an infield single off former Mariner Randy Johnson of Arizona. But the national highlight was reserved for Baltimore's Cal Ripken Jr., playing in his 19th and final All-Star Game. Stepping to the plate in the bottom of the third inning, he received one of the longest standing ovations ever accorded an All-Star. Ripken tipped his cap and then hit the first pitch from Chan Ho Park over the left field wall, sparking the American League to a 4–1 victory. The Mariners erected a plaque in the left-field bullpen to mark the spot where Ripken's homer landed.

2. Heavyweight boxing championship, Sicks' Stadium, August 22, 1957. Popular champion Floyd Patterson found himself defending his belt in an unlikely setting against an unlikely opponent in a minor league ballpark in Seattle's Rainier Valley against Pete Rademacher, the 1956 Olympic gold medalist, the first time in boxing history an amateur had challenged for the title in his first pro bout. Patterson took on the fight for an obvious reason—a $250,000 guarantee, big money then, to fight a local favorite. A Yakima Valley native and former Washington State lineman, Rademacher stunned himself, Patterson and the crowd of 16,981, with a second-round knockdown of the champ. But Patterson rallied to knock down Rademacher once in the third round, four times in the fifth and twice in the sixth before Patterson was declared the winner. Rademacher went on to a 17–6 pro career, including fights against some of the more notable pugilists of the early 1960s such as Karl Mildenberger, Zora Foley, Archie Moore and Brian London.

1. Three Kingdome NCAA men's basketball Final Fours: March 31–April 2, 1984; April 1–3, 1989, April 1–3, 1995. College basketball's showcase helped establish Seattle's modern credentials for hosting big-time events. As a spectacle, the Final Four was growing in prestige in the 1980s, and took a leap ahead with the first Seattle event. The pre-event party drew thousands to the cavernous, eight-year-old Kingdome for a smoky indoor feast of barbecued salmon, followed by two days of blockbuster hoops on a sunny spring weekend that drew more than 40,000 patrons from around the country. Seattle promoter Bob Walsh's presentation was given credit for boosting the event into the same big-time realm as the pro championships. In an epic big-man title clash, Georgetown, led by Patrick Ewing, beat Hakeem Olajuwon's University of Houston 84–75. In 1989, Michigan guard Rumeal Robinson's two free throws with three seconds left in OT gave the Wolverines an 80–79 victory over Seton Hall, led by future Sonics coach P.J. Carlesimo. In 1995, Ed O'Bannon's 30 points and 17 rebounds helped UCLA to an 89–78 win over Arkansas, the Bruins' 11th national title.

What I Love about Soccer :: Drew Carey

Comedian, actor, game show host, Drew Carey added another line to his resume in 2008: Seattle sports team owner. He's part of the group that owns the 2009 Major League Soccer expansion Seattle Sounders FC. He explains his seduction by "The Beautiful Game."

5. The more you learn, the more you like it. It changes the appreciation. When I started a few years ago, I didn't know about offside, or what the lines meant. I started reading, talking and looking up stuff. And, as I tell my friends, now I can heckle with authority.

4. It's not always about who is stronger, or faster or smarter. The beauty of the game is all about trickery. It's about finding space and going somewhere, when your defender forgets about you for a moment, and all of a sudden you're open in front of the goal with the ball at your feet.

3. The surprising physical nature. Sometimes I get a field pass and photograph from the sidelines. What I first noticed up close is how physical the game gets at the higher levels. I had no idea. Guys really come after you. Nothing is held back. If all you know about soccer is watching your kids play, you've never seen a soccer match.

2. Being a fan means being tough, 24/7. I watch an English game at the pub at 6:45 in the morning. The place is packed; people singing and chanting. They're having fun and they're into it.

1. Non-stop action. When you don't know anything about the sport, it may seem like 11 guys trying to kick a ball around. But as you learn, you'll notice a thousand things. There's always something happening. Players are always trying to get position. The defense is trying to keep its form together. Attackers are trying to exploit a gap. The ball moves around; guys are making runs and dummy runs. When you know all those things, it's fun to watch.

No, not little computer pictograms, nor religious images. This is the real deal – sports figures that transcended the deeds of the game to become larger than life to a community looking for heroes. Ego is OK, as long as it's gilded with a little endearing humility, which is why Brian Bosworth is not on this list.

15. Fred Hutchinson, Seattle Rainiers.

As a 19-year-old out of Seattle's Franklin High, Hutchinson won 25 games and was the biggest box-office draw for the 1938 debut of the Seattle Rainiers Triple A team. After a successful major league pitching career, he managed the 1955 Rainiers to the Pacific Coast League pennant. The force of Hutchinson's reputation was such that in 1999 the *Seattle Post-Intelligencer* named him Seattle's athlete of the 20th century. The eponymous Cancer Research Center in Seattle, one of the world's finest, is dedicated to his memory.

14. Bob Robertson, broadcaster.

Even more than the decades of athletes and coaches he described, Robertson is the face and voice of Washington State sports. In 2008, he began his 42nd year as Cougar football's play-by-play man. His raspy baritone also was heard for 25 years on WSU basketball, as well as 25 summers calling Pacific Coast League baseball in Seattle and Tacoma. Additionally he has done pro soccer, hockey, boxing, wrestling, hydroplanes and a few Mariners games in the late 1990s. His corny sign-off, "Always be a good sport, and be a good sport all ways," is such a comforting fixture at the end of each WSU broadcast that if he didn't say it, there is speculation that the entire Palouse would disappear in a cleave in the space-time continuum.

13. Jack Thompson, Washington State quarterback.

Although he grew up in the Seattle area, the Throwin' Samoan is a Cougar down to his South Pacific roots. The three-time All-Pac-8 quarterback ended his WSU football career in 1978 as the most prolific passer in NCAA history (7,818 yards). As one of the most storied, popular figures in school history—one of only two WSU players to have his number retired – Thompson is a fixture at every Apple Cup, gently trash-talking his rivals from Washington.

12. Johnny O'Brien, Seattle U.

As a five-foot-nine center, O'Brien made Seattle University basketball a headline all across the country, and became a lifelong local celebrity, on January 21, 1952. He led the Chieftains, scoring 43 points, to a stunning 84–81 upset victory over the Harlem Globetrotters (when they were serious) in an exhibition game at Hec Edmundson Pavilion. He and twin brother Eddie also played major league baseball. Johnny later became operations director at the Kingdome.

11. John Stockton, Gonzaga basketball.

One of the greatest point guards in NBA history, Stockton played from 1984 to 2003 with the Utah Jazz, more games with the same team than any player in pro ball. But he's really Spokane through and through, having graduated from the city's Gonzaga High and Gonzaga University. After his NBA career, Stockton returned home with his wife and six kids. They live next door to his parents. His father Jack's tavern is one of the premier joints in the Inland Empire.

10. Slick Watts, Sonics. He arrived in Seattle in 1973 as an obscure, undrafted free agent from Xavier-New Orleans and invited the city to embrace him with open arms. Infatuated with his grit, hustle, bald pate, colorful headbands and creative use of English, it did. He once led the NBA in assists and steals and was cool way before the Sonics became cool. Watts, retired almost 30 years, still makes numerous public and charitable appearances around town.

9. Edo Vanni, Rainiers. Vanni embodied baseball in Seattle for more than three decades. A Queen Anne High graduate and freshman football player at UW, he signed up for the first Rainiers team in 1938, and was a key member of their pennant-winning teams of 1939, 1940 and 1941. He managed the last Rainiers club in 1964, served as general manager of its successor, the Seattle Angels, from 1965–68 and worked in the front office for the 1969 Seattle Pilots. The Mariners may have made the most significant statement about Vanni's place in Seattle's sporting food chain: They gave him a lifetime pass to Safeco Field and his own parking place.

8. Fred Brown, Sonics. "Downtown" Freddy Brown, who joined the Sonics as the seventh pick in the 1971 NBA draft, played his entire 13-year career in Seattle. He captained the 1978–79 world champions, scored more points than any player in franchise history (14,018) and endeared himself to fans by annually purchasing as many as 200 season tickets and distributing them to disadvantaged youth. Former Mayor Charles Royer proclaimed February 11, 1985 as "Fred Brown Day" in Seattle, and Brown's No. 32 was retired on November 6, 1986. A post-hoops career as a bank vice president kept him in town and in touch with generations of Sonics fans.

7. Nate McMillan, Sonics. A scared, skinny kid when he arrived in 1986 from North Carolina State, the self-effacing McMillan grew to become "Mr. Sonic." He spent his entire 13-year playing career in Seattle as a point guard dedicated to passing, defense, floor burns and, later, mentoring. He quickly moved from Sonics assistant to head coach. In four-and-a-half years before leaving to coach the Portland Trail Blazers, he had a 212–183 record that included in 2005 the Sonics' only playoff-series win since the end of the George Karl era in 1998. An intense player and a demanding coach, McMillan frequently showed the other side with numerous public appearances and charity work.

6. Lenny Wilkens, Sonics. Top player, personnel director, championship head coach, general manager, broadcaster and briefly, president, Wilkens' mark was all over Seattle's oldest sports franchise. From the streets of New York's Bedford-Stuyvesant neighborhood, Wilkens upon his 1968 arrival was Seattle's first superstar pro athlete. He became part of the moss-covered firmament when he coached the Sonics to Seattle's only major pro sports title in 1979. A Hall of Famer as a player and coach, he went on to coach five other teams and became the winningest and losingest coach in NBA history.

5. Sonny Sixkiller, Washington football. Sixkiller's popularity can be traced, in part, to the politics of his era. When Sixkiller arrived in 1970, Washington football had experienced three years of racial strife and a string of awful teams. Sixkiller, a Cherokee Native American from Ashland, OR, led a UW revival by becoming the first Husky quarterback since Don Heinrich in 1952 to lead the nation in passing. His talent, name, heritage and personality became the subject of sufficiently large affection and curiosity that he made the cover of Sports Illustrated. A longtime Huskies booster, he's involved with UW football and basketball broadcast.

4. Ken Griffey Jr., Mariners. Without him, there would be no Mariners. From the time of his major-league arrival in 1989, he was the reason many casual fans entered the Kingdome cave to watch baseball. His All-Star exploits for a hapless franchise in the 1990s led the momentum to create Safeco Field. The full measure of Griffey's impact on the local sporting scene didn't emerge until eight years after he left Seattle. Returning to Safeco Field in 2007 with the Cincinnati Reds, Griffey spent an entire weekend series as the focus of a lovefest, receiving literally dozens of standing ovations.

3. Steve Largent, Seahawks football. The Seahawks' first and only Hall of Famer, Largent had only average size and speed, but exceptional instinct, determination and concentration. A man of intense religious faith, he also had the self-effacing humility that plays well in Seattle, making him a 14-year beacon. He retired after a 200-game career in 1989 as one of the greatest receivers in pro football history, holding six major NFL records, which subsequently made him the first player inducted into the team's Ring of Honor. Upon his retirement, Largent returned to his native Oklahoma, where he was appointed to fill a Republican vacancy in the U.S. House of Representatives, winning re-election three times.

2. Don James, Washington football. James defined coaching excellence in his tenure at Washington from 1975–92. He came off as distant and colorless, but results certified him a legend among a generation of Huskies fans, creating a standard that his successors have not reached. He inherited a program that had not been to a bowl game in 12 years and led the Huskies to 14 bowl appearances over the next 18 seasons (six Rose Bowls) and the 1991 co-national championship. *Sports Illustrated* famously listed the top three coaches one year as 1. Don James 2. Don James 3. Don James. He resigned just before the 1993 season.

1. Edgar Martinez, Mariners. Men wanted to be him, women wanted to marry him, children wanted to be adopted by him. The Mariners designated hitter, two-time batting champion and all-time nice guy made seven All-Star Game appearances and will be the Mariners' first Hall of Fame candidate in 2010. In 1995, he hit .571 against the New York Yankees in the first American League Division Series after the 1994 strike, making the nation aware of what Seattle sports fans had come to love. The city named a street after him (Edgar Martinez Drive, next to the ballpark) and the American League named a major award after him (Edgar Martinez Designated Hitter Award). During and after his final game at Safeco Field, on October 3, 2004, he received eight standing ovations, one lasting nearly four minutes.

Not all the key figures in sports are 300 pounds, seven-foot, speak Japanese or sport tats, cornrows and baggy shorts. Some wear ties and are rich from other amusements. Without them, big-time sports don't happen.

10. Ron Crockett, horseman and UW booster. Crockett's initiative and $10 million investment helped open Emerald Downs in 1996, bringing back thoroughbred racing to the Puget Sound area following the closure of Longacres in 1992. He served as president of the track for more than a decade and ranks among the most successful racehorse owners in state history. Crockett is also one of the most influential boosters of the University of Washington, donating large sums to athletics and the business school.

9. Daniel Dugdale, baseball owner and entrepreneur. Dugdale arrived in Seattle in 1898 on his way to the Klondike gold rush in Alaska, and never left. A former big league catcher, Dugdale amassed a minor fortune by speculating in local real estate and used his wealth to build two Seattle baseball stadiums, notably Dugdale Park (1913) at the intersection of Rainier Avenue and McClellan Street. It was the home for five championship teams and also hosted some of baseball's greatest players, including Babe Ruth and Ty Cobb. Dugdale formed and managed some of Seattle's earliest teams, including the Klondikers (also known as Rainmakers, Clamdiggers and Chinooks) and Siwashes (later known as the Turks and Giants).

8. Lloyd Nordstrom, civic activist. Nordstrom headed a consortium of business leaders and entrepreneurs operating under the name Seattle Professional Football that was awarded an NFL franchise on December 5, 1975. In addition to Nordstrom, patriarch of the Nordstrom department store chain, the group included industrialist Ned Skinner, contractor Howard S. Wright, retailer M. Lamont Bean and entrepreneur Herman Sarkowsky. Two years after the group paid $16 million for the franchise and one year after the Seahawks were named, Nordstrom died while vacationing in Mexico. A former University of Washington tennis player (1930–32), Nordstrom made a $2.5 million posthumous donation that served as the principal funding for the UW Tennis Center, which bears his name.

7. Emil Sick, Rainiers owner. A dynamic civic booster who owned and operated the Rainier Brewery, Sick purchased the Seattle Indians of the Pacific Coast League in 1937, renamed them the Rainiers and built a new ballpark in the Rainier Valley. Sicks' Stadium not only served as home to the Rainiers and their successor teams through 1968, it was where the ill-fated Pilots played during their one season (1969) in Seattle.

6. Herman Sarkowsky, entrepreneur. Owner of Sarkowsky Investments, a real estate development and private investment firm, Sarkowsky's interest in sports included football, basketball and thoroughbred racing. He had a long run as managing partner of the Portland Trail Blazers and Seattle Seahawks, invested in Northwest Racing Associates, which developed Emerald Downs in Auburn, and owned numerous thoroughbreds of prominence, including Phone Chatter, the champion two-year-old filly of 1993 and winner of that year's Breeders' Cup Juvenile Fillies.

5. Joe Gottstein, horseman and entrepreneur. A Seattle native and Brown University graduate, Gottstein initiated and presided over the second and longest thoroughbred racing era in state history. The Meadows, Washington's first major race track, closed in 1903 due to an anti-gambling movement. In 1922, Gottstein lobbied the state Legislature to legalize pari-mutuel wagering, an effort that paid off in 1933 when Gov. Clarence Martin approved. The new track, Longacres, was built in just 28 days. Gottstein inaugurated one of the Northwest's greatest traditions, the Longacres Mile, in 1935 and also played a major role in the formation of the Washington Horse Breeders Association.

4. Bob Walsh, promoter. Walsh, who came to Seattle in the 1970s as assistant general manager of the Sonics, organized a group of investors and civic activists to bring to the region more than 80 sports, business and cultural events during the 1980s and early 1990s. The high-profile events included the 1984, 1989 and 1995 NCAA Final Fours, the 1988–89 NCAA women's Final Fours, and the 1990 Goodwill Games, which included the largest cultural exchange (USA and USSR) in U.S. history. Walsh also orchestrated a public relations campaign in the mid-1980s that resulted in Seattle accepting a nickname change from "Queen City" to "Emerald City."

3. Paul Allen, Seahawks/Blazers owner, entrepreneur. In 1997, the Microsoft co-founder and Seattle native, who already owned the Portland Trail Blazers, exerted his greatest Seattle sports influence when he purchased the Seahawks after former owner Ken Behring threatened to move the franchise to Los Angeles and then financed a statewide election that approved construction of Qwest Field and an exhibition center that would replace the Kingdome. His investment not only gave the Seahawks a new home by 2002, it led to the awarding in 2007 of a Major League Soccer expansion franchise to a group of Seattle and Hollywood investors, including Allen.

2. Slade Gorton, politician/lawyer. The two-term Republican U.S. senator made three major interventions to save major league baseball in Seattle. When the Pilots moved to Milwaukee following the 1969 season, Gorton, as state attorney general, successfully sued the American League in 1975, which resulted in the awarding of an expansion franchise (Mariners) in 1977. In 1991 as senator, he forced Mariners owner Jeff Smulyan to sell the club to a local group headed by Hiroshi Yamauchi of Japan, whom he solicited. In 1996, when the club's local owners, angry with local politicians over stadium funding issues, threatened an out-of-town sale, Gorton barged in and beat up the local pols, creating a deal that completed Safeco Field, which opened in 1999.

1. Torchy Torrance, booster and civic activist. A turn-of the-20th century baseball player at the University of Washington, Torrance was a tireless booster of all UW and Seattle athletic teams. He helped raise funds to build Husky Stadium (1920), helped Joe Gottstein launch Longacres (1933), helped acquire the land upon which Sicks' Stadium was constructed, served as executive vice president of the Triple A Seattle Rainiers (he signed pitcher Fred Hutchinson to a one-year, $2,500 contract in 1938), helped found Greater Seattle Inc., which produced the Seafair celebration, played a prominent role in recruiting Hugh McElhenny and Don Heinrich to the UW and ran the Greater Washington Advertising Association, which helped recruit and pay athletes to attend the UW. The disclosure that the GWAA maintained a slush fund for Huskies jocks led the NCAA to place Washington on its first-ever probation in 1956.

As a columnist for the *Spokesman-Review* in Spokane, John Blanchette has been amused and bemused by the Cougs—and Cougings—since 1981. He coined the phrase "to Coug it" and has thus been given oracle status by his newspaper's readers, although perhaps not so much by the more overwrought fans of Washington State athletics.

Go ahead. Keep thinking that "to Coug it" is merely a snarky, Dawg-centric way of saying "choke." But then, you probably also think peruse means to skim and that irony is just an amusing coincidence.

The athletic disposition at Washington State University should not be so blithely misapplied just because it can't be precisely defined. Yes, the Cougars have had their share of landings in pieces multiple and fiery. So what? Game-ending gag jobs collect dust in every team's attic.

Couging is not just losing spectacularly or suddenly without consolation – though that certainly is a part of it.

It's more like this: You're at the convenience store with only enough cash for either a lottery ticket or a 16-ounce can of, oh, Schmidt. You buy the beer. The guy in line behind you gambles on the ticket you passed on and wins a million dollars. You Couged.

But, hey, the Schmitty went down pretty good, too. And it makes for a hell of a story.

Nor is it always an unhappy ending. Take the 2002 locker-room ambush in which little-used linebacker Ira Davis broke the jaw of standout cornerback Jason David over some campus femme fatale. True Couging. Yet David's callow replacement, Karl Paymah, played splendidly and Wazzu romped on Saturday.

But it rarely works out so well. Before the 1991 Apple Cup, Mike Price admitted voting Miami No. 1 in the coaches' poll rather than the Huskies because of his friendship with Hurricanes coach Dennis Erickson. "That's being a featherhead," said UW's Beno Bryant after a 35-point skewering.

The comic possibilities in Couging are endless, but for this exercise we'll settle on five:

5. Phantom Devil vs. Cougar math, 1985. Down a touchdown in the fourth quarter against Arizona State, Wazzu has the Sun Devils pinned on their own 5. The visitors report to the huddle without a running back, so there is no one to retrieve quarterback Jeff Van Raaphorst's pitchout except WSU linebacker Maury Metcalf. Alas, while ASU has just 10 men on the field, the Cougars have 12—and the penalty nudges along a 21–16 loss.

4. But if you knew him, you'd like him. Trying to prop up the doomed basketball regime of Kevin Eastman, athletic director Rick Dickson says two prominent coaches, Eddie Sutton and Roy Williams, tell him Eastman is going about things "the right way" and suggest any WSU success of the previous 20 years was tainted by coachly jaywalking, or worse. To recap: The AD spatters mud on his own school and cites Sutton, who once resigned in disgrace at Kentucky, as an arbiter of what's right. The next day Williams tells a reporter: "I wouldn't know (Dickson) if he were to walk in my office."

3. Palouse justice. Stanford is crushing the Cougs at Spokane's Albi Stadium in 1970 with Eric Cross steaming toward the end zone again when Terry Smith, a beered-up 27-year-old Wazzu student, vaults over the railing and tackles Cross at the goal line. Fans pass the hat for Smith's $40 bail and come up with $900—the excess purportedly deposited in a "Rose Bowl fund" should the Cougars ever make it. No trace of the principal or interest is ever found.

2. The incredible lightness of being ahead. Wazzu leads the Huskies 27–14 with three minutes to go in 1975 and coach Jim Sweeney accedes to the urgings of quarterback John Hopkins, who wants to pile on another touchdown. Hopkins' pass is intercepted by Al Burleson and returned 93 yards, and a minute later Warren Moon finds Spider Gaines on a tipped 78-yard scoring pass. The Huskies prevail 28–27 and Sweeney resigns the next Monday.

1. Does anyone remember the tourney was for charity? Nooo . . .We're back to Price, the self-proclaimed "King of Poop Island." First he spoils Wazzu's second Rose Bowl in six years when he accepts a new job at Alabama, but insists on coaching the bowl game, a humiliation at the hands of Oklahoma. Four months later, he gets tanked at a golf event, visits a Pensacola topless club, passes out with one of the employees in his hotel room and leaves her to charge $1,000 worth of room service the next morning. He is fired before coaching a game, and forfeits the better part of $14 million because he hasn't signed his contract.

Now that's giving generations of future Cougs something to shoot at.

Long before Bill Gates and Paul Allen became known as Seattle's big-idea guys, local sports figures invented new ways to do fun things. Ten who made their mark:

10. Eddie Bauer, down parka. In 1936, the Seattle retailer and outdoorsman invented and patented the quilted down jacket, which he named "The Skyliner," after suffering through a day of fishing in wet garments made of wool.

9. Bill Kirschner, fiberglass skis. Kirschner founded K2, the legendary ski manufacturer, in a shed on Vashon Island in 1961. After testing his revolutionary skis on Crystal Mountain, he produced the first professional model in 1965. The skis gained world-wide attention in 1969 when Marilyn Cochran won the World Cup title in the giant slalom using fiberglass skis made by Kirschner.

8. Ole Bardahl, engine additives. A Norwegian immigrant who arrived in Seattle in 1922 with $32 in his pocket and no ability to speak English, Bardahl founded Bardahl Manufacturing in 1939, producing an oil treatment for automobiles that increased engine performance. He named the additive "Bardahl," and sold all of $188 worth of product in his first year. By 1952, Bardahl was the top-selling engine additive in the U.S. Bardahl also gave his product to local racers to test. He sponsored a variety of competitive vehicles, including motorcycles, snowmobiles and race cars, but became best known for his sponsorship of unlimited hydroplanes. Between 1957 and 1969, Bardahl-sponsored boats won five APBA Gold Cups and six national championships.

7. Hiram Conibear, the Washington stroke. When Conibear hired on as Washington's crew coach in 1907, he had never been involved with the sport. He was a quick study. Conibear read up on physics and decided that the traditional Oxford style of rowing, in which oarsmen put their maximum power at the end of a long "layback" stroke, was unsound and uncomfortable. Experimenting with a broom instead of an oar, Conibear came up with a shorter stroke that provided more power and eliminated drag. By the time Conibear's career ended in 1917, Washington was a national rowing power, and his "Washington stroke" was used throughout the world.

6. Don Coryell, "I" formation. A UW graduate and the only coach to win 100 games at both the college and professional levels, Coryell invented the "I" formation offense while he coached at San Diego State. Coryell later contributed to the development of the West Coast offense, which Bill Walsh of the San Francisco 49ers refined, and was later adapted by Mike Holmgren in his 10-year tenure as Seahawks head coach.

5. Hec Edmundson, West Coast fast break. A middle distance runner of distinction at the University of Idaho—he ran in the 1908 Olympic Games in London and in the 1912 Games in Stockholm—Edmundson became the UW basketball coach in 1921. He used his track background to install a new offense—one that utilized the fast break instead of the slow-tempo style in vogue at the time. Edmundson is credited with being the first coach west of the Mississippi River to run the fast break.

4. Ray Flaherty, plays and platoons. A Gonzaga graduate who played with the Los Angeles Wildcats of the first AFL and the New York Yankees and New York Giants of the NFL, Flaherty coached the Washington Redskins to a pair of NFL titles (1937, 1942). In the 1937 championship game, Flaherty introduced a behind-the-line screen pass against the Bears, which enabled quarterback Sammy Baugh to throw three touchdown passes against the unprepared Chicago defense. Flaherty later developed a two-platoon system in which one unit emphasized the passing game while the second featured the running game. Flaherty's two-platoon was effective in the 1942 NFL title game when the Redskins beat the Bears 14-6.

3. Ted Jones, hydroplane racing. A Boeing engineer, Jones had a good idea but not the cash to carry it out. So he linked up with Seattle auto dealer Stanley Sayres, who was rebuilding his 225-cubic inch hydro, Slo-Mo-Shun II. Jones persuaded Sayres to fund the building of a new 225-class hydro to test his theory. The new boat, Slo-Mo-Shun III, seemed so promising that Sayres shelved it and built a full-fledged unlimited, Slo-Mo-Shun IV, the first prop-riding thunderboat to run successfully. The boat ushered in the "modern era" of hydroplane racing when, in 1950, it broke the previous world water-speed record of 141 mph by nearly 20 mph and became the first Seattle boat to win the APBA Gold Cup. Between 1950 and 1966, Jones-designed unlimiteds won 75 major races, including 14 Gold Cups and 10 consecutive national championships.

2. Ted Lucero, turbine powered hydroplane. The backing of entrepreneur Dave Heerensperger allowed Lucero to create the first successful turbine-powered hydroplane. Named Pay 'N Pak after Heerensperger's chain of stores, the new ride was almost 2,000 pounds lighter than previous turbine boats due to its extensive use of aluminum honeycomb and its single, more powerful T-55 turbine.

1. George Pocock, unique racing shells. Pocock Racing Shells has been an integral part of American rowing. The University of Washington helped popularize the Seattle company by using a Pocock shell in 1923 when it won the school's first national championship at the Intercollegiate Rowing Association Regatta at Poughkeepsie, N.Y. For the next 50 years, Pocock supplied nearly every college and university in the country with his shells, many of which were used by gold-medal crews in the Olympic Games.

UW's most successful coach made it look easy over the years. But there were guys who made it tough on him. This list is unranked.

Jim Sweeney, Washington State, 1968–75. We won the Cougar game (1975) 28–27 but should have lost by two or three touchdowns. Jim could get a team up for big games, especially if he was the underdog.

Frank Kush, Arizona State, 1975–79. We lost 35–12 (1975) in Tempe. With two seconds left on the clock, ASU called a time out on our goal line to score again. I was upset about this for three years. We got back at them in 1978 in Seattle, 41–7. In 1979, he was fired the day of the game. We lost 21–7. His players carried him onto the field prior to kickoff. Later, we were declared the winner by forfeit. He was one tough coach.

Bear Bryant, Alabama, 1975–78. We lost 52–0 (1975) on a very hot day. This was my first year at UW. In 1978 we lost 20–17 in Seattle. We played a great game against a legend. Alabama had great athletes and they were well coached. Bear was always gracious to me.

Lee Corso, Indiana, 1976, 1978. He beat me three times, once at Kent State when he was with Louisville, and twice when he was at Indiana. He ran a limited-play offense and sound defense against us. I think the Woody Hayes offense had an influence on him.

Bill Walsh, Stanford, 1977–78, 1992. We beat his Stanford teams all three times we played them. He was an offensive genius. Whatever defense we were in, he seemed to always have the best and toughest call ready for us.

Bob Toledo, Oregon, 1983–88. He was an assistant at Oregon, the offensive coordinator and play caller. He was a lot like Bill Walsh, always well prepared and seemed to have the best call up against the defense we had on.

Homer Smith, UCLA, 1980–86, 1990–93. He was another offensive coordinator (for Terry Donahue) that had a great plan against our fine 1990 blitzing defense. We lost 25–22 but still went to the Rose Bowl that year and won. He put in a quick passing series from the shotgun and three-step quarterback drop. Our pressure wasn't quite as effective against this plan.

Terry Donahue, UCLA, 1976–92. His teams always seemed to be talented and well coached. We had a great rivalry with UCLA and we also got a big victory in 1975 over Dick Vermiel, 17–13. Against Terry we won six, lost seven, and had one tie.

Bill McCartney, Colorado, 1989, 1992. We caught Bill with his two best teams. In 1989, we lost 45–28 and in 1990 we lost 20–14. They were tough, talented, and well drilled. The 1989 Colorado team won the national championship, and the week of our game their quarterback, Sal Aunese, passed away. It was quite an emotional game for them. Bill was selected National Coach of the Year in 1989. We did beat them in the Freedom Bowl in 1985, 20–17.

Jim Walden, Washington State, 1978–86. We had a number of great Apple Cup games when Jim was the coach. His 1982 and 1983 teams cost us two trips to the Rose Bowl. We were better than them in 1982 and it was quite an upset, 24–20. In 1983, they won in Seattle 17–6 and at the end of the season they were the best team in the Pac-10 in my opinion. Jim did a good job of preparing for all teams but especially against the Huskies. One of the great quotes by Bob Rondeau (voice of UW football) was that I went into the Apple Cup each year as a 2,000-word underdog.

Despite a paucity of big-time championships, the list of quality coaches was so chubby we created three categories: Seattle, state and high schools. And we still left off coaches of great accomplishment. Our prime criteria were sustained excellence and impact (in this market, if you count only championships, the list gets short).

10. Gil Dobie. Never heard of him? The University of Washington football coach from 1908–1916 was 58–0–3. Take that, Bear Bryant. He was fired by UW president Henry Suzzallo, who thought college football was getting out of hand. In 1916.

9. Lenny Wilkens. The first big-time player for the 1967 expansion franchise, he went on to become the winningest and losingest coach in NBA history. Won his, and the Sonics', lone title in 1978–79. Player-coach from 1979–82 and sideline only from 1977–85, Wilkens had a record of 478–402 (.543). Inducted into the Basketball Hall of Fame as a player in 1989 and a coach in 1998.

8. Chuck Knox. In 1983, 1984 and 1985, Knox took the Seahawks to their first playoff appearances. The first included a 27–20 Orange Bowl shocker over of the eight-point favorite Miami Dolphins. In 1986, the Seahawks missed the playoffs, but two of their 10 wins came over the Giants and Broncos, that season's Super Bowl entrants. From 1983 to 1991, Knox's "Ground Chuck" offense morphed into a pass-happy outfit behind quarterback Dave Krieg to create a sports phenomenon that had a 20,000-person waiting list for tickets.

7. George Karl. The volatile, voluble Karl rode herd on a wild group of drama queens to the best years in club history. Sonics made the playoffs in each of his six full seasons through 1998, compiling a franchise-best record of 384–150 (.719) and 40–40 in the playoffs. Made the 1996 Finals against the 72-win Chicago Bulls of Michael Jordan. Had an epic playoff failure in 1994, losing to eighth-seeded Nuggets, and numerous verbal scraps with team president Wally Walker. Reporters wore black armbands after Karl was ushered out of town, knowing his wonderfully loose cannon would never be aimed their way again.

6. Marv Harshman. Truly a man of the state, Harshman coached 13 years at his alma mater, Pacific Lutheran in Tacoma (1945–58), 13 years at WSU in Pullman (1958–1971) and 14 years at UW (1972–85), where his teams went 246–146. His 642 wins at the three schools put him 34th on the all-time college list. Made three NCAA tourney appearances at UW and won Pac-10 titles in his last two seasons. National coach of the year in 1982, Harsh was inducted into the National Basketball Hall of Fame in 1985.

5. Cliff McCrath. From 1970 to 2007, McCrath's Seattle Pacific University men's soccer teams won nearly 600 games, made the NCAA tournament 30 times and won five championships. The all time Division II coaching victory leader, "Uncle Nubs" (he lost a few fingers in a childhood accident), also one of the great characters in Seattle sports history, is in the U.S. Soccer Hall of Fame.

4. Al Ulbrickson/Dick Erickson/Bob Ernst. The area's most enduring tradition of athletic success is University of Washington crew, which had three major figures. Ulbrickson's crews won six Intercollegiate Rowing Assn. regattas in the 1930s and 1940s, coached crews that won Olympic gold in 1936 and 1948, and stunned the Russians in Moscow in 1958. Erickson (1968–87) won at Henley and a U.S. national title, and helped found the women's program. Ernst is the only coach to win national titles with men's and women's eights, coached the U.S. women to Olympic gold in 1984, and at the 2007 IRA regatta became the first coach since 1950 to have men's varsity, junior varsity and frosh crews win gold. To know Seattle sports, you have to know a little row.

3. Mike Holmgren. "The Big Show" helped produce the big deed—a Seahawks appearance in Super Bowl XL, a dream almost unimaginable for a team that had the most 7–9, 8–8 and 9–7 seasons since the AFL-NFL merger. Even though the Seahawks lost to the Pittsburgh Steelers in sour fashion, Holmgren, who ended his 10-year run in Seattle with an 86-74 record and four division titles, restored franchise credibility that vanished after Chuck Knox left.

2. Lou Piniella. Piniella broke a culture of losing for a franchise with the slowest crawl (15 seasons) to a winning record in the modern history of major league sports. An improbable comeback from 13 games down in August 1995, helped launch the suddenly popular Mariners into the top echelon of baseball business success. Piniella's highlight-reel tantrums masked a deep knowledge of game strategy and a deeper understanding of ballplayer psychology. His 10 years in Seattle produced four playoff appearances, a regular season of 116 wins in 2001, and the emotional momentum to get built one of the finest modern-era ballparks. His biggest regret upon departure in 2003 was no World Series for Seattle. Without Piniella, there would have been no baseball team.

1. Don James. The "Dawgfather" of University of Washington football revived a floundering program into a national power. In 18 years, his 153–57–2 record included a mythical co-national championship in 1991 with Miami, four wins in six Rose Bowl appearances and a preposterous upset over Oklahoma in the 1985 Orange Bowl. James was national college coach of the year in 1984 and 1991 and inducted into the college football Hall of Fame in 1997. The intensely organized James seemed to some a distant CEO looming in his coaching tower, but he rarely missed a detail in practice or in games. The ending wasn't clean: he quit 12 days before the 1993 season in a dispute over pending sanctions from the Pac-10 and NCAA. But that's often how it is in college sports. Husky football hasn't been the same since.

The pro teams and the University of Washington dominate the Seattle sports culture. But lots of commendable commandants have enriched the state elsewhere and deserve no place in the shadows.

11. Vincent Borleske. In 32 years at Whitman's small campus in Walla Walla, Borleske led the NAIA Missionaries to four Northwest Conference football titles, but his best work was in baseball. In winning 10 NWC titles, Borleske had a record of 530–368. Basketball wasn't bad either—seven titles. After retiring in 1947, he served two terms as mayor of Walla Walla.

10. Dick and Tony Bennett. After a long period of moribund hoops, WSU hired the father-son coaching tandem from Wisconsin in 2003 and improbably converted the Cougs into a hoops machine. Dick coached three seasons (36–49) while installing a relentless defense and patient offense, then retired, laying the groundwork for son Tony. In 2007, he took WSU to its best record in 60 years, a 26–8 mark and second place in the Pac-10—after being picked ninth in the preseason poll. He became only the second coach in NCAA history to win the national coach of the year award in his first season. In 2008, the Cougars (26–9) for the first time in school history had back-to-back tourney appearances, reaching the round of 16.

9. O.E. "Babe" Hollingberry. One of the few football coaches at WSU with a career winning record, Hollingberry's 17 seasons (93–53–14 from 1926 to 1942) included a Rose Bowl appearance in 1931. He coached two of the greatest players in Cougars history, eventual All-Pros Mel Hein and Turk Edwards.

8. Chuck "Bobo" Brayton. He began his WSU career in 1936 by hitchhiking to Pullman from his home in Birdsview, near Mount Vernon. Eventually, he coached 1,162 baseball victories. His teams from 1970–79 won every Pac-10 Northern Division title and his 1965 and 1976 teams reached the College World Series. Among his pupils were Ron Cey, John Olerud and Scott Hatteberg.

7. John Chaplin. The gregarious wild man of the Palouse won WSU's only official NCAA championship when his Cougars track and field team took the 1977 title. From 1981–85, his teams were undefeated in dual meets, and his 21-year dual-meet record was 202–15 (.931). He coached 73 All-Americans and was the U.S. head coach in the 2000 Olympics.

6. Dean Nicholson. From 1964 to 1990, the Central Washington basketball coach compiled a 609–219 record, reaching the NAIA national tournament a record 22 times, winning 38 games, another record. The Wildcats reached the Final Four six times, finishing second in 1970 when he was named coach of the year with a 31–2 team. A standout basketball and baseball player himself at CWU (1946–50), he followed into CWU hoops coaching his father, Leo (505–281 from 1930–64). An Ellensburg High grad, Nicholson coached at Puyallup High for 14 years before succeeding his father. He also coached the Yakima Sun Kings of the CBA and Yakima Valley CC.

5. Fred "Doc" Bohler. Beginning in 1908, Bohler spent 42 seasons at WSU, where he was athletics director and coached basketball, track, baseball, wrestling, boxing and skiing. From 1909 to 1926, his hoops teams went 226–177. The campus gym bears his name.

4. Jack Friel. From 1928 to 1958, "The Prune" became the winningest basketball coach in Cougars history (495–377, .568), including five conference titles and an appearance in the NCAA championship game in 1941 (lost to Wisconsin 39–34). Long active on the rules committee, he persuaded the Pacific Coast Conference to adopt the one-and-one free throw rule in the 1950s. His top player was Gene Conley, who became the first to play on championship teams in two pro sports (Boston Celtics, Milwaukee Braves).

3. Mike Price. When Price took over WSU football in 1989, the regional talk was that the Cougars, because of remote location, lesser facilities and low budget, no longer belonged in the Pac-10. Price halted that talk by compiling an 83–78 record that included three 10-win seasons and five bowl appearances. The capper was in 1997, when the Cougars beat the rival Huskies in Seattle to advance to the Rose Bowl for the first time since 1931. The Cougs lost to Michigan, but Price was named national coach of the year.

2. Mark Few. An unheralded assistant when he took over Gonzaga basketball in 1999, Few set an NCAA record with 81 wins in his first three years (including consecutive Sweet Sixteen appearances), converting Gonzaga's image from cute interloper to perennial power. The Zags made the 64-team tourney field in each of Few's nine years through 2008. Few was West Coast Conference coach of the year from 2001 to 2006, and had four players—Adam Morrison, Dan Dickau, Blake Stepp and Rony Turiaf—make it to the NBA. Success allowed Gonzaga to build a new, 6,000-seat arena in downtown Spokane.

1. Frosty Westering. The legendary football coach liked to say, "Make the big time where you are." For 32 seasons at tiny Pacific Lutheran University (3,000 students) south of Tacoma, he made it a happenin' place. In 40 seasons at two non-scholarship schools, he had a 305–96–7 record that included three NAIA Division II titles, the 1999 Division III championship as well as four national runner-up finishes. A member of the NAIA and college halls of fame, Westering's homilies and life lessons that came with more standard zone blitz packages seemed cornball to some. But when the entire football team piled into a fast-food place post-game, they would serenade the harried counter staff with chants of "Good job, Andy!" and "Well done, Sue!" More cornball, please.

College basketball Hall of Famer Marv Harshman won 642 games during a 40-year career a three schools: Pacific Lutheran, Washington State, and Washington. He earned 1984 National Coach of the Year honors after leading the Huskies to the Sweet 16. He's also the answer to the trivia question, "Who was the last guy to beat John Wooden?"

10. Slats Gill, Oregon State. Zone specialist, teacher of the basics. Excellent teacher of post play, good at controlling tempo.

9. Ralph Miller, Oregon State. Excellent style of play and recruited to it. Very tough to beat with a lead in the second half. Spread court specialist.

8. Ned Wulk, Arizona State. Team oriented, very versatile, good teacher, strong fundamentalist, good fast-break teams.

7. Lute Olson, Arizona. Great recruiter and teacher, up-tempo offenses, excellent bench coach, teams always prepared, a real winner.

6. Don Monson, Idaho/Oregon. Great teacher of fundamentals. Good at analyzing situations. Teams always very competitive. Good recruiter.

5. John McClendon, North Carolina Central. Offensive mastermind. Excellent pressure teacher. Tough to defend. System worked in college and the pros.

4. Jud Heathcote, Montana/Michigan State. Super teacher and motivator. Defensive innovator with the 2–3 match-up zone. Fine recruiter. Great bench coach.

3. Bob Knight, Indiana. Very tough to play, extremely disciplined teams, did not beat themselves. Excellent teacher.

2. Pete Newell, Cal. Very adaptable. He would change style of play to suit his talent and to also meet opponents' offenses and defenses.

1. John Wooden, UCLA. Greatest ever. Master teacher. He took good players and made them great, resulting in super teams.

Craig Smith, who wrote the "Sideline Smitty" prep sports column in *The Seattle Times*, is a Washington native who worked at the newspaper from 1976–08. He knows the state prep scene as well as anyone, and offers the best coaches in state high school history.

10. Elton Goodwin, baseball, South Kitsap. Talk about the perfect sendoff. Goodwin's final win was in the 2003 4A state-championship game. He was 491–136 at South Kitsap from 1976–2003 and produced dozens of college players and four major leaguers: Willie Bloomquist, Sean Spencer, Jason Ellison and Jason Hammel. Goodwin never stopped his quest for baseball knowledge and always grilled pros and his returning college players for tips and drills.

9. Al Hairston, boys basketball, Garfield. In 12 years as head coach, Hairston's teams won the big-school title five times. A sign in the Garfield gym proclaimed, "Al's House," to honor the coach and former SuperSonic.

8. Pat Tyson, cross-country, Shorecrest (Seattle) and Mead (Spokane). Tyson was a former teammate and roommate of Oregon distance legend Steve Prefontaine. From 1986–2005, Tyson's Mead cross-country squads amassed a dual record of 145–6, and he won 12 boys state cross-country team titles. His runners combined for 26 individual state titles in track and cross-country.

7. Nola Ayres, girls gymnastics, Sehome (Bellingham). Under Ayres, the Bellingham school owned state gymnastics. Sehome won 20 of 21 big-school titles from 1973–93 and added four more before she retired in 2000.

6. Linda Sheridan, girls basketball/volleyball, Shadle Park (Spokane). In the 1987–88 and 1988–89 school years, Sheridan coached volleyball and basketball teams of her alma mater to state big-school titles. She won three other state volleyball crowns and is credited with inspiring many girls to enter coaching. The school named its gym in her honor.

5. Butch Goncharoff, football, Bellevue. The most significant high-school football victory in the state since World War II didn't come in a state-championship game. It was Bellevue's 39–20 victory over De La Salle of Concord, CA, at Qwest Field in 2004, because it snapped De La Salle's national-record winning streak at 151 games. Goncharoff's teams won five of six 3A state titles from 2001–2006.

4. Al Aldridge, girls basketball, Prairie (Vancouver). Aldridge's record starting the 2008–09 season was 613–118 with five state titles. Before retiring as a full-time teacher, Aldridge taught band, which helped his hoopsters: Near the end of tight games, the band knew not to play because Aldridge wanted to make sure his players heard his instructions. He also had hand signals with his lead trumpet players during games to indicate pitch adjustments. Speaking of pitches, he also coached softball at Prairie and won two state titles.

3. Dick Hannula, boys swimming, Wilson (Tacoma). No team in state history has been more dominant than Wilson swim teams. The school won 24 consecutive big-school state titles from 1960 to 1983 and had an unbeaten (one tie) streak of 323 meets in that span. One year, they made shirts that read, "20 years, still no fears." Hannula had a pipeline of talent from the Tacoma Swim Club and also benefited from having a pool on the Wilson campus.

2. Ed Pepple, boys basketball, Mercer Island. Pepple's mother caught him skipping school in the 1940s to attend the state basketball tournament. "She grabbed me by the ear and dragged me back to school," he said. He played in the tournament title game in 1950 for a Lincoln-Seattle team that lost in overtime to South Kitsap. As a coach, Pepple won four titles as MI coach. His record entering the 2008–09 season—his 42nd at Mercer Island—was a state-best 936–296. An ex-Marine, Pepple made his players get haircuts and wear Mercer Island maroon blazers to road games.

1. Terry Ennis, football, Stanwood/ Renton/Cascade (Everett)/Archbishop Murphy. Son of legendary Everett coach Jim Ennis, Terry won every place he coached in his 36-year career. He was 287–87 with three state titles. In the final five days of his life, he coached from a chair on the sidelines. He won on Saturday night and died Wednesday. His 2007 Archbishop Murphy team later was disqualified from the state 2A playoffs because a player's physical exam had lapsed. It was the oversight of a dying man but there was no mercy. Rick Reilly of *Sports Illustrated* wrote: "The smallest-brained crustaceans are water fleas. The smallest-brained parasites are flatworms. And the smallest-brained mammals are the men and women who run high-school athletics in the state of Washington." A state rule allowing mercy for clerical errors was adopted eight months later.

Every major sports market has had some doozies, but we like to think that if Seattle hasn't been the motherlode of misguided field/floor management, we pity the fools where it resides.

10. Mac Duckworth, Washington basketball. Of all coaches in UW hoops history who lasted more than a season, only Duckworth had a losing record. From 1964–68, he compiled a 53–74 mark, including 24–47 in conference play, a winning percentage of just .417. Duckworth resigned after going 12–14 in his final season.

9. Paul Graham, Washington State basketball. Starting in his first season of 1999–2000, Graham's teams were 6–22, 12–16, 6–21 and 7–20, the worst coaching record in WSU history, including just nine Pac-10 wins in those four years. After his firing, when the program never looked more helpless, WSU hired Dick and Tony Bennett and were in the NCAA tourney four years later.

8. Paul Westphal, Sonics. Westphal inherited a team that won 61 games in 1997–98 under George Karl and managed to win just two playoff games over the next two years. His tenure, which came to an end 15 games into his third season, was marked as much by discord as losses. His players questioned his ability while he questioned their commitment and work habits. Westphal's dismissal came days after an on-court shouting match with star guard Gary Payton during a game with Dallas. The coach suspended Payton for a game, then hours later rescinded it, effectively losing control of the team.

7. Tom Nissalke (1972), Bob Hopkins (1977), Bob Weiss (2005). These three each coached the Sonics a half-season or less. Hopkins lasted 22 games, Weiss 30 and Nissalke 45. Nissalke was the only man named ABA (Dallas) and NBA (Houston) coach of the year, but in Seattle, owner Sam Schulman, after a 13–32 start, called his hiring "a blunder." Hopkins succeeded his cousin, Bill Russell, but didn't succeed with a 5–17 record, then was succeeded by Lenny Wilkens, who took nearly the same group of players to the 1978 NBA Finals. Weiss, an original Sonics player, was promoted from assistant on a 52-win team coached by Nate McMillan, but started off 13–17, failing to make the jump from players' pal to players' boss.

6. John Cherberg, Washington football. The quintessential disciplinarian, Cherberg alienated his players by making them sit erect on the bench and wouldn't even allow them to whistle. His players openly mocked him and finally instigated a mutiny, which led to his termination. After compiling a 10–18–2 record from 1953–55, Cherberg had a long stint as the state's lieutenant governor.

5. Lynn Nance, Washington basketball. An FBI agent and an NCAA investigator before he became UW basketball coach, Nance was so paranoid that he once refused to tell Bud Withers, then of the *Seattle Post-Intelligencer*, where one of his recruits, Mark Pope, played high school basketball. In Nance's four years at Washington (1990–93), the Huskies won only 50 of 112 games despite playing 10 contests against non-Division 1 opponents.

4. Every Mariners manager not named. Maury Wills or Lou Piniella. Darrell Johnson, Rene Lachemann, Del Crandall, Chuck Cottier, Marty Martinez, Dick Williams, Jim Snyder, Jim Lefebvre, Bill Plummer, Bob Melvin, Mike Hargrove and John McLaren combined for 1,480 wins and 1,862 losses, or 382 games below .500. Sure, some of these guys did OK, but we lumped them together as a salute to the renegade mediocrity that gripped the franchise for so many years. The Mariners were the slowest major team to a winning season—15 years—in the modern history of American sports. It certainly wasn't all the fault of the managers, but you know how it goes in baseball. We exempted Wills from this spot for a reason (see No. 1).

3. Andy Russo, Washington basketball. Russo replaced Marv Harshman after guiding the Karl Malone-led Louisiana Tech to a 29–3 record in the 1984–85 season. He never came remotely close to replicating that success at Washington. In four years, his teams went 61–62 (.496), including 12–16 and 10–19 in his final two years. Russo's clubs served up some of the epic losses in school history. On December 20, 1988, UW lost to Arizona 116–61. Two nights later, they lost to a mediocre Arizona State team missing both of its starting guards, 121–90. That's the most points ever scored against Washington, erasing a record that had lasted 48 hours. On New Year's Day, 1989, Russo told writers covering the Huskies, "We'll be all right. It's like an egg when it breaks. You glue it back together. It's stronger."

2. Tom Flores, Seahawks. Flores won a pair of Super Bowls while coaching the Raiders, but his Seattle tenure amounted to squat as he went 14–34 from 1992–94. At 2–14, his 1992 team was the worst in franchise history. In one six-game stretch, the Seahawks scored 22 points. Flores' tenure was so brutal that he holds the distinction of being one of four head coaches in NFL history (Jimmy Johnson, George Seifert, Mike Shanahan) to win two Super Bowls and not get inducted into the Pro Football Hall of Fame.

1. Maury Wills, Mariners. The worst coach/manager in Seattle sports history, Wills, legendary base stealer for the Dodgers, took over for Darrell Johnson late in the 1980 season and was canned after starting the 1981 campaign with six wins in 24 games. Wills did himself in not so much because of his record, but because of his erratic behavior and bizarre decisions. Before a game against Oakland in the Kingdome, he tried to change the lines of the batter's box. Caught by Oakland manager Billy Martin, Wills was fined and suspended. Another time, he made out a lineup card that had two third basemen and no center fielder. He attempted to send a pinch hitter to the plate who had already played. He tried to insert a pitcher into a game who had already pitched. Once, when asked whom he expected to play center field, Wills said, "I wouldn't be a bit surprised if it was Leon Roberts." Roberts had been traded to Texas five weeks earlier. After his firing, Wills underwent treatment for cocaine addiction.

The word "classic" in sports has been bludgeoned to death. But there are times when a game or event carries meaning and memory beyond a big result. It's when conditions or circumstances, often unanticipated, combine with pinnacle moments to create an experience that will stay on tongues and in minds of all who bore witness.

10. Seattle Metropolitans win Stanley Cup, March 26, 1917. None of us were there, OK? Guess who was—Royal Brougham, the *Seattle Post-Intelligencer's* sports editor who lived long enough to hand off his typewriter ribbon to Rudman and Thiel. A cub reporter then, Brougham wrote the Mets "went through the invaders' defense like a tornado on wheels in huckleberry time." Seattle's 9–1 victory over the Montreal Canadiens, in front of 2,500 fans at the downtown Ice Arena, enabled the Mets to win Seattle's first pro sports championship and become the first American team to win the Stanley Cup.

9. First Monday Night Football game, October 29, 1979. It wasn't so much that the three-year-old Seahawks, making their first appearance on Monday Night Football with Giff, Dandy Don and Howard, trailed 14–0 early and rebounded for a 31–28 victory as much as it was the improbable nature of Seattle's comeback. Coach Jack Patera utilized several trick plays against the Atlanta Falcons, which included a fake field goal attempt that turned into a 20-yard pass from QB Jim Zorn to kicker Efren Herrera, the first catch of the kicker's career. The original play-calling made the Seahawks a hit locally and nationally.

8. George Wilson vs. Ernie Nevers, November 7, 1925. No game in the first 40 years of Husky football fascinated fans more than the Washington-Stanford matchup of 1925, because it featured the first and only meeting of Washington's George Wilson and Stanford's Ernie Nevers, two of the three backs, along with Red Grange of Illinois, that Walter Camp named to his All-America backfield. While both teams averaged 40 points per game, the defenses held sway until the second period when Wilson put Washington ahead by throwing a 26-yard TD to George Guttormsen. Late in the third quarter, after Washington scored on an interception return by Louie Tesreau, Stanford reached the UW 9. On instructions from Stanford coach Pop Warner, Nevers cracked the line three times, reaching the 3, and each time was met head-on by Wilson and Elmer Tesreau. On fourth down, Nevers again hit the line, only to be smashed by Wilson and Tesreau for no gain. Nevers was knocked unconscious, and both he and Tesreau were carted off the field. With Nevers out, Stanford could make no dent in Washington's 13–0 lead.

7. Mercer Island-Shadle Park, March 14, 1981. The AAA boys' state basketball title game remains the most controversial finale in the 85-year history of the tournament. It ended when Shadle Park's Greg Schmidt hit a short jump shot from the baseline either before or after the buzzer, giving the Spokane team a 66–65 victory over the suburban Seattle school at the Coliseum. One referee, Chris Manolopoulos, ruled Schmidt's shot good. But the other, Dave George, signaled no basket, creating instant bedlam. Fans from both schools stormed the floor, thinking they had won. Soon shoving matches broke out, Mercer Island players bellowed and cried, and Shadle Park players stood in a collective daze. Finally, Manolopoulos's ruling stood, after which he left the Coliseum with a police escort. Lost in the confusion was the fact that Shadle Park's Mark Rypien, a future Super Bowl Most Valuable Player, was named the tournament's MVP.

6. Blanchet wins "game of the century." November 7, 1975. The *Seattle Times* ranked Blanchet's 42–35, four-overtime victory over Garfield, played in front of 12,951 fans at Memorial Stadium, as the prep "Game of the Century." Hard to argue. The Seattle schools each were 8–0 (Blanchet had a 25-game winning streak over three seasons) and both featured high-profile players who would later star for the Washington Huskies—Joe Steele and Ken Gardner for Blanchet, Anthony Allen and Bruce Harrell for Garfield. Tied at 35 in the fourth overtime, Blanchet tried a halfback pass. Steele, who had already run for two touchdowns and caught a five-yard pass for a third, got the pitch, saw Steve Williams cutting across the middle, and tossed the winning 11-yard touchdown.

5. Washington over Duke, March 1984. Playing one of the most storied programs in college basketball in the West Regionals of the NCAA Tournament, the Huskies never cowered. They opened hitting 10 of their first 12 shots, finished it by connecting on 10 of their last 11, and wound up making 71 percent (31 of 44) overall, a school record. Two players stood out: Junior forward Detlef Schrempf dropped in 11 of his 14 attempts en route to a game-high 30 points, and Reggie Rogers, moonlighting from the UW football team, scored 10 points and made the game's most important shot, a free throw with six seconds to play that gave the Huskies their final point in an 80–78 victory.

4. Moon leads UW to Rose Bowl win, January 2, 1978. The Huskies seemed dead in the water after four games—they were 1–3 and had lost to a couple of cupcakes. But Washington won five of its final six and, despite being 14-point underdogs, polished off Michigan in the Rose Bowl 27–20 in probably the most important game of the Don James era. Because of the success of the 1977 Huskies, James was able to recruit to the UW the nucleus of players who took Washington to the 1979 Sun Bowl, the 1981 and 1982 Rose Bowls, and the 1982 Aloha Bowl.

3. Snow Bowl in Pullman, November 21, 1992.
No Apple Cup classic is more memorable than the 1992 "Snow Bowl" in Pullman's Martin Stadium. In a blizzard for the books, future NFL stars Drew Bledsoe and Mark Brunell hooked up in a remarkable passing duel, Bledsoe finally winning the day by throwing for 260 yards and two touchdowns as the Cougars shellacked the defending national champions 42–23. On the occasion of its 10th anniversary, Bledsoe said, "That's still my most favorite game I've played in."

2. An Orange beats a Rose, January 1, 1985.
Washington lost only one game in 1984, a 16–7 setback to USC in Los Angeles that kept the Huskies out of the Rose Bowl. But they were the first Pac-10 team to receive an invitation to the Orange Bowl in Miami. The "consolation" nearly resulted in Washington winning the national championship. The 10–1 Huskies entered as a seven-point underdog to the No. 2-ranked Oklahoma Sooners. But quarterback Hugh Millen came off the bench to direct two scoring drives, game MVP Jacque Robinson ran for 135 yards and a TD, and the Husky defense stymied the Sooners' wishbone offense. The 28–17 Washington victory gave the Huskies a claim to No. 1 in the final polls. The only unbeaten, BYU, played an easy schedule and defeated a mediocre 6–5 Michigan team in the Holiday Bowl. At 11–1, Washington finished No. 2, the highest wire-service ranking for a Husky team up to that time.

1. How baseball was saved in Seattle, October 8, 1995.
No moment in Seattle sports was more dramatic or significant than Game 5 of the American League Division Series. By now, Edgar Martinez's double that drove in Ken Griffey Jr. with the winning run in the 11th inning of the 6–5 victory over the Yanks has been played a thousand times on the Safeco Field screen, which owes some part of its existence to the drama that launched a thousand lobbyists to the state capital. In contrast to the historic feebleness of the Mariners franchise, the resulting frenzy over the club possibly moving to Florida created a political freight train that led to the $380 million public funding of Safeco Field, the implosion of the Kingdome, and long-term stability and profitability for the franchise.

Every sports team knows these woes. But each time, palms slam to foreheads of die-hard fans: How did that happen? Here are the best 10 confounding dumbfounders, whether by a single play or game-long failure, which left no jaw undropped.

10. Oregon 30, UW 21, October 22, 1994. Oregon freshman DB Kenny Wheaton picked off a Damon Huard pass with 49 seconds to play and returned it 97 yards for a touchdown—the second-longest interception return ever against Washington—to lift the Ducks to victory at Autzen Stadium. Equally bad for UW fans, the momentum of the victory propelled Oregon to its first Rose Bowl appearance in 37 years.

9. Arizona 31, UW 28, October 3, 1998. In one of the more improbable endings in UW football history, Arizona QB Ortege Jenkins scored on a 9-yard run with four seconds to go to give No. 14 Arizona the victory. Jenkins directed Arizona's 13-play drive, during which he was the quarterback for all but one play. On that play, replacement Keith Smith threw a 22-yard completion to Jenkins. From there, Jenkins marched the Wildcats to the end zone, scoring on second down when, on a play that became known as "The Leap by the Lake," he hurtled toward the end zone, cleared three defenders with a somersault and landed on his feet.

8. Indians 15, Mariners 14 (11), August 5, 2001. The greatest team in Mariners history inexplicably also had the greatest single-game swoon. Leading 12–0 after three innings and 14–2 after five, the M's were outscored 13–0 from the seventh through the 11th innings. On only two other occasions in major league history had a team climbed out of a 12-run hole to win. What made the rally even more astonishing was that Cleveland pulled starters Roberto Alomar, Juan Gonzalez and Ellis Burks by the seventh inning. The Indians scored three in the seventh, four in the eighth and five after two were out in the ninth, the last three on Omar Vizquel's bases-loaded triple off closer Kazuhiro Sasaki. On three occasions in the ninth, the Indians were down to their final strike.

7. Miami 65, UW 7, November 24, 2001. Top-ranked and eventual national champion Miami (9–0) entered the game having buried two Top 15 teams by a combined 124–7 the two previous weekends, then buried the 12th-ranked Huskies (8–2 at the time) with a 30-point second quarter, the most Washington ever surrendered in one period. The Huskies, with quarterback Cody Pickett throwing a career-worst five interceptions, turned the ball over seven times in the second-worst defeat in school history.

6. Nuggets 168, Sonics 116, March 26, 2008. A season designed for wretchedness nevertheless punched through a new frontier for futility when the Sonics laid down and quit against the Nuggets. "It's unbelievable," said Nuggets forward Kenyon Martin. "A lot of people are going to think it's a misprint. There are no words for it." Records galore fell for both teams, but what told the tale in the worst game of the worst season in the Sonics' 41 years was that Nuggets star Allen Iverson took time during the game to sign autographs for fans.

5. Jets 41, Seahawks 3, August 31, 1997. Because they had a new owner, a new stadium on the way and a horde of new players, the Seahawks had a new motto for the season: "A Whole New Ball Game." Except it wasn't. A game the Seahawks expected to win turned into one of the most forgettable three hours in franchise history. Against a middling Jets team (eventually 9–7), it was so bad—five dropped passes, four false starts, an intentional grounding penalty—that new coach and hometown hero Dennis Erickson apologized for his team's lack of effort and execution. "It was pretty pitiful," Erickson said. "I apologize to everybody for that performance."

4. Arizona 116, UW 61, December 20, 1988. Wildcat coach Lute Olson's 35–3 team that reached the Final Four, led by Steve Kerr and Sean Elliott, came in ninth-ranked against a 4–2 Washington team and delivered the worst margin of defeat in Pac-10 hoops history. "I have never been in this position before," said coach Andy Russo, who was fired after the 12–16 season, his second consecutive loser. "I thought we were definitely beyond being beaten this bad."

3. Rangers 12, Mariners 10, April 6, 1992. The Mariners, celebrating the start of their first full season of new, local ownership, played the most dubious home opener in franchise history, allowing the Rangers nine runs with two outs in the eighth inning. "I don't think I've ever seen nine runs with two outs in the eighth inning," complained manager Bill Plummer. Closer Mike Schooler played the goat, giving up four runs, including a pinch-hit three-run homer.

2. Rams 24, Seahawks 0, November 4, 1979. The final score became inconsequential compared to the most ghastly statistic in franchise history: a minus 7 yards total offense, which remains the NFL record. The Seahawks lost an average of 7.2 inches on each play, made only one first down, and never had the ball for more than 1:58 on any of their 12 possessions. "We did a hell of a job," said Rams DE Fred Dryer. "I'm sure when we look at the film we'll find someone who made a mistake, but who cares?"

1. Oregon State 21, UW 20, October 19, 1985. Oddsmakers had Washington as a 37-point favorite to make easy work of the hapless Beavers, who were working on their 28th consecutive losing season. They hadn't scored a touchdown in more than a month and were featuring a walk-on freshman quarterback, Rich Gonzalez, who had never been involved in a college touchdown, let alone a victory. What oddsmakers failed to account for was the umbrage that ran deep through the OSU squad after a Seattle columnist (author Rudman) dismissed the Beavers as "the Barney Fife of college football." The Beavers stayed all game with the more talented Huskies (4–2) until, with 1:46 to play and Washington facing fourth-and-9 at its 30, a blown block allowed Oregon State's Andre Todd to race in and stuff Thane Cleland's punt. The ball rolled into the end zone, where Lavance Northington recovered it for the game-tying touchdown. The extra point not only gave Oregon State the biggest upset victory in terms of point spread in college history (since eclipsed), but the biggest win in school history. (After the game, one Oregon State player was still so steamed at author Rudman over the Barney Fife crack that he jabbed a finger into author Thiel's chest and gave him a good what for.)

Nothing like local kids making good to tug at the heartstrings of sports fans. Perhaps more than any other in the book, this list of improbable moments by teams and individuals captures the joy of sports, when the big underdog masters the formidable foe.

10. Bellevue snaps De La Salle's 151-game win streak, September 4, 2004.
The Wolverines turned one of the most anticipated games in state high school history—the matchup with De La Salle of Concord, Calif., the nation's top prep team—into what more closely resembled an ordinary Kingco Conference 3A romp. Bellevue ran the ball at will (Bellevue, in fact, did not even attempt a pass), delighting an Emerald City Kickoff Classic crowd of 24,987 at Qwest Field. The 39–20 victory, coming against a team that had shut out seven opponents a year earlier, snapped De La Salle's national record 151-game winning streak that began in 1992.

9. Lindgren upsets the Russians, July 25, 1964.
Spokane's Gerry Lindgren won 11 of the 12 NCAA cross-country events he contested while a student at Washington State, set a six-mile world record in 1965, held national records at 3,000 and 5,000 meters, and was national champion at 10,000. But nothing Lindgren did gained him more enduring fame than his performance in the USA-USSR track meet when, as a largely unknown 17-year-old, he outran two seasoned Russians, Leonid Ivanov and Anatoly Dutov, to win the 10,000 in front of 50,515 fans at the Los Angeles Coliseum. Lindgren opened up a 20-yard lead at the four-mile mark and steadily widened his margin, finally winning in 29:17.6, with more than 100 yards to spare.

8. UW finally beats a No. 1, February 22, 1979.
Brad Holland put the Huskies (11–13) in the soup with 15 seconds to play with two free throws to give UCLA (eventually 25–5) its first lead of the night. Washington's first option was seven-foot-one center Petur Gudmundsson. But the Bruins defense forced UW to a second option, Stan Walker, who hit a jumper over All-America Keith Wilkes, giving Washington a 69–68 victory—the first time a UW basketball team beat the No. 1-ranked team in the nation.

7. Huskies hand Wooden last loss, February 22, 1975.
John Wooden won 10 NCAA basketball titles during his tenure at UCLA. His last defeat came at Hec Edmundson Pavilion when the Huskies (16–7), led by Larry Johnson's 27 points and 14 rebounds, built a 52–44 halftime lead, went on a 10–0 run in the second half and up-ended the Bruins 103–81, UW's first win over the Bruins in 12 years. Undeterred, UCLA (28–3) regrouped to win another national championship, and Wooden retired.

6. Cope wins Daytona 500, February 18, 1990. A lightly regarded racer from little Spanaway, south of Tacoma, Derrike Cope had never come close to winning a NASCAR event in 71 career attempts, and was given no shot in a field that included Dale Earnhardt, desperate to win the only race that had eluded him. Earnhardt led for 155 of 199 laps and seemed certain to win when the flag dropped for one final spin around the oval. Cope, remarkably, put himself in a position—he led laps 194–195—to take advantage of any trouble. Cope got his break when Earnhardt ran over debris that nearly caused him to lose control. Cope sped by for a win that, in 2008, on the occasion of the 50th anniversary celebration of the race, was voted the greatest upset in the history of Daytona.

5. Seahawks 27, Dolphins 20, December 31, 1983. No one expected the Seahawks to give Dan Marino and the Dolphins much of a game, especially at the Orange Bowl in an AFC divisional playoff game. At 9–7, Seattle narrowly made the playoffs, was in only its second postseason contest, and an eight-point underdog. Trailing 20–17 halfway through the final period, the Seahawks went 66 yards in five plays, including one of the seminal plays in team history—a 40-yard pass from Dave Krieg to Steve Largent—that set up rookie Curt Warner's two-yard, game-winning TD inside two minutes. The 27–20 victory was the first playoff win in franchise history.

4. Larry Owings over Dan Gable, March 28, 1970. Dan Gable never lost a wrestling match in high school (64 consecutive victories), nor at Iowa State University. When he stepped onto the mat at McGaw Hall on the Northwestern campus, he was a three-time All-America, two-time NCAA champion and the winner of 181 consecutive matches, including his previous five by pins. His seemingly in-over-his-head opponent in the 142-pound NCAA final: University of Washington sophomore Larry Owings. Owings trailed Gable 10–9 with 25 seconds left but had a near pin and a takedown to win the match. An eight-minute video of Owings' triumph was subsequently placed on permanent display in the Wrestling Hall of Fame in Stillwater, OK.

3. Whammy in Miami, September 24, 1994. Oddsmakers installed the Hurricanes as 14-point favorites over UW for at least two good reasons: No. 5 Miami had not lost at the Orange Bowl in 58 games over eight years, and had not lost at home to a team outside of Florida in more than a decade. Miami also had a defense anchored by Warren Sapp (in his Outland Trophy season) and Ray Lewis (future All-Pro linebacker). Miami held a 14–3 halftime lead, but sparked by a 75-yard touchdown pass (Damon Huard to Richard Thomas), a 34-yard interception return (Russell Hairston) and a fumble recovery TD (Bob Sapp), the Huskies (2–1) went on a 22-point scoring spree to break open the game. Miami head coach Dennis Erickson, an Everett native coaching against fellow Snohomish County native Jim Lambright, labeled the 38–20 loss "a fluke." Erickson resigned after a 10–2 season to take the head coaching job with the Seahawks.

2. Seattle U. derails undefeated Texas Western, March 3, 1966. The Miners entered the Coliseum with a 23–0 record and a No. 2 national ranking. With 11,557 watching, the Seattle U. Chieftains, after changing leads 19 times, handed Texas Western (later Texas-El Paso) its only defeat, 74–72, when Tom Workman swished a shot with 53 seconds left. The visitors missed three shots and a free throw in the waning seconds. Less than a month later, the Miners became the first all-black team to win the NCAA title when they upset heavily favored Kentucky in the championship game. Texas Western's loss in Seattle was its only one of the year.

1. UW rowers beat the Russians, July 19, 1958. A scandal in the University of Washington football program—boosters paid players, resulting in NCAA sanctions against all of the school's teams—prevented coach Al Ulbrickson's rowers from taking part in the 1958 national collegiate championships. So the Huskies accepted invitations to take part in the Henley Royal Regatta on the Thames River in London, and in an international competition on the Khiminskoe Reservoir outside Moscow that had been arranged by the State Department as part of a cultural exchange. At Henley, the UW eight drew defending world champion Trud Club of Leningrad, Russia, and lost by a length and a quarter. Trud went on to win the Grand Challenge Cup. Fifteen days later, the Huskies lined up against four Russian crews—Trud Club, Soviet Army, Moscow Spartak and Kiev Dynamos. With KOMO sports director Keith Jackson broadcasting the race live—the first broadcast of a sports event from behind the Iron Curtain—the UW caught and passed the Soviet Army shell at the 500-meter mark. At 1,000 meters, Washington opened up a one-length lead over Trud and went on to win by one and three-quarters lengths in 6:18.06, one of the greatest upsets in rowing history.

Reasons Miami Would Have Beaten UW In 1991
:: Dennis Erickson

Everett native Dennis Erickson was hanging his coaching hat at the University of Miami in 1991 when the Hurricanes fashioned an 11–0 record. More than 3,000 miles away, Don James was doing the same thing with the 1991 Washington team. In pre-BCS days, Miami went to the Orange Bowl and Washington to the Rose Bowl. What if UW quarterback Billy Joe Hobert's suggestion had been taken: That the UW "dog the Rose Bowl" to play Miami? Who would have won?

I would have loved to see that game. It would have been tough for Washington, maybe too tough. It probably would have been as good as any game that was ever played. I never talked to Don (James) about it, but Gilby (1991 UW offensive coordinator and fellow Snohomish County native Keith Gilbertson) and I still argue about it. No one ever wins the argument.

5. Coaching. Truthfully, this is one area where you'd have to give the edge to Washington. I mean, age over beauty, right? Don James is a good guy, a great person and a tremendous coach. His teams were always tough, organized, and disciplined. That's how he won as many games as he did.

4. Special teams. Our punting, kicking, and return units were sensational. Kevin Williams was an outstanding returner. Carlos Huerta is considered the greatest kicker in Miami history.

3. Attitude. I loved our attitude. Play hard and have fun playing. I learned more at Miami about how to play as far as attitude than anyplace. Our players didn't think of it as hot-dogging. They just had fun. That gave them an edge and they enjoyed that. We intimidated people. Defense creates intimidation when you fly around and knock the living crap out of people. They never let up. Our practices were harder than games and spring ball was ugly.

2. Explosive offense. We had several plays that would score from long distance. Our skill players called themselves "The Ruthless Posse."

1. Speed on defense. Speed was the name of our game. On defense in particular, guys could run. We were just really good. So was Washington. Both teams would have had trouble moving the ball.

Bob Rondeau has been the radio voice of the Huskies for 32 years, and on behalf of Washington adherents, he respectfully disagrees with Erickson.

9. Um, because they were bigger and stronger. In a vast majority of the individual match-ups, Washington would have been superior. This team had everything in terms of physicality. They knew it and so did their opponents. It's interesting to note how healthy the Dawgs stayed in the 1991 season. Just lucky? Doubtful. Bigger, stronger players tend to overpower smaller, weaker players. Funny how unhealthy the Huskies' opponents tended to be, after the game. Miami would have been no exception.

8. Speed doesn't always kill. Granted, the Hurricanes might have had better overall team speed. But in this case, it would not have been lethal. It would have been immaterial. Washington's defensive pressure would have negated anything Miami brought to the table. Michigan's Heisman Trophy winner that year, Desmond Howard, was a fast wide receiver as well. How many catches did he have in the Rose Bowl against UW? One. Further, quarterbacks lacking mobility were cannon fodder for that Husky defense. As I recall, Gino Torretta wasn't exactly Vince Young. Which brings us to . . .

7. Quarterbacks. I don't care if Torretta would later win the Heisman. Had the 'Canes and Huskies played, Mr. T. would have been the third-best quarterback on the field. Billy Joe Hobert was better and so was Mark Brunell, who was coming back from a knee injury. Don't believe me? Compare the pro careers of the three guys in question. Which brings us to...

6. Pros. If better players make for better teams, Washington was clearly superior with 11 players chosen in the 1992 NFL draft, including No. 1 overall. Miami had seven players selected, three of whom were taken in the 12th round. By the way, the Hurricanes MVP in 1991 was, drum roll please, the kicker, Carlos Huerta. The kicker???

5. O Line? Oh, my! In case you thought the Miami defensive line and a corps of linebackers labeled among the school's best would have been difference-makers against Washington, think again. The Huskies' offensive line was massive and massively talented. Including the tight end, five of the six Husky starters would go on to the NFL. Washington's offense was a study in balance, and the Dawgs would have moved the ball nicely against the Hurricanes.

4. Steve Emtman. Since he was the best player in America in 1991, is there reason to believe he would not have been the best player on the field in a game against Miami? Worry not, 'Canes, no one else could block him, either.

3. The Nebraska comparison. Miami will claim its 22–0 shutout of Nebraska in the Orange Bowl trumped Washington's 36–21 win over the Cornhuskers during the regular season. The Orange Bowl was played in, yes, Miami, while the Huskies' win came at Lincoln. We can only imagine the count had the Huskies played Nebraska in Seattle.

2. Tomey says 'Canes weren't able. Dick Tomey's Arizona Wildcats lost to Washington 54–0 in Seattle and to Miami 36–9 in Tucson. Tomey (now head coach at San Jose State) says of the games: "We hung in with Miami for a while. Washington? We were never in it; they could have named their score. That Husky team was incredible. Their defense was suffocating and their offensive variety extraordinary. I thought that team was better than Miami." Final score? "I think it would have been a relatively low-scoring game. Washington 21–17." Works for me.

1. Etched in stone. The Huskies and Hurricanes were invited to the White House after the 1991 co-championship. History favored Washington. Trust me, it was common knowledge in the nation's capital which school had the better team. After all, has it ever been called…the Miami Monument? Case closed.

If you were there, or caught the telecast, we hardly need remind you. But we will, because these games were so much fun, then and now.

10. Seahawks 13, Cowboys 10, October 3, 2005. Trailing 10–3 with less than a minute to play, the Seahawks scored a touchdown—pass from Matt Hasselbeck to TE Ryan Hannum—and a 50-yard field goal by Josh Brown with five seconds remaining. It marked the first time in the team's 30 seasons that the Seahawks had scored twice in the final minute to win a game.

9. Seahawks 17, Chiefs 16, November 11, 1990. For 59 minutes, the Seahawks' Arrowhead Stadium jinx played out perfectly: Derrick Thomas sacked Dave Krieg an NFL-record seven times, officials flagged Seattle 13 times for 102 yards, and the Seahawks gave up two fumbles. But Krieg orchestrated a final-minute drive that finally reached the Kansas City 25-yard line. With four seconds remaining, Krieg spun away from Thomas, avoiding an eighth sack, and hit a leaping Paul Skansi with a game-winning touchdown with no time left. It marked the first time in Seahawks history that they won a game on the final play.

8. UW 28, Cal 27, November 12, 1988; UW 24, Cal 23, October 9, 1993. Same teams, same circumstances, same one-point outcome, five years apart. In 1988, Huskies fell behind 27–3 before rallying behind QB Cary Conklin for 25 points in 20 minutes. John McCallum's 25-yard field goal with seconds remaining made for the largest comeback in Huskies history. In 1993, UW trailed 23–3 in the third after four interceptions of Damon Huard. But Huard completed 12 of his final 14 passes to lead three TD drives, two in the final 2:06.

7. Seahawks, 23, Oilers 16, November 3, 1996. Houston field goal kicker Al Del Greco was one relatively easy one away from beating the Seahawks at the Kingdome. Instead, his 37-yard attempt in final seconds caromed off Seattle DE Michael McCrary. He collected the ball and dished to FS Robert Blackmon, who ran 61 yards for an improbable game-winning TD.

6. UW 103, Oregon St. 99 (OT), January 17, 2004. Washington's basketball season seemed on the brink of collapse when the 6–8 Huskies (0–5 in Pac-10 play) fell behind Oregon State by 16 in the second half at Gill Coliseum. Then 5–8 G Nate Robinson scored 13 points in a six-minute span, sparking a 29–13 Husky run, and Tre Simmons drilled a 3-point shot with five seconds to play to trail 81–80. Following a pair of Chris Stephens free throws, Robinson picked up the inbounds pass at midcourt, dribbled to the 3-point arc and hit a jumper with a half second left to force OT, which UW dominated. The victory served as the impetus for 15 wins in the next 17 games, which earned Washington a place in the NCAA tournament.

5. Sonics 114, Bucks 113 (OT), April 8, 1980. With six seconds remaining in overtime, Milwaukee's Marques Johnson seemed to have ended a game that had been played in a Coliseum atmosphere of utter bedlam when he dunked off a steal to give the Bucks a 113–111 lead. Then Sonics guard Dennis Johnson shocked all by weaving through 70 feet of the best defense Milwaukee could muster and chucking up a 26-foot grenade with one second to go that gave the Sonics a victory in Game 1 of the Western Conference semifinals.

4. UW 38, Purdue 35, September 18, 1971. Washington came from behind four times to beat the Boilermakers, with the final four minutes among the wildest in UW history. At the four-minute mark, UW quarterback Sonny Sixkiller, who finished with a career-high 387 passing yards, threw an 18-yard TD pass to Jim Krieg to give Washington a 31–28 lead. On the next scrimmage play (3:39 remaining), Purdue's Gary Danielson connected with Darryl Stingley on an 80-yard TD pass to put the Boilermakers ahead 35–31. With 2:29 to go, Sixkiller threw a 33-yard TD pass to Tom Scott to put the Huskies ahead 38–35. Danielson had the Boilermakers on the move in the final two minutes, but UW linebacker Rick Huget sealed the victory when he intercepted Danielson with 1:49 left.

3. Seahawks 21, Cowboys 20, January 6, 2007. They don't call it a wild-card game for nothing. Trailing 20–13 in the fourth quarter at home, the Seahawks were stopped at fourth-and-goal at the Cowboys 2-yard line. But on the next play, CB Kelly Jennings forced WR Terry Glenn to fumble into the end zone for a safety. The Seahawks took the kickoff and turned the drive into a 37-yard touchdown pass to TE Jerramy Stevens, whiffing on the two-point PAT. With 1:20 left, the Cowboys attempted a 19-yard field goal, but QB/holder Tony Romo, who was downed at the 2-yard line, bobbled the snap.

2. UW 28, WSU 27, November 22, 1975. No Apple Cup ever had a wackier windup. With 3:01 to play, Washington State had a 27–14 lead and the ball on the UW 14-yard line. Staring at fourth-and-one, the Cougars needed only a first down or a field goal to win. Instead, Cougars players opted to rub it in, convincing coach Jim Sweeney they should throw the ball. Oops. Washington's Al Burleson returned the interception 93 yards to a touchdown, the longest return of a pilfered pass in school history. Inspired, the Huskies forced WSU to punt, and the UW took over on its 22 with 1:56 to play. On first down, QB Warren Moon hurled the ball in the direction of a mob in the center of the field. It hit WSU's Tony Heath on his helmet and ricocheted into the hands of Spider Gaines, who gleefully turned the boink into a 78-yard touchdown.

1. Mariners 6, Yankees 5 (11), October 8, 1995. You knew this one was here—the most captivating game in Seattle sports. Once trailing 0–2 in the ALDS against the Yankees, and 4-3 in the 11th inning of the deciding game at the Kingdome against New York ace Black Jack McDowell, pitching in relief. Joey Cora had a bunt single and went to third on a single by Ken Griffey Jr. Up came Edgar Martinez, whose .356 average that won the AL batting title was the highest for a right-handed hitter since Joe DiMaggio in 1939. Martinez ripped a double to left that plated Cora and Griffey and nearly brought down the concrete roof with what manager Lou Piniella later said was the "hit, the run, the game and the series that saved baseball in Seattle."

A closer needs three things to succeed: (1) A good out pitch; (2) A cool entrance song; and (3) A fearless nature combined with no conscience. The former Mariners closer scored on each count. After fooling around with a couple different songs, he settled on "Thunderstruck" by AC/DC. This staple of rock radio blasted out over the PA while a thunderbolt-themed light show appeared on the stadium scoreboards. Fans would cheer along as Putz tried to pin down a win or a save. It was a sensational show. If we acknowledge that "Thunderstruck" is the best entrance song, what are the other good ones? Here's J.J.'s list of his five favorites used by other closers.

5. Joe Nathan, Twins. "Stand Up" by Steel Dragon, the fictional band featured in the movie "Rock Star," written by Sammy Hagar for the movie.

4. Bobby Jenks, White Sox. "Boom" by P. O. D. M's fans will recognize this song as Bret Boone's at-bat music for several years.

3. Eric Gagne, Brewers. "Welcome to the Jungle" by Guns N' Roses. This obviously had a little more impact during his great Dodger seasons. Also, the song was warm-up music for Randy Johnson when he was in Seattle, including his entrance into Game 5 of the 1995 Yankees playoff series.

2. Mariano Rivera, Yankees. "Enter Sandman" by Metallica.

1. Jonathan Papelbon, Red Sox. "Bodies" by Drowning Pool. "Let the bodies hit the floor" seems an appropriate lyric for Papelbon's ability to retire batters.

There are butt-kickings, and then there are times when the boot gets buried into an opponent's soul. Such times as these:

10. Mariners 15, White Sox 4, May 2, 2000. After Jon Rauch plunked Ichiro with the game's first pitch, Bret Boone launched Rauch's next offering over the right-field fence. Mike Cameron then waited two pitches before belting a Rauch fastball over the center-field wall. By the end of the first inning, Boone and Cameron had become the first pair of teammates to twice hit back-to-back homers in a game's first inning, and the Mariners had a 10–0 lead. When it ended, Cameron had become the 13th player with four homers in a game and the fifth to do it in consecutive at-bats.

9. UW 72, California 0, November 6, 1915. Allen Young scored three times and Hap Miller, Walter Shiel and Cy Noble added two TDs each as Washington handed California its worst football beating ever. Purple and Gold rooters sang "Bow Down to Washington" for the first time.

8. Sonics 149, 76ers 93, March 6, 1993. During one phenomenal 15-minute stretch in the first half, the Sonics outscored the 76ers 51–11. During that run, the Sonics scored 18 consecutive points and held Philadelphia without a field goal. Seattle, which led by as many as 59 points, had seven players in double figures, including Dana Barros, who contributed 15 points, eight assists and six rebounds in 29 minutes off the bench.

7. UW 66, Oregon 0, October 26, 1974. Washington rolled up 508 yards and held Oregon to just 55 and two first downs in recording the biggest victory of the Jim Owens era. Quarterback Chris Rowland and fullback Robin Earl each scored two TDs, as did reserve halfback Mike Vicino.

6. Sounders 9, Drillers 0, August 1, 1979. Derek Smethurst, with four goals, opened and closed the scoring in front of 12,395 fans at the Kingdome. His first came at 14:54 and his last with 16 seconds remaining. John Ryan, Alan Hudson, Micky Cave, Tommy Ord and Jimmy McAlister also zinged balls past Edmonton goalkeeper Peter Arnautoff as the Sounders set team records for points in a half (16), points in a game (30), goals in a half (5), assists in a game (12) and largest margin of victory (9).

5. Mariners 22, Tigers 6, April 29, 1999. The remarkable thing was that the Mariners trailed 6–1 before putting up 21 unanswered runs. Eleven came in the fifth inning, setting a team record (the Tigers had not allowed 11 runs in an inning in 40 years). A grand slam by Ken Griffey Jr. capped the fifth, and he added a solo shot in a six-run sixth. In all, the Mariners used 12 batters, and each had a hit.

4. UW 92, Seattle U. 70, March 13, 1953. The first basketball meeting between the Huskies and Chieftains came in the NCAA Tournament West Regionals at Corvallis, Ore. NCAA Player of the Year Bob Houbregs scored 45 points to lead the Huskies. Who knew that the two schools would not play again for 17 years?

3. Sonics 136, Rockets 80, December 6, 1986. The Sonics scored seven points in a 37-second span of the first quarter, built a 13–6 lead, and never looked back against a Houston team missing Hakeem Olajuwon. By halftime, Tom Chambers and Dale Ellis combined to match the 42-point output by the Rockets. Seattle's lead dipped below 30 points three times in the second half, but each time the Sonics built it back up, finally winning by 56, the largest winning spread by a visiting team in NBA history.

2. Seahawks 42, Eagles 0, December 4, 2005. The Seahawks gained just 194 yards—they had been averaging 386—but didn't need to do much offensively after taking a 35–0 halftime lead, built, in part, on interception returns for touchdowns by Andre Dyson and rookie Lofa Tatupu. It marked the largest road win and largest road shutout in franchise history.

1. UW 44, Wisconsin 8, January 1, 1960. Two factors made this rout unlikely: Washington hadn't been to a Rose Bowl in 22 years, and West Coast teams had served as New Year's fodder for the Big Ten for as long as anyone could remember. But if Washington gave no inkling that history was about change, the first quarter removed any doubt. Don McKeta scored on a six-yard run, George Fleming kicked a 36-yard field goal and returned a punt 53 yards for another TD, and the rout was on. Big Ten teams had won 11 of the 12 previous Rose Bowls. Beginning in 1961, when Washington beat Minnesota 17–7, Pacific Coast Conference teams won 11 of the next 17.

No postseason loss is good, but some are way more aggravating than others, the kind that leave a big steaming pile in the middle of a sports fan's soul. It's one thing to lose as an underdog, but to have an upset in hand, or a big lead as a favorite, then crap out . . . well, get the Maalox out for this list.

10. Rams 27, Seahawks 20. January 8, 2005. In their first home playoff game since after the 1999 season, the Seahawks had a chance to tie in the closing seconds, but Bobby Engram could not handle Matt Hasselbeck's pass in the end zone on fourth-and-4, the ball boinking off his facemask. By losing, the Seahawks extended their playoff drought to 21 years. By winning, the Rams became the first 8–8 team to win a playoff game. Three of the four previous 8–8 teams had lost by double-digit margins.

9. Texas 47, Washington 43, December 28, 2001. The Huskies, who led the Holiday Bowl with Texas by 19 points following Willie Hurst's four-yard touchdown with 3:51 to play in the third quarter, came apart in the fourth as Longhorns quarterback Major Applewhite directed a 27–7 scoring binge, which included 20 unanswered points. On Texas' game-winning drive, Applewhite, who finished with 473 yards and four touchdown passes (both bowl records against the Huskies), completed passes of 12, 25 and 32 yards.

8. Yankees 3, Mariners 1, October 21, 2001. Winners of a record 116 games during the regular season, the Mariners trailed the series 2–1, but led 1–0 in Game 4 of the ALCS after second baseman Bret Boone homered in the eighth inning off reliever Ramiro Mendoza. In the bottom of the eighth, Bernie Williams hit a wind-aided home run off Arthur Rhodes, and then Alfonso Soriano won it with a walk-off blast off Kazuhiro Sasaki in the ninth. Soriano's home run became the turning point in the series as the Yankees went on to win it 4–1 and deny the Mariners their best opportunity in franchise history to reach the World Series.

7. Yankees 5, Mariners 0, October 14, 2000. Back in the postseason after a three-year absence, the Mariners opened the ALCS with a 2–0 victory at Yankee Stadium, but were blown out in Games 2 and 3, losing 7–1 and 8–2. Looking to even the series, the Mariners ran into Roger Clemens at his postseason best. He allowed just one hit (a seventh-inning double to Al Martin) and fanned 15, pitching the first-ever LCS one-hitter. The Mariners lost the series 4–2.

6. Dolphins 20, Seahawks 17, January 9, 2000. In the last game played in the Kingdome, the Seahawks took a 17-point lead over the Dolphins, but couldn't contain 38-year-old Dan Marino, who rallied Miami by completing 12 of 21 passes for 158 yards in the second half. The Seahawks had enough time to pull out the victory late, but went backward on three consecutive plays.

5. Miami of Ohio 59, Washington 58, March 12, 1999. The favored Huskies seemed in control of their first-round, Midwest Regional matchup in the Louisiana Superdome after guard Donald Watts scored 12 consecutive points in a four-minute stretch in the second half that gave the UW a 43–37 lead. But Wally Szczerbiak, who finished with 43 points, shot the Redhawks back into the lead. With Miami clinging to a 59–58 lead, Watts went for the game winner but was stripped. The ball popped to teammate Greg Clark, whose shot was snuffed by Szczerbiak.

4. Packers 33, Seahawks 27 (OT), January 10, 2004. Facing Green Bay at Lambeau Field in an NFC wild card game, the Seahawks rallied to tie at the end of regulation on a one-yard run by Shaun Alexander. On the opening series of OT, the Seahawks were on the move after quarterback Matt Hasselbeck delivered his famous boast, "We want the ball. We're going to score," just before the coin toss. Facing a third-and-11, Hasselbeck threw the ball into the left flat toward little-used receiver Alex Bannister, who failed to run his route properly. Green Bay cornerback Al Harris intercepted and returned it 52 yards for the winning touchdown.

3. Connecticut 75, Washington 74, March 19, 1998; Connecticut 98, Washington 92 (OT), March 24, 2006. Twice the Northwest Huskies have met the Northeast Huskies in the NCAA men's hoops tourney, and twice the Seattles were denied upsets at the last moments. In 1998, the Huskies entered the East Regional semifinal against Connecticut as nine-point underdogs and seemed on the verge of falling out of contention on multiple occasions. But the UW rallied for its only lead, 74–73, with 29 seconds to play. In the final moments, Richard Hamilton put back his own wild miss to vanquish Washington. In the Sweet Sixteen of 2006, Washington fought through brutal officiating for the late lead, only to see UConn's Rashad Anderson hurl a three with 1.8 seconds left to force OT, then walk away in the extra period.

2. Nuggets 98, Sonics 94 (OT), May 7, 1994. The Sonics, who started the 1993–94 season winning 20 of their first 22 games, finished the regular season at 63–19 and, with Chicago's Michael Jordan off playing baseball, were favored to win the NBA title. In the first round, the Sonics took a predictable 2–0 lead over the eighth-seeded Denver Nuggets, but lost Games 3 and 4 in Denver, sending the series back to Seattle for the finale. The Sonics had won 14 in a row at home and lost only four times in Seattle all season. But Game 5 went into overtime. Shawn Kemp put Seattle ahead 94–93 with 2:29 to play, but the Sonics didn't score again. A couple of blocked shots by Dikembe Mutombo, who had 32 for the series, preserved Denver's unprecedented victory—the Nuggets became the first No. 8 seed ever to defeat a No. 1 seed.

1. Lakers 98, Sonics 93, April 27, 1980. The defending world champion Sonics trailed in the series 2–1, but held a 21-point lead (69–48) with 6:36 left in the third quarter at Hec Edmundson Pavilion (the Coliseum was not available). That's when Lakers coach Paul Westhead switched to his "small" lineup of Michael Cooper and Norm Nixon at guard, rookie Magic Johnson and Jamaal Wilkes at forward and Kareem Abdul-Jabbar at center. The Sonics wilted. Los Angeles went on a 24–2 rampage to take the lead. The Sonics hit only one of 11 shots during LA's scoring spree (Fred Brown wound up 0-for-11). The Sonics not only lost the game and the series, their 21-point blown lead in the second half was, at the time, the largest in NBA playoff history.

As a member of the NFL's competition committee in the 1990s, former Seahawks head coach Mike Holmgren lobbied hard to institute instant replay. So it doesn't seem fair that he's been victimized several times by gaffes in the replay system. It's to his credit that he laughs easily when telling these stories. Except for the last one.

8. February 4, 1996, Pro Bowl. I coached the NFC team. The NFL invited two retired coaches to sit in the press box and monitor the game. The Pro Bowl is set up so only basic offenses and defenses can be used, in order to prevent injuries and promote scoring. If either team lined up in an illegal formation, coaches in the box could buzz the field and point it out. Ted Marchibroda was coaching the AFC, and on the first play he lined up with his receivers in a trips formation. You can't do that, because the defense that would be used to stop that formation isn't allowed in the game. So the first play was an 80-yard touchdown. I wait a second, and I'm not hearing anything on my headset. So I call upstairs and I'm yelling at Wayne Sevier (longtime NFL assistant), one of the coaches that were supposed to be watching for this stuff. And I hear Wayne say, "Hang on a second, Mike. Hey! Can I get more chili on my hot dog?" I couldn't believe it. I said, "Wayne! This is what you're here for! Didn't you see that formation?" He says, "No, I was putting more relish on my hot dog. I'm sorry."

7. December 6, 2004, Cowboys vs. Seahawks. Keyshawn Johnson caught a TD pass late in the game to pull Dallas to within three (39–36). He had one foot out of bounds but I couldn't do anything because it's in the final two minutes. They chose not to replay it. Afterward, I couldn't figure it out because he was clearly out of bounds. Later, I found out the guys responsible for replay had to catch a flight. So they'd taken down their equipment and couldn't review the play. Dallas got the ball back, scored again and completed a comeback win. I don't think this particular replay guy worked for the league much longer.

6. January 12, 2008, Seahawks at Packers, NFC playoffs. Green Bay was short on a first down by three inches. The Packers challenged the spot and (referee) Mike Carey went under the replay hood, using that tiny monitor. He comes back and moves the ball five inches, then measures again. I yelled at him, "It's hard enough to look in that box, how can you possibly make a five-inch difference?" It killed me. They knew Green Bay was three inches short because they measured. Then they moved it five inches. Then they measured again. They knew (the new measurement) was a first down.

5. October 28, 2001, Dolphins vs. Seahawks. It was a close game and Shaun Alexander fumbled. The officials ruled he was down and it's Seattle ball. Bob McElwee was the official. Miami challenged the play. So Bob went under the hood, came back and announced we had retained possession. But all of a sudden, Bob looks like he's having an out-of-body experience. He's standing behind our guys, shaking his head. Then he stopped the clock, ran back over to the hood and came back to say, "I made a mistake, Miami ball." I said, "Bob, why?" He says, "I just got mixed up." What had happened was (an official in the booth) buzzed him, which is not allowed. On replay, the ref is not supposed to get outside help. They don't want an "eye in the sky" mentality.

4. November 4, 2007, Seahawks at Cleveland. We're driving in overtime. They gave us a first down on a third and eight. It was challenged upstairs. The rule is there must be indisputable visual evidence to overturn the call. On this play, on every replay angle, you can't see where the ball is. But they overturned it. The ref told me, "I can't conceive that the ball made it to the line." I said, "How can you say that when you can't see where the ball is? How do you know where the ball is?" He said, "I can't see the ball." I said, "THAT'S my point."

3. November 23, 2003, Seahawks at Ravens. We've got the game won. We're going to run out the clock and take a knee. We've got it timed so the Ravens are going to have three seconds left. We sent in Chop (lineman Floyd "Pork Chop" Womack) as a third tight end. (Ravens head coach Brian) Billick says to the official nearest him, "You gotta make sure he reports." The guy runs out and asks the ref if Chop reported. He did. But now, instead of running the clock, they stop it. I said to Tom White, the ref, "You've got to run the clock." He said, "No, this was an administrative stoppage." I said, "That's for a guy running on the field or starting a fight. They asked a question about something we didn't do wrong. You run the clock." If ANY official in the crew knows the rule, it's his job to speak up. No one did. None of them knew the rule. Baltimore got the ball back with 39 seconds left instead of three. They scored on the final play of the game and then won in overtime.

2. December 8, 2002, Eagles at Seahawks. They threw a pass on first down after an interception and it bounced three yards in front of the wide receiver. It's not a scoop call, it's nothing. It happened right in front of me and it's ruled incomplete. Andy Reid (Eagles coach) challenges. It's not even close. Bill Carollo, who is a good ref, said the call on the field was overruled. I remember thinking, "How can that be? Didn't you see the same thing I did?" They go on to win the game. Next day I'm on the phone to director of officiating Mike Peirera. Before I get started, Mike said, "I'm sorry, I'm really sorry. That wasn't a catch." I told him that in my mind it didn't even seem close. He said, "Carollo went under the hood and we accidentally showed him the wrong play." They showed him the play before, an interception, which was clearly a catch. I said, "Wait a second, you mean they just go in there and no one says what's going on?" I was speechless.

1. February 5, 2006. Seahawks vs. Steelers, Super Bowl XL. Matt Hasselbeck was called for blocking below the waist while tackling Ike Taylor after Taylor intercepted him. In my wildest dreams, I'll never understand that call. How can you block below the waist when you're tackling? One in a series of bad calls that happened that day.

One of the primal appeals of spectator sports is the spontaneous opportunity to witness something unimagined or unprecedented. The Northwest has been blessed to witness some astounding games for which the ticket buyer that day had no notion.

10. Elgin Baylor's 51 points, 37 rebounds, February 28, 1958. During his two-year Seattle University career, Baylor scored 40-plus points nine times, 50-plus points four times, and had one game in which he knocked down 60 (January 30, 1958 vs. Portland). But his most dominant statistical performance came against Pacific Lutheran at the Seattle Civic Auditorium. Baylor took 32 shots, made 21 (66 percent) and set a school record with 37 rebounds in a 94–60 victory.

9. Tom Chambers' All-Star show, February 8, 1987. The 6–10 Sonics forward wasn't even supposed to be in the game in Seattle, but he ended up stealing the show. A late addition to the Western Conference All-Star team when Houston's Ralph Sampson sustained a knee injury, Chambers became the brightest star in an incredible galaxy of talent. He scored 34 points, including 14 in the fourth quarter, as the West defeated the East 154–149. The game featured 12 players who became Hall of Fame inductees, and two others—Michael Jordan and Hakeem Olajuwon—who are awaiting enshrinement.

8. Rueben Mayes' 357 yards vs. Oregon, October 27, 1984. With his final carry of the game, a 50–41 Washington State victory over Oregon at Eugene, Mayes eclipsed the NCAA single-game rushing record of 356 by Georgia Tech's Eddie Lee Ivery in 1978, and also broke the Pac-10 single-game record of 347 yards, set by USC's Rickey Bell in 1976 against the Cougars at the Kingdome. Mayes, who had three touchdowns, also broke the Pac-10 single-game all-purpose record with an additional 18 yards on kickoff returns for a total of 375.

7. Fred Brown's 58 points against Golden State, March 23, 1974. Brown not only hit 24 of 37 shots (no 3-pointers then) to break Spencer Haywood's team record of 51, he won the game at the buzzer with a twisting, 20-foot turnaround jumper from the right side that banked perfectly off the backboard, giving Seattle a 139–137 victory. Brown had nine points in the first period, 23 in the second, eight in the third and 18 in the fourth. "You hope to make every shot you take," Brown told the *Seattle Post-Intelligencer.* "It never happens, but that's why you shoot. And I'll admit I was very tired."

6. Hugh McElhenny's spree against WSU, November 25, 1950. In a 52–21 UW victory over WSU in Spokane, McElhenny ran for a school-record 296 yards and scored five TDs on runs of 23, 39, 7, 14 and 84 yards. McElhenny's 296 yards remain 38 yards more than the No. 2 effort in UW history (Credell Green had 258 against the Cougars in 1955), and his 14.8 yards per carry established an NCAA record.

5. Shaun Alexander's 30 points—in a half, September 29, 2002. Thirteen players in NFL history had scored 30 or more points in a game before Alexander did it in a 48–23 victory over the Minnesota Vikings at Qwest Field. But the Seahawks running back became the first to score five TDs in a half. Alexander, who rushed for 139 yards, scored on an 80-yard pass from Matt Hasselbeck and ran for TDs of 2, 20, 3 and 14 yards.

4. Mike Cameron's four home runs, May 2, 2002. Just one day after a Major League Baseball report revealed that home runs were down 19 percent from the previous season, Cameron single-handedly tried to reverse the trend. Entering a game against the White Sox with four hits in his previous 32 at-bats, the Mariners center fielder became the 13th player to homer four times in one contest, and just the fifth to do it in consecutive at-bats. Cameron and Bret Boone hit back-to-back homers twice in the first inning, becoming the first teammates in history to accomplish that feat, and then Cameron added home runs in the third and fifth innings. In the seventh, pitcher Mike Porzio plunked Cameron on the left leg, leaving him one more chance in the ninth. After taking six pitches, Cameron sent a ball to deep right, where Jeff Liefer caught it, ending Cameron's bid to become the first player to hit five home runs in a game.

3. Randy Johnson's 9–1 win over the Angels, October 2, 1995. Prior to a one-game playoff against the Angels to decide the AL West title, the Mariners sensed a championship the moment they saw Johnson stroll into the clubhouse. "You could see by the scowl on his face that Randy had a bad attitude," third baseman Mike Blowers said. "When he has that look, you know what you're going to get." The Mariners got it, Johnson delivering a masterpiece. Working on three days rest, Johnson retired the first 17 batters, striking out nine. His complete-game three-hitter with 12 strikeouts sent the Mariners into the postseason for the first time in franchise history. "You couldn't write a better story," said Johnson.

2. Marques Tuiasosopo's NCAA record, October 30, 1999. In a 35–30 victory over Stanford, the University of Washington quarterback, despite smarting from a severely bruised tailbone, passed for a career-high 302 yards and ran for a career-high 207, becoming the first player in NCAA history to accomplish the 300/200 double. Prior to Tuiasosopo, only three other players in NCAA history had rushed and passed for more than 200 yards in a game, and only six other quarterbacks had managed a 300–100 double. Tuiasosopo also ran for a pair of touchdowns and threw a TD pass to Gerald Harris.

1. Edgar Martinez's 7 RBIs, October 8, 1995. More famous for hitting the double that won Game 5 and the 1995 ALDS against the Yankees, Martinez's performance in Game 4 prompted him to say, "I thought that was the greatest game I ever played." In the third inning, Martinez hit a three-run homer to cut the Yankees lead to 5–3. In the eighth, he belted a grand slam off John Wetteland to put the Mariners ahead 10–6 in a game they eventually won 11–8. Martinez became the first player to drive in seven runs in a playoff game. He finished the series with a .521 batting average.

Danny Ainge once said, "Nobody wants to admit it, but we all choke at one time or another." That truth plays out annually before our eyes, although exactly what psychological state in great players creates such debacles is an open question. Whether from pressure, fatigue or bad beans, we know it, as with pornography, when we see it.

10. Mike Schooler, Mariners, September 6, 1992. One out away from nailing down an extra-inning victory over Cleveland, the Seattle closer yielded a 12th-inning grand slam to Carlos Martinez that gave the Indians a 12–9 win over the Mariners. The grand slam was the fourth allowed by Schooler in 1992, a total that matched the major league record.

9. Lauren Jackson, Storm, August 17, 2002. With the Storm facing playoff elimination in Los Angeles, the All-Star forward turned in 1-for-9 shooting performance, scored four points, committed five fouls and added two turnovers in 69–59 loss that bounced Seattle from WNBA playoffs.

8. Randy Johnson, Mariners, April 26, 1991. Johnson walked seven batters, including five in the first three innings, gave up a long home run to Chili Davis on an 0–2 pitch, and committed an error in a 6–0 loss to the Twins at the Metrodome. Johnson compounded his problems by twice failing to cover first base. Said Big Unit, "I guess I was in a Twilight zone all night. Beam me up, Scotty."

7. Matt Hasselbeck, Seahawks, October 24, 2004. The Seahawks quarterback completed just 14 of 41 passes and threw a career-high four interceptions in a 25–17 loss to the Cardinals. Hasselbeck's passer rating for the first half was 6.7; for the game, 18.9.

6. Mark Langston, Mariners, April 19, 1988. Langston surrendered a franchise-record five home runs in a 7–2 loss to the White Sox at the Kingdome. Langston yielded long balls to Carlton Fisk in the seventh and eighth innings, to Ken Williams in the fifth, former Mariner Ivan Calderon in the sixth and Harold Baines in the eighth, breaking the club record.

5. Steve Trout, Mariners, April 6, 1988. In a 29-pitch farce at the Oakland Coliseum, Trout walked five batters, threw two wild pitches, plunked a hitter and made a throwing error before pitching coach Billy Connors yanked him after two-thirds of an inning. "My man just vapor-locked," said Connors. "Boy, was he bad! He was ca-ca! He had no clue! He was hitting guys on 0–2 pitches and not even hurting them."

4. Eddie Johnson, Sonics, May 28, 1993. In an amazing tour de farce, Johnson went 0-for-6 from the field, including an air ball from eight feet, and committed eight turnovers in the Sonics' 104–97 loss to the Phoenix Suns in Game 3 of the Western Conference finals.

3. Jim Zorn, Seahawks, October 24, 1976. In what became a 41–14 Detroit victory over Seattle at the Kingdome, the Seahawks quarterback watched in frustration as two of his tosses were returned for TDs while four other picks killed promising drives. "I hoped to make those plays work, but this isn't a game of hope," said Zorn. "It's a game of percentages." It remains the most dubious single-game record in franchise history.

2. Jerramy Stevens, Seahawks, February 5, 2006. One of the main pre-game storylines surrounding Super Bowl XL involved Pittsburgh's Jerome Bettis, who was returning to Detroit to play his final NFL game. The networks made much fuss over "The Bus," but Seattle's tight end would have none of it. "It's a heartwarming story and all that," said Stevens, "but it will be a sad day when he leaves without the trophy." Super Bowl XL turned out to be a sadder game for Stevens. His three calamitous drops negated what would have been big gains, largely abetting Seattle's 21–10 defeat.

1. Dennis Johnson, Sonics, June 7, 1978. One year later, Johnson would be named the Most Valuable Player of the NBA Finals. But in 1978, no player ever came up lamer in an NBA championship game than the Sonics guard, who missed every one of his 14 shots in Seattle's 105–99 Game 7 loss to the Washington Bullets. "I just messed up," said Johnson. "I couldn't hit anything."

Most Impressive Record Breakers

Some prodigious individual feats, single-season and career, have been rung up by state athletes, made all the more impressive when they are stacked together.

10. Brian Sternberg's three world records, 1963. A 1961 graduate of Seattle's Shoreline High, Sternberg set the world record in the pole vault three different times in 1963, including a top clearance of 16–8 at the Compton Relays, making him the only state athlete since World War II to hold a world track and field record. Sternberg was paralyzed below the neck on July 2, 1963, in a trampoline accident.

9. Shaun Alexander's 28 touchdowns, 2005. Only three running backs in NFL history—Jim Brown, Emmitt Smith and LaDainian Tomlinson—scored touchdowns at a faster clip than Alexander, whose 28 in the Seahawks' Super Bowl season of 2005 broke Priest Holmes' record of 27 in 2003.

8. Chip Hanauer's 12 APBA Gold Cups, 1982–99. Until Hanauer, of Seattle, no driver dominated the "Indianapolis 500 of unlimited hydroplane racing" more than Bill Muncey, who recorded eight victories in the race between 1956–79. Starting in 1982, Hanauer won seven consecutive Gold Cups, matched Muncey's mark in 1992, and added four more before he retired. Hanauer's dozen, on five different waterways (Detroit River, Ohio River, Columbia River, Lake Washington, San Diego's Mission Bay), can be placed in the following perspective: since Hanauer's retirement, no driver has won more than three.

7. Jeff Jaeger's 80 field goals, 1983–86. Jaeger not only departed the University of Washington owning the NCAA record for career field goals (he still ranks tied for second), he made 19 more three pointers than No. 2, Chuck Nelson.

6. Doris Brown's world cross-country titles, 1967–71. Since 1932, only two women have won the World Cross Country Championship five different times, Seattle Pacific's Doris Brown and Norway's Grete Waitz. Brown was the first American woman to win the race in 1967 when she triumphed at Barry, Wales. She added four more victories in 1968 at Blackburn, England; in 1969 at Clydebank, Scotland; in 1970 at Frederick, Md.; and in 1971 at San Sebastian, Spain, making her the only woman to win the race for five consecutive years.

5. Al Worley's 14 interceptions, 1968. The remarkable thing about Worley's record—still the top single-season total in NCAA history—is that the UW defensive back set it while playing in only 10 games. To put the mark in context, only eight other players in college football history had as many as 12 interceptions in a season (including Washington's Bill Albrecht in 1951), despite the fact that schedules have expanded to as many as 13 games.

4. Phil Mahre's 27 World Cup victories, 1976–84. The White Pass skier's total stood as the American record for nearly a quarter of a century, until Bode Miller eclipsed it during the 2007–08 World Cup season. Mahre's three World Cup overall titles (1981–83) also remain the most by an American.

3. Steve Largent's Triple Crown, 1976–89. When Largent retired after 14 years with the Seahawks, his 819 pass receptions ranked No. 1 in the history of the NFL. So did his 13,089 yards and his 100 receiving TDs. That made Largent the second receiver in NFL annals, following Don Hutson (1935–45), to retire owning the "Triple Crown" of receiving (all of Largent's records were subsequently eclipsed by Jerry Rice).

2. John Stockton's assists and steals, 1984–03. During his 18 seasons with the Utah Jazz, the Spokane native and Gonzaga graduate not only established NBA career records for assists (15,806) and steals (3,265), he posted five of the top six assists seasons in history, finishing his career having averaged a double-double (13.1 points and 10.5 assists per game). Stockton's assists record in context: (1) Stockton handed out 5,483 more assists than anyone in NBA history; (2) only 33 players had more than 5,483 assists in their entire careers.

1. Ichiro's 262 hits, 2004. Ichiro gave no indication in April that he was about to launch a season for the ages, producing just 26 hits (only three for extra bases) for a .255 average. Even after a 50-hit month of May, he tailed off again, delivering only 29 hits in June. But once the All-Star break passed, no pitcher could contain the Seattle right fielder. He had 51 hits in July and 56 in August, reaching the 200 mark before the month had elapsed. Two days before the end of the season, Ichiro broke George Sisler's 84-year-old major league record of 257. His 262 total was 46 more than runner-up Michael Young of Texas, marking the largest differential in MLB history between the No. 1 and No. 2 hitters in the league.

In addition to turning the infield grounder into instant drama, Ichiro has often offered to his American audience surprising perspectives, full of wisdom and whimsy, on matters of baseball and life. We asked the Mariners' franchise player for a list of what struck him as odd about American ball and American people.

1. The weaker the human, the more likely he is to join a herd and lick each other's wounds.

2. The more foolish the person, the more likely he is to belittle others to build his own confidence.

The first two are similarities between Americans and Japanese. The more players on a team who fit those characteristics, the more likely the team will lose. The next three are things I have noticed – not of all people, but an overall impression – about Americans, not Japanese.

3. When a person gives a gift to another, it is expected the gift will be treated well. But baseball players throw and kick their baseball gloves that have been given to them by makers of baseball equipment. I feel that is a contradiction.

4. Although it is a tradition to shake hands in America, people don't wash their hands when they go to the bathroom.

5. The fashion sense Americans have is a crime.

The most difficult feat in sports is not achieving excellence, but maintaining it. The most aggravating deed in sports is not a single failure, but a whole fetid slew of them. In these parts, hearts have been set aflutter by sustained soaring and crashing. The best jaw-droppers:

12. UW's 19-Game Win Streak Against California, 1977–01.

To begin with, the streak never would have reached 19 if, in five separate games, the Bears hadn't blown second-half leads of 27–3, 23–3, 24–10, 24–13 and 21–10. (Or if, in two other games, the Huskies hadn't connected on last-second field goals to win.) By the time the Huskies ran the streak to 19, it marked the second-longest Pac-10 winning streak involving one school beating another, trailing only USC's 26-game run of success against Oregon State that started in 1968.

11. Washington football's 63-game unbeaten streak, 1907–17.

The streak is seven games longer than the next best in NCAA history—56 by Michigan between 1901–05—and 15 longer than the longest in modern college football history—48 by Oklahoma (1953–57). During the 63 games, Washington posted 43 shutouts, including eight in a row, and held its opponents to one touchdown or less in all but one of the games. Washington outscored its opponents 1,944 to 124, an average winning margin of 30.1 to 1.9, and posted 10 shutouts each with a winning margin of 50 or more points.

10. Chip Hanauer's seven consecutive APBA Gold Cups, 1982–88.

When Hanauer won in the Miss Circus Circus in 1988 on the Detroit River, he broke the previous unlimited hydroplane record of five consecutive wins, set by Gar Wood from 1917–21. Hanauer's seven came in the Atlas Van Lines from 1982–84, in the Miller American from 1985–87, and the finale in the casino wagon.

9. Seahawks 11-game winning streak, 2005.

Because of enforced parity in the NFL, winning streaks are hard to come by. This one was three longer than the club's previous best in 1984. It started in Week 5 (October 9) with a 37–31 victory over St. Louis and ran through Week 16 (December 24) with a 28–13 win over the Indianapolis Colts. The streak featured two improbable victories at Qwest Field. In a 13–10 win over the Cowboys in Week 7, the Seahawks scored twice inside the final minute. In a 24–21 victory over the Giants in Week 12, New York, after committing a record 11 false-start penalties, amazingly missed three game-winning field goal attempts in the fourth quarter and overtime.

8. Randy Johnson's 16-game winning streak, 1995–97.

Encompassing 25 starts over parts of three seasons (injuries limited him to 14 starts n 1996), the Big Unit's streak started August 1, 1995, at California and lasted until May 8, 1997 at Baltimore, ending one victory shy of the American League record. The streak ended oddly. Johnson allowed two runs in the first inning at Camden Yards and was locked in a 2–1 duel with Mike Mussina through five when the game was delayed for 57 minutes due to rain. Both starters returned, and Johnson promptly gave up a three-run homer to Chris Hoiles in the sixth and left losing 5–1.

7. Chuck Nelson's 30 consecutive field goals, 1981–82. From November 14, 1981, to November 20, 1982, University of Washington's Chuck Nelson attempted and made all 30 field goals, an NCAA record that still stands. Nelson obliterated the NCAA mark of 16 shared by Dale Castro of Maryland (1970) and Ish Ordonez of Arkansas (1978–79).

6. Steve Largent's 177 consecutive games catching a pass, 1977–89. The streak started November 20, 1977, against the Houston Oilers, with a four-yarder, and ended December 23, 1989, when he caught two passes for 41 yards in the final game of his career. During the streak, Largent made multiple catches 159 times, or 89.8 percent of the time. His 177 consecutive games with at least one reception, an NFL record at the time of his retirement, remains 106 consecutive games more than the No. 2 mark in Seahawks history, 71 by Joey Galloway from 1995–99.

5. Mariners lose 15 of 17 games, 2007. In their dreary early history, the Mariners had some swoons that were doozies, but the move to Safeco vaulted them into baseball's high-revenue category, which made this collapse all the more aggravating. The M's and their club-record $114 million payroll were just a game behind the AL West-leading Angels on August 25, but by September 11, were 9 ½ games out thanks largely to a collapse by a young bullpen that was overused earlier in bailing out a weak starting rotation. A second-place, 88-win seasonal finish didn't do much to heal the gaping wound.

4. Ichiro's Eight Consecutive 200-Hit Seasons, 2001–08. When Ichiro collected his 200th hit of 2008 (he finished with 213), he joined Wee Willie Keeler (1894–1901) as the only players in major league history to amass 200 or more hits in a season for eight consecutive years. In doing so, Ichiro also became the first player in history to post eight 200-hit seasons in a row in the first eight years of a career, and joined Lou Gehrig as the only players in history to put up eight years of 200 or more hits and 100 or more runs scored.

3a. UW football's 13 consecutive Pac-10 football losses, 2004–05. For a team that dominated the Pac-10 in the early 1990s and went to the Rose Bowl as recently as 2000, the scandal-ridden Huskies' abrupt conference collapse was one of the darkest periods in its football history. The firing of coach Rick Neuheisel, the forced appointment of his senior assistant, Keith Gilbertson, and the forced retirement of the AD who hired Neuheisel, Barbara Hedges, plunged the UW into chaos, killed recruiting and made the Huskies a conference joke. The first seven losses were on the watch of Gilbertson, the last six under his successor, Tyrone Willingham. Worst loss: September 10, 2005, Cal 56–17. Average margin of defeat: 20 points.

3b. UW Footballs 14-game losing streak, 2007-08. While Willingham weathered calls for hhis ouster after 13 consecutive Pac-10 losses, Washington's 14-game losing streak through the end of 2008—second longest in conference history—finally did him in and ushered in the Steve Sarkisian era.

1. Ken Griffey Jr.'s eight homers in eight games, July 20–28, 1993.

Over a nine-day span, the Mariners superstar tied a major league record by hitting a home run in eight consecutive games, becoming the third player to accomplish the feat, joining Dale Long (1950) and Don Mattingly (1987) as masters of the daily dramatic. Griffey's eight blasts:

Date	Pitcher/Team	Distance	Count	Type
7/20	Paul Gibson / NYY	430 feet	2–1	Solo
7/21	Jimmy Key / NYY	420 feet	1–2	Solo
7/22	Jeff Mutis / Clev	403 feet	1–2	Solo
7/23	Albie Lopez / Clev	407 feet	1st pitch	Solo
7/24	Matt Young / Clev	340 feet	3–2	Solo
7/25	Jose Mesa / Clev	392 feet	1–1	2-Run
7/27	Kevin Tapani / Minn	441 feet	1–1	GS
7/28	Willie Banks / Minn	404 feet	1st pitch	Solo

If you bore live witness to any of these moments, you begin by telling your friends, "Oh, man, you shoulda been there," and they will be more jealous of you than if you showed up with Jessica Biel.

15. Jay Buhner's bullpen tumble, July 29, 1997. Buhner made two great plays in a 4–0 loss to Boston. Almost nobody remembers the first—he robbed Mike Stanley of a home run in the fourth inning—but anyone who saw the second recalls it. Scott Hatteberg hit a long fly to right, Buhner retreated, then retreated again, then caught the ball and tumbled—butt over teacups—over the five-foot wall into the Red Sox bullpen, making the greatest catch of his career. "It was the kind of play outfielders always dream about," Buhner said.

14. Ichiro in right, May 2, 2005; Ichiro in center, May 26, 2008. In the seventh inning against the Angels (2005), Ichiro chased after a Garret Anderson fly ball that looked like a sure double and maybe a home run. As Anderson's shot neared the fence, Ichiro made a gravity-cheating scale of the wall, adjusted his body in mid-climb, then reached over the fence and robbed Anderson of a home run. "I don't know that I've ever seen a better catch," said Angels manager Mike Scioscia. In the fifth inning against the Red Sox (2008), Jason Varitek drove a ball to deep center. Ichiro got on his horse and made a basket catch with his back to the plate before crashing into the wall and somersaulting. "That was one of the greatest catches I've ever seen," said Varitek.

13. Fred Couples, No. 12, The Masters, April 12, 1992. The Seattle native often called it "the biggest break of my life." Fact was, though, he hit the perfect shot. After birdies at No. 8 and No. 9 put him into the lead on the final day of the Masters, Couples arrived at No. 12, which had been the undoing of several players whose shots continually plopped into Rae's Creek. For a tense, few moments, it appeared No. 12 would also serve as Couples' downfall. His tee shot landed on a bank inches above the creek, started a slow roll toward the water, and then stopped. The ball should have rolled in, wrecking Couples' chances of winning the Masters. Instead, Couples recovered for the key par that enabled him to win his only major championship.

12. Ignition of the Mariners' tear, August 24, 1995. Ken Griffey Jr. hit 398 home runs while wearing a Mariners' uniform, none more significant than this blast against the Yankees. The Mariners trailed the Angels by 11 ½ games in the AL West and seemed hopelessly out of contention, until Griffey came to bat with two outs and one on in the bottom of the ninth. Griffey's first-pitch, two-run, walk-off homer off John Wetteland gave the Mariners a 9–7 victory that started their amazing run to the playoffs. The significance of the feat became greater later as events played out, but the thrill button was pushed that day.

11. Hugh McElhenny's 100-yard punt return, October 6, 1951. Of the three 90-yard scoring plays that Hugh McElhenny manufactured in his University of Washington football career, this one against USC was the most unlikely. After fielding a Frank Gifford punt at his own goal line, McElhenny went sideline-to-sideline, occasionally retreated so he could go forward, knocked people down and left tacklers flailing in racing 100 yards to a touchdown. Recalled Gifford, a USC All-America and NFL all-pro, years later: "Suddenly, there was only one man between him and the goal—me. And he left me flat on my face." McElhenny's 100-yard return remains the only one in Pacific Coast Conference history.

10. Ken Griffey Jr.'s Spiderman acts, April 26, 1990; May 26, 1995. In a 6–2 victory over New York in 1990, Griffey brought the Yankee Stadium crowd to its feet in the fourth inning when, after a long sprint from right-center, he made a leaping catch over the center-field wall to rob Jesse Barfield of what would have been his 200th career home run. In 1995, against Baltimore, as soon as Kevin Bass sent a pitch screaming to the wall in right-center field at the Kingdome, Griffey got on his horse, did a Spiderman crawl along the wall and made the catch, one of his most spectacular ever. Griffey made the snatch despite breaking his wrist, forcing him to miss 73 games.

9. Dennis Johnson's Bucks-beating bomb, April 8, 1980. With Milwaukee leading Seattle 113–111 in a Western Conference semifinal playoff game, the Sonics had one possession remaining, 70 feet separating them and the hoop, and six seconds to do something about it. All five Bucks took turns impeding Johnson's progress as he dribbled up court. None succeeded. When Johnson, a mediocre outside shooter, was 26 feet away, he launched and hit at the buzzer, giving Seattle a 114–113 victory.

8. "Everybody scores!" October 2, 1995. In a one-game playoff at the Kingdome to decide the AL West title, the Mariners held a 1–0 lead over the Angels heading into the bottom of the seventh inning. Mike Blowers opened with a single and Tino Martinez reached on a bunt. After Dan Wilson moved runners up with a sacrifice bunt, Angels starter Mark Langston hit Joey Cora with a pitch, loading the bases. Vince Coleman lined out to right, bringing Luis Sojo to the plate. Sojo slapped a ball down the first base line that eventually rolled underneath the bench in the Mariners bullpen. By the time the Angels dug it out, Blowers, Martinez and Cora had scored, and 52,356 fans were in full spasm. Then Sojo scored on an error at the plate by Langston, prompting team broadcaster Rick Rizzs, practically drowning in his own glee, to yelp, "Everybody scores!"

7. Nate Robinson's cosmic dunk, January 29, 2004. The little guy's epic two-handed baseline slam, coming off a back-door lob from Curtis Allen, electrified a sold-out Hec Ed and helped Washington shatter Arizona, 96–83. *Post-Intelligencer* columnist Art Thiel had this reaction to Robinson's dunk: "Every once in a while, a moment happens in a sports event that is so majestic it blows past the brain and burns right into the soul. So if he's five-foot-eight (in thick socks), and the rim is 10 feet, and his eyes are above it that means Oh. My. Goodness."

6. Ichiro guns down Terrence Long, April 11, 2001. Rarely does a throw make for a defining baseball highlight, but rarely does one see a meteorite in daylight. In the eighth inning of what became a 3–0 Seattle victory at the Oakland Coliseum, the A's Terrence Long attempted to advance from first to third on a single by Ramon Hernandez. After fielding the ball in right, Ichiro, just a few games into his American baseball career, unleashed a screamer that traveled about three feet off the ground all the way to third, easily nailing a shocked Long, who said, "It was going to take a perfect throw to get me, and it was."

5. Steve Largent's payback, December 11, 1988. On September 4, during the Seahawks' season opener at Mile High Stadium in Denver, Largent ran a pass route over the middle only to get crushed by Broncos safety Mike Harden, who delivered an illegal forearm smash that caved in Largent's facemask, dislodged a couple of his teeth and knocked him unconscious. The NFL fined Harden $5,000. Now fast forward to Week 15 for the Denver-Seattle rematch at the Kingdome. Early in the first half, Harden picked off a Dave Krieg pass and began running it back. As he moved from the middle of the field toward the left sideline, Harden had his eyes fixed ahead and was, apparently, the only person in the Kingdome who did not see Largent streaking across the field, bearing down on him. In a moment that still delights Seahawks fans, Largent's blindside blast lifted Harden off his feet, forcing a fumble that Largent recovered. The play brought everyone in the Kingdome—save Harden—to their feet. For years afterward, NFL Films featured the play among its all-time greatest hits.

4. The "Lister Blister", April 28, 1992. Every Internet video collection of Shawn Kemp's greatest dunks features one he labeled "The Lister Blister." It occurred in Game 3 of a Western Conference first-round playoff series in Oakland. Late in the game, with the score tied, Kemp delivered a vicious tomahawk dunk right over seven-foot Alton Lister, and then pointed at him. Kemp always said it was his favorite dunk.

3. Steve Emtman eats Arizona, October 5, 1991. Emtman won the Outland Trophy, the Lombardi Award, was a consensus All-America and the No. 1 overall pick in the NFL Draft. Two plays summarize his essence. On the first scrimmage play against Arizona, Emtman shook off a double team, broke through the line and flattened Wildcat quarterback George Malauulu before he could hand the ball off. Emtman then said to Malauulu, "I'll be back." Replied Malauulu, "I know." Next play, same thing. Before the third play, Malauulu called a timeout. The roar at Husky Stadium was never louder. "It's ridiculous," Arizona coach Dick Tomey told reporters after the game. "We think we've got the schemes to handle him and he's in our backfield the first two plays of the game."

.2. The Griffey family goes back-to-back, September 14, 1990. The Cincinnati Reds asked Ken Griffey Sr. to retire on August 23, 1990. Instead, Griffey Sr. secured his release and latched on with Seattle. Two days after joining the Mariners, Griffey Sr. and Ken Griffey Jr. became the first father-son combination to hit in the same lineup. Senior singled, then Junior singled. Two weeks later, in Anaheim, Senior took the Angels' Kirk McCaskill deep in the fourth inning. Not to be outdone, Junior also took McCaskill deep, marking the first time in major league history that a father and son had hit home runs in the same major league game.

1. The double, October 8, 1995. The most famous, dramatic and important play in Seattle pro sports history began to unfold in the bottom of the 11th of the final game of the ALDS when Joey Cora led off by bunting his way aboard against New York's Jack McDowell. After Ken Griffey Jr. reached with a single, sending Cora to third, Edgar Martinez strode to plate. At stake: Game 5 of the ALDS and maybe the future of the franchise in Seattle, especially given that King County voters rejected building the Mariners a new ballpark. Oblivious to the larger burden, Martinez promptly roped a McDowell fastball down the left-field line, sending Cora home and Griffey on the run of his life. "When I saw the ball land near the line," Griffey said later, "I ran as fast as I could and for as long as I could. When I got to third, Sammy (third base coach Sam Perlozzo) said, 'Keep going.' So I did." As Griffey slid across the plate with the winning run, teammates bounded out of the dugout and piled on him, sending 57,411 fans into delirium that echoes to this day in Safeco Field, the yard that emerged from the din.

He's been behind the mike for the Mariners since game No. 1 (April 6, 1977) and has seen every high and low in franchise history. Among his signature calls is the versatile "My Oh My!" which can be used at top volume for an exciting play or in a more subdued style to punctuate some terrible thing perpetrated on the M's.

7. The life, times, and death of the Kingdome. It was laboratory baseball. There are no elements to bother the baseball; no wind, no high sky. But it was never an ugly old lady to me. It will always be a huge part of my life. She was a dowager. When you consider what happened there: it got us a new baseball team in 1977. First time you walked into the Kingdome it was like "Wow!"

6. A night talking baseball with Casey Stengel. It was in 1958 or 1959. He'd come in the pressroom at Yankee Stadium after the game and have a couple of drinks. He drank scotch. As the evening wore on he had a few scotches and said, "Where do you live, son?" "I live in Kew Gardens." I was an E2 at the time I don't think I even had a stripe. I wasn't even a private first class. (Niehaus worked for Armed Forces Radio.) He said, "Would you like to come over to my place and have a drink?" I said, "Are you kidding me?" So his chauffeur took us down to the Essex House where he lived and we sat there and talked baseball and drank until the sun was coming up. When I told him I was planning on taking the subway home, he went downstairs with me and gave a cabbie a 20-dollar bill, which was like $100 today, and he said, "Make sure this young man gets home safely." I ended up going to his funeral. It was a celebration more than anything else. They played "Take Me out to the Ballgame." It was a happening.

5. Jay Buhner's defensive skills. The way he played that carom off the right field wall in the Kingdome—he would nail guys going to second base and he'd nail guys going from first to third. He played that like a Stradivarius, those bounces that would come off the wall out there whether they were high, or in the middle, or low. I've never seen anybody play the outfield like that, except maybe Joe Rudi in Oakland. Jay was a master. It was like going to a fronton to watch jai alai. He was unbelievable out there.

4. Helping Lou Piniella with his crossword puzzle. We lost a tough game in Boston on a hit and run that backfired. We were on our way home, flying across country. I had introduced him to crossword puzzles. So he comes down the aisle of the plane still upset about the game, complaining about how we lost. Then he says, "By the way, the clue is 'movie alien,' and it's only two letters." And I said "ET, Lou. ET." And he says, "How do you spell that?"

3. Junior. He deserves a whole "My Oh My!" section to himself. He in his prime is the best pure talent I've ever seen. We're at Tiger Stadium; the deepest centerfield in baseball. Junior is in right center and a left-handed batter slices the ball into left-center field and, man, Griffey is flying over there and he gets his glove on the ball and the ball goes off his glove. Just a tremendous effort, and I said, "Junior usually makes that catch." So we go to New York and the next afternoon he yells at me, "Hey Niehaus! My people tell me you said I should have made that catch last night in Detroit." I said, "Your people tell you wrong." He said, "What did you say?" I said, "I said you USU-ALLY make that catch." He got a grin on his face and said, "Yeah, I usually do, don't I?"

2. The great plays. Cammy's four home runs . . . Randy's no-hitter . . . Bosio's no-hitter, which featured Omar Vizquel's incredible play on a chopper over the mound; one of the most exciting final outs in the history of no-hitters . . . Randy coming in from the bullpen in Game 5 of the 1995 Yankees series . . . Edgar's double in that same game . . . Brian Holman losing the perfect game . . . Marc Newfield hitting into an unassisted triple play at Fenway Park . . . Ichiro breaking the hits record.

1. Opening night 1977. I had come up here from Anaheim. Sen. Henry M. Jackson threw out the first pitch. It was my first chance to be a No. 1 announcer.

1A. From the fans. In July of 2008, Dave was inducted into the broadcaster's wing of the Baseball Hall of Fame in Cooperstown, N.Y.

No matter the devotion to practice, scouting, film study, game planning and work-outs, there's no accounting for the wonder, and the blunder, of human nature.

11. Jake's Mistake By The Lake, September 6, 2008. The UW quarter-back was penalized 15 yards for celebrating what could have been a game-tying touchdown run with two seconds left against Brigham Young—Locker tossed the ball in the air and chest-bumped a teammate—and the Cougars' Jan Jorgensen blocked the ensuing 35-yard extra-point attempt to help the Cougars hold on to a 28–27 victory. Locker's celebration—game officials insisted they had no choice but to enforce the celebration rule—was so tame compared to others that it drew the condemnation of sports fans, coaches and others (even an NFL referee) all across the country, including former NBA star Charles Barkley, who said, "That official in the Washington game, if I ever see his ass, I'm going to beat him like a drum. That was atrocious."

10. Huskies' last-play "miscommotion," October 7, 2006. With 1:34 remaining at the L.A. Coliseum and UW trailing third-ranked USC 26–20, the Huskies (4–1) took the ball at their own 19-yard line and moved to the Trojans' 15-yard line with one play left for a major upset. Amazingly, the UW could not get off a pass into the end zone as 30 seconds ticked off the clock. The referees debated whether to add time, and Huskies coaches switched from a spike call to a play, but when the clock started, quarterback Isaiah Stanback was not under center and the game ended. Wide receiver Sonny Shackelford told it well to the *Seattle Times*: "It was all miscommotion."

9. Bench jockey, October 18, 1930. Late in a 0–0 tie between Washington and Oregon in Portland, a Ducks tailback broke loose and raced down the sidelines. Since no Husky was going to catch him, Larry Westerweller decided it was time to act. The only problem was that Westerweller wasn't in the game. He shot off the bench and made the tackle at the Washington 20-yard line. The officials awarded Oregon the TD that beat Washington 7–0.

8. Omar Vizquel bunts into a triple play, July 3, 1992. The Mariners had Dave Valle on third and Harold Reynolds on first when Omar Vizquel stepped to the plate to face Detroit reliever Walt Terrell. On the first pitch, Valle charged from third and Reynolds broke for second. Vizquel's squeeze bunt attempt looped down the third-base line, directly into the glove of onrushing third baseman Skeeter Barnes. Vizquel was the first out. Barnes tagged Valle for the second out and threw to first for the third out, nailing Reynolds. This marked the only time in Mariners history that they bunted into a triple play.

7. Seahawks' original 12th Man, October 29, 1978. When Denver PK Jim Turner missed an 18-yard chip shot in overtime, the Seahawks thought they averted a loss. Instead, they were penalized for having 12 men—DE Dave Kraayeveld being the extra party—on the field, allowing Turner a re-take. He drilled it, giving the Broncos a 20–17 victory.

6. Nelson shanks the Apple Cup, November 20, 1982. UW placekicker Chuck Nelson, who entered the game with 15 national, 14 conference and 14 school records, including an NCAA-record 30 consecutive field goals, uncharacteristically missed from 33 yards in Pullman and the Huskies lost to Washington State 24–20, ending their Rose Bowl hopes.

5. Showboating against Showtime, December 29, 1994. The Sonics had a fourth-quarter, four-on-none breakaway against the Los Angeles Lakers led by guard Gary Payton, who could have taken it to the hoop himself. But when Payton saw Shawn Kemp trailing him, he started thinking street. Payton flipped the ball underhanded off the backboard, figuring that Kemp would grab it and dunk. Instead, Kemp clanked his dunk off the back of the iron. The Sonics lost 96–95.

4. Dave Krieg's unchecked passion, September 1, 1991. Officials nailed the Seattle quarterback with a 15-yard unsportsmanlike conduct penalty for running from the sideline into the end zone to argue a call during a Seahawks-Saints game in New Orleans. Krieg's blunder forced John Kasay to attempt a game-tying field goal from 37 yards instead of 22. Kasay pushed the kick wide left and the Seahawks lost 27–24.

3. Two M's out at home on same play, July 9, 1985. It's one thing to get thrown out at home plate, but twice on the same play? And when the catcher has a busted leg and a broken ankle? In the third inning against Toronto, Seattle's Phil Bradley attempted to score from second on Gorman Thomas's single to right. Jesse Barfield threw to catcher Buck Martinez in time to nail Bradley, but Bradley bowled over Martinez in a collision that broke Martinez's leg. Thomas went to second on the throw and, seeing Martinez writhing in agony, tried to take third. Martinez, prone, threw wildly to third. Thomas took off for home. Left fielder George Bell threw perfectly to Martinez, who caught the ball half-sitting up and tagged out the runner, suffering a broken ankle in the process.

2. Moon throws it away on fourth down, November 6, 1976. The Huskies were driving late in a game against California, hoping to even the score at 7. But on a fourth-down play, UW quarterback Warren Moon, having momentarily lost his head, intentionally threw the ball out of bounds and that was the game.

1. Huskies' 12th man blunder, August 31, 2002. Seconds away from upsetting Michigan at Ann Arbor, Washington was whistled for having 12 men on the field, giving the Wolverines the 15 penalty yards they needed to allow junior Philip Brabbs, who earlier missed from 36 and 42 yards, to boot a 44-yard field goal as time expired. What could have been one of the UW's more unlikely wins instead turned into a 31–29 defeat. Said coach Rick Neuheisel, "It's a nightmare loss."

You won't find these facts in any sports record book, because they really aren't records. But that's why you're reading this book – to be enlightened by stuff in ways you won't get anywhere else. Since this collection of dubious gems is so weird as to defy ranking, we offer them in chronological order.

13. Largest fine for cheating in a salmon derby—$1,500, six months, William and Joan Parks, 1981. In an affair that became known as "Salmonscam," the husband and wife were convicted of attempted first-degree theft, sentenced to six months and fined $1,500 for trying to claim first and second place in the 44th annual Port Angeles Salmon Derby with bogus fish. Instead of entering salmon that had been caught during the contest, the couple submitted a 43-pound salmon and a 36-pound salmon that had not only been frozen, but caught in fresh water.

12. Most errors committed by a player who refused to pinch-hit because he was playing a video game in the clubhouse—48, Rey Quinones, Mariners, 1986–88. In 1987, Quinones refused manager Dick Williams' order because he was on the last level of Super Mario Brothers.

11. Largest contract buyout received by a coach who then applied for unemployment—$204,000, Andy Russo, UW, 1989. When Russo resigned as UW basketball coach, he was given $204,000 to settle his contract. But when he couldn't immediately get another job, he filed for unemployment. He was actually receiving checks until a Washington state agency discovered the situation and squawked. Russo and the UW battled out the issue in the State Unemployment Department, and Russo lost his case.

10. Possibly the shortest punt in NFL history—minus-2 yards, Ruben Rodriguez, Seahawks, Oct. 22, 1989. In the Seahawks' 24–21 overtime loss to Denver, Rodriguez's ceiling-high blooper in the windless Kingdome led to the Broncos' second touchdown.

9. Most fans Maced during an Apple Cup melee—too many to count, 1989. Dozens of UW students tried to tear down the goal posts at Husky Stadium following Washington's 20–9 victory over Washington State, and were sprayed by campus police in riot gear. Two students were arrested and several others taken to University Hospital.

8. Highest salary earned by a player who rammed his car into a guardrail, was convicted of DUI, had a sidewalk brawl with a teammate and then blamed the media—$1.25 million, Dale Ellis, 1992. "I despise you guys, I really do," the Sonics swingman told Seattle reporters after a Milwaukee-Seattle game on February 2, 1992.

7. Longest stay by a drifter in a Seattle athlete's apartment—one week, Chris Bosio, Mariners, 1993. During spring training, Bosio received news that a drifter had broken into his apartment and lived in it for a week, pretending to be a gardener. The drifter took Bosio's moped out for a spin and crashed it. He also stole Bosio's clothes, fax machine and kitchen utensils. The police arrested the man, but released him. Undeterred, the drifter returned to Bosio's house, kicked in the garage door and stole more belongings. Next, a woman who lived in an apartment below Bosio's shot her daughter and killed herself. Then Bosio's grandfather died. After Bosio threw a no-hitter on April 22, he said, "Things happen for a reason." Apparently so. In his next start, Bosio suffered a broken collarbone while trying to cover first base.

6. Most times pitching for the cycle in one inning—1, Dave Fleming, Mariners, April 8, 1994. After Fleming allowed two runs in the first inning against Toronto, in the second he pitched for the cycle, allowing a home run (Carlos Delgado), a triple (Devon White), a double (Alex Gonzalez) and a single (Paul Molitor).

5. Most runs allowed by a reliever in 1/3 of an inning—9, Jose Mesa, Mariners, May 28, 2000. With the M's and Devil Rays tied at 3, Senor Smoke took over for Arthur Rhodes in the bottom of the eighth. After serving up a gopher ball to Mike Difelice, Mesa gave up a walk to Felix Martinez, a single to Randy Winn, a single to Gerald Williams, a double to Jose Guillen, a single to Fred McGriff, a single to Vinny Castilla and a double to Ozzie Guillen. After walking Difelice, up for the second time, Mesa argued with the umpire and was ejected. He allowed a club reliever-record nine earned runs in 0.1 innings pitched, shattering the mark of five by Mike Schooler against the Yankees, September 7, 1989.

4. Most career money made by a player who whined he wasn't being taken care of—$100 million, Gary Payton, Sonics, 2002. When the Sonics star made it plain he wanted a contract extension, the Sonics made it plainer that he couldn't have one. Said Payton's agent, Aaron Goodwin, "Gary's hurt. Yes, he's hurt that he hasn't been taken care of for the future. He's hurt that the team hasn't done what it can to give him security."

3. Least value received from a $20 table dance—minus $10 million, Mike Price, 2003. A drunken soiree to Arety's Angels, a Pensacola, FL, strip club, and a subsequent entanglement with a stripper cost the former Washington State football coach his new gig at Alabama, worth $10 million.

2. Largest NBA fine for telling the truth—$250,000, Auburey McClendon, Sonics, August 13, 2007. When the partner of Sonics owner Clay Bennett told an Oklahoma newspaper, "We didn't buy the team to keep it in Seattle, we hoped to come to Oklahoma City", NBA Commissioner David Stern fined McClendon a quarter-mil, but never explained why. Subsequent e-mails discovered in a lawsuit by the city suggested that relocation was the undisclosed agenda by the ownership group, underscoring the old bromide that there is no money in the truth.

1. Most times throwing a wild pitch in one inning—4, R.A. Dickey, Mariners, August 17, 2008. The knuckleballer tied a major league record when he uncorked four in the fifth inning of an 11–8 loss to the Minnesota Twins. Not only did Dickey become the just the fifth major league pitcher to throw four wild pitches in an inning, he broke the Mariners' single-game record for wild pitches, which had been three.

Cool Things That Happen When You're a Guitar Hero :: Mike McCready

Mike McCready is a Pearl Jam guitarist and full-time baseball addict.

8. On our 2003 tour, we got baseballs from all the places we played. For my birthday, Ed (lead singer Ed Vedder) gave me a display case to put them in.

7. Watching Ed sing "Take Me Out to the Ball Game" at a Cubs game—twice!

6. Playing the Star Spangled Banner for the Crohns and Colitis Foundation at a Seattle Thunderbirds game.

5. Hanging out with Richie Sexson, Raul Ibanez and Mariners' strength coach Allen Wirtala in Toronto after our show in 2005.

4. Playing the "Star Spangled Banner" at a Mariners game. This hasn't happened . . . yet!

3. Taking batting practice at Fenway Park and watching Jeff Ament and Ed hit well. Our security guard, Big Pete, crushed a few (I was fielding).

2. Having Tim Wakefield of the Red Sox throw knuckleballs at Jeff and I in Boston (thanks, Theo!).

1. Taking batting practice with the Mariners in 2005, and actually hitting a foul down the first base line! Being down on the field and hanging out with my friends was amazing.

When Seahawks defensive tackle Craig Terrill isn't chasing down quarterbacks, he's playing guitar, and writing and performing his own music. His first CD, "CT93," was released in 2008. It's a solid hit. He and his band have had numerous live gigs around town. Here's who inspired him:

5. Angus Young. I would not be in the NFL without the sounds of AC/DC inspiring my workouts. The ultimate rock and roll sound. Plus, nobody else could play such a mean guitar dressed in a schoolboy outfit. Favorite song: "Thunderstruck."

4. Jimi Hendrix. How can you not have Jimi in your top five? He transformed the guitar from a musical instrument into a piece of art. Favorite Song: "Hey Joe."

3. Derek Trucks. I had the pleasure to meet and watch Derek play. Unbelievable tone and, in my opinion, the best slide player ever. Favorite song: "Revolution."

2. Joe Walsh. Such a cool sound. I love all of his work with the Eagles as well as his solo career. Favorite song: "Funk #49."

1. Eric Clapton. My all-time favorite. The precision, soul and innovation that he brings to the guitar are unmatched. No other guitarist has had the longevity and immense success of Clapton. Favorite song: "White Room."

Not exactly the tired or the poor in a huddled mass, these guys nevertheless yearned to be free to show what they could do. When Seattle teams gave them a chance, they delivered (includes undrafted rookie free agents as well as veterans.)

10. Chad Brown, Seahawks, 1997. Because contracts are not guaranteed in the NFL, football free agents are often short-timers. Not this guy. The Seahawks lured the Pro Bowl linebacker away from the Pittsburgh Steelers by giving him a six-year contract that featured a $7 million signing bonus, largest in club history at the time. Brown made good, playing in Seattle for eight years, finishing his career ranked among the club's all-time top 10 in tackles (744), sacks (48) and yards lost on sacks (284.5).

9. Slick Watts, Sonics, 1973. Back in the day when the draft was 10 rounds, nobody spotted Watts, an unknown from Xavier of Louisiana whose bald head became a Seattle symbol long before the non-hairstyle was trendy. The native of Rolling Fork, Miss., was never an all-star and lasted only six NBA seasons, but was an endearing character who not only won the NBA's citizenship award in 1976 for his community work, but twice served as Grand marshal of the annual Seafair Torchlight Parade. Watts was the first Sonic named to the NBA's All-Defensive first team (1975–76), and also that season was the first player to lead the league in assists (661) and steals (261).

8. Joe Nash, Seahawks, 1982. After the undrafted Nash signed with the Seahawks out of Boston College, he played 14 seasons and started 169 of 218 games, the most appearances by any player in franchise history. From 1982 through 1995, Nash missed just one game due to injury. A defensive tackle before switching to nose tackle, Nash was voted to the Pro Bowl in 1984.

7. Mack Strong, Seahawks, 1993. Has there been a better name for a fullback? Signed out of Georgia, Strong had one of most durable careers for a punishing position in NFL history before a neck injury forced him to retire after five games of the 2007 season. A valuable locker room guy and versatile figure in the backfield, Strong played in 201 games, second most in Seattle history, and started 111. He made Pro Bowls in 2005 and 2006 after serving as the lead blocker for RB Shaun Alexander.

6. Norm Charlton, Mariners, 1995. Released by the Phillies at midseason with a 7.36 ERA, Charlton signed with the Mariners following a 10-minute audition in the Kingdome in front of Lou Piniella, his former manager in Cincinnati. For the rest of the season, Charlton recorded 14 saves while posting a 1.51 ERA as the Mariners made up 13 games on the Angels and won their first American League West title. "The Sheriff" had 34 saves for the Mariners in 1996–97.

5. Jim Zorn, Seahawks, 1976. The team's first quarterback (1976–84), the left-handed scrambler from Cal Poly-Pomona signed with the Seahawks after a training-camp fling with the Dallas Cowboys. He became their most recognizable player as he led the NFL in passing attempts (439), set a rookie record by throwing for 2,571 yards and was named the NFC's Offensive Rookie of the Year. The Seahawks inducted Zorn into their Ring of Honor on August 30, 1991.

4. Gus Williams, Sonics, 1977. The Mount Vernon, N.Y., native signed with the Sonics in 1976–77 after the Warriors refused to give him a three-year contract. For the next six years, he never averaged fewer than 18.1 points per game. A two-time All-Star (1982–83) and a one-man fast break, "The Wizard" led the Sonics in scoring (26.6) during their NBA title run in 1979, and was Seattle's leading scorer in all five Finals games against the Washington Bullets. The Sonics retired Williams' No. 1 jersey in 2004 as part of their celebration of the 25th anniversary of the 1979 championship.

3. Dave Krieg, Seahawks, 1980. His obscure background is as much a part of his legend as the football achievements in 19 NFL seasons, the first 12 with the Seahawks. The club's all-time leader in 31 career, season and single-game passing categories when he left after 1991, Krieg "walked on" at the Seahawks' 1980 training camp after a modest career at Wisconsin's tiny Milton College, which has since gone out of business. "Mudbone" displaced the franchise's original QB starter, Jim Zorn, in 1983. A three-time Pro Bowler, Krieg was the only Seattle quarterback with a playoff victory until Matt Hasselbeck led the Seahawks to the Super Bowl following the 2005 season. The Seahawks inducted Krieg into their Ring of Honor on September 26, 2004.

2. Ichiro Suzuki, Mariners, 2001. Not a mystery find by any means, Ichiro was the best hitter in Japan, having won seven consecutive batting titles when he became an object of an MLB bidding war under the Japanese system of posting. The Mariners' winning bid of $13.1 million seemed high for a player without MLB experience, but Ichiro justified the investment quickly by winning the 2001 batting title and MVP award in a season in which the club won 116 games. Including 2001, he has led the major in hits and multi-hit games every year and is one of the game's best defensive outfielders.

1. Edgar Martinez, Mariners, 1982. Martinez spent his entire 18-year career with the Mariners, retiring after the 2004 season as the most popular player in franchise history. Martinez won two batting titles (1992, 1995), played in seven All-Star Games, won three Silver Slugger awards and joined Babe Ruth, Ted Williams, Rogers Hornsby and Lou Gehrig as the only players with 300 home runs, 500 doubles, a career batting average higher than .300, an on-base percentage higher than .400 and a slugging percentage higher than .500. Among his numerous achievements, Edgar was named AL Designated Hitter of the Year five times, which led MLB to rename the award the "Edgar Martinez Designated Hitter Award."

Most Galling Free Agent Busts

The major pro sports leagues have a wicked system for getting well or sick quickly—veteran free agents. Here's a gruesome list of Seattle's ill pills.

10. Cedric Woodard, Seahawks, 2000. A defensive tackle, Woodard signed a five-year, $15 million contract and then did almost nothing for the next two years. He made 12 starts in 2003 and just 28 for his entire Seattle tenure, which ended in 2004 when the Seahawks cut him.

9. Mike Felder, Mariners, 1993. Although GM Woody Woodward trumpeted the signing (for a then-munificent sum of $1.8 million over two years) of Felder as the dawn of an "exciting" Mariners era, it merely added evidence for the case that if a .211 hitter could be located anywhere in the world, the Mariners would find him.

8. Carlos Silva, Mariners, 2008. Due to a bankrupt farm system, the Mariners tried to re-tool for 2008 by signing Silva, a free-agent right-hander, to a four-year, $48 million contract. It turned out to be one of the most expensive mistakes the Mariners ever made. After starting out 3–0, Silva went a Magooish 1–15 the rest of the way as batters pounded him like a piñata. In nine of his 28 starts, Silva surrendered at least five earned runs, enabling him to finish a botched season with a 6.46 ERA.

7. Rich Aurilia, Mariners, 2004. The Mariners not only paid Aurilia $12,068 per at-bat in return for a .241 average in the half-season that they employed him, they traded away future All-Star shortstop Carlos Guillen to the Detroit Tigers to make room for him.

6. Nate Odomes, Seahawks, 1994. He starred on Buffalo Bills teams that made four Super Bowls, but after the Seahawks lavished a $2.2 million signing bonus on the Pro Bowl defensive back, he never played a down. He injured his right knee in a pick-up basketball game, then after serious repair surgery, blew out the same knee in mini-camp.

5. Calvin Booth, Sonics, 2001. Nicknamed "Puss 'n' Booth" by a sportswriter, Booth was terrible, which should have been no surprise. The Sonics stunned the NBA when they signed a guy who had played for four teams in four years to a six-year, $34 million contract. He played sparingly in 133 games over the next three and a half years, averaging 3.5 points per game.

4. Jim McDaniels, Sonics, 1972. Famous for once telling *Sports Illustrated* that he returned a Cadillac he had purchased because "the steering wheel didn't tilt the right way," McDaniels was the Sonics' second-round pick in 1971, but began his pro career in the rival American Basketball Association with the Carolina Cougars, who signed him to a $1.35 million contract payable over 25 years. Soon disgruntled with that deal, McDaniels jumped to the Sonics. But his career tanked. McDaniels, who had averaged 26.8 points per game in the ABA, averaged just 5.5 in two Seattle years, which ended when coach/GM Bill Russell cut him.

3. Scott Spiezio, Mariners, 2004. Signed to a three-year, $9.3 million contract, the third baseman hit .198 during his 141-game stint with the club (2004–05). By contrast, Mario Mendoza (he of the infamous Mendoza Line), the all-time poster player for inept batting, compiled a .218 average in his 262-game Seattle career (1979–80). Spiezio hit .064 in 2005 when the Mariners had to eat $3 million of his salary after releasing him. Besides being a waste of roster space, Spiezio and his girlfriend assaulted a Chicago taxi driver not long after the Mariners got rid of him.

2. Vin Baker, Sonics, 1999. After the first year of the less-than-legendary Baker-Shawn Kemp trade in 1997, the Sonics thought they did all right—the six-foot-eleven Baker had an All-Star year and averaged 19.2 points. But following the 1998–99 labor lockout, Baker ballooned to nearly 300 pounds and was frequently hurt. Nevertheless, when he opted for free agency, the Sonics, seeing no other worthy stiffs, on August 18 re-signed him to a six-year deal worth $86.7 million—one of the greatest fleece jobs in franchise history. Baker lasted three years in a state of semi-torpor before a trade to Boston. Years later, he revealed that he had become an alcoholic who binged in hotel rooms and at home after playing poorly.

1. Jim McIlvaine, Sonics, 1996. After a season with Washington in which he had averaged only 2.3 points and three rebounds, Sonics president Wally Walker, who three years later would offer Vin Baker $86.7 million, gave the seven-foot center a seven-year, $33.6 million free-agent contract. It not only quickly became the most idiotic free-agent signing in the history of the franchise because McIlvaine couldn't play, it backfired in another way. The signing angered team star Shawn Kemp, causing a rift from which the team never recovered. It led to the trading of Kemp to Cleveland in a three-way deal that brought Baker from Milwaukee, another huge, expensive mistake.

In a town often fussy about who moves here, we take it hard when a top athlete leaves, especially with nothing coming back. Here's a list of prime-timers who took the money and ran, which is their right, but Alex Rodriguez will never get a drink bought for him in this town again. Not that he can't afford to pick up a tab . . . (Rankings based on career after leaving Seattle).

11. Marvin Webster, Sonics, 1978. Webster, who came to Seattle in a trade from Denver, averaged 14.0 points and 12.6 rebounds in his lone season with the Sonics and earned the moniker "The Human Eraser" by blocking two shots per game. More importantly, the seven-foot-one center figured prominently in the Sonics reaching the NBA Finals for the first time (they lost in seven games) by significantly raising the level of his game (16.1 points, 13.1 rebounds, 2.6 blocks). But when the season ended, Webster skipped to the New York Knicks. His move didn't harm the Sonics as much as they feared. They won the NBA Finals the year after Webster bolted, and he had only one decent season (averaged 11.3 points in 1979) the rest of his career, which ended in 1987.

10. Rashard Lewis, Sonics, 2007. After nine seasons in Seattle, the last with a career- high 22.4 scoring average, Lewis took a six-year, $118 million offer from the Orlando Magic, a maximum contract many considered absurd for a one-time All-Star. Local resentment was not directed at Lewis, but at new Sonics owner Clay Bennett, who was tearing down a roster he couldn't afford after paying $350 million for the franchise—another figure many considered absurd. Lewis averaged 18.4 points for the Magic, who made the 2008 playoffs as a No. 3 seed. The deal became a sign-and-trade when the Sonics obtained a second-round pick and a trade exception under the salary cap, but it meant nothing for the disastrous 2007–2008 season.

9. Pete Kendall, Seahawks, 2001. A first-round draft choice from Boston College in 1996, Kendall, a guard, became an unrestricted free agent and signed a five-year, $18 million deal with the Arizona Cardinals. The Seahawks attempted to re-sign him, but he stood to make more in the first three years of his deal with the Cardinals than he would have made in the five-year contract the Seahawks offered. Kendall, one of the game's most outspoken players, left the Cardinals and continued on with the Jets and Redskins, complaining steadily about his contracts.

8. Floyd Bannister, Mariners, 1983. Although lefty Bannister, a Seattle native, had a 51–68 record in six major league seasons when he became a free agent, several teams made significant bids for him. The Mariners under owner George Argyros not only were not one of them, they had no inclination to make a near-millionaire out of any player. So Bannister chose the Chicago White Sox, who offered $4.5 million over five years. Bannister won 66 games for the White Sox over those five seasons. The Mariners lost 457 games over the same span, including 102 the year after Bannister bolted.

7. Sam Adams, Seahawks, 2000. The Seahawks, specifically coach/GM Mike Holmgren, had decided against re-signing the huge defensive tackle even before Adams let it be known he wanted $3 million per year. Seattle's 1994 No. 1 draft pick eventually signed with Baltimore, and helped lead the most dominating defense in the league to a victory in Super Bowl XXXV.

6. Shawn Springs, Seahawks, 2004. Seattle's first-round draft choice in 1997 and a Pro Bowl cornerback in 1998, Springs played seven years before jumping to the Washington Redskins for $30 million over six years. It wasn't just the money that lured Springs, a D.C. native: "Playing up there in the Pacific Northwest," he said, "is like playing in Egypt, it's so far away."

5. Kevin Mawae, Seahawks, 1998. The Seahawks lost their starting center when Mawae accepted a five-year, $17 million offer from the New York Jets that included a $5 million signing bonus, making him the NFL's highest-paid center. Re-signing Mawae had been a priority for the Seahawks, but they could not match the Jets. Mawae played in seven Pro Bowls after departing Seattle and had a 15-year career with three teams through 2008.

4. Nate McMillan, Sonics, 2005. The jilt came as a coach, not a player, when his 12 seasons were so selfless and dedicated he became known as "Mr. Sonic." His five additional years as assistant and head coach made him the longest-tenured Sonics employee, but that made no difference when the club failed to extend his contract prior to 2005. After the Sonics that season won 52 games and a playoff series, management offered him $18 million over four years. But Portland owner and Seattle native Paul Allen offered $27 million over six to coach the rival Trail Blazers, embarrassing the Sonics by valuing their heart and soul more than the club that raised him.

3. Tom Chambers, Sonics, 1988. Chambers, a six-foot-ten forward and MVP of the 1987 All-Star Game in Seattle, as well as a five-year Sonic, became the first unrestricted free agent in NBA history to change teams by signing a five-year, $10 million contract with the Phoenix Suns. He departed not because he wanted to, but because head coach Bernie Bickerstaff no longer wanted him after pulling a draft-day maneuver to obtain forward-center Michael Cage. Chambers exacted revenge on March 24, 1990, when he scored 60 points against the Sonics.

2. Steve Hutchinson, Seahawks, 2006. One of Seattle's two first-round draft choices in 2001, Hutchinson was voted to two All-Pro teams in his first five years. Given that, and given that he helped form the best left-side offensive line tandem in the league with tackle Walter Jones, Hutchinson wanted a top-shelf contract extension. The Seahawks wouldn't do it. Rather than designating him a franchise player for a one-year contract, the Seahawks tagged him a "transition" player, making him vulnerable to free agent offers. That opened the door to the Vikings, whose offer of seven years and $49 million would make him the game's highest-paid guard. Hutchinson jumped, in what turned out to be one of the largest screw-ups in Seahawks history. In the 2005 season that ended in the Super Bowl, the Seahawks averaged 153 rushing yards per game. In less than two years, thanks to Hutchinson's absence and a fading Shaun Alexander, they had one of the puniest running attacks in the league.

1. Alex Rodriguez, Mariners, 2001. The Mariners, who passed on the chance to trade him, were prepared to make Rodriguez, already recognized as one of the game's greatest, the highest-paid ever. But the Texas Rangers surpassed Seattle's offer by five years and more than $150 million, handing the All-Star shortstop a sports-record 10-year, $252 million contract. "Texas made the decision easy for me," said Rodriguez, who after departing Seattle won five home run titles and three Most Valuable Player awards. But his annual returns as a Ranger and a Yankee are greeted with heavy boos that have become a Seattle tradition, despite the fact that taking the Rangers' offer is what every one of the hecklers in a similar position would have done.

Rod Long is a Seattle comedian, writer and photographer. He has been called "Seattle's longest suffering sports fan." His musings on some frequent topics:

Indian burial ground theory. In hindsight, the Mariners 2008 season was over by Mother's Day weekend. It's a cold bowl of chili. But, it's a rule, rather than exception, that Seattle teams find a way to always fall short. Are Seattle sports teams cursed? Did that herd of dead chinchillas draped across the back of Jerramy Stevens as he deplaned in Detroit for Super Bowl week doom the Hawks before kickoff? It's been rumored that Safeco and Qwest fields are built on Indian burial grounds. It would explain how mojo turned to doo-doo. No amount of casino profits can erase the karma. If the ground is indeed sacred, the city and the teams must make amends. Have a traditional cleansing ceremony at both stadiums and invite families of the departed. At this point, what do we have to lose – except more games and hope?

Brian Bosworth. Years ago, I saw his Saturday work on ABC. It was like watching a Tasmanian Devil in a football uniform—with excited narration provided by Keith Jackson. He pursued running backs with pit bull tenacity from sideline to sideline, often out of bounds, with loogie. Boz brought a special brand of nasty and outrageous. Plus, he wore a blond Mohawk and earrings. So coveted was this menace, the *Post-Intelligencer* ran an ongoing column called "Boz Watch." It gave eager fans a look into the daily antics of our soon-to-be superstar. Strangers sent salmon, coffee and hair products. The man hadn't made a tackle, yet was getting more local love than Kenny G. Then, boom—quicker than you can say $11 million WHOOPS, Boz was gone. Off to Hollywood, with a quick stopover in court. It was the performance of his life. Through tears, he explained the bum shoulder actually started hurting shortly after he signed the contract. In the movie *Stone Cold,* Boz played a biker who was actually an undercover cop. Since he played an undercover linebacker for the Seahawks for three years, it was perfect.

Jack Sikma. When the Sonics traded Jack Sikma to Milwaukee it cost me about three minutes and a couple of callbacks in my monologue. In the early 1980s, I was living and working in Los Angeles. Three or four times a week, I played basketball in a league I called, "The West Hollywood All-Negro Argument Tournament." It was spirited combat, with 20-minute debates between plays. I wore a Lonnie Shelton No. 8 Sonics jersey. I often channeled Lonnie's butt, to help me box out and rebound. It was all about representing Seattle. One afternoon, in a discussion of the NBA's great centers, Rudy, the designated park spokesman, diagnosed Sikma's game: "Sikma's that white dude in Seattle with the Jeri-curl hairstyle. And got game too. Sikma likes to get a brother to go for that first move. Then he's got you in the popcorn machine. Sikma turns and puts the rock way up high. Got a funky shot that's hard to check. Yeah, man…Sikma's good! He can't mess with Kareem, but Sikma's good!" Rudy became a mainstay in my act. He even called Seahawks coach Chuck Knox's old radio show and suggested that what the Hawks needed was a player like Jack Sikma.

Dan McGwire. A trademark of Seahawk first-round draft choices during the Ken Behring era was tall, stiff quarterbacks. During a blowout loss at Dallas, Dan spent much of the afternoon on his back studying cloud patterns over Texas Stadium. I was doing a weekly update every Sunday night at the Comedy Underground called "First & Long." I opened that night saying President Kennedy had better protection in Dallas that Dan McGwire.

Lou Piniella. No manager ever got his money's worth after being ejected from a baseball game like former Mariner skipper Lou Pinella. In a passive/aggressive town where you can't wear a "Yankees Suck" T-shirt to the ballpark, Lou told you who sucked and why. One night against the Orioles, Lou got the boot in the fifth inning. After emptying all bats and the water cooler from the Mariner dugout, Lou grabbed third base and went home.

This list is about the wow factor—lots of names coming and going—not necessarily how it worked out for all parties. Seattle has seen some star-power doozies, but as you will see, not a lot of them worked in favor of the local side.

10. December 12, 1980. Number of players: 11

Deal: In the second biggest trade in Mariners history (they collaborated with the Mets and Indians on a 12-player trade on December 13, 2008, that's too soon to judge) in terms of the number of players involved, the club sent LHP Rick Honeycutt, C Larry Cox, DH Willie Horton, SS Mario Mendoza and OF Leon Roberts to the Texas Rangers for DH Richie Zisk, INF Rick Auerbach, RHP Ken Clay, LHP Jerry Don Gleaton, P Brian Allard and minor leaguer Steve Finch.

Next: The Mariners gave up a lot of nothing and got mostly nothing in return. Gleaton, Allard and Clay combined to win nine games in two years before the Mariners deemed them expendable. Auerbach hit .155 in 38 games. Zisk became the key acquisition, hitting 49 home runs and driving in 141 from 1981–83.

9. June 24, 2004. Number of players: 4

Deal: The Mariners traded RHP Freddy Garcia and C Ben Davis to the White Sox for OF Jeremy Reed, C Miguel Olivo and minor league INF Michael Morse.

Next: The trade of Seattle's staff ace amounted to the Mariners pulling the plug on a dismal 2004 season (99 losses). In exchange, the Mariners received an outfielder (Reed) who couldn't hit, a catcher (Olivo) who couldn't hit either (.151 in 54 games in 2005), and a player (Morse) for which the Mariners could never find a position.

8. June 29, 2007. Number of players: 4

Deal: The Sonics traded All-Star G Ray Allen and the 35th overall pick in the 2007 draft to the Boston Celtics for F Wally Szczerbiak, G Delonte West and the No. 5 overall pick, which the Celtics had used on Georgetown's six-foot-nine F Jeff Green.

Next: The Sonics traded Allen, their best player, because new owner Clay Bennett wanted nothing to do with his $80 million contract. He helped transform the Celtics into a premier team. West was a bust, traded at midseason; so was Szczerbiak, but he could play. Green had a decent first season as Kevin Durant's running mate, but they suffered through the worst season in Sonics history.

7. September 25, 1997. Number of players: 5

Deal: The Sonics traded All-Star F Shawn Kemp in a three-team swap that saw Milwaukee G Sherman Douglas go to Cleveland, Cleveland G Terrell Brandon and F Tyrone Hill go to Milwaukee, and Milwaukee F-C Vin Baker land in Seattle.

Next: Kemp was a superstar anchor of six consecutive 55-win teams but self-destructed, getting fat and into drugs. Baker, an All-Star, had one good season and then got fat and into alcohol, becoming one of the biggest and most expensive disappointments in Sonics history.

6. October 23, 1975. Number of players: 2

Deal: The Sonics traded All-Star F Spencer Haywood to the New York Knicks for a 1979 first-round draft choice (G Vinny Johnson) and $2 million.

Next: Although Haywood averaged 24.9 points in his five years in Seattle and made four All-Star teams, his personality conflicts with head coach Bill Russell became intolerable. To help expedite Haywood's departure, Russell told reporters Haywood was unhappy in Seattle and probably disgruntled because he didn't make enough outside income, which he could make in New York. Haywood declined steadily after he arrived in New York, and never made another All-Star team.

5. February 20, 2003. Number of players: 5

Deal: Sonics traded All-Star G Gary Payton and F Desmond Mason to the Milwaukee Bucks for All-Star G Ray Allen, G Kevin Ollie and rookie G-F Ronald Murray.

Next: At 34, Payton had no more All-Star seasons left when the Sonics essentially swapped him for Allen, one of the most accomplished shooters in the league. But the Sonics had little help for Allen, and made the playoffs just once in his four years in Seattle. Payton went on to win his lone NBA title as a reserve with Miami.

4. July 31, 1998. Number of players: 4.

Deal: The Mariners traded LHP Randy Johnson to the Houston Astros for RHP Freddy Garcia, SS Carlos Guillen and LHP John Halama.

Next: Johnson went on to star for Arizona and the Yankees, winning four Cy Youngs and a 2001 World Series co-MVP. Garcia developed into Seattle's staff ace, but never came close to duplicating Johnson's post-Seattle feats. The main crime involved Guillen, whom the Mariners literally gave away to Detroit as he was evolving into an All-Star.

3. May 3, 1977. Number of players: 5

Deal: The Seahawks traded their first pick in the draft, No. 2 overall, to the Dallas Cowboys for Dallas' first-round pick and three second-round picks. The Cowboys used Seattle's No. 1 on Heisman Trophy winner Tony Dorsett of Pittsburgh. The Seahawks used Dallas' No.1 on OT Steve August and the three second-round picks on OT Tom Lynch, LB Terry Beeson and LB Peter Cronan.

Next: The first-year team believed it needed several high draft picks to become competitive. But the players they selected turned out to be ordinary, while Dorsett became a Hall of Famer.

2. December 12, 1938, Number of players: 5

Deal: The Rainiers traded RHP Fred Hutchinson to the Detroit Tigers for OF Jo-Jo White, 1B George Archie, INF Tony Piet, minor league pitcher Ed Selway and $50,000.

Next: When the Rainiers sent Seattle native Hutchinson, coming off a rookie season in which he went 25–7 with a 2.48 ERA and 29 complete games, to the Tigers, it marked the biggest deal involving a minor leaguer in more than a decade. The talent the Rainiers received in return for Seattle's first sports icon not only brought them three consecutive Pacific Coast League pennants, it enabled the Rainiers to become Seattle's most popular summer entertainment during and after the war years.

1. February 10, 2000. Players involved: 5.

Deal: The Mariners traded OF Ken Griffey Jr. to the Cincinnati Reds for OF Mike Cameron, RHP Brett Tomko, INF Antonio Perez and minor leaguer Jake Meyer.

Next: The trade of the greatest player in Seattle sports history was shattering for many. After 11 seasons, 10 All-Star appearances and 398 home runs, Griffey forced the Mariners to trade him, conceding Seattle had drawn "the short straw." On pace to break Babe Ruth's home run record at the time of the trade, Griffey proceeded to miss 3 ½ of the next seven seasons with a variety of injuries. Cameron proved to be an excellent defensive replacement, but was allowed to go into free agency after the 2003 season when the Mariners found his asking price too high. None of the other throw-ins did much with Seattle.

Fans always seem to remember the bad trades—acutely so in Seattle, because of their preponderance—but the local squads also have come out on top on a number of key deals that were difference makers.

10. Three draft picks for Curt Warner, April 24, 1983.
For the first seven years of their existence (1976–82), the Seahawks never had a marquee running back. That changed at the 1983 draft when the Seahawks sent their first-, second- and third-round choices to Houston for the Oilers' No. 3 overall pick. They used it on Penn State running back Curt Warner, who in his first year led the AFC in rushing yards (1,449) and went on to post three more 1,000-yard seasons as he helped make the Seahawks a playoff team for the first time. He was inducted into the team's Ring of Honor in 1994.

9. Ron Villone and Marc Newfield for Andy Benes, July 31, 1995.
Although RHP Benes, an impending free agent, had a 4–7 record before the trade by GM Woody Woodward with San Diego, he soon became the most important rent-a-player in franchise history. Benes went 7–2 down the stretch as the Mariners rallied from a 13-game deficit on August 2 to win their first division championship. LHP Villone, a first-round draft pick in 1992, became a steady middle-relief man for 11 teams (including a second tour with the Mariners) over 13 seasons. OF Newfield, also a No. 1 draft pick (1990), never had more than 200 at-bats in five marginal MLB seasons with three teams.

8. Fredd Young for two No. 1 picks, September 8, 1988.
When the Seahawks could not satisfy the linebacker's contract demands, they sent him to Indianapolis for the Colts' No. 1 picks in 1989 and 1990. The Seahawks used the 1989 No. 1 on OL Andy Heck, who started 70 games at three positions during five Seattle years. The Seahawks used the 1990 No. 1, plus their own No. 1, to move up in the 1990 draft to select DT Cortez Kennedy, who became an eight-time Pro Bowl player and 1992 NFL Defensive Player of the Year. Young, who had 15 sacks in his two seasons as a starting linebacker in Seattle, had two in his three seasons with the Colts—then was done.

7. Ken Phelps for Jay Buhner, July 21, 1988.
Buhner, a wild-swinging Texan, was 23 with little major league experience when the Yankees sent him and pitchers Rick Balabon and Troy Evers to the Mariners for Phelps, a 34-year-old designated hitter. New York owner George Steinbrenner believed the addition of Phelps virtually guaranteed the Yankees would win the AL. But Phelps, who hit .284 with 14 home runs in Seattle, hit just .224 with 10 home runs, and the Yankees faded to fifth place. A year later, the Yankees dealt Phelps to Oakland. Buhner went on to hit 307 home runs, drive in 951 and win a Gold Glove during 14 seasons with the Mariners. So lopsided was the trade that it was mentioned in a Seinfeld episode that aired January 26, 1996.

6. Jamie Moyer for Darren Bragg, July 30, 1996. When Woodward sent young OF Bragg to the Boston Red Sox for LHP Moyer, they were acquiring a journeyman starter who had bounced among five teams, never winning more than 13 games in nine seasons. From mid-1996 through mid-2006, Moyer became the winningest pitcher in Mariners history, twice reaching 20 victories and failing to pitch at least 200 innings only once. Bragg, a career .255 hitter, played for nine teams in 11 seasons, only in one of which did he reach 500 at-bats.

5. Rick Mirer for what became Walter Jones and Shawn Springs, starting February 18, 1997. Although QB Mirer had a solid rookie season in 1993 after the Seahawks made him the No. 2 overall choice, he regressed into one of the worst picks in franchise history. VP of football ops Randy Mueller sent Mirer and a fourth-rounder to the Bears for their first-rounder in the 1997 draft. That gave the Seahawks the 11th and 12th overall picks. A couple of months later, Mueller sent the 11th pick, along with their second-, third- and fourth-round choices, to Atlanta for the third overall pick and the Falcons' third-rounder. On the day of the draft, Mueller sent the Falcons' third-rounder and their own first to Tampa Bay for the sixth overall choice. The Seahawks then drafted CB Shawn Springs with the No. 3 pick and OT Walter Jones with the No. 6 pick. Springs started 88 games over seven seasons. Jones became the best offensive lineman in franchise history (nine Pro Bowls). Mirer played in just seven games for the Bears.

4. Mark Langston for two pitchers and a Big Unit, May 25, 1989. When Woodward traded pending free agent LHP Langston, who had just rejected a three-year, $7.1 million contract offer, to the Montreal Expos for RHPs Gene Harris and Brian Holman and LHP Randy Johnson, 3B Jimmy Presley described it as "the saddest day in Mariner history." One of the Mariners' few star attractions, Langston won 74 games in six seasons and would go on to win 105 more with the Expos, Angels, Padres and Indians. He also collaborated with Mike Witt to no-hit the Mariners less than a year after the trade. While neither Harris nor Holman spent more than three years in Seattle, the six-foot-ten Johnson lasted a decade, becoming a Cy Young Award recipient (1995) and the winner of one of the most significant games in franchise history, a one-game playoff against the Angels October 2, 1995, to beat Langston and put the Mariners in the postseason for the first time.

3. Tom Burleson and Bobby Wilkerson for Paul Silas, Marvin Webster and Willie Wise, May 24, 1977. When new Sonics coach Bob Hopkins and player personnel director Lenny Wilkens collaborated to deal underachieving seven-foot-four C Tom Burleson and six-foot-six G Bobby Wilkerson to the Denver Nuggets for seven-foot-one C Webster, aka "The Human Eraser," six-foot-seven F Silas and six-foot-four G Willie Wise, it didn't create much of a stir. But it proved to be one of the franchise's most astute deals. With Webster manning the middle and Silas providing rebounding and veteran leadership off the bench, the Sonics reached the NBA Finals for the first time in franchise history in 1978. Webster then left for the Knicks, who compensated with PF Lonnie Shelton, and the Sonics went on to their first and only NBA championship in 1979. Burleson washed out after four more seasons. Wilkerson did OK, playing for four teams in seven seasons.

2. The Hasselbeck-Hutchinson heist, March 2, 2001. Only a few trades in Seahawks history could be classified as "heists." But the one that Mike Holmgren pulled off at the expense of the Green Bay Packers, his former employer, qualifies amply. Holmgren traded Seattle's first-round (10th overall) and third-round (72nd overall) picks to the Packers for Green Bay's backup quarterback and its No. 1 pick (17th overall). That's how Holmgren got three-time Pro Bowler Matt Hasselbeck and guard Steve Hutchinson, who would play in four Pro Bowls with the Seahawks. Green Bay used Seattle's draft picks on DE Jamal Reynolds and LB Torrance Marshall, to little end.

1. An 8th-round pick for a Hall of Famer, August 26, 1976. Selected by the Houston Oilers in the fourth round of the 1976 draft, WR Steve Largent of Tulsa was slated to be cut after four exhibition games. At the recommendation of offensive coordinator Jerry Rhome, the Seahawks sent an eighth-round draft pick to get the greatest receiver in franchise history. By the time Largent retired in 1989, he was the NFL's career leader in receptions (819), yards (13,089) and touchdowns (101). In 1995, Largent became the first Seahawk inducted into the Pro Football Hall of Fame. The Oilers used the eighth-round pick on WR Steve Davis of Georgia, who never played in the NFL.

Things I Have to Have at Training Camp
:: Matt Hasselbeck

As an NFL veteran, nothing excites Seahawks quarterback Matt Hasselbeck more than the thought of training camp.

10. EAS Muscle Armor. It only comes in one flavor (lemon lime) but it is THE premier safe-to-take drink. Hydrate, hydrate, hydrate!

9. Anti-inflammatories. Advil, Icy Hot, Ben Gay. The older I get the longer the list gets.

8. Refrigerator. With a six-pack of beer for the night that curfew is extended to midnight. (Maybe a 12-pack, if we're being honest.)

7. Flip-flops. For starters, community bathrooms. Enough said. You actually get fined for showering without flip-flops. I don't even walk around the room without them. We used to stay in college dorm rooms, and college dorm rooms never change.

6. Family photo. The worst part of camp was being away from the family. It's fun to be at camp, hanging out with your buddies. But you miss your kids. Come to think of it, at camp we all get treated like kids.

5. Bike with lock! Before my first training camp with the Hawks at Eastern Washington University in Cheney, Christian Fauria told me to rent a bike. Instead, I just bought one. I've had the same bike for every season I've trained in Seattle. I think I've ridden it once outside of training camp. You need a lock because bikes get stolen, usually as part of a prank. You want to do the least amount of walking possible. Being on your feet is no good.

4. A good book. Because the playbook is so boring. And the meetings are the same. The talks are the same every year. I've got it all memorized.

3. Massage chair. I rent it out to other players. Beds are bad and everyone aches. Another thing about the massage chair is that no matter which assistant coach comes to enforce curfew, 100 percent of the time his back hurts. So they'll hang out for a while and use the chair. Which gives us a few more minutes. But they've gotten wise. They've started coming to my room first to announce lights out.

2. Eight alarm clocks for my go-to prank. First, you need a clock. Then, I hesitate to tell you the rest, because no one knows it's me. In camp, you never want to get caught starting the prank because the victim will come after you. I've done this one several times. The best guy to get with it was former long snapper J. P. Darche. He wore contact lenses, otherwise he was nearly blind without them. I hid eight alarm clocks in his room, set to go off at one-hour intervals. 1:08, 2:08, 3:08, 4:08, etc. The 4:08 one was the best because it was a talking alarm clock: "4:08! 4:08! 4:08!" Since he didn't have his contacts in, he couldn't find the clocks. Best thing was he thought Robbie Tobeck did it. The two would always go at it. I think because Darche was from Canada, somehow he offended Tobeck. He still blames Tobeck for the alarms.

1. Sega Genesis with NHL 95. Everyone brings video games. X Box. Play Station 2. PSP. Games where eight can play at once. It's ridiculous. I can't keep up. I bring Sega Genesis, which is what I played in college, and NHL 95. It's the greatest game ever invented. Games are only five minutes long and there's only two control buttons so anyone can learn to play. But here's the problem. I'm one of the oldest guys on the team now. No one knows what Sega Genesis is anymore. One camp, Trent Dilfer, J. P. Darche, Isaiah Kacyvenski and I played NHL 95 every free moment. Eventually, my arm got so sore I almost missed practice. Before camp the first year I was in Seattle, I went shopping for video games. I was looking at all the old stuff, Madden 96, Kung Fu, World Cup Soccer, Bill Walsh College Football 1996 and 1997. I took the Walsh games and asked the clerk how much. He said 48 for the 1996 and 46 for the 1997 Bill Walsh. I told him I'd take the 1997. He said, "You know I mean 46 cents, right?" I couldn't believe it. I bought every old game they had.

There are big trades, which we've discussed, and there are good trades, which we've discussed. Then there are trades that no one in Seattle wants to discuss. We're here to discuss. All these deals must have had some point, but hindsight suggests only an attempt to annoy sports fans' digestive systems.

10. Derek Lowe and Jason Varitek for Heathcliff Slocumb, July 31, 1997. As the trading deadline approached, Mariners GM Woody Woodward moved to shore up the club's most glaring weakness, the bullpen. For reasons known only to his psychiatrist, Woodward fixated on Heathcliff Slocumb, who had an 0–5 record, five blown saves and a 5.79 ERA as Boston's closer. Woodward sent the Red Sox rookie RHP Derek Lowe and minor league C Jason Varitek, Seattle's first-round pick in the 1994 free agent draft. Slocumb saved 13 games for Mariners over the second half of 1997 and made 57 appearances in 1998, but never could get his ERA under 5.00, and was cut. Lowe won more than 100 games and saved more than 80 for the Red Sox and Dodgers following his departure from Seattle, twice becoming an All-Star. Varitek became a hero in Red Sox Nation, earning two All-Star appearances and two World Series rings.

9. Tino Martinez and Jeff Nelson for nothing close, December 7, 1995. Following their dramatic 1995 postseason run, the Mariners cut costs by trading to the team they beat in the playoffs, the Yankees, popular 1B Martinez, setup man Nelson and pitching prospect Jim Mecir for LHP Sterling Hitchcock and 3B Russ Davis. For the Yanks, Martinez hit 251 of his 339 career home runs, and Nelson won four World Series rings before the Mariners re-acquired him in 2001. Hitchcock went 13–9 in 35 starts with the Mariners in 1996, but his 5.35 ERA jettisoned him to San Diego after the season for RHP Scott Sanders, who allowed so many home runs early in 1997 (16 in six starts) that he was dumped to Detroit at mid-year. In return came pitchers Omar Olivares and Felipe Lira, both of whom were gone within a year—with the Mariners receiving nothing in return. Davis hit 61 home runs between 1997–99, including the first home run at Safeco Field (July 17, 1999), but his 71 errors cashiered him after 1999.

8. Spike Owen and Dave Henderson for nothing close, August 19, 1986. In an attempt to improve their pallid pitching, the Mariners sent OF/DH Henderson and SS Owen to the Red Sox for RHPs Mike Brown and Mike Trujillo, SS Rey Quinones and OF John Christensen. None of the Seattle additions amounted to much, Quinones lasting the longest (two and a half seasons). Henderson played eight seasons after leaving Seattle, was an All-Star in 1991, and reached the World Series four times (1986 with Boston, 1988–90 with Oakland). Owen played nine years with four teams. Yankees owner George Steinbrenner was so livid, he called the trade "the robbery of the century." Added Steinbrenner: "The Mariners probably just handed the pennant to the Red Sox." Indeed, Boston won the AL pennant.

7. Carlos Guillen to Detroit for nothing, January 8, 2004. Because he had acquired Rich Aurilia in free agency (one year, $3.1 million), Mariners GM Bill Bavasi reasoned he had no further need for the oft-injured SS. So Bavasi sent Guillen to Detroit for a pair of minor league infielders, Ramon Santiago and Juan Gonzalez. Aurilia bombed, hitting .241 in 73 games before the Mariners gave up on him at mid-season. Guillen went on to become a multi-year All-Star in Detroit. Neither Santiago nor Gonzalez played for the Mariners, both eased out of the club's minor league system. Ironically, both also ended up back with Detroit.

6. Scottie Pippen for Olden Polynice, et al, June 22, 1987; Polynice and two No. 1s for Benoit Benjamin, February 20, 1991. Polynice, a six-foot-ten center with a great body, iron hands and dubious head, was part of two colossal bungles by Sonics GM Bob Whitsitt. On 1987 draft day, Central Arkansas F Scottie Pippen was taken by the Sonics with the fifth overall pick and traded to Chicago for a trio of selections that became Polynice, a second-round pick in 1988 (F Sylvester Gray), and a future choice who morphed into C Brad Sellers. Enthused one Seattle newspaper: "This is a deal that would make Red Auerbach Celtic-green with envy." Not quite. Polynice, a decent defender and rebounder, started just seven of 289 games over four years with the Sonics; Gray and Sellers did nothing. Pippen played on six NBA championship teams in Chicago and, in 1996, was named one of the 50 best players in history. To make matters worse, Polynice was traded to the Clippers in 1991 along with two first-round picks for Benoit Benjamin. The most memorable part of Benjamin's legacy was that he once tried to enter a game with two left shoes.

5. The Kevin Mitchell fiasco, December 11, 1991. In acquiring Mitchell (and LHP Mike Remlinger) from San Francisco for starting pitchers Billy Swift and Dave Burba and reliever Mike Jackson, the Mariners departed from their penurious payroll policy, figuring Mitchell's power would enhance their offense and attract fans. Many predicted Mitchell might smack 50 home runs playing in the dead-air Kingdome, a reasonable assumption considering, from 1989–91, he had the most HRs (109) in the majors. Alas, in 1992 with the Mariners, 110 players hit more home runs than Mitchell. Not only did Mitchell hit just nine HRs, he was paid $3.7 million, then unloaded on Cincinnati. Remlinger never pitched for the Mariners. The Mariners later re-acquired both Swift and Jackson. The pair and Burba all had long careers in the majors.

4. Three picks (honest!) for Kelly Stouffer, April 22, 1988. The Seahawks originally tried to dispatch All-Pro SS Kenny Easley to the Cardinals for Stouffer, who had sat out what would have been his rookie year in a contract imbroglio. But Easley, suffering from failing kidneys, flunked his physical, nixing the swap. The Seahawks tried again, sending three draft picks—a No. 5 in 1988 and a No. 1 and a No. 5 in 1989—for Stouffer, whom they promptly signed to a four-year deal. "This guy has all the tools," Seahawks coach Chuck Knox told the Seattle media, "as far as we perceive the tools to be." But not only could Stouffer not displace starter Dave Krieg, he started just 16 games in five years, and was released after a 1992 season in which the Seahawks featured one of the worst offenses in NFL history.

3. Dennis Johnson for Paul Westphal, June 3, 1980. Although Johnson averaged 19 points and four assists in the 1979–80 season while making the All-Defensive first team, Sonics coach Lenny Wilkens grew weary of the moody guard, calling the MVP of the Sonics' 1979 NBA championship team "a cancer." So the Sonics shipped Johnson to Phoenix for Westphal, a five-time All-Star himself, and a couple of draft picks. While Johnson went on to flourish in Phoenix, and later in Boston, where he won a string of championship rings, Westphal's career derailed. He averaged a career-low 16.7 points per game in his only season in Seattle (1980–81) while playing just 36 games before getting hurt, and the Sonics finished 22 games worse in the standings than they had in Johnson's final year.

2. Five Players For Erik Bedard, February 9, 2008. The Mariners figured they were getting a staff ace when they dispatched former No. 1 pick Adam Jones, left-handed reliever George Sherrill and three minor league prospects to the Baltimore Orioles for Bedard, a 13-game winner in 2007. Instead, they got an uncommunicative odd duck (at 29 years of age he was still living in the basement of his parents' home) who couldn't stay healthy. When he did throw, the moody Bedard rarely exceeded 100 pitches. Worse, he failed to communicate the extent of a shoulder problem to the team's medical staff and finally had to undergo surgery. Meanwhile, Jones became Baltimore's everyday center fielder, Sherrill saved 31 games (five against Seattle), and young pitchers Chris Tillman, Tony Butler and Kam Mickolio, who could have progressed nicely in Seattle's farm system, instead progressed nicely in the Orioles organization.

1. Lenny Wilkens for Butch Beard, August 23, 1972. No trade in Seattle sports history riled the populace as much as the decision by Sonics owner Sam Schulman to deal five-time All-Star Wilkens and throw-in Barry Clemens to the Cleveland Cavaliers for guard Butch Beard. Wilkens, who arrived in Seattle three years earlier in a trade for guard Walt Hazzard, was the first superstar in Seattle sports. He led the club to a team-record 47-win season, just missing the playoffs. The trade was a catastrophic mistake. Without Wilkens, who had been the team's player-coach, the Sonics slipped to 26–56. His coaching replacement, Tom Nissalke, was fired after 45 games. His playing replacement, Beard, averaged just 6.6 points per game and lasted one year. Sonics fans expressed their displeasure over the deal the first time Wilkens returned to Seattle. They booed Beard and their own team—4–10 at the time—and wildly cheered Wilkens with a two-minute pre-game standing ovation. Wilkens had 22 points, nine rebounds and nine assists to lead the Cavaliers to a 113–107 victory.

Dreadful Draft-Day Debacles

Given the soaring mediocrity that has visited Seattle pro sports teams over their histories, it stands to reason that they have had a lot of high draft picks. It also stands to reason that to maintain mediocrity, teams have to blow a lot of those picks. Herewith lies a sad sampling of the worst.

10. (tie) Ryan Anderson, Mariners, 1997, Robert Swift, Sonics 2004. Both were first-round, big-upside giants ruined mostly by injuries. The Mariners were hoping for a duplicate of "Big Unit" Randy Johnson when they picked the quickly monickered "Little Unit", a six-foot-ten left hander out of Southfield, MI. But two shoulder surgeries and a dubious work ethic prevented Anderson from reaching the majors. Swift, 7–1 and 270, was taken out of high school in Bakersfield, CA, with the 12th pick. In his first three seasons he played in 71 games, thanks largely to injuries that included a torn knee ligament.

9. Tito Nanni, Mariners, 1978. Selected in the first round, sixth overall, Nanni never even made it out of the low minors. Instead of drafting Nanni, the Mariners could have had Ryne Sandberg, Cal Ripken Jr., or Dave Stieb, In fact, a top Seattle scout at the time, Jerry Krause, who went on to some basketball success with the Chicago Bulls, futilely insisted the club take a slugger named Kirk Gibson.

8. Frank Oleynick, Sonics, 1975. Selected with the 12th overall pick, Oleynick was a popular choice because he starred at Seattle University. But he did nothing in his two years with the Sonics, never starting and averaging just five points per game. Instead, the Sonics could have had Joe Bryant, Ricky Sobers, Kevin Grevey, World B. Free, Dan Roundfield or even Gus Williams, whom they signed as a free agent two years later.

7. Roger Salkeld, Mariners, 1989. Selected in the first round, third overall, Salkeld spent parts of two seasons (1993–94) with the Mariners, going 2-5 in 15 career starts. The Mariners traded Salkeld and his 7.17 ERA to Cincinnati in 1995 for Tim Belcher. Salkeld pitched one year for the Reds (1996). Although he went 8–5 in 19 starts, he washed out of the league with a 5.61 career ERA.

6. Patrick Lennon, Mariners, 1986. A high school shortstop and the eighth overall pick, Lennon played just 10 games with the big club. Bo Jackson, still on the board when the Mariners selected, not only became a major league All-Star, he became a Pro Bowl football player. Lennon's troubles nearly scared the Mariners away from taking another high schooler in the 1987 draft, but owner George Argyros was finally prevailed upon to allow the selection of Ken Griffey Jr.

5. Owen Gill, Seahawks, 1985. A fullback from Iowa, Gill was the first player taken by the Seahawks with the No. 53 overall (no first-rounder) choice. Gill not only didn't play a down in a regular-season game, he didn't make it through training camp. Gill came to symbolize the bankruptcy of the entire 1985 draft. From the second through the fifth rounds, the Seahawks selected Gill, WR Danny Greene, TE Tony Davis, C Mark Napolitan, CB Arnold Brown and RB Johnnie Jones. The six combined to play just six games for the Seahawks.

4. Rich King, Sonics, 1991. Selected in the first round, 14th overall, out of Nebraska, the seven-foot-two, 260-pound King barely registered during four unproductive seasons. In 72 games, he made just two starts and averaged 1.9 points per game. He never played in the league after the Sonics released him.

3. Andre Hines, Seahawks, 1980. Seahawks bosses planned to use their second-round pick on Brian Holloway, an All-America tackle from Stanford. Instead, in an epic case of mistaken identity by bullheaded head coach Jack Patera, who refused to admit he was wrong, Holloway's pudgy backup was picked. Once drafted, Hines freely admitted he rarely played at Stanford. He rarely played for the Seahawks—nine games, starting none. In one memorable Seahawk embarrassment, a 51–7 blowout loss at Dallas on Thanksgiving Day, 1980, Patera inserted Hines late, whereupon Cowboys' defensive end Harvey Martin immediately drew Hines off-sides by yelling "Boo!"

2. Al Chambers, Mariners, 1979. The first pick in the first round, Chambers knocked around in the minors for nearly seven years before the club gave up on the outfielder and released him. He played just 57 career games at the major-league level, batting .208 with two home runs. Rather than taking Chambers, the Mariners could have selected Andy Van Slyke, an outfielder who made three All-Star teams.

1. Dan McGwire, Seahawks, 1991. Younger brother of baseball star Mark McGwire, the tallest (six-foot-eight) quarterback in NFL history made only five starts and played in 12 games after the Seahawks—or, rather, meddlesome owner Ken Behring—made him the 16th overall pick out of San Diego State. Despite needing a successor to Dave Krieg, coach Chuck Knox objected furiously to taking McGwire, who by 1993 could not even beat out Stan Gelbaugh to back up another bust, Kelly Stouffer. Not only was McGwire a terrible choice, but on the draft board below him was Brett Favre.

Cornerback Marcus Trufant was an All-State selection at Tacoma's Wilson High School and a second-team All-America after four stellar seasons at Washington State. The Seahawks took him with the 11th pick in the 2003 draft. He made his first Pro Bowl in 2007. Usually a quiet guy, his job is to deny the noisiest players in the game—NFL wide receivers. Here are 10 opponents, in alphabetical order, whom he says like to burn the ground and the ears with equal passion.

Anquan Boldin, Arizona. Running back in a wide receiver's body. Smash-mouth type. Competes so hard it forces you to keep on edge every play.

Isaac Bruce, San Francisco. His play backs his talk and his talk backs his play. Very tricky and smart. Can't have less than an A-game with him.

Plaxico Burress, New York Giants. Caught the game-winning pass in the Super Bowl and will let everyone know about it. Plays hurt and knows how to get it done.

Braylon Edwards, Cleveland. An up-and-coming, big-play receiver who's not afraid to dish it out. So big and so athletic, it's very difficult to guard him. I have to use my quicks.

Chad Johnson, Cincinnati. Always has something up his sleeve to get his team-mates and crowd into the game. One of the best at making you guess on his moves.

Santana Moss, Washington. Small, strong guy who is an in-your-face type. Great competitor. Always wants the ball. You love to have a guy like him on your team.

Muhsin Muhammad, Carolina. Savvy veteran whose hard work pays off. Tough guy who has been doing it well for a while and has not lost a step.

Terrell Owens, Dallas. Everyone wants to know what T.O. is doing. People focus a lot on his off the field stuff, but this guy can really play. Makes any team he's on better.

Antwaan Randle El, Washington. All-around intense game for four quarters. He goes 110% in everything, and does so many different things well—pass, run, catch. A hard match-up.

Steve Smith, Carolina. Lets you know that he's on the field, and lets you know when he catches the ball. A spark plug, and he's all over the field.

Boxing locally and nationally rarely is on the mainstream radar anymore. But in Seattle's less dilettante days, thanks to crusty boxing promoters and trainers such as Jack Hurley and George Chemeres, there were a good number of nationally ranked pugilists, including Olympic champs, who brought excitement and big names to town.

10. Leo Randolph vs. Ricardo Cardona, May 4, 1980. Only a tiny gathering—1,109 at the Seattle Center Arena—saw it, but those who did witnessed Randolph's finest professional fight, a 15-round TKO for the world junior featherweight title. Randolph, a 1976 Olympic gold medalist from Tacoma, administered such a pummeling that Cardona departed on a stretcher after lying on the canvas some 20 minutes after the bout was stopped with 90 seconds remaining in the nationally televised fight.

9. Greg Haugen vs. Julio Cesar Chavez, February 20, 1993. Heading into the fight, Haugen, of Auburn, made a comment that many of Chavez's wins "came against Tijuana taxi drivers that my mom could whip." This generated a huge uproar in the Mexican community and was partially why 132,247 customers paid their way into Mexico City's National Stadium to watch it. They thoroughly enjoyed the pummeling Chavez administered in winning the WBC world light welterweight title.

8. Eddie Cotton vs. Harold Johnson, August 29, 1961. Cotton, a popular light heavyweight contender from Seattle who also labored as a tool and die maker at Boeing, had two shots to claim a National Boxing Association title during his long career (1948–67). His first, in 1961, was his best. In front of 4,000 fans at Sicks' Stadium, Cotton lost most of the early rounds, then launched a furious assault on the defending champion in rounds 12 through 15, but dropped a split decision.

7. Boone Kirkman vs. Jimmy Ellis, December 12, 1973. In front of 10,072 fans at the Seattle Coliseum, Kirkman, a Renton heavyweight, recovered from a stunning first-round knockdown and a severe third-round beating to score a narrow split decision over the Angelo Dundee-trained Ellis, only the second ranked fighter Kirkman encountered.

6. Boone Kirkman vs. Ken Norton, June 25, 1974. A partisan crowd of 11,039 at the Seattle Coliseum agonized as Kirkman paid for his share of the $100,000 purse. Kirkman won the first round, but Norton dominated thereafter, snapping uppercuts to Kirkman's chin, scoring almost at will. As the bell clanged ending the seventh round, Norton, who had already beaten Muhammad Ali, dropped Kirkman with a savage blow to the head, rendering Kirkman incapable of answering the bell for the eighth.

5. Greg Haugen vs. Vinny Pazienza, February 6, 1988. After Haugen won the obligatory pre-fight war of taunts heading into their world IBF lightweight title bout—Haugen said Pazienza's face looked like pizza and that he dressed like Liberace—he had Pazienza's number from the opening bell. Haugen had Pazienza bleeding in every round starting with the third after opening up a 10-stitch cut over Pazienza's right eye, and Pazienza did not land a punch of significance in the final 11 rounds.

4. Sonny Liston vs. Eddie Machen, September 7, 1960. Liston, the No. 1 contender to heavyweight champion Floyd Patterson, had to go the distance to earn a unanimous decision over Machen, the No. 2 contender. It was the first nationally televised fight from Seattle (ABC), held on a ring built over the mound at Sicks' Stadium. Liston, who had disposed of his previous nine opponents by knockout, never got a clear shot at Machen, much to the disappointment of the 7,682 on hand.

3. Al Hostak vs. Freddie Steele, July 28, 1938. More than 35,000 fans paid nearly $100,000 to watch Seattle's Hostak make quick work of Tacoma's Steele in a world middleweight title fight at Civic Stadium. Hostak took the fight right to Steele, landing the first punch, then knocking Steele down three times in the first round before delivering the winning blow. Hostak's last punch, a short, perfectly timed left hook to the button, sent Steele to the canvas. Referee Jack Dempsey, the former heavyweight champion, counted the decisive 10. "One of the greatest punchers I've ever seen," Dempsey said of Hostak.

2. Harry "Kid" Matthews vs. Rocky Marciano, July 28, 1952. No Northwest boxer ever fought on a bigger stage, or against a tougher opponent, than Matthews, an Everett native. Matthews took the first round from Marciano, the defending world heavyweight champion, but unwisely decided to trade punches with the Bronx slugger in the second round. Marciano kayoed him at the 2:04 mark. The fight drew 20,000 fans to Yankee Stadium, including both Washington senators, Democrat Warren Magnuson and Republican Harry Cain.

1. Pete Rademacher vs. Floyd Patterson, August 22, 1957. A former Washington State football player and an Olympic gold medalist (1956), but a fighter that critics had written off as an unskilled humpty-dumpty, Rademacher stepped into the ring determined to become the first man to win the world heavyweight title in his first professional fight. In the second round, Rademacher, from the Yakima area, sent the Sicks' Stadium crowd of 16,961 into a frenzy when he surprised Patterson by knocking him to the canvas. A wary Patterson, working from a crouch, began to connect with fast combinations. He scored his first knockdown in the third round, four more in the fifth and the last two in the sixth, when Rademacher's rubber legs would no longer support him.

Over the years some of the game's biggest names have competed in the longest-running professional sports event in the state. The race has been run every year except 1943 when the track was closed due to a World War II blackout. The track's infield was used that year as an Army barracks.

12. August 29, 1948. For the first and only time in Mile history, one trainer saddled the win, place and show horses. Allen Drumheller's Amble In became the first horse to win the race twice. Amble In's stable mates Minstrel Boy and Hank H finished second and third.

11. August 25, 1991. Idaho native and *Seabiscuit* star Gary Stevens got a Mile win aboard Irish bred Louis Cyphre. The Hall of Fame jockey listed the Mile win as among his favorites and said his career would have been "incomplete" if he had failed to win it at least once.

10. August 28, 1949. The story behind this race wasn't the winner, Blue Tiger. It was second-place Irene's Angel, ridden by 18-year-old apprentice Bill Shoemaker. "Shoe" was just beginning his legendary 41-year riding career. Twenty-nine years later he returned to Longacres to win the 1978 Mile aboard Bad N Big.

9. August 25, 1985. The Mile has always had a division among entries with clear rooting interests. The division falls along the lines of Washington horses versus horses bred elsewhere, usually California. On this day, one Washington horse went to post against eight invaders. Chum Salmon looked like he was out for a leisurely stroll, falling 15 lengths behind. The Washington star then staged a great comeback to win by a length and a half.

8. August 18, 1996. After three years at Yakima Meadows following the closing of Longacres, the Mile returned to the Seattle area at the new Emerald Downs. Appropriately, the track's first Mile witnessed the dawn of a new powerhouse team as Mike Pegram and Bob Baffert brought Isitingood to the Auburn oval. He won by a neck, and Pegram and Baffert began a run of success that continues to this day.

7. August 24, 2003. Skyjack was the Chris Bosio of horses: A gutty competitor whose huge heart allowed him to compete despite chronic knee problems. He ran the fastest Longacres Mile in history at 1:33 to win the race. Trainer Doug O'Neil praised the wild crowd at the Downs, comparing the atmosphere to one you'd expect to see at a college football game.

6. August 29, 1971. Here's good advice for people who get angry when they lose at the track: Remember, you ARE betting on animals. That phrase would be applicable to people who had tickets on Titular II. Local sportsman Herman Sarkowsky's horse was the favorite and running easily to the win when he glimpsed the starting gate in the infield. At Hollywood Park, where he had always run, the gate was hauled off to the outside of the track after the race started. At Longacres, the gate was hauled into the infield. Titular II saw the gate and freaked. He came to a near stop before regaining speed, but by then could do no better than third. Pitch Out won the race.

5. August 23 1981. A star-studded field of jockeys (Bill Shoemaker, Laffit Pincay Jr., and Sandy Hawley) all took a back seat to Gary Baze, who rode legendary Washington thoroughbred Trooper Seven to his second consecutive Mile win. The race was run in front of an all-time record crowd of 25,931 fans.

4. August 21, 2005. Thirty-four years after Titular II's disastrous finish, No Giveaway found an opening at the top of the lane and roared through a crowd to nab Sarkowsky's first Mile win. Fans went nuts as No Giveaway made up 20 lengths. And fans lucky enough to hold a winning ticket beamed at the longest shot ever to win the Mile, 60 to 1.

3. August 21, 1983. Perhaps the most impressive horse/jockey combo in Mile history teamed as Laffit Pincay Jr. rode Chinook Pass to a wire-to-wire victory. Chinook Pass was considered the world's best sprint horse and indeed would be named the top sprinter of 1983 at the Eclipse Awards. But on this day the only Washington-bred horse to win an Eclipse proved he could handle two turns and won the race by a then-record six lengths.

2. August 24, 1986. Eventual 1986 Breeder's Cup Classic winner Skywalker won the Mile with Laffit Pincay Jr. aboard. Skywalker ran in the 1985 Kentucky Derby but suffered a leg fracture in that race and finished sixth. Bedside Promise dueled Skywalker the length of the stretch but lost by a neck.

1. August 20, 2006. No trainer had ever won five times until Jim Penney pulled it off with Flamethrowintexan, and no horse worked harder to get the win as Tex and California invader Papi Chulo staged a remarkable stretch duel before Tex prevailed by whatever is less than a nose.

He parlayed money from a string of fast food restaurants in Western Washington into success in horse racing, particularly with trainer Bob Baffert. Mike Pegram has a reputation for naming horses after people and events in his life.

10. Isitingood (winner, 1996 Longacres Mile). We bought the horse and came to find out he had a fractured sesamoid bone. We told the consignor the horse was damaged goods. He wouldn't help us. We got a super hometown job on that horse. He's the son of Crusader's Sword. What's the crusader say when the sword is in? "Is it in good?" The sword was in us.

9. Icecoldbeeratreds (top California two-year-old, 2002). We were sitting at Red's bar across the street from Del Mar watching UW in the 1999 Holiday Bowl. Tracy Tracton, who owned the bar, said, "When are you going to name a horse after me?" I said, "Get me a beer and we'll think about it." Then I said, "We just named the horse: Ice cold beer at Red's!"

8. The Beer Runner. Named after my son, Timmy. At Del Mar you had to be in the turf club to get beer. We found out you could bring your own in, but in a small cooler. I'd come to the track with five cases. Timmy was 18 at the time and he'd run the empty cooler back to the truck where we had the rest of the beer in a huge fish cooler. That's when I switched from Bud Light to Coors Light. Because of the shape of the can, you could fit more in the cooler: 22 vs. 19.

7. Silverbulletday (winner, 1998 Breeders' Cup Juvenile Fillies). Could have been Budlightday if more Bud Lights fit in a cooler.

6. Love on the Rail. We had won the Breeders' Cup Sprint in 1992 at Gulfstream with Thirty Slews and we (including a lady friend) were the last ones out of the hospitality tent. Walking back to the barn, we got to the eighth pole and got bored and decided what we needed was a little love on the rail. There's still a security report on that incident on the books at Gulfstream.

5. Zipper's Up (longshot entry in the 1996 Breeders' Cup Juvenile). This was another name the Jockey Club (the body that regulates names and tries to prevent double entendres) had problems with. The best part about this horse is that at the Breeders Cup, people kept yelling at Bob Baffert, "Your zipper! Your zipper! Zipper Up!" Bob thought they were just talking about the horse and didn't realize that he walked around for two races with his fly down.

4. Captain Steve (winner, $6 million Dubai World Cup). Baffert won the 1997 Kentucky Derby with Silver Charm. The next day my girlfriend gave me a birthday present and told me I should check it. I didn't take time to open it, just tossed the package in my carry-on bag. I'm going through security and all hell breaks loose. My girlfriend decided I needed a .357 magnum. I'm yelling, "That ain't my gun." But it is my bag. You know how most of the time, when you see guys in handcuffs, they've got their heads down? Well I've got my head up. I'm looking for anyone who can help. They take me in to search me. Since Silver Charm had won the Derby the day before I've got a pocket full of cash. So it doesn't look good. I called Baffert at the track. He thought I was joking. I said, "This ain't no joke. I'm in jail." Baffert found Julian Wheat, the horseman's liaison at Churchill Downs. He calls a guy he knows named Steve Thompson. He was a captain in the Louisville police department. He came down to the airport and got me out.

3. Preachinatthebar. Named for my good friend, Nola, the bartender at Santa Anita. She became born again. She's the only person I know who'll serve you whiskey, tout horses, cuss like a sailor when they're coming down the stretch, and then give you a sermon. I originally named a horse Holy Nola. Holy Nola won a race while I was locked up in Louisville. Her first offspring was Preachinatthebar.

2. Midnight Lute (winner, 2007 Breeders' Cup Sprint). Named after Lute Olson. We bought the horse the day before the Arizona-Illinois NCAA tourney game in Chicago in 2005. UA lost in double overtime after blowing a big lead. Paul Whiteman is my partner in the horse and he's a friend of Lute's. So after the game, Paul tells Baffert he's backing out. I said, "Tell Paul if he doesn't buy into this horse I'll name him Chicago Meltdown and every time the horse runs he'll think about the game." Midnight Lute was actually a nickname given to Olson by Jerry Tarkanian.

1. Danthebluegrassman. Dan Chandler was Happy Chandler's son (former MLB commissioner who was in office when Jackie Robinson broke the color barrier). He played for Adolph Rupp at Kentucky and used to boast that he held the UK all-time free throw record since he went 2-for-2 during his career. He was a character. He was fired seven times from Caesar's Palace. He was a casino host and somehow he kept getting his job back. Rick Pitino did the eulogy at Dan's funeral. He's buried with Danthebluegrassman's saddlecloth.

NOTE: 1998 Kentucky Derby winner Real Quiet isn't on this list because he was already named when Pegram bought him from Eduardo Gaviria. Gaviria didn't like the horse because he had crooked knees and Pegram got him for the astounding price of $17,000. "He's the only Kentucky Derby winner in history who didn't have an under bidder. I was the only guy with 17 grand and a set of balls," said Pegram. Considering Real Quiet earned $3.2 million in his career and sired the above-mentioned Midnight Lute, the investment worked OK.

A member of the International Motor Sports Hall of Fame, Seattle native Hanauer won the APBA Gold Cup a record 12 times. His wise, wry counsel was sought for novice drivers, fans, and broadcasters for a safe, happy celebration of the annual August chaos on Lake Washington.

8. Approaching a seagull in a boat far faster than seagulls are used to dealing with. Seagulls are arrogant birds, practiced and confident in timing their watery take off. They are used to seeing boats approaching them at not more than 20 mph. Just as your boat arrives, they take off and gently bank to one side, allowing your boat to pass harmlessly, with only a few feet to spare. A boat approaching 10 times faster throws timing off lethally. Two problems for the parties: The gull suffers catastrophic injuries, rendering the bird unrecognizable to the most educated ornithologist, and the crew spends a considerable amount of time separating gull guts from the unlimited hydroplane.

7. Having the steering on your 200 mph hydroplane be opposite of what is otherwise considered normal and desirable. When leaving the pit area for a test session in your hydroplane, it is helpful that when you turn the boat left, the boat responds by going left. If the people who built your hydroplane were up extremely late, finishing a new boat for the big race, are exceptionally tired from weeks of little sleep and hard work, they may, by mistake, hook up the steering backward. This can make the otherwise simple job of steering a 200 mph race boat around a two-mile oval more complicated than it needs to be.

6. Spending millions of dollars to broadcast the Seafair race for television, but renting generators from a company that forgets to put oil in them. Hundreds of skilled technicians and millions of dollars worth of sophisticated equipment, standing by to begin an eight-hour race broadcast, can be brought to a screeching halt if the generators stop running due to a lack of oil. I've also learned that when computers and equipment stop running minutes before an all-day live broadcast, professional people begin using unprofessional language.

5. Seeing Mt. Rainier in an inverted position while driving an unlimited hydroplane. Above Lake Washington on Seafair Sunday, there are an extraordinary number of aircraft in which seeing Mt. Rainier inverted is not a problem. In fact, this view of the mountain is even desirable. Such things as a Pitts aerobatic biplane or an F-18 fighter jet do it on purpose, on queue and on television. These vehicles land a short time later and neither pilot nor plane are worse for the experience. An unlimited hydroplane has many of the same abilities as the previously mentioned flying machines, but is not equipped with the proper landing apparatus. Hydroplanes simply fall from their brief encounter with the sky and land on the surface of Lake Washington with the grace of a raw egg upon the kitchen floor.

4. Not having the coveted pit area parking pass or losing the one you were issued. It is easier to find an abandoned lane on I-5 at 7 a.m. Monday than it is to find a place to park within four miles of the pit area on Seafair Sunday. Doesn't matter if you are recognized as one of the most successful racers in Seafair history, the mayor, or Christ. No pass, no park. Best option is to pay an amount greater than the amount a driver might win at the race for a place on what was a local resident's front yard the Thursday before race weekend.

3. Having the escape hatch under your ass fail at any speed above 30 mph. In the cockpit there is an escape hatch that runs from ankles past buttocks. If the boat were to flip and land upside down, the escape hatch is the rescue portal. If the hatch fails during a race, water pressure at 150 mph takes your legs and places them over the top of your head. The problem is your ass is belted tightly to the bottom of the boat, not allowing the spine to flex. The water pressure overcomes the strength of the spine and breaks lumbar vertebra one through four. This smarts.

2. Waiting to use the portable toilets, five minutes before you get into a 200 mph hydroplane for the "big race." You would think Seafair would provide race drivers with restrooms not accessible to the general public. You would be wrong. This is commensurate with an NFL player being forced to use the concourse toilet facilities during a game. Imagine a Seahawk running into the stands, hoping the line is not so long that he either soils himself or misses his team's next possession.

1. Bringing your sister who just joined a convent to spend the day on the log boom. Your friends, who ordinarily conduct themselves like respectable professionals, will begin to treat your sister as they would a sophomore woman from Washington State on spring break. This is the result of your sophisticated friends consuming large amounts of alcohol beginning at around 6:30 a.m., when you all met at the boat that subsequently ties up to the log boom, the floating spectator party area. Two things tend to happen: The sister petitions a court later for only-child status, or the debauchery is so compelling that she becomes a race groupie willing to be a porta-potty line stand-in for a driver.

Despite the fact a major auto race has never been run here, there's an impressive list of native sons who've become stars in the sport.

7. Kevin Hamlin, Snohomish. Hamlin had a successful early career in Northwest Series racing (youngest driver to win a race when he won at age of 19 in 1999). Two years later he became the circuit's youngest champion ever. Since 2005, he's worked for Chip Ganassi Racing and has driven in both Nationwide and Truck Series events.

6. Chad Little, Spokane. Little raced in NASCAR for 16 years without a win although he did have 44 top 10's, including six wins in nine years of Busch series racing. Well known on Washington's short track circuit in the 1980s, he moved on to the Winston West series where he was Rookie of the Year in 1986 and tour champ in 1987.

5. Dominic Dobson, Seattle. The 1986 CART Rookie of the Year competed in seven consecutive Indy 500s with a best finish of 11th in 1990. He was born in Stuttgart, Germany, and raised in Seattle, where he runs Dobson Motorsport, a company specializing in investment opportunities in classic sports cars.

4. Derrike Cope, Spanaway. The 1990 winner of the Daytona 500, he captured NASCAR's biggest race after Dale Earnhardt ran over a hose clamp and cut a tire with less than a mile left. The opportunistic Cope skillfully guided his car through the field of debris from Earnhardt's blowout and rolled, shockingly, into victory lane. Famously (or perhaps infamously) the race was not shown on live TV in the Seattle area.

3. Greg Biffle, Camas. A multiple winner on the NASCAR Sprint Cup circuit, Biffle finished second in the point standings in 2005 when he won six races. He's already the only driver to win both the NASCAR truck and Busch/Nationwide series titles, and in 2008 made a serious run at winning "The Chase."

2. Kasey Kahne, Enumclaw. A multiple winner on NASCAR's top circuit, Kahne is considered one of the sport's biggest young stars. He's already replaced one legend, succeeding Bill Elliott in the number 9 car (2003). In 2008 he replaced Dale Earnhardt Jr. as Budweiser's primary driver. Winner of the 2008 Coca-Cola 600, Kasey's got a street named after him in his hometown of Enumclaw. Gastineau, who emceed that event, said that it seemed as if every one of the thousands of people there on Labor Day 2005 had a personal story about knowing him as a kid. After he won his first race at the Sprint Cup level, an announcer stated that he was from Seattle. Kahne quickly corrected him: "I'm from Enumclaw." THAT'S the kind of move that gets your hometown to name a street after you.

1. Tom Sneva, Spokane. The first man to qualify for the Indy 500 over 200 mph, Sneva broke that barrier in 1977. Nicknamed "The Gasman," he won the 500 in 1983, the only Washington native to capture the world's biggest race. His win didn't come easily. A bad pit stop dropped him from first to second with 25 laps to go. His car was clearly faster than Al Unser's, who was leading the race. Problem was a rookie named Al Unser Jr., who was a lap down on the field but positioned on the track between his father and Sneva. For 16 laps he ran interference for his old man weaving back and forth in an attempt to block Sneva. Sneva finally got Little Al at about the start/finish line on lap 190 and then passed Al Sr. in the third turn of lap 191. Nine laps later he had the win.

Favorite NASCAR Tracks :: Kasey Kahne

The Enumclaw native has become one of the most popular and accomplished young drivers on the NASCAR circuit.

5. Bristol. It's tight, rough racing. 160,000 fans watching.... It's all out for 500 laps.

4. Texas. It's just a fast, fun racetrack with a great group of fans.

3. Charlotte. This is No. 3 because it's close to team member homes, employees and crew members. It's nice to race and win in front of all the people that work so hard on the car.

2. Indy. It's my second favorite because all four corners are different and that makes it difficult to get your car perfect there. To win at Indianapolis Motor Speedway is prestigious and would be huge.

1. Atlanta. It's great because it's fast, rough and you can race anywhere on the track—from top to bottom.

Olympic glory is the hardest won in sports. The chance comes only every fourth year. The athlete has to survive difficult national trials and must peak at the perfect time, free of injury, illness and distraction, to be the best in the world. The state's athletes have represented well in Summer and Winter Games, including some who scored at multiple Olympics. A list of the most impressive medal winners from Washington:

15. Rebecca Twigg, Los Angeles 1984; Barcelona, 1992. A native of Spokane, Twigg won a silver medal in the cycling road race at Los Angeles, then returned to the Games eight years later and added a bronze in the 3,000-meter individual pursuit. Twigg won six world championships during her career. In 1995, she set a world record in individual pursuit.

14. Pete Rademacher, Melbourne, 1956. A 1950–51 Washington State football letterman from the Yakima area, Rademacher won the super heavyweight boxing gold medal, defeating Lev Mukhin of the Soviet Union. Rademacher never gave Mukhin a chance, knocking him down in the first 50 seconds and twice more in the next 80 seconds.

13. Debbie Armstrong, Sarajevo, 1984. A star at Seattle's Garfield High in basketball and soccer (1976–80), Armstrong achieved athletic celebrity as an alpine skier when she became the first USA woman to win Olympic gold in the giant slalom, and the first American woman to claim any alpine skiing gold since Andrea Mead-Lawrence won double gold in 1952.

12. Jonathan McKee, Los Angeles, 1984; Sydney, 2000. Seattle native and Shorecrest High graduate McKee won the Flying Dutchman gold in 1984. In 2000, he teamed with brother Charlie at age 40 to capture a bronze in the 49er class. A three-time All-America sailor at Yale (1981–83), McKee is also a three-time world champion (Flying Dutchman, Tasar, 49er).

11. Richard Wailes, Melbourne, 1956; Rome, 1960. A Washington native and Yale graduate, Wailes captured a gold medal in the USA's eight-oared boat in 1956 and returned to Rome in 1960 to earn another gold in fours. He is a member of the Rowing Hall of Fame and the Yale Athletic Hall of Fame.

10. Jack Medica, Berlin, 1936. The UW's greatest swimmer—he won NCAA championships in the 220-, 440- and 1,500-yard freestyle races three years in a row (1934–36), Medica won the 400 freestyle gold and earned silver medals in the 1,500 freestyle and 4x200 freestyle relay.

9. Kaye Hall, Mexico City, 1968. Hall, of Tacoma, earned two golds (100 backstroke, 400 medley relay) and a bronze (200 backstroke). Her 1:06.2 clocking in the 100 backstroke set a world record. Once a holder of six American records, Hall is a member of the International Swimming Hall of Fame.

8. Traci Ruiz, Los Angeles, 1984; Seoul, 1988. A native of Hawaii, a graduate of Arizona State and a longtime Seattle-area resident, Ruiz won the solo gold in synchronized swimming and teamed with Candie Costie to win another gold in duet. Ruiz captured a silver in the solo event at Seoul.

7. Mary Wayte, Los Angeles, 1984; Seoul, 1988. Although raised on Mercer Island, Wayte did most of her swimming at the University of Florida. At Los Angeles, Wayte defeated archrival Sippy Woodhead in the 200 freestyle final, then added another gold as a member of the 4x100 freestyle relay team. Wayte returned in 1988 and won silver as a member of the 4x100 medley relay and a bronze as a member of the 4x100 freestyle relay.

6. Apolo Anton Ohno, Salt Lake, 2002; Turin, 2006. Seattle's most decorated Winter Olympian, the Federal Way short-track speed skater earned five medals, including two gold, in the 2002 and 2006 Winter Olympics. Ohno's three medals in Turin, including a gold in the 500, made him just the fourth American to win at least three medals in a single Winter Olympics, following long-track speed skaters Eric Heiden, Sheila Young and Chad Hedrick.

5. Hope Solo, Beijing, 2008. The former University of Washington goalkeeper posted three shutouts in the women's soccer tournament, including a 1–0 extra-time victory over Brazil in the gold-medal game. Solo's six saves, including a point-blank stop of a shot by Brazilian striker Marta, earned her "Woman of the Match" accolades.

4. Anna Cummins and Mary Whipple, Athens, 2004; Beijing, 2008. By winning the gold medal in women's eight in Beijing, Cummins (No. 5 seat) and Whipple (cox), both University of Washington graduates, became the first female rowers from the state to medal in consecutive Olympics. Teammates since 1999, when they were freshmen at the UW, Cummins and Whipple were also part of the USA's silver-medal eight in 2004 in Athens.

3. Mac Wilkins, Montreal, 1976; Los Angeles, 1984. Wilkins' career spanned 23 years, four Olympic teams and included four world records. A 1973 Oregon graduate who attended Tacoma's Clover Park High, Wilkins achieved his greatest fame in 1976 when he won the gold in the discus after setting an Olympic record of 224–0 in the prelims. He also finished second at the 1984 Games and fifth at the 1988 Games.

2. Phil Mahre, Sarajevo, 1984. The most successful Alpine skier in U.S. history, Mahre won a silver medal in the 1980 Olympics at Lake Placid and capped his career with a gold medal in the slalom at the 1984 Olympics in Sarajevo. He was inducted into the U.S. Olympic Hall of Fame in 1992 along with Seattle swimmer Helene Madison.

1. Helene Madison, Los Angeles, 1932. Madison won the 100-meter freestyle, anchored the U.S. team to victory in the 4x100 freestyle relay and also captured a third gold medal in the 400-meter freestyle, making her the only athlete from Washington state to win three golds in the same Olympics. After winning her third gold, Madison celebrated by dancing at the Coconut Grove with Clark Gable.

Though the major spectator team sports draw most of the attention, the region's abundance of mountains and seas have also helped inspire great athletes to epic adventures and achievements (listed alphabetically).

Alan Jones, endurance adventurist. In his heyday in the 1970s and 1980s, Tacoma-based "Captain America" performed numerous feats of endurance, strength and daring to call attention to human potential, and often to benefit worthwhile causes. Among the stunts of Jones, a native of Iowa and an ex-Marine and Vietnam vet: Completed 48,010 consecutive rope skips in six hours without a miss (Chicago, 1975), swam 700 miles of the Mississippi River (Minneapolis to St. Louis, 1976), dove 30 feet into a 2 ½-foot pool that contained 22 piranhas (1978), swam the English Channel handcuffed (1980), executed 8,214 karate kicks above his head in six hours for a Guinness Book of World Records feat (1980), swam the Straits of Juan de Fuca handcuffed (1981), set a Guinness record by doing 27,000 jumping jacks in six hours (Burien, 1981), carried a 310-pound barbell four miles uphill (Everett, 1982), did 7,000 jumping jacks in six hours for another Guinness mark (1983), swam the 27-mile length of Lake Washington (Seattle, 1983), swam 60 miles from Port Townsend to Seattle (1984), set a Guinness record by making 236 parachute jumps in 23.5 hours (Issaquah, 1985), and set a parasail record of 2,000 feet over Tacoma's Commencement Bay (1985).

Scott Jurek, ultra runner. A Minnesota native and current Seattle resident, Jurek took up distance running as a way to get in shape for cross-country ski racing, and then took his new skill to incredible lengths. He competed in his first "ultra run" in 1994, a 50-mile race, finishing second. In 1999, he won the Western States 100-mile Endurance Run for the first time, then won it again every year through 2005. In 2005 and 2006, he won the Badwater Ultramarathon, a particularly grueling run starting in California's Death Valley in temperatures up to 130 degrees and ending 135 miles away and more than 11,000 feet higher on Mount Whitney. In 2007, he won the Hard Rock Hundred, a 100-mile race in southwest Colorado that is contested at an average elevation of 11,000 feet, setting a course record of 26 hours, 8 minutes. Jurek also won Greece's Spartathlon (2006 and 2007), a 152.9-mile run from Athens to Sparta over elevations ranging from sea level to 4,000 feet.

Karen Thorndike, solo sailor. It took Thorndike eight years of planning and three different attempts over a four-year span (1995–98) for the Snohomish resident to become the first American woman to sail solo around the five Southern Hemisphere capes. Thorndike's first attempt, in 1995, ended when a storm off the Oregon Coast damaged her boat. Her second try was rebuffed near Nicaragua when her boat was struck by lightning. Her third attempted took her to Hawaii, Tahiti and South America. After rounding Cape Horn, Thorndike had to be rescued in stormy seas off the Falkland Islands when she became ill. Four months later, she resumed her voyage, only to run into another delay—waiting out the Southern Hemisphere winter near Argentina. Thorndike resumed her journey on November 1, 1997, and made a successful return to San Diego on August 18, 1998, having sailed 33,000 miles.

Ed Viesturs, mountaineer. When Viesturs, a Bainbridge Island resident, reached the summit of Nepal's Annapurna on May 12, 2005, he became the first American and the fifth person in the world to climb all 14 of the world's highest mountains (above 8,000 meters) without the use of supplemental oxygen. Viesturs' quest, entitled "Endeavor 8000," took him 18 years to complete and included 29 separate Himalayan expeditions. Viesturs reached the summit of Mt. Everest six times, making him just one of two non-Sherpa to accomplish that feat.

Jim Whittaker, mountaineer, sailor. Best known for a single feat—the first American to summit Mt. Everest on May 1, 1963—the Seattle native's mountaineering career goes well beyond that achievement. In 1978, he led the first American ascent of K2, the world's second-highest peak, after five previous American failures spanning 40 years. Against formidable political and logistical odds, he organized the 1990 Mt. Everest Peace Climb, which placed 20 men and women from the U.S., China and the Soviet Union on the top of the world's highest mountain. In addition to his mountaineering exploits, Whittaker became an accomplished scuba diver and bluewater sailor, twice skippering his own boats on the 2,400-mile Victoria, B.C., to Maui race. In a four-year span, Whittaker also sailed his 54-foot steel pilothouse ketch, Impossible, from his home in Port Townsend to Mexico, throughout the South Pacific to Australia and back, a journey of more than 20,000 miles.

One of the toughest tasks in sports is succeeding a legendary figure popular with fans. It almost never works, but there are exceptions. Whether player or coach, these 10 did the hard job about as well as could be expected.

10. Raul Ibanez, 2005–2008. Ibanez replaced the most popular Mariner in team history, Edgar Martinez, as its designated hitter. Ibanez hit .280 with 20 home runs (Edgar banged 12 in his final season) in his only year as Seattle's primary DH, then moved to left field. He couldn't fill the role of civic hero, but no one could, and still managed to become a popular, productive figure on his own.

9. Freddy Garcia, 1999–2004. One of three players acquired from Houston in the controversial 1998 trade of Randy Johnson, Garcia, as a 23-year-old rookie, had to replace the Big Unit as staff ace. All he did was lead AL rookie pitchers in wins (17–8 record), opponents batting average against (.263), ERA (4.07), games started (33) and strikeouts (170), finishing second in AL Rookie of the Year balloting.

8. Jim Lambright, 1993–98. Lambright, the senior assistant coach, had the unenviable task of replacing the best coach in UW football history, and do it 12 days prior to the start of the season. Don James' abrupt resignation, to protest pending Pac-10 sanctions, threw the program into tumult from which it has yet to recover. Lambright went 7–4 his first year, the first of a two-year bowl ban. Although he went 44–25–1 over six years, including a remarkable 38–20 win at Miami in 1994, his 1–3 mark in bowls, including a 45–25 loss in 1998 to Air Force in Honolulu, helped usher him out.

7. D'Marco Farr, 1992–93. He had to replace Outland Trophy and Lombardi Award winner Steve Emtman, the No. 1 player taken in the NFL draft, on Washington's defensive line. Farr was no Emtman. But he wasn't bad, either. In 12 games the year after Emtman departed, Farr had 10.5 tackles for loss and five sacks. His seven-year pro career with the St. Louis Rams outlasted Emtman's injury-shortened tenure.

6. Chuck Carroll, 1926–28. Carroll replaced George Wilson, a two-time Walter Camp All-America running back at Washington, who led the Huskies to their first two Rose Bowls (1923, 1925). Carroll scored 33 TDs in his UW career and became the school's second All-American, but never played in a bowl game.

5. Mike Cameron, 2000–03. Obtained in the trade from Cincinnati that sent away franchise icon Ken Griffey Jr., Cameron, instead of being overwhelmed, became an instant hit with fans on April 7, 2000, when he climbed the center-field wall in Griffey-esque fashion to rob Derek Jeter of a home run. Although he never hit better than .267 nor more than 25 homers in his four years in Seattle, Cameron was healthier than Griffey, earned a Gold Glove, became a 2001 All-Star and proved a popular figure.

4. Ray Allen, 2003–2007. The Sonics didn't want to extend the contract of 34-year-old legend Gary Payton, so they traded him and swingman Desmond Mason to Milwaukee for Allen and some throw-ins. Allen, seven years younger and more offensive minded, became the team's All-Star and averaged 24 points a game in his five Seattle years.

3. Chip Hanauer, 1982–94. Following the death of Bill Muncey, who won a record 62 unlimited hydroplane races, in a 1981 accident in Acapulco, Hanauer replaced him as the driver of the Atlas Van Lines and went on to win a record 12 APBA Gold Cups.

2. Jeff Jaeger, 1983–86. A walk-on, Jaeger became Washington's placekicker after the departure of first-team All-America Chuck Nelson (also a walk-on) following the 1982 season. Jaeger kicked an NCAA-record 80 field goals and became first-team All-America himself.

1. Don James, 1975–1992. The third choice of Washington athletics director Joe Kearney to replace Jim Owens, the man who transformed Washington and West Coast football, James started shakily with 6–5 and 5–6 seasons. But he won the Pac-8 conference title in 1977 as well as the Rose Bowl, launching a career (153–57–2) that would rank him among the best college football coaches in history.

Sue Bird arrived in Seattle from the University of Connecticut as the No. 1 pick in the 2002 WNBA draft. One of six women to win Olympic gold, an NCAA title and a WNBA crown, she's been an integral part of the Storm's success. She's also a gal with a sense of humor. Here's her collection of bad opening lines.

5. Lose-lose. In college a guy pulls out the old, "You want to play one-on-one sometime?" I've heard this one a million times, but before I could answer he followed it with, "If you win, I take you to dinner. If I win, I take you to dinner."

4. What made you think I cared? Once guys learn that I play basketball, I have to listen to stories about their "careers." I've had people tell me about rec league games, when they played JV, how they were good in middle school, but then stopped growing, so they never made it past high school. Four words: Live. In. The. Now.

3. The high price of gas. This was set-up by my friends. A guy came up to me in a bar and asked, "Do you mind if I stand here?" I said it was all right. He said, "Okay, good, because I just farted over there." I look over and all my friends were laughing. I later learned that the line works for this guy all the time.

2. Make it "to go" the night before. I was asked how I like my eggs. I asked why. He said, "So I know what to make for you in the morning."

1. Sometimes, bad is good. I was at a bar when a cute guy came up to me and asked if I had a boyfriend. When I responded no, he said, "Well, can I stand next to you and be yours for the night?" This is on my list because it's the worst one I ever fell for! I laughed and actually dated the guy for a few months.

Most Memorable Things Said

Philosophical utterances, bon mots, wry wit and spontaneous, unintended genius factored heavily in the most memorable things that Washington athletes—and their tormentors—had to say (listed chronologically):

"Explaining to your wife why she needs a penicillin shot for your infection."

Mike Heath, Pilots outfielder, in response to this question in 1969: 'What's the most difficult thing about playing major league baseball?'

"Quick guys get tired. Big guys don't shrink."

Marv Harshman, UW basketball coach, explaining his preference for size to speed in 1972.

"Opening Day."

Bob Stinson, Mariners catcher, after he was asked by Hy Zimmerman of the Seattle Times during 1977 spring training (Mariners inaugural season) when the team would be eliminated from the pennant race.

"When the athletic director said I should recruit more whites to keep the folks in Pullman happy, I signed Rufus White and Willie White."

George Raveling, Washington State basketball coach, in 1980.

"He was absolutely the worst manager I've ever seen. He didn't even know how to argue."

Ken Kaiser, American League umpire, after the Mariners fired manager Maury Wills early in the 1981 season.

"Sometimes things happen, and when they start happening they just keep on happening."

Henry Lawrence, Raiders offensive lineman, after Jacob Green beat him for 3½ sacks in the Seahawks' 38–36 victory over Oakland on October 16, 1983.

"San Diego is just about the luckiest city since Beirut."

Jim Street, *Seattle Post-Intelligencer*, after Mariners owner George Argyros announced in 1987 that he was going to sell the Mariners and buy the San Diego Padres.

"He has a face like pizza and he dresses like Liberace."

Greg Haugen, Auburn boxer, when asked to describe Vinny Pazienza, Haugen's opponent in a 1987 International Boxing Federation championship bout.

"Probably the Beatles White Album."

Steve Largent, Seahawks receiver, after he was asked in 1989 which of his records he cherished the most.

"All I saw was purple."

Todd Marinovich, USC quarterback, after the Huskies defeated the Trojans 31–0 on September 22, 1990.

"I think we should just dog the Rose Bowl and go play Miami."

Billy Joe Hobert, UW quarterback, after both the Huskies and Hurricanes finished the 1991 regular season with perfect records.

"I've reached the epitome of grand slamness."

Mike Schooler, Mariners closer, on matching the MLB record for grand slams served up in a season (1992).

"Ted Bernhardt should be shot."

George Karl, Sonics coach, after a two-point loss to Charlotte in 1995 in which he felt the NBA official had a bad night.

"He left one high and I was able to make contact with that one and now we're just celebrating."

Edgar Martinez, Mariners DH, on ABC-TV about a minute after hitting "the double" in 1995.

"We gave up Babe Ruth."

Chuck Armstrong, Mariners president, after the club traded Ken Griffey Jr. to the Cincinnati Reds on February 10, 2000, for a package of four players.

"They made it personal so we had to make it back personal."

Gary Payton, Sonics guard, on his anger towards Seattle owner Howard Schultz after he was traded to Milwaukee in 2002.

"Fifty-one hits! That's unbelievable. Even 40 hits in a month is a heck-uva year."

Ron Fairly, Mariners broadcaster, after Ichiro finished July 2004 with 51 hits.

"Ichiro changes your mind about what's possible."

Raul Ibanez, Mariners outfielder, as Ichiro approached George Sisler's record for hits in a season in September of 2004.

"Sometimes, you've just got to let guys score."

Jerome James, Sonics center, explaining his NBA defensive philosophy in 2005.

"I have never thrown a warm-up pitch before with a tear in my eye."

Jamie Moyer, Mariners pitcher, after catcher Dan Wilson warmed him up before the start of the second inning at Safeco Field on September 30, 2005, in what was Wilson's last appearance with the Mariners.

"I am a man possessed! Will do everything we can. Thanks for hanging with me, boys. The game is getting started."

Clay Bennett, Sonics owner, in a 2007 e-mail to his fellow Oklahoma investors on plans to move the Sonics.

When we say "back in the day," we're not talking 2005, as some athletes suggest. We mean back in Herbert Hoover's day. If you don't know who Herbert Hoover is, well, read on for a little of what it was like in sports when the Depression didn't refer to Sonics fans.

10. Dick Gyselman, Indians/Rainiers. Gyselman, aka "The Needle," became a fan favorite in Seattle after the Boston Braves traded him to the Indians in 1935. He hit .303 and knocked in 100 runs in his first year with the team and went on to play 10 years at third base, appearing in 1,649 games. Like Edgar Martinez, his specialty was the double (he hit 300), but unlike Edgar, he could run (134 stolen bases).

9. Mike Hunt, Indians/Rainiers. Long before Ken Griffey Jr. pounded majestic home runs for the Mariners, Hunt delivered pokes for the Indians and Rainiers. Seattle's premier slugger of the 1930s, he led the Pacific Coast League in home runs and RBIs in 1936 and 1937 and whacked 124 long balls in just four seasons.

8. "Brick" Eldred, Indians. Eldred hit above .350 for three consecutive years (1922–24) and never hit lower than .319 in the eight seasons he spent in Seattle. He was inducted into the Pacific Coast League Hall of Fame in 2003.

7. Bernie Morris, Metropolitans. Morris arrived in Seattle via a trade with Victoria prior to the start of the 1915–16 season. He led the Pacific Coast Hockey Association in scoring in his first season and in points the next year, when he became famous for one of the most dominating performances in Stanley Cup history. In four games against the Montreal Canadiens, Morris tallied 14 goals, outscoring the entire Montreal team for the series. His five goals in Game 4 remain a Stanley Cup record. In all, Morris led the Metropolitans in scoring five times and was an All-Star every year. The Mets traded him to Calgary in 1923.

6."Seattle" Bill James, Giants. James certified himself a local hero in 1912 after the Seattle Giants spent the first two months of the season in last place in the Northwestern League. En route to 27 wins for the year, the pitcher went on a 15-game victory spree as the Giants won 27 of their final 31 to finish 99–66 and clinch the pennant. After the season, Giants owner Dan Dugdale cashed in on James by selling him to the Boston Braves.

5. "Kewpie" Dick Barrett, Indians/Rainiers. Voted as the all-time most popular Rainier in a 1954 poll conducted by the *Post-Intelligencer*, Barrett won 20 or more games seven times between 1935 and 1942. He averaged 25 complete games during that span.

4. Bill MacFarland, Americans/Totems. MacFarland had a superb nine-year playing career in Seattle, totaling 299 goals split between the Americans and Totems. In 1961–62, his 46 goals led the Western Hockey League, and he was named the league's Most Valuable Player. Following his retirement, MacFarland coached the Totems to back-to-back WHL championships in 1967 and 1968.

3. Steve Anderson, UW. Anderson matched the world record in the high hurdles five times during his University of Washington track career (1928–30), won the U.S. Olympic trials and earned a silver medal at the 1928 Stockholm Olympic Games. Anderson also led the Huskies to a pair of second-place finishes at the NCAA Track and Field Championships, winning the 220 low hurdles in 1929 and the 120 highs in 1930. He won the 120 high hurdles at three consecutive AAU national championship meets (1928–29–30) and set a world indoor record of 9.8 for the 80-yard hurdles in 1929.

2. Frank Foyston, Metropolitans. A forward who occasionally played center, Foyston was the second-leading scorer and Most Valuable Player on the 1917 Metropolitans, who defeated the Montreal Canadiens for the Stanley Cup, becoming the first American team to accomplish the feat.

1. Jack Medica, UW. The Seattle native won nine national collegiate championships and set 11 world records at various strokes and distances during his four years at the University of Washington (1933–36) when he became the school's first All-America swimmer. At the 1936 Olympics in Berlin, Medica won gold in the 400 meters and a silver in the 1,500 meters.

You under-30 types may be surprised to learn the local sports world hasn't always been Mariners, Seahawks, Sonics and UW. And you over 50s might smile at the teams you've forgotten. And you business-people, take note that just because sports are popular doesn't mean they will be successful.

10. Seattle Smashers, 1978–79. The salient points about the Smashers, a two-year entry in the co-ed International Volleyball Association: they played in the Center Arena, charged $2–$4 for tickets, played in the West Division with the Santa Barbara Spikers (Seattle's big rival), Orange County Stars and San Diego Breakers, used a blue, white and gold ball, were owned by Seattle attorney Robert Mussehl (he bought the club for $110,000), had a player payroll of $150,000, and needed to draw about 3,000 fans per game to break even. That didn't happen, and the Smashers ceased operations in May, 1980, citing the lack of an operating budget.

9. Seattle Cascades, 1977–78. A World Team Tennis franchise first known as the Sea-Port Cascades (1977) and then the Seattle Cascades (1978), the team was captained by former Seattle University star Tom Gorman and played its home matches in the Coliseum, drawing between 1,000 to 2,000 fans per match, and sometimes less. While the team (Gorman, Betty Stove, JoAnne Russell, Sherwood Stewart) was competitive, the owner, Don Kelleher, a California lumber baron, refused to promote his product or take any interest in it. In the words of former Cascades public relations director George Hill, Kelleher "ran the franchise like a lemonade stand." It folded after the 1978 season.

8. Seattle Steelheads, 1946. The Negro Leagues phenomenon didn't quite catch on in Seattle. A charter member of the six-team West Coast Negro League, the "Steelies" were barnstorming players from Abe Saperstein's Harlem Globetrotters baseball team. The club made its debut on June 1, 1946, by splitting a doubleheader with the San Diego Tigers at Sicks' Stadium in front of 2,500 fans, and was supposed to play a 110-game schedule with home games in Seattle, Tacoma, Bremerton, Spokane and Bellingham. But the league went out of business a month after it formed due to lack of interest.

7. Seattle Reign, 1996–98. Seattle's first women's pro basketball team—the American Basketball League entry—played at Mercer Arena and occasionally at Key Arena. Over two and a half seasons, the Reign featured such players as 1996 Olympian Venus Lacy, Tacoma's Kate Starbird and Shalonda Enis, the ABL's Rookie of the Year in 1997–98. The Reign went out of business on December 22, 1998, when the ABL, unable to withstand competition from the new WNBA, folded.

6. Tacoma Stars, 1983–92. The Stars represented the best of several efforts (Tacoma Tides, FC Seattle Storm, Seattle SeaDogs) to return professional soccer to the Puget Sound region in the wake of the demise of the original Sounders. The Stars, featuring numerous players and coaches who had associations with the Sounders, as well as All-Star imports Steve Zungul and Preki, were members of the Major Indoor Soccer League and played home matches at the Tacoma Dome. Although the Stars reached the MISL championship series in 1987, they folded briefly later that year before being revived under new ownership. When losses reached $4 million in June 1992, the team folded for good.

5. Seattle Pilots, 1969. The franchise isn't actually defunct—it was reincarnated as the Milwaukee Brewers in 1970—and the Pilots will never really be defunct as long as copies of Jim Bouton's *Ball Four*, a tell-all diary about the 1969 season, still exist. Featuring Tommy Harper, Gene Brabender and no-hit shortstop Ray Oyler, the Pilots went 64–98 in their only season at Sicks' Stadium, then declared bankruptcy and departed for bratwurst heaven.

4. Seattle Metropolitans, 1915–24. The Metropolitans—the first professional hockey team in Seattle—played in the Pacific Coast Hockey Association (PCHA), a league founded in 1912 by Frank and Lester Patrick. The 1917 Metropolitans became the first American team to win the Stanley Cup by defeating the National Hockey League's Montreal Canadiens three games to one and by a combined score of 19 to 3. The Metropolitans also played in the Stanley Cup finals in 1919 (cancelled due to the Spanish influenza pandemic) and in 1920, when they lost to the Ottawa Senators. The Mets, and the PCHA, went out of business following the 1923–24 season, mainly due to low attendance.

3. Seattle Totems, 1957–75. The Totems, who evolved out of the Seattle Ironmen (1945–52), Seattle Bombers (1952–55) and Seattle Americans (1955–57), finished first only once in their first 10 seasons, but they played for the Western Hockey League championship five times, coming away with three titles. During the best years of the franchise, Guyle Fielder led the league in points six times, and Fielder and Bill MacFarland combined for five MVP awards. During the worst years of the franchise— the last six seasons—the Totems made only two trips to the playoffs and failed to win a series. They folded due to financial reasons following a failed attempt by co-owner Vince Abbey to lure an NHL franchise to Seattle.

2. Seattle Sounders, 1974–83. The original Sounders, a member of the North American Soccer League, had an intriguing 10-year run. The team was popular and successful for its first seven years, attracting numerous sellout crowds (including 58,128 for the first-ever sports event in the Kingdome in 1976) and twice playing for the league championship. Featuring several former English First Division stars, including Roger Davies, Tommy Ord, Alan Hudson and Bruce Rioch, the Sounders outdrew (on a per-game basis) the Mariners from 1977 through 1981, but began to implode when a series of coaching changes and embarrassing ownership gaffes alienated the fan base. Three years after going 25–7 and averaging more than 25,000 fans per game (1980), the Sounders went out of business. "If you wanted to write a book about how to screw up a professional soccer franchise," NASL President Howard Samuels told the *Seattle Post-Intelligencer*, "we could write it. The Seattle franchise has been a horror story, a mass of bad decisions and mistakes."

1. Seattle Rainiers/Angels, 1903–06, 1919–68. Named after team owner Emil Sick's Rainier Brewery, the Triple A Pacific Coast League entry won pennants in 1939, 1940, 1941, 1951 and 1955 and for three decades served as Seattle's best summertime entertainment. Sick sold the Rainiers to the Boston Red Sox in 1960, and the Red Sox, in turn, sold the club to the California Angels, who renamed the team the Seattle Angels, as they were known during the final four years of their existence. The franchise ended with the arrival of major league baseball in 1969.

Surprises from the Pages of *Ball Four*

The 40th anniversary of the Seattle Pilots' absurd one-year stint in the American League will be commemorated (celebrated isn't quite right, is it?) in 2009. Thanks to pitcher Jim Bouton's sensational book, *Ball Four*, memories of the Pilots live forever. Here's 16 highlights from the book many consider the best ever written on baseball.

Things from *Ball Four* that surprised fans in 1969:

8. Yankees clubhouse man Pete Previte often forged Mickey Mantle's autograph on baseballs.

7. Mickey Mantle occasionally played with a hangover.

6. A rookie named Lou Piniella had a heated argument with manager Joe Schultz over his arm strength.

5. Beaver shooting—the art of watching pretty girls surreptitiously in various stages of dress.

4. Page 45. March 11, 1969. "Baseball players will take anything. If you had a pill that could guarantee a pitcher 20 wins but might take five years off his life, he'd take it."

3. Players routinely used amphetamines, called "greenies," they bought from dubious characters who hung around teams.

2. Players often discussed trying to empower a player's union.

1. The Pilots had trouble drawing fans, yet were instructed to tell kids that they weren't allowed to sign autographs.

Things from *Ball Four* that would surprise a first-time reader in 2009:

8. Bouton made $22,000 pitching in 1969. (Alex Rodriguez made approximately 18k per inning in 2008.)

7. When Gary Bell was traded to Chicago, he told his wife that they would have to take the big TV they bought back to the store because they couldn't afford to ship it across the country.

6. The only time a manager told Bouton to hit an opposing batter was in 1968 with the Seattle Angels of the PCL. The manager was Joe Adcock. The catcher who delivered the news was John Olerud. In August that year, Olerud's son, John, a future major league star and batting champion, was born in Seattle.

5. A steady source of frustration for Bouton was an inability to find anyone to catch him when he wanted to practice his knuckleball. (Today's teams have full-time, paid bullpen catchers.)

4. Bouton paid $50 to buy a case of a new product called Gatorade so his teammates could try it. Bouton suspected it might be good. The team refused to reimburse him.

3. Pilot Fred Talbot flew to Gladstone, OR, to be interviewed on radio shows after a Gladstone resident won $27,000 in a team promotion when Talbot hit a grand slam. Talbot was not paid for the trip. (Today's players are regularly compensated for various promotional activities.)

2. After being traded to Houston, Bouton worried about getting killed by the tougher players in the NL.

1. Bowie Kuhn, commissioner of baseball when *Ball Four* was published in 1970, derided the book as "detrimental to baseball." In a radio marketing pitch in 2008, the Mariners used the phrase, "You spend a good piece of your life gripping a baseball, and in the end it turns out it was the other way around all the time." That is the final line in *Ball Four*.

It wasn't just the Kingdome, pal. Seattle has gone through a lot of ballyards, arenas, digs, joints and venues as the city kept growing and the appetite for sports went unsated.

10. Denny Field, 1895–1920. Located on 45th Street on the northeast corner of the UW campus, this is where the legendary Gil Dobie compiled most of his 58–0–3 record. Sitting at a piano in the middle of Denny Field on November 13, 1915, songwriter Lester J. Wilson first played "Bow Down To Washington" at halftime of the California game. Washington last used the field on November 13, 1920, then moved into Husky Stadium. Today, Denny Field is used for intramural sports.

9. Recreation Park, 1903–06. When the then-outlaw Pacific Coast League set up shop in Seattle in 1903, the Siwashes played in a new park, hastily constructed on a site that eventually first became a Metro bus barn and later the SuperSonics training facility. The first game, on April 29, 1903, attracted 3,000 spectators, who watched Seattle wallop San Francisco 11–1. On the same day, the Dan Dugdale-owned Seattle Chinooks defeated Portland 5–4 at Athletic Park.

8. Yesler Way Park, 1907–18. Nicknamed "Band Box Park" due to its small size, this venue was located at Yesler Way between 12th and 14th avenues and was home to the Siwashes, who became the Turks in 1909 and the Giants in 1910. It was one of two major Seattle construction projects completed in 1907. The other: Pike Place Market.

7. Seattle Ice Arena, 1915–24. Located across from what is now the Fairmont Olympic Hotel on Fifth Avenue between University and Seneca streets, the first Seattle Ice Arena was home to the Seattle Metropolitans hockey team. The arena, where the Mets won the Stanley Cup in 1917, was torn down after the team folded.

6. Civic Auditorium, 1928–62. Funding for a future Civic Auditorium began with a gift of $20,000 made by Pioneer Square saloonkeeper James Osborne. The facility was used for a variety of sports events, including Seattle U. basketball games (Elgin Baylor played there), concerts, community ceremonies and an occasional boxing match. Jack Dempsey fought three exhibitions in the building in August 1931.

5. Dugdale Park, 1913–32. Named after Seattle baseball guru Dan Dugdale, who funded the project, the all-wood structure served as home to a variety of teams, including the Northwestern League Giants (1913–17), Ballard Pippins (1914), Pacific Coast International League Giants (1918), International Northwestern League Drydockers (1919), Pacific Coast League Purple Sox (1919), Rainiers (1919–20) and Indians (1920–32). Located at Rainier Avenue and McClellan Street, future site of Sicks' Stadium, then a Lowe's home improvement store, Dugdale Park was the first stadium on the West Coast with double-decked stands. One of the most famous moments in the stadium's history was an October 19, 1924 exhibition when Babe Ruth hit three long home runs over the right-field fence. An arsonist torched the park on July 4, 1932.

4. Civic Stadium, 1928–45. Originally built to host boxing matches and high school football games, Civic Stadium became home to the Rainiers baseball team after Dugdale Park burned down. The future site of Memorial Stadium at the Seattle Center, Civic Stadium had no grass, wire fences, huge wooden light poles that were in play, and a left-field line that measured just 285 feet. Local boxer Freddie Steele won the world middleweight title over Eddie Risko on July 11, 1936, at Civic Stadium, and lost the title there to Al Hostak on July 26, 1938, in a match that drew 35,000, the biggest local boxing match in Seattle history. The stadium was torn down in 1945.

3. Sicks' Stadium, 1938–69. Built by Emil Sick, owner of the Rainier Brewery, for an outlay of $350,000, the ballpark was used by the minor league Rainiers, Angels and Indians of the Pacific Coast League, and also by the major league Seattle Pilots when they became the newest member of the American League in 1969. Between 1938 and 1957, the Rainiers led the PCL in attendance nine times and outdrew San Francisco's PCL team, the Seals, 14 times. Sicks' Stadium hosted a charity game on October 7, 1945, that featured Satchel Paige and Bob Feller, but the biggest event held at the stadium was either (a) Pete Rademacher's world heavyweight title fight against Floyd Patterson on Aug. 22, 1957, or (b) an Elvis Presley concert a year earlier. Two notable Sicks' Stadium sidelights: Italian farmers raised produce for the Pike Place Market just across the outfield fence, and the slope beyond the outfield became known as "Tightwad Hill" because fans could view games for free.

2. Longacres Race Track, 1933–92. The brainchild of Seattle real estate mogul Joseph Gottstein, Longacres opened in Renton on August 3, 1933, after a crew of 3,000 constructed it in just 28 days. The first meet lasted 40 days. The next four decades featured visits by such renowned jockeys as Bill Shoemaker, Laffit Pincay, Chris McCarron and Sandy Hawley, racing favorites Grey Papa, Chinook Pass, Belle of Rainier and Captain Condo. Two years after the track's opening, Gottstein, who borrowed $85,000 to build it, instituted the Longacres Mile, with a purse of $10,000. By 1992 it was $250,000. In terms of entertainment value and ambience, no sporting venue in Seattle beat it. Wrote Valley Daily News reporter Eric Lucas during the oval's final days: "Longacres has more nooks and crannies than a medieval castle, a wilderness of seating areas, bars, lounges, cafes, restaurants, cupolas, boxes and bleachers added helter-skelter over the years." Victimized by the state lottery and a slumping economy, Longacres closed September 21, 1992.

1. The Kingdome, 1976–2000. Built to "last a thousand years," the Kingdome didn't make it to its 25th birthday. Often castigated by the teams housed in the concrete cavern—Seahawks, Mariners, Sonics and Sounders—as gloomy and not enough of a revenue generator, the engineering marvel nevertheless gave rainy Seattle the dry spot it needed to become a major league city. More than 73 million people entered to witness, among other events, three NCAA Final Fours (1984, 1989, 1995), an AFC-NFC Pro Bowl (1976), a Major League All-Star Game (1979), an NBA All-Star Game (1987), plus a Billy Graham Crusade, the Rolling Stones, an Evel Knievel bus jump, a paper airplane contest, numerous prep football championships and a passel of home, boat, auto and outdoors shows. Before a Mariners game in 1994, a leaky roof caused interior ceiling tiles to fall into the seating bowl, presaging a large civic fight over the building's long-term safety and economic viability that ultimately led to its demise. The Kingdome was imploded on March 26, 2000, to make way for Qwest Field.

Best Sports Arenas for Rock Shows :: Jeff Ament

Pearl Jam has been described as the little Seattle band with the big heart. The group has toured the world for nearly two decades, and in addition to playing great music, it has maintained a philanthropic attitude with numerous acts of charity toward its fans. The band's popularity dictates live shows at sports venues. On behalf of the band, Jeff Ament, bassist, skateboard fiend, NBA wannabe and frequent courtside observer at Sonics games before their move to Oklahoma City, offers Pearl Jam's list of favorite venues in which to play a show.

Says Jeff:

What make these arenas great are 80 percent sentiment and 20 percent sound of the room. Five of the choices were places my heroes played basketball. The old arenas generally sound way better than the new ones. Being on stage at Madison Square Garden, between songs, your mind wanders to Ali, Willis Reed, Earl the Pearl, Clyde, the great Knicks/Celtics/Lakers battles . . . Wilt, Kareem, Bird, Magic, Jordan and Isiah Thomas. Not to mention all the great rock shows: Springsteen, Zeppelin, Kiss, The Who, to name just a few.

10. Boca Juniors Stadium, Buenos Aires, Argentina

9. Fila Forum, Milan, Italy

8. Crisler Arena, Ann Arbor, MI

7. Montreal Forum, Montreal, Canada

6. Spectrum, Philadelphia, PA

5. Los Angeles Forum, Los Angeles, CA

4. Madison Square Garden, New York, NY

3. Chicago Stadium, Chicago, IL

2. Boston Garden, Boston, MA

1. Washington-Grizzly Stadium, Missoula, MT

Honorable Mention: Rupp Arena, Lexington, KY; Purdue's Mackey Arena, West Lafayette, IN; Cow Palace, San Francisco, CA; Qwest Arena, Boise, ID; XCel Energy Center, St. Paul, MN

A myriad of teams, sports and events cavorted upon Seattle playgrounds over the years but have gone away, largely for reasons financial. They are not forgotten.

10. Seattle Bowl, 2001–02. The Seattle Bowl had no chance from the get-go in a cold-weather city. A continuation of the discontinued Oahu Bowl run out of Hawaii, it matched the fifth-place teams from the Atlantic Coast Conference and Pac-10. The 2001 game, at Safeco Field, drew 30,000 for Stanford-Georgia Tech. The 2002 game did better, attracting 38,241 for Oregon-Wake Forest. When Seattle Bowl promoters missed two deadlines for providing a $1.5 million letter of credit to secure the 2003 game, it was canceled.

9. PGA tour stops, 1936, 1945, 1948; 1961–66. There was a time (mid 1930s–late 1940s) when the PGA's top golfers made semi-regular visits to the Puget Sound region, and another era (1961–66) in which the PGA made an annual tour stop in Seattle. The first major PGA event in Seattle occurred in 1936 when McDonald Smith outdueled Byron Nelson for the $1,200 first prize in the Seattle Open at Inglewood Country Club. Subsequent events included the 1945 Tacoma Open (Fircrest/Jimmy Hines), 1945 Seattle Open (Broadmoor/Byron Nelson) and 1948 Tacoma Open (Fircrest/Porky Oliver). The PGA didn't return to the region until 1961, when Dave Marr won the Seattle Open at Broadmoor, collecting $3,500. The Seattle Open continued as a regular PGA encampment through 1966: 1962, Jack Nicklaus, $4,300 (Broadmoor); 1963, Bobby Nichols, $5,300 (Inglewood); 1964, Billy Casper, $5,800 (Broadmoor); 1965, Gay Brewer, $6,600 (Inglewood); 1966, Homero Blancas, $6,600 (Everett). After that, sponsors fell away and the tour has never come back.

8. Rainier Tennis Classic, 1972–76. For four years in the early 1970s, the Association of Tennis Professionals experimented with an indoor West Coast circuit that included Seattle, San Francisco, Portland and San Diego. Seattle hosted four events that drew the likes of former Seattle University All-America Tom Gorman, two-time Grand Slam champion Rod Laver, Ilie Nastase, Charles Pasarell and Tom Okker. But with a top purse of $20,000 and almost no enthusiasm expressed by Seattleites, the ATP discontinued the event.

7. Buchan Bakers basketball, 1948–61. A Northwest amateur basketball team whose rosters were rife with ex-Huskies and former Cougars, the Bakers peaked in 1956 when they won the national AAU tournament and also became the first American team to compete behind the Iron Curtain by playing in a series of games in Poland and Czechoslovakia. Sponsored by the Buchan Baking Co., a Seattle bread wholesale business, the Bakers featured former Huskies Joe Cipriano, Charlie Koon, Dean Parsons and Bruno Boin, former Seattle U. stars Stan Glowaski, Dick Stricklin and Charlie Brown, and former WSU players such as Larry Beck. The Bakers played exhibitions against the Huskies and Chieftains, participated in the 1956 U.S. Olympic trials, beat the Soviet national team in 1959, placed third in the 1960 National AAU Tournament, and fourth in 1957.

6. Virginia Slims of Seattle women's tennis, 1979–82. Most of the best players on the WTA circuit came to town during the five-year run—sponsored first by the cigarette maker, later by Avon—among them Chris Evert, Martina Navratilova, Billie Jean King, Virginia Wade, Betty Stove, Hana Mandlikova, Tracy Austin and even transsexual Renee Richards. The event, held every February at both the Center Arena and Coliseum, perished due to a lack of interest. The tournament usually drew between 1,000–3,500 per session, and the title matches rarely attracted more than 6,000.

5. Leilani Lanes, 1961–06. Home to numerous editions of the PBA's Seattle Open, and dozens of matchups between Hall of Famers Earl Anthony and Dick Weber, Leilani Lanes was a popular Greenwood fixture for 44 years until the property was sold to a developer in 2006. Often called the "Cheers" of bowling, Leilani played host to thousands of bowling leagues, whose members were drawn to the giant bowling pin outside and the Lani Kai Restaurant & Lounge inside.

4. Hairbreadth Husky cartoon, 1959–92. Artist Bob McCausland worked at the *Seattle Post-Intelligencer* for 33 years, and for 22 of them produced a wildly popular cartoon titled "Hairbreadth Husky" that chronicled the University of Washington's football triumphs and travails. McCausland first produced the cartoon in 1959, a year in which the Huskies always seemed to win in the final minutes, by a "hair." The *P-I* carried two Hairbreadth Husky cartoons weekly, before and after each game. The Hairbreadth Husky character sported a booster hat and a large letterman's jacket.

3. Safeco Classic LPGA tour stop, 1982–99. Played annually at the Meridian Valley Country Club in Kent, the event featured decent purses ($400,000–$650,000) and strong fields—Julie Inkster, Patty Sheehan (three-time winner), Nancy Lopez, Annika Sorenstam, and Karrie Webb, etc. But Safeco discontinued its sponsorship in 1999 after determining it wasn't getting enough bang for its buck. No replacement sponsor was found.

2. NCAA basketball Final Fours. Well, they still exist, but not in Seattle. Back when the men's college championships were not so much, the University of Washington hosted the Final Fours of 1949 and 1952. But the modern version received a big boost in 1984 when the Kingdome became the second domed stadium to host. The crowds, parties and general spectacle received rave reviews, elevating the prestige of the event. The tourney came back in 1989 and 1995. But the Kingdome was imploded in 2000, so Seattle no longer has a site big enough to contain the monster it helped create.

1. Kingbowl prep football, 1977–94. All five high school classifications in the state played their championships games on the same Saturday in December, at the same venue, the Kingdome, for 17 years. Created by Seattle sports promoter Michael Campbell, the Kingbowl came to an end when the games were moved to the Tacoma Dome—the venue switch saved the Washington Interscholastic Activities Association $50,000 a year in rent—and renamed the "Grid Classic."

Lou Piniella is a crafty, shrewd baseball strategist. But no TV network videotape logger would ever guess that about their hero. Piniella's tantrums in New York, Cincinnati, Seattle, Tampa and Chicago have made him a legend, often much to his chagrin. Sometimes he plans it, sometimes he can't help himself. Either way, Mariners fans were greatly entertained by one of the game's most passionate, competitive characters.

9. First Seattle ejection, June 6, 1993. A 20-minute brawl in Camden Yards between the Mariners and Orioles began when Baltimore pitcher Mike Mussina plunked Seattle catcher Bill Haselman. Seven players were ejected along with Piniella, who was highly agitated because Mussina wasn't booted. "That's why I got ejected, because he didn't," said Piniella, who kicked dirt on home plate and then played the game under protest.

8. Flagged for delay of game, April 8, 1997. With a crowd of 24,348 egging him on, Piniella went jaw-to-jaw with home plate umpire Darryl Cousins in what became a 14–8 victory over the Cleveland Indians at the Kingdome. Infuriated at being thumbed by Cousins for holding up play, Piniella repeatedly kicked dirt on home plate. Not satisfied with that, Piniella shoveled more dirt on the chalk lines of the batter's box.

7. Bat trick, July 25, 1999. During a 4–3 loss to the Twins at the Metrodome, Piniella erupted over a call by plate umpire Durwood Merrill, who ruled Raul Ibanez left third base too early on a sacrifice fly. Instead of the standard kicks of dirt and hat, Piniella decided to uproot third base. But he couldn't do it. So he retreated to the dugout and began tossing bats on the field—seven by unofficial press box count. When asked why he couldn't uproot third base, Piniella said, "My back's been bothering me, so I didn't try too hard."

6. Tired of his own act, August 26, 1996. One of most intense periods in Piniella's Seattle tenure came in late August and early September of 1996, during a battle for the AL West flag, when he was booted three times in 10 games. The most theatrical of the three occurred in a 2–1 win over the Yankees when Piniella went ballistic after the umpires ruled a home run by Edgar Martinez was a double because of fan interference. Piniella steamed out of the dugout to go nose-to-nose with umpire Durwood Merrill. Piniella threw his hat, kicked it, returned to Merrill's grill, kicked at dirt and missed, then kicked at dirt and connected. After being booted, he kicked dirt two more times. Afterward, he said, "I'm getting tired of getting run out of games."

5. A splendid Seattle home kickoff, May 17, 1994. Piniella managed the Mariners for one year and one month before he recorded his first Kingdome ejection. During a 4–0 loss to Kansas City, Piniella kicked his cap 16 times and deposited four loads of dirt on home plate.

4. Short trip to stardom, August 22, 1999. Notable about this Piniella nut-out was the first moment. When a call went against the Mariners in a game against the Indians, Piniella attempted to storm out of the dugout, but tripped and stumbled on the steps, drawing a huge laugh from Indians manager Mike Hargrove. When Piniella finally reached the field, he put on another dirt-kicking spree that lasted long enough for ESPN to break in and show the tantrum live on a split screen.

3. Earth Day, May 28, 2002. Outraged when Tropicana Field's big screen began showing highlights of a five-run inning that put Tampa Bay ahead 5–0, Piniella got into plate umpire John Schulock's face, then kicked up a dirt storm that partially covered home plate. With Schulock unmoved, Piniella dropped to his hands and knees and scooped dirt on the plate. Mariners catcher Dan Wilson borrowed Schulock's brush to sweep the plate clean, which didn't sit well with Piniella. "If I was the catcher, we would have played with a dirty home plate," said Piniella, adding, "I should be in the landscaping business. If I were the catcher, I would have buried home plate. I would have gotten one of those wheelbarrows full of turf and dumped it on the plate."

2. Don't forget to test the manager too, August 26, 1998. Late in a 5–3 loss at Cleveland, Piniella rushed from the dugout to protest when third baseman Russ Davis was called out by umpire Larry Barnett for running outside the basepath. After briefly arguing, Piniella returned to the dugout. Then, to his amazement, Piniella found out he'd been ejected. Out he came, throwing his cap on the ground, whiffing with a kick. On his way back to the dugout, he kicked his hat five more times. After the third, Mariners broadcaster Dave Niehaus said, "He got some distance on that one! That was a three-pointer right there." He tossed it into the stands, but a quick-witted Cleveland fan tossed it back. Said Cleveland manager Mike Hargrove: "I don't know how anybody can think of that many things to yell." Said Piniella, "I don't blame anyone for laughing. Everyone likes to see someone make a fool of themselves in front of 40,000 people." Two days later, Piniella told reporters, "You know the andro stuff (androstenedione) everyone's talking about for muscles? If I was on that, I'd have kicked my hat out of the stadium."

1. "Get my fuckin' hat!" September 18, 2002. In his most theatrical tantrum, Piniella launched into a two-minute, six-second tirade at Safeco Field after a close call at first base that was exacerbated when Piniella determined umpire C.B. Bucknor smirked. After a series of yelps and bleats so wild his coaches had to restrain Piniella, Bucknor had seen enough and tossed the Seattle manager, who said later, "The ump had the nerve to have a smirk on his face." After two hat kicks and two throw-downs, a solid boot sent his chapeau 10 feet. To first base coach Johnny Moses, he yelled (plain to lip-readers everywhere): "Get my fuckin' hat!" Moses obliged, whereupon Pinella applied his footwear to it again. That was followed by an uprooting of first base, which ended up in foul territory down the left-field line. When he retrieved the base, he threw it again and stomped off the field to chants of "Lou! Lou!" After the game, Piniella admitted to reporters, "My hamstring hurts and my shoulder is sore." Said bench coach John McLaren, witness to a majority of Piniella career tirades, "That one was the best. Lou had all his greatest hits in it." A few days later, a reporter showed Piniella a photograph of him kicking his hat. Said Piniella: "I'm going to send the picture to Jon Gruden (coach of the NFL Tampa Bay Buccaneers). I'm ready for the season. That's good form there."

It could be argued that from 1994 to 2002, no one in Seattle sports had a tougher job than Dan Wilson. How would you like to be the in-game conduit between manager Lou Piniella and his pitchers? The M's decade of success was in no small part fueled by Wilson, who spent 12 solid years behind the plate.

4. "That Yaz was a great player." One of Lou's finer moments came after a series in Boston. Our bus driver was having trouble getting to the airport. The usual route was blocked with barricades. The driver circled for another 20 minutes with no luck. Lou told the driver to go back to the barricades and he'd see what he could do. When we arrived again at the barricades, there was a policeman standing guard. Lou asked the driver to open the door and he jumped out to talk to the policeman. The cop was astounded that it was actually THE Lou Piniella. After a brief conversation about how well Lou knew Carl Yastrzemski, the cop moved the barriers and we were on our way.

3. Peacemaker. We were leaving the stadium in Kansas City after a win, and everyone was feeling chipper. Off to the side of the parking lot were two fans in a pretty good fight, throwing blows and wrestling around. Lou went into action. He yelled for the bus driver to stop the bus and open the door. When Lou got out he ran over to the two guys and began breaking it up. Again, upon seeing Lou, the guys were astounded. They both stopped fighting and began apologizing profusely. From a seat on the bus, it was truly hilarious.

2. The 9/11 tribute. A more serious moment from Lou came in 2001 when baseball resumed after 9/11. Before the game when we would clinch the division at Safeco, Lou called me and a couple of others into his office to discuss what he thought should happen after the game if we won. He wanted to handle this in an appropriate, considerate fashion. He thought that we had accomplished something outstanding (eventually, 116 wins), but the people of New York were really on his mind. With seriousness and compassion that I had not witnessed from him to this degree, he drew up plans for how we were to proceed if we won. He was the architect of what is, in my mind, one of the classiest and most inspirational moments in baseball history. I'm sure you remember the moment of silence and then a carrying of the American flag around the infield. Fans, players, coaches were all crying. The moment was so captivating. Lou was the hero of that night.

1. He knows from tantrums. I typically did not snap after a tough circumstance, but one particular day I was angry about striking out. As I came back to the dugout I took off my helmet and tried to slam dunk it into a bucket we used to carry the game balls. When I let go of the helmet (which was traveling at a good velocity), I watched as it hit the rim of the bucket and careened off, hitting Lou right in the hand. As well as being mad about the strikeout, now I'm feeling bad I hit Lou. I immediately apologized to Lou, who by now is shaking his hand in the air from the blow. He looked at me and said, "That's all right, son. You can be mad you struck out, but I'm okay."

Five Barrys, Three Coaches, One Great Party
:: Kevin Calabro

The enormously skilled and entertaining former play-by-play voice of the Sonics worked through three ownership groups and alongside a half a dozen coaches.

Five Favorite Barrys

Brent (brother). I asked him once in an interview what he was supposed to do on offense: "Go stand in the corner with a finger up my nose and hope Gary sees me."

Rick (father). He worked with me in 1989. He was a hoot to go to dinner with. If the meal wasn't perfect he'd make a stink. I don't care it was a five-star place or Taco Bell.

Drew (brother). He played a short time with us. Uncanny how similar were the personalities of Drew and Brent.

Jon (brother). J.B. and I ended up the last two to leave a Spurs NBA championship victory party in 2007 in Cleveland. We drank all their wine. I have no idea how we got into the party but we were walking back to the hotel at 5 a.m.

Ackerley (boss). I lost count of the number of times I thought the old man would fire me. One time he called our radio producer while we were on the air. We were complaining about how high our seats were. He said if there were any more references to the nose-bleed seats he'd banish me and color guy Mychal Thompson to the men's room permanently.

Three Favorite Coaches

Bob Kloppenburg. A brilliant basketball man and perfect gentleman, but he was also the absent-minded professor. His wife, Gail, would send him on the road with his suitcase packed with outfits. She would pin instructions to the clothes, and inevitably Klop would forget and leave a pinned note on his tie or coat. We coined a word, "kloppage," for any food particle (usually popcorn) that fell and stuck to the front of a red sweater he was fond of wearing.

George Karl. An absolute beauty. Our first road trip with George was to Phoenix. We ended up closing a sports bar at 2 a.m. George didn't touch a drop of alcohol but we did have meat loaf sandwiches while sitting on a curb waiting for a cab. George kept things loose with shooting games, constant banter and baiting of players, staff, management, broadcasters. A very fun guy.

Paul Westphal. He could have had me fired one year. I mouthed off to a reporter after a bad loss in Dallas that left Gary Payton screaming at the coach and his team. Gary refused to get off the floor and I commented to the reporter after the game that Paul had lost the team. I thought it was off the record. It wasn't. It got published. A few days later I apologized to the GM, assistant GM and to Paul. He said he respected me for coming clean with him and admitted that things had been difficult with Gary as well as Vin Baker.

Favorite Street Party

Game 7, 1996 Western Conference Finals, versus John Stockton, Karl Malone and the incredibly efficient Utah Jazz. The Sonics led by eight with 5 ½ minutes left. Utah pulled to within one with 30 seconds left. Kemp was fouled and hit two free throws with 14 seconds left. Malone missed two free throws with eight seconds left. Hersey Hawkins grabbed the miss and was fouled. He split two free throws and the Sonics were in the NBA Finals against Michael Jordan and the Chicago Bulls.

Marques Johnson and I continued our radio coverage as the players, coaches and fans mobbed one another. I hopped over the scorer's table with a microphone and beat Jim Gray and national TV to Sam Perkins. Afterward, along with stat man Ernie Tobey, we went up to the owner's suite. We figured if anybody had free beer, it would be them. I was disappointed in the somewhat subdued scene with owner Barry Ackerley's twin sons, Ted and Chris. I politely dumped two full beers on them, as well as team president John Dresel. After the initial shock, they quickly got in the spirit and returned the favor. Dresel would later tell me the carpet was ruined but they'd take care of it. Attaboy! Hanging around with management wasn't what we had in mind.

We eased out of the building in M.J.'s rental and headed to Jalisco's restaurant, where a party section had been fenced off in the back parking lot. We walked into a maelstrom. You'd have thought we played the game. After sifting through the crowd, I got to the back parking lot where the hard-core was holding court. Our flagship station, KJR, had most of their staff back there. A man I call "the foghorn," Dave Grosby, assisted by fellow host Mike Gastineau, was about to climb on a chair and make some pronouncement. Without proper decorum, I walked up to Groz and dumped a fresh beer right on his head. The Gasman, seemingly chagrined that he hadn't been given the same courtesy, was next. So it went. Someone took a grande margarita and unloaded on me. We yelled and screamed incoherently through the night. The fine celebration culminated with an $80 cab ride back to my home in Redmond.

No surprise that among the highly competitive, occasional disputations occur. Be it over love, money or loud music, teammates, agents and judges sometimes have to be summoned to play referee.

12. John Brisker vs. Joby Wright, 1973. During a training camp practice on September 15 in Port Angeles, the two Sonics forwards got into a shoving match that ended with Brisker landing a roundhouse right that knocked out four of Wright's teeth and shattered his jaw. Brisker's punch effectively ended Wright's NBA career.

11. Barry Ackerley vs. Bob Whitsitt, 1994. The ill-will between the Sonics' owner and his team president and GM grew so rancorous that Ackerley not only placed Whitsitt on administrative leave, he had Whitsitt's office stripped of its computer terminal, telephone, VCR, television set and fax machine, making it impossible for Whitsitt to function. Said Ackerley's son, Bill, the president of Ackerley Communications, "We didn't feel it was appropriate for Bob to be using company assets when he has been placed on a paid administrative leave."

10. Randy Johnson vs. David Segui, 1998. The Big Unit became angry at Segui when the first baseman turned up the volume on the Mariners clubhouse stereo while Johnson was entertaining guests in front of his nearby locker. Johnson said something sarcastic to Segui, who replied in kind. Johnson went after Segui and the pair wrestled, but before teammates broke it up, Segui hurt his wrist.

9. Gary Payton vs. Vernon Maxwell, 2000. The Sonics guards were involved in a fierce altercation March 26 that ended practice and injured two teammates. Their confrontation began during a scrimmage, in which the pair hurled barbs at each other. It spilled into the locker room and became so intense that Payton picked up a chair and threatened to bash Maxwell, which prompted Maxwell to storm into the team's training room to grab a free weight. Payton didn't swing the chair. Instead, he threw a TV remote control at Maxwell. During the fracas, center Horace Grant suffered a bruised left shoulder while trying to help separate the pair. Swingman Chuck Person aggravated an already injured left knee while attempting to play peacemaker.

8. Fred Couples vs. Deborah Couples, 1993; Greg Haugen vs. Karen Haugen, 1994. The PGA Tour golfer's marriage, already crumbling when Couples won the 1992 Masters, became a public absurdity when Deborah told a Palm Beach, FL, divorce court that she required $168,000 per month in living expenses—at least until the conclusion of her polo season. Couples, from Seattle, told the court that his wife's obsession with polo had ended their marriage. "If she had not gone overboard in polo we would probably still be married," said Couples. The court determined that Mrs. Couples should receive $52,000 per month. Meanwhile, in Henderson, NV, the relationship between Haugen, 34, a former lightweight boxing champion from Auburn, and his estranged wife reached its nadir when the pair were arrested when she tried to run the fighter over with her car and shoot him. Henderson police said the incident ended when the cops found the Haugens wrestling for a gun in the front yard of their home.

7. Joey Galloway vs. Mike Holmgren, 1999. The Seahawks wide receiver said he was willing to sit out the entire NFL season if the club did not give him a more lucrative contract. When Holmgren, in his first season as Seahawks coach and GM, balked at offering more money and refused to trade Galloway, he boycotted training camp and returned to his native Ohio. He spent his NFL Sundays playing flag football in a public park. Galloway held out for 101 days, accumulating $837,117 in fines. He returned to the team only so he would be credited for playing the season and could become an unrestricted free agent. Holmgren finally traded Galloway on February 12, 2000, to the Dallas Cowboys for first-round picks in 2000 and 2001.

6. Monique Ellis vs. Bobbi Jo Lister, 1988. On March 1, Monique Ellis, wife of Sonics guard Dale Ellis, and Bobbi Jo Lister, wife of center Alton Lister, became embroiled in a fight outside the Seattle locker room 10 minutes after the Sonics beat the Lakers 114–100. The fight began when Nadia Gordon of Bellevue, claiming to be the sister of Monique Ellis, kicked and punched Bobbi Jo. Bernita Horton of Seattle tried to stop Gordon and was kicked and punched by Monique. "As far as I'm concerned, I was mugged," Horton told Seattle police. "I just tried to stop a fight and Monique attacked me." The rift between the wives apparently began when Alton Lister signed a $4.2 million contract while Ellis could not successfully renegotiate the final year of a contract worth $325,000 per year. Earlier in the season, Monique and Bobbi Jo had engaged in a hair-pulling incident in the Coliseum parking lot.

5. Dale Ellis vs. Xavier McDaniel, 1990. On November 21, the Sonics stars engaged in a full-blown donnybrook that drew blood in front of the team's offices at 190 Queen Anne Ave. N. When Ellis emerged from an elevator in the building's lobby, he spotted McDaniel standing in front of the building. The two argued heatedly and punches were thrown while a Sonics' employee tried to restrain the pair. As they went at it, the fight moved up the street. When it ended, the Sonics suspended Ellis for five days with no pay, but took no action against McDaniel, who said, "We've played seven games without him and God knows how many more we'll have to play without him. All his practice shots are short anyhow."

4. Dennis Johnson vs. Lenny Wilkens, 1980; Gus Williams vs. Sam Schulman, 1980–81. Johnson, a 24-year-old guard with big hopes and big freckles, had led the Sonics to their only NBA championship in 1979. Often a moody sort, Johnson was given a big contract, but spent much of the 1979–80 season playing to the contract instead of with his teammates. At the urging of head coach Lenny Wilkens, the Sonics traded Johnson to the Phoenix Suns on June 3, 1980, for guard Paul Westphal. Wilkens later described Johnson as "a cancer," but the deal was fatal to the Sonics. Westphal, injured, played only 36 games for Seattle. A maturing Johnson went on to stardom with Phoenix and the Boston Celtics, where he won two more titles. Meanwhile, Johnson's backcourt mate, superquick all-star Gus Williams, demanded a top-tier contract after the 1979–80 season. Owner Sam Schulman refused. In the prime of his career, Williams sat out the entire season. Without Johnson and Williams, the Sonics record plunged to 34–48, the quickest fall from grace in history for an NBA champion.

3. Phil Shinnick vs. USA Track and Field, 1963–03. On May 25, 1963, at the Modesto Relays, the University of Washington's Phil Shinnick, an Eastern Washington farm boy of 20, broke the world record in the long jump with a leap of 27–4—or so he thought. Meet officials soon disqualified Shinnick's jump, assuming it was wind-aided even though no wind gauge was in use. After much debate, the same meet officials voted to recognize Shinnick's jump, but never submitted his mark to the International Association of Athletics Federation (IAAF) for ratification. Shinnick then launched what would become a 40-year crusade to get the record recognized. Finally, in 2003, at the United States Amateur Track Federation's annual meeting in Greensboro, NC, Shinnick was informed that his previously disavowed leap would be recognized as a one-time American record. The IAAF has yet to recognize it as a one-time world record.

2. George Karl vs. Wally Walker, 1994–98. Whether it was because Walker was a Virginia grad and Karl was a North Carolina Tar Heel, or the fact that Walker was buttoned-down and Karl was opened up, the two feuded early and often after Walker's ascension to the Sonics president/GM job in 1994. Walker resisted some pressure to fire Karl after the top-seeded Sonics lost to No. 8 Denver in the first round of the 1994 playoffs, and the tandem helped the Sonics reach the NBA Finals in 1996. Still, after the 1997–98 season, Walker refused to renew Karl's contract, despite a winning mark of 70 percent over six seasons. Walker said he could no longer trust his head coach to keep quiet about team business. Karl launched into a series of criticisms of Walker that got him fined $25,000 by the NBA for making "disparaging remarks" and $50,000 for "negative remarks" about Sonics management, specifically Walker. Said Karl, "My recommendation would be to blow up the management and keep the team."

1. Gil Dobie vs. Henry Suzzallo, 1915–16. Suzzallo, the UW president, did not like football, believing it to be an unnecessary and violent distraction from the school's core mission—education. Suzzallo, who started in 1915, also did not like the highly successful Dobie, resenting his city-wide popularity. So when one of Dobie's players, star tackle Bill Grimm, was accused—but not found guilty—of cheating on an exam, Suzzallo and the UW faculty senate suspended him from the final game of the year against California. That action provoked a two-day strike by Washington players, which Dobie publicly supported. Because Dobie sided with his players rather than with Suzzallo and the faculty senate, the president fired him. Dobie's nine-season record: 58–0–3.

Nifty Nicknames

Clever nicknames seem to have gone the way of great big men in pro basketball and great base stealers in baseball. Sexy for Richie Sexson? C'mon. But a few of these monikers are worthy of recall:

14. The Inspector—Bill Caudill. The Mariners' closer in 1982–83 enjoyed stalking through the clubhouse in full Sherlock Holmes regalia and inspecting the bat rack with a magnifying glass for "missing hits." Also known as "Cuffs," Caudill frequently handcuffed unsuspecting victims to railings in the Kingdome—and left them there.

13. Lord of All Indoors—Steve Zungul. One of the greatest scorers in the defunct Major Indoor Soccer League, the native of Croatia played for the Tacoma Stars from 1986–88.

12. Bye Bye—Steve Balboni. If his life story gets turned into a movie, Dennis Franz will have the lead role. The lumpy slugger played only 97 games for the Mariners in 1988, but numerous of his 21 homers justified his nickname.

11. Pork Chop—Floyd Womack. The oft-injured Seahawks offensive lineman, a fourth-round draftee in 2001 from Mississippi State, earned the nickname not long after birth because his mother thought he resembled a local wrestler in Cleveland, MS, named Pork Chop Cash. Be happy he didn't look like Brussels Sprouts Johnson.

10. Big Smooth—Sam Perkins. The laconic, heavy lidded six-foot-nine forward from North Carolina, acquired in a trade by the Sonics in 1993, loved to unfurl his ultra-long arms beyond the arc to hoist threes with an effortless grace.

9. Big Paper Daddy—Ricky Pierce. From 1990–94, nobody on the Sonics took and made more clutch jumpers than their money shooter. One of many handles dished by the Sonics' ace play-by-play voice, Kevin Calabro.

8. The Glove—Gary Payton. The toughest, most volatile, trash-talkingest player in Sonics history was a legend on the defensive end. The story is that a cousin told him during the 1993 Western Conference finals against Phoenix, "You're holding Kevin Johnson like a baseball in a glove."

7. Big Unit—Randy Johnson. The second-tallest pitcher in baseball history, Johnson, a five-time Cy Young Award winner, anchored the Mariners rotation from 1989 to 1998. Before his trade to Seattle, he was a little-known in the Montreal Expos organization. During batting practice, he collided head-first with teammate Tim Raines, who said, "You're a big unit!"

6. Yoda—Steve Largent. Steve Raible, a wide-receiver teammate who became the team's play-by-play voice, fastened Largent with the Stars Wars moniker. Seems that Largent and his wife attended a Halloween party as Yoda and Princess Leia—only his wife came as the diminutive green warrior. But calling an NFL wide receiver "Princess" wasn't going to work, Raible said.

5. Reign Man—Shawn Kemp. Another contribution by Calabro, who popularized the nickname when he saw it on a poster. Other accounts say it was a play on Kemp's enjoyment of Seattle's dubious winter weather, as well as one of his favorite movies, *Rain Man*, starring Dustin Hoffman. Whatever the source, Kemp in his prime was a menacing presence over the heads of his defenders.

4. Human Eraser—Marvin Webster. The seven-foot-two center from Morgan State was a formidable shot blocker on the Sonics' utterly unexpected run to the 1978 NBA Finals.

3. Mudbone—Dave Krieg. Sometimes nicknames aren't enjoyed by the recipient, which was the case for the longtime Seahawks quarterback (1980–91). He had no choice. Then-offensive coach Jerry Rhome liked to break training camp monotony with a little fun, so veterans would vote players nicknames without negotiation. Mudbone was a character in one of comedian Richard Pryor's more famous routines, and it fit well Krieg's scraggly QB pedigree.

2. Downtown—Freddy Brown. The land of the NBA long shot has been dubbed "downtown" ever since Brown's marksmanship became legendary (1971–84). The nickname's rhyme and style were perfect for the franchise's best shooter, whose 58 points on March 23, 1974, remains the club's single-game record.

1. Throwin' Samoan—Jack Thompson. Longtime Spokane columnist Harry Missildine probably never banged two words together better than when he identified the Washington State quarterback great, a native of Samoa and a graduate of White Center's Evergreen High, by his heritage and premier skill.

Honorable mention—Jay (Bone) Buhner, Don (Dawgfather) James, Jeffrey (Hack Man, Penitentiary Face) Leonard, Hugh (The King) McElhenny, Jose (Senor Smoke) Mesa, Gus (The Wizard) Williams.

Better Known for Another Gig

We all know the stereotype of an athlete peaking in his 20s, then struggling the rest of his life. Here are 10 local people who beat the stereotype.

10. Matt Rogers, UW football. An offensive lineman who played on the 2000 Rose Bowl team, Rogers became famous in 2004 when he was named one of the 12 finalists on the third season of the reality/talent-search television series *American Idol* (he was the second of the 12 finalists voted off the show). Rogers' *American Idol* appearances subsequently landed him correspondent gigs on *Access Hollywood* and *Entertainment Tonight*.

9. Bob Sapp, UW football. After winning the Morris Trophy as the Pac-10's best offensive lineman in 1996, the six-foot-five, 250-pound Sapp washed out of the NFL but soon found fame as a wrestler, kickboxer and mixed martial arts master, mostly fighting in Japan. Sapp parlayed his enormous popularity as a fighter into appearances in more than two dozen commercials, some 200 product endorsements that featured his name or image, a music CD, four books and an appearance on *The Tonight Show*.

8. John Cherberg, UW football. After he was fired as Washington's football coach in 1955, Cherberg served as the state's lieutenant governor for 32 years— longer than any other lieutenant governor in U.S. history. First elected in 1956, he never lost a statewide election.

7. Bobby Galer, UW basketball. Considered one of the UW's all-time scoring greats from 1933–35, the former All-America distinguished himself with a brilliant military record, retiring as a Marine Corps general and a holder of the Congressional Medal of Honor.

6. George Fleming, UW football. Fleming starred for the Huskies on the 1960 and 1961 Rose Bowl teams, then spent 22 years in the Legislature, actively campaigning for civil rights, housing and minority business opportunities.

5. Fred Shero, Ironmen. The legendary Philadelphia Flyers coach played 43 games for the 1951–52 Seattle Ironmen, a forerunner of the Totems. Shero coached the Broad Street Bullies when they won Stanley Cup titles in 1974 and 1975. Shero also coached of the New York Rangers when they reached the Stanley Cup Finals in 1979.

4. Arnie Weinmeister, UW football. A Husky lineman in 1942–47 who starred as a defensive tackle for the New York Giants (he played in four Pro Bowls and was elected to the Hall of Fame), the Portland native became one of the most powerful voices in the Teamsters union. For 19 years he was international vice president, making him the most powerful Teamster in the West.

3. Jim Bouton, Pilots. Struggling to master a knuckleball, Bouton went 2–1 with a 3.91 ERA in 57 appearances for the 1969 Pilots, then was traded to the Houston Astros. His diary of that Pilots season, published in 1970 and titled *Ball Four*, not only became the biggest best seller in the history of sports books, but the most influential book in the history of sports.

2. Herman Brix, UW football. After completing his Husky career in 1927 and participating in the Stockholm Olympics (1928), Brix became the first movie Tarzan, selected personally by creator Edgar Rice Burroughs. Brix, under the stage name of Bruce Bennett, followed up his appearance in *The New Adventures of Tarzan* (1935) with *The Lone Ranger* (1938), *The Man With Nine Lives* (1940), *Sahara* (1943), *Cheyenne* (1947), *The Treasure of The Sierre Madre* (1948) and *Daniel Boone* (1956).

1. Norm Dicks, UW football. An offensive-line letterman in 1961 and 1962, Dicks was first elected to the House of Representatives in 1976, representing the 6th Congressional District in Tacoma. He won 17 consecutive terms thereafter while serving on a variety of coveted committees, including the House Appropriations Committee and the Committee on Homeland Security.

"Most" Moments From Schrempf Celebrity Golf
:: The Groz (Dave Grosby)

In 2006, Seattle City Council member Nick Licata infamously said that NBA basketball would not be missed when it left since it offered little cultural value. Though he later apologized, damage was done. On the side of value, I offer Detlef Schrempf and wife, Mari. They created the Detlef Schrempf Foundation in 1993, which has raised more than $7 million for numerous local charities. The primary fundraiser is a charity golf tournament, which annually features a bizarre group of celebrities and pseudo-celebs. As the tournament's unofficial mascot and KJR radio host, I'd like to share the nine "most" moments from this Seattle institution.

9. Most durable pseudo-celeb. Remember the O.J. Simpson trial? At the beginning, there was the L.A. cop on the stand who kept saying, "This is wrong, O.J.," and "This is a shame, O.J." His name is Ron Schipp. He was invited in 1994 and has been back every year.

8. Most gutsy celeb move. Ex-NBA star David Robinson, the Admiral, on his back in the tee box with a golf tee and ball clenched in his mouth as the Golfing Gorilla (a local pro who performs stunts in a gorilla suit) sweeps his driver just above Robinson's face and pounds the ball down the fairway.

7. Most surprising celeb winner. This book's co-author, Mike Gastineau, went left when he should have gone right and flipped his golf cart into a ravine. Afterwards, a wobbly, scratched-up Gasman turned in his scorecard and found his team had won the tourney.

6. Second-most surprising celeb winner. Daredevil Robbie Kneivel. The madman from Sequim partied all night one year on the eve of tournament. After arriving at the course, he passed out on the putting green for three hours. Then won.

5. Most inappropriate and funny line. Knievel, that same morning on the ferry ride to the course. He and I were standing on the stern when he looked out and loudly exclaimed, "Fuck!" "What, what is it?" I said. "Awww," he growled. "My ex-wife just bobbed to the surface."

4. Most embarrassing moment. Many contenders here. How about NBA legend Bob Cousy teeing off in borrowed loafers and rented clubs because his were mysteriously lost? Did I mention he was wearing a coconut shell bra?

3. Is Groz full of crap or what? Our favorite KJR radio quiz show features me making bold statements. Listeners guess whether I'm telling the truth and win prizes. Play along: Half these statements are true. See if you can pick the fabrications.

A. Ex-NFL star Thurman Thomas showed up at the tournament with zero golf equipment and subsequently bought clothes, shoes, and clubs at the course.

B. Sonics play-by-play man Kevin Calabro once hit a hole-in-one.

C. Former Sonics coach George Karl never played in the tournament.

D. Actor Brian Doyle Murray spent an hour with me at a bar telling inside stories about filming *Caddyshack*.

E. Ex-NBA player Brian Grant quit the tournament four holes in when it occurred to him that he'd never played golf.

F. Nick Licata has a real handle on the cultural value of basketball.

2. Most insane celeb move. Robbie Knievel bet Patrick Warburton (Puddy, from "Seinfeld") that he wouldn't jump off the second level of the ferry to the lower deck. This is not just frowned upon, but illegal. Warburton jumped and somehow survived. After many loud threats, the captain agreed to sail us all home.

1. Most amazing fans. The family on the course that provides a Margaritaville-style rest stop in their back yard for players. They've even moved a few times and the party moves with them.

By the way, B, C, and F are full of crap.

We know that Clay Bennett belongs with this bunch for hijacking the Sonics to Oklahoma City, but we deal with that clown on other pages. Seattle's most notorious prevaricators and defrauders:

10. Ken Behring, Seahawks, 1996. Trying to explain, if not justify, the Seahawks' sudden move to Los Angeles, the team's owner said he was so concerned about a major earthquake hitting the Kingdome that he would no longer permit the Seahawks to play in the facility. Behring based his fears on a seismic study that had never been released. "It's kind of ironic that Behring talks about earthquake risk and then he's locating to a stadium (Rose Bowl) that sits on the San Andreas fault," said Mariners president Chuck Armstrong.

9. Howard Schultz, Sonics, 2003. The Sonics owner told forward Desmond Mason on February 15 that he was a valued part of the franchise, which Mason interpreted to mean that he would not be traded. But the Sonics traded Mason, along with Gary Payton, days later to the Milwaukee Bucks. Said Mason, "If you feed me it, be true about it. Or just tell me you don't know. It's up in the air. Don't give me, `You will be here, or this is what we're going to do.' Just tell me you don't know, or don't say anything at all."

8. Jeff Smulyan, Mariners, 1990. Asked to respond to an *International Herald Tribune* report that the Mariners were in the process of being sold to a Japanese conglomerate, Smulyan said the story was, "absolutely and totally preposterous," adding, "We have no interest in selling this team. I have been dealing with newspapers for a long time and I've never seen a story make as little sense as this one. It's outrageous." Two years later, Smulyan sold the Mariners club to a group whose primary owner, Hiroshi Yamauchi, lived in Japan.

7. Rick Honeycutt, Mariners, 1980. During the third inning of a September 30 game against Kansas City in the Kingdome, the Royals grew suspicious of the special effects of Honeycutt's pitches and asked ump Bill Kunkel to check the ball and Honeycutt's gloved hand. Kunkel discovered a thumbtack taped to Honeycutt's index finger and also found a piece of sandpaper attached to the tape. Kunkel threw Honeycutt out of the game. As Honeycutt walked off the field he forgot about the tack and wiped his hand across his brow, opening a gash. Said Honeycutt after he was fined $250 and suspended for 10 days, "I haven't been in trouble like that since the last time I was sent to the principal's office."

6. George Argyros, Mariners, 1987. The Mariners owner declared on February 18 that his aim was not to move the team, telling reporters "that's our intent, to stay in Seattle." What he didn't say was that he had already contacted San Diego Padres owner Joan Kroc about purchasing her franchise.

5. Gaylord Perry, Mariners, 1982. The legendary spitballer and future Hall of Famer, pitching on a month-to-month contract, was ejected during the seventh inning of an August 23 game against the Red Sox for throwing a spitball. It marked the first—and only—ejection of Perry's career.

3. Al Martin, Mariners, 2001. For reasons known only to him, the Mariners outfielder compared a collision with teammate Carlos Guillen to the time he tried to tackle Michigan RB Leroy Hoard in 1986, a year in which Martin claimed to have played strong safety for the USC Trojans. Said Martin, "For some reason, I decided I could make a head-on stop of Hoard. I hit him, or rather he hit me. You remember those big tree-truck legs Hoard had? That's what hit me." Martin not only made this claim for years, he frequently talked about making other big tackles in USC games. But some elementary gumshoeing revealed that USC and Michigan did not play in 1986, that he had never attended USC, and that Martin had been an outfielder in the Atlanta Braves' system in 1986.

2. Rick Neuheisel, UW football, 2003. On February 10, Neuheisel denied he had met with San Francisco 49ers officials about the team's head coaching position, explaining that he had made a trip to San Francisco instead to play golf with a friend. "I have not been contacted by anyone from the 49ers organization about the position," Neuheisel said. "Categorically, no. Absolutely not." When it was discovered he had made the trip, and had talked to the 49ers about becoming their coach, Neuheisel issued a public apology through the University of Washington.

1. Maury Wills, Mariners, 1981. Prior to a Kingdome game on April 25, and in full view of Oakland manager Billy Martin, Wills instructed groundskeepers to enlarge the batter's box to aid Tom Paciorek's at-bats against Rick Langford. Martin waited until after the first pitch was thrown to lodge a protest. A "shocked and dumbfounded" Wills was suspended for two games and fined $500.

Guys Who Were Going Good, Then Went Elsewhere

The careers of numerous Seattle and state athletes blossomed away from the local gaze. Thanks to the splendid sweep of their careers, TV brought many of their achievements back home, even if they didn't visit often enough.

12. Tim Lincecum. The University of Washington graduate, San Francisco's first-round draft pick in 2006, played his first full season in the major leagues in 2008, went 18–5, led the National League in strikeouts (265), finished second in wins and ERA (2.62), set a bundle of Giants records, and won the NL Cy Young Award.

11. Grady Sizemore. The Cascade High (Everett) graduate signed a letter of intent to play football at the University of Washington, but opted instead for a career in major league baseball. After spending four years in the minor leagues, he became Cleveland's leadoff hitter, a *Sports Illustrated* cover boy (May 11, 2007), and a two-time All-Star. In 2008, his fifth year in the majors, Sizemore received MVP consideration after hitting 33 home runs from the leadoff position.

10. Mel Stottlemyre. In an 11-year career with the New York Yankees, the righty from little Mabton, near Yakima, had a 164–139 record with a 2.97 ERA, including three 20-win seasons. A five-time All-Star, he led the majors in innings pitched in 1965 with 291, which included 18 complete games. He became a popular pitching coach, serving stints with the Astros, Mets and Yankees, joining Joe Torre's staff in 1996 for a run of four World Series titles in five seasons. A resident of the Seattle suburb of Issaquah, Stottlemyre joined his adopted hometown team, the Mariners, in 2008.

9. Ron Santo/Ron Cey. The two Rons were All-Star third basemen, Santo from Seattle's Franklin High, Cey from Tacoma's Mount Tahoma High. Santo had a 14-year career with the Cubs starting 1960 in which he made 10 All-Star teams and won five Gold Gloves. Cey, who went to Washington State, had a 17-year major league career, 12 with the Dodgers. He was a six-time All-Star, as well as co-MVP of the 1981 World Series. "The Penguin" hit 316 home runs, Santo 342.

8. Earl Averill. The "Earl of Snohomish" was among the princes of baseball in the 1930s. An All-Star outfielder with Cleveland from from 1933–38, he hit over .300 in eight consecutive seasons. His most famous baseball moment was freakish—his line drive in the 1937 All-Star Game broke the toe of legendary pitcher Dizzy Dean, thwarting his career. The veterans committee selected Averill to the Hall of Fame in 1975.

7. Charlie Greene. An Arkansas native and an O'Dea High School grad (9.5 seconds in the 100 yard dash in 1963) who ran for the University of Nebraska, Greene was a star in the 1968 Olympics in Mexico City. He won a bronze in the 100 meters and, despite a hamstring injury, led off the 4x100 U.S. relay team that won gold. After his athletic career, he joined the Army and coached track at West Point. After retiring as a major, he headed Special Olympics International.

6. Don Coryell. A UW football player of no great distinction from 1949–51, Coryell became the first coach to win more than 100 games at the pro as well as collegiate levels. In 12 years at San Diego State, he had undefeated seasons in 1966, 1968 and 1969. In the NFL, he won division titles with the St. Louis Cardinals in 1974–75, and three more with the San Diego Chargers (1979–81). The "Air Coryell" passing scheme helped revolutionize the offensive game. He also tutored two coaches at San Diego State who did fairly well on their own—John Madden and Joe Gibbs.

5. Earl Anthony. If you were transfixed by bowling on TV in the 1970s—who wasn't?—and you saw the buzz haircut and the black horn-rims, you knew you were about to witness greatness. Anthony was the pre-eminent bowler of his era, perhaps ever. Born in Kent and raised in Tacoma, Anthony was a minor league pitcher until an ankle injury forced him to switch careers. "Square Earl" won 41 PBA titles and became the first pro bowler to win $1 million for a career. Bowler of the Year six times, he won the ABC Masters in 1977 and 1984 and is a member of the Bowling Hall of Fame. Anthony died in 2001 from a fall at age 63.

4. Tom Gorman. A graduate of Seattle Prep, where he was state champ three years in a row, and Seattle University, Gorman was the opposite of the pouty-brat stereotype common on tour. He was a part of the pro tennis world's elite in the 1970s. He won seven singles titles and nine doubles titles, was a member of the U.S.'s winning Davis Cup team in 1972 and ranked among the world's top 10 in 1974. He went on to coach the Davis Cup team for eight years, winning twice.

3. Gary Stevens. Born in Caldwell, Idaho, into a horse racing family, Stevens won riding titles at Longacres in 1983 and 1984 to launch a spectacular career as one of horse racing's greatest figures. He won more than $221 million in purses during his career, which included the Eclipse Award as the nation's best jockey in 1998. A three-time Kentucky Derby winner, Stevens starred as legendary jockey George Woolf in the 2003 movie *Seabiscuit*, which was nominated for an Academy Award.

2. Ryne Sandberg. A three-sport star at Spokane's North Central High, Sandberg passed on several college scholarship offers, including one from WSU to play quarterback, and was chosen in the baseball draft by the Phillies. In 1982, "Ryno" was traded to the Cubs in a deal Phillies fans still rue because by 1984, he was the National League's MVP. The Cubs saw him as a third baseman, but when they made a big free-agent signing, Tacoma native Ron Cey, Sandberg was bumped to second, where he adjusted well for 15 seasons. His stellar career was rewarded in 2005 with his selection to the Hall of Fame.

1. Fred Couples. He went from a Seattle muni-course rat to a star career on the PGA Tour. Couples graduated from Seattle's O'Dea High and won the Washington State Open at 19. Nicknamed "Boom Boom" for the big drives flying from his slim five-foot-eleven frame, Couples attended the University of Houston, then made a big mark on the tour, winning 15 events, including the Masters in 1992—a year in which he spent 16 weeks rated the world's No. 1 player—and the Players Championship in 1984 and 1996. He was twice named PGA Tour Player of the Year and twice won the Vardon Trophy for lowest scoring average. The king of the TV-created "Skins Game," Couples won five times in 11 invitations. His easygoing, self-effacing manner won him many fans in the galleries and within the tour.

An Odd Affair with the Sonics :: John Keister

A Seattle native, funnyman John Keister won numerous Emmy Awards when he hosted the locally legendary sketch comedy TV show, *Almost Live*. Less known are his perverse little moments with the team he used to root for, the Sonics.

3. Glove love. In the early 1990s, I was booked to do a TV commercial with The Glove himself, Gary Payton. After keeping us waiting for hours, Gary finally arrived and the first words out of his mouth were, "I can't be here too long!" I'd been on some commercial shoots that had taken eight hours, so in a way I was grateful that he cut it off after half an hour. "That's it. We're done!" he said. One more thing. They wanted him to sign my bald head. He looked at them, then at me, then back at them. "Sign his head?" He shrugged, I shrugged. He signed my head then the make-up person wiped off the ink. As he sped off in his Porsche I walked over to the executive producer. "Just out of curiosity," I asked, "How much did he get paid for what just happened?" "Twenty-five thousand dollars," he said. Silence. Then he seemed to feel the need to make me feel better. "We pay you what we pay Detlef Schrempf."

2. A.P. ocalypse. After college I got a job assisting a friend of mine who was working as a stringer for the *Associated Press* covering the Sonics. I was the "quote man" who ran between the locker rooms for quotes from the coaches and players. As I turn the corner into the Sonics locker room, I ran into a crowd of gigantic, naked men screaming at each other with early 1980's funk erupting from ghetto blasters. I couldn't hear anything and I didn't recognize most of the players. I had been warned: You don't realize how much you rely on jersey numbers to keep track. Then I spot the coach, Lenny Wilkens. My boyhood hero. Good old Lenny. He's always so nice on interview shows. He'll be nice to me. But Lenny is pissed. He's pissed at the players, pissed that Gus Williams is still holding out, pissed that the Sonics are in a slump. So pissed he sizzles like one of those bug zappers. I'm the first moth to flutter over. I mumble a question. Lenny fixes me with a stare. "What!" I turn and run. No quotes that night. To this day when I see Lenny Wilkens on television, a few drops of pee leak out of me.

1. Lost Key. A friend bought tickets to what figured to be the final Sonics season in Seattle. He invited me to a game. The seats were way up in the rafters. I looked over at the press table where my nerves long ago had been shot. The luxury suites I had been invited to when I was elevated to host of "Almost Live." The court where I had been asked to throw out the first ball during a number of playoff seasons. The team that had brought Seattle its only big-time national championship. The Sonics of the late 1960s–early 1970s were the bright spot in an economically devastated city. Forty years later, the Concorde, rival to Boeing's much-touted SuperSonic Transport (the team namesake that was never built), was a mothballed curiosity at the Museum of Flight at Boeing Field. The city's then-abandoned houses had been transformed by high-tech millionaires. Seattle was awash in money. At the opening tip, the crowd cheered and my friend leaned over and said, "Can you believe all this is going to go away?"

Didn't think this could be a list? Hah! Given our familiarity with rain, one would think we are experts on roofs. But no. Our two biggest indoor sports palaces leaked. But we have other ways to get out of games . . .

10. War, what is it good for? February 8, 2003. Due to the USA's impending war against Iraq, Major League Baseball canceled the Mariners' season-opening trip to Japan, where they had been scheduled to play the Oakland A's in a two-game series.

9. Earth day, May 2, 1996. An earthquake that registered 5.4 on the Richter scale rocked Seattle and the Kingdome, causing suspension of a Mariners game with Cleveland in the bottom of the seventh inning. The Mariners trailed 6–3 when the quake struck, forcing evacuation of the facility (the game resumed the next day when inspectors declared the Kingdome safe). "The earthquake freaked me out," said Mariners DH Edgar Martinez. "I didn't know whether to run or to stay."

8. Excuse me, is this arena taken? April 27, 1968. Seattle, champion of the Western Hockey League, and Rochester, the American Hockey League champion, were scheduled to meet in a championship series at the Seattle Coliseum, only to find out that the facility was booked. So was the Seattle Center Arena. With no venue available, the series was canceled, costing the disappointed Totems players at least $750 (guaranteed loser's share) and as much as $1,000 (guaranteed winner's share) from the playoff purse.

7. The absurd-inable snowmen, Cleveland, April 6–9, 2007. Ask the Mariners about global warming, and they will say bring it on. A classic Lake Erie snow dump lasting four days wiped out an entire Mariners series in Cleveland. Since it was the only time the teams were booked to play in Ohio, all games had to be made up one at a time during mutual off-days. The Mariners, who traditionally travel more air miles than any other MLB team, claimed the extra travel was a burden on their season. It also ranked as one of baseball's strangest weather-related developments since May 1945, when torrential rains wiped out every American League contest on the schedule for four consecutive days.

6. What part of "wet paint" don't you understand? April 11, 1969. In advance of the arrival of major league baseball in Seattle, workers began refurbishing—and expanding—Sicks' Stadium months before the April 11 Pilots' season opener. But by Opening Day, only 6,000 new seats had been added, less than half the number that was supposed to be installed. As the Pilots took the field for the first home game in franchise history, many fans had to wait outside while seats were put into place (some didn't get inside the stadium until the third inning). Those who did get in found workers still hammering nails and applying paint.

5. Hey, it's Seattle—you expected the Gobi Desert? October 29, 1924.
The nine-game Junior World Series, a minor-league matchup pitting manager Red Killefer's Seattle Siwashes against the St. Paul Saints, may as well have never been scheduled. Ten consecutive days of rain in Seattle virtually wiped out the series, which was called on October 29 after St. Paul won the only game played, 12–4, in front of 8,000 fans.

4. Doesn't rain like this in Seattle, Kansas City, October 4, 1998. At Arrowhead Stadium, Seattle and Kansas City played what was arguably the worst-weather game in Seahawks' history. The contest had to be suspended for 54 minutes due to lightning accompanying the monsoon. Standing water threatened to reach low-level electric panels. Rain was so fierce that the game was nearly impossible to see—either from the stands or on television. Halftime lasted just six minutes in an effort to assure the game's completion.

3. Basketball game, ppd. rain, January 5, 1986. Officials postponed a game between the Sonics and Phoenix Suns in the Coliseum on account of rain leaking through the arena roof, the first "rain out" in NBA history. The Suns led the Sonics 35–24 in the second quarter when water began to pour through the roof. A tarp duct-taped to the roof earlier that day during a construction project had blown off and the trickle of raindrops soon turned into a steady stream at halfcourt. Some of the 5,679 fans pulled out their umbrellas to protect themselves. The game was re-started the next day and the Suns won, 117–114.

2. Just a little pandemic—everyone stay calm, March 18–27, 1918. The Seattle Metropolitans' second consecutive appearance in the Stanley Cup Finals turned into a real-life disaster when the championship series with the Montreal Canadiens, tied at 2–2–1, was cancelled due to the worldwide Spanish influenza pandemic, which felled most of the Montreal players. One Canadiens player, Joe Hall, died in a Seattle hospital, and Montreal manager George Kennedy was bedridden for months and never fully recovered, dying a few years later. Montreal offered to forfeit the Cup to Seattle, which refused. So for the only time since the trophy's inception in 1893, the Stanley Cup was not awarded.

1. Roof, roof, roof for the home team, July 19, 1994. A few hours before the start of a Mariners-Orioles game in the Kingdome, four acoustic ceiling tiles weighing 26 pounds each came loose from the underside of the Dome's concrete roof and crashed into the seats behind home plate as the Mariners were taking batting practice. The game was postponed and the Kingdome shut down for four months, forcing the Mariners to play the remainder of what became a strike-shortened season—20 games over the next 22 days—on the road. The repair bill came to $55.1 million. In addition, the urgent work also claimed the lives of two workers, who were killed in a crane accident. King County was forced to pay the Mariners $4.1 million and the Seahawks $2.7 million for the inconvenience of having no place to play. The building's vulnerability was exposed, giving leverage to each team that wanted its own publicly funded stadium. They got them, and the Kingdome was imploded six years later.

In a capitalist society, almost everything can be given a value. In a sports-mad society, almost anything of value will be traded, discarded, extorted, devalued and overvalued in pursuit of an edge.

9. Gaylord Perry's quirky contract, 1983. Figuring that the 44-year-old pitcher didn't have much left in his tank, the Mariners signed Perry, a future Hall of Famer, to a month-to-month contract instead of the usual guaranteed year. When Perry's record fell to 3–10 on June 27, the Mariners cut him, owing him only for three months' work. Somehow, the idea never caught on with the players' union.

8. A manager dealt for players, 2002. When the Mariners allowed Lou Piniella to forego the final year (2003) of a three-year contract so he could manage in a city closer to his Tampa, Fla., home, they did so with the understanding they would get value in return. They did. When Piniella signed with the Tampa Bay Devil Rays, the Mariners received All-Star outfielder Randy Winn and infielder Antonio Perez—the first known players-for-a-manager swap since 1976, when the Pirates traded catcher Manny Sanguillen to the A's for their manager, Chuck Tanner.

7. Rick Mirer's end-of-world contract, 1993. After Notre Dame quarterback Rick Mirer, selected No. 2 overall in the NFL draft by the Seahawks, signed five, one-year contracts worth $15.6 million, it came to light that the deal included 59 off-the-wall incentive bonuses, including one that called for Mirer to receive $3 million if the Seahawks improved by just one game on its 2–14 record in 1992—whether Mirer played or not. The contract also contained a clause guaranteeing Mirer's deal "up to and including the end of the world." Commissioner Paul Tagliabue voided the package, calling it a "sham" that violated the league's labor agreement.

6. Jeff Nelson's bone chips on eBay, May 23, 2002. After the Mariners reliever underwent surgery to remove chips from his pitching elbow, he placed them in an eBay auction at the urging of KJR sports talk show host Dave Mahler. Nelson didn't think anyone would bid on his bone chips, but a lot of people did. The opening bid was $250. In the span of an hour, 68 additional bids were made, pushing the price to $12,000. When bidding peaked at $23,600, e-Bay called a halt, saying that it was against its policy to list body parts on its web site.

5. Mariners play Chicken, 1979. Following a 104-loss season in 1978, the Mariners figured they needed to do something to attract some customers (they drew 877,440 fans and had alienated thousands of potential ticket buyers by relocating the inexpensive bleacher seats to the nether reaches of the Kingdome's third deck). So they teamed up with broadcast partner KVI radio and offered a three-year, $250,000 contract offer to the San Diego Chicken, hoping to lure the popular mascot to Seattle. The Chicken wasn't impressed. Had he accepted, the Chicken would have made $75,000 for the 1979 season. That year the average Mariner made $61,830.

4. Extortion, Huskies booster style, 2007. Ed Hansen, a lawyer, multimillionaire, University of Washington alum, former three-term Everett mayor and big-money football booster, did not want the University of Washington to retain football coach Tyrone Willingham (Hansen believed Willingham had completely mucked-up the program). He sent an e-mail to President Mark Emmert that said, "I hereby pledge to contribute a minimum of $100,000 towards a law school scholarship within 90 days, conditioned upon the termination of Ty Willingham as football coach. In addition, I hereby pledge a second $100,000 towards a law school scholarship within 90 days, conditioned upon the termination of Todd Turner as athletic director." The UW elected to retain Willingham, but fired Turner. As for the twin $100,000 offers, Emmert called them "grossly inappropriate."

3. Psst, wanna buy a player? 1990. Long before the Mariners were able to command one of the richest local cable TV packages in the major leagues, they had this situation: owner Jeff Smulyan asked broadcast partner KSTW-TV to buy free agent first baseman Nick Esasky as part of the franchise's attempt to get more benefits from its TV contract. The idea was abandoned as unworkable.

2. Paparazzi and Ichiro, 2001. Shortly after Ichiro Suzuki joined the Mariners, a Japanese web publisher reportedly offered a $2 million bounty for anyone who could provide a picture of him in the buff. The Mariners dismissed the story as a crazy rumor, but Ichiro apparently wasn't so sure. He took precautions by putting his uniform on behind closed doors, behind pillars and in obscure hallways—anywhere but at his locker. Half-joked Seattle pitcher Paul Abbott, "Guys are trying to figure out how to get a mini-camera in here and then split the money."

1. Traded for a team bus, 1983. In one of the goofier barters in sports history, the Seattle Breakers (Western Hockey League) traded the rights to left-winger Tom Martin to the Victoria, B.C., Cougars for a down payment on a team bus. Martin was playing at Denver University and said he wished to play professionally in his hometown of Victoria. The Spokane Flyers originally purchased the bus from Trailways in 1981 for $60,000. When the Spokane franchise folded, the Cougars purchased the bus, but it remained in the U.S. because Victoria could not afford to pay customs, excise and sales taxes. The Breakers finally obtained the bus for Martin as well as $35,000. "I didn't think much about it at the time," Martin recalled later. "But it was a real nice bus."

KJR-AM radio host Dave Mahler makes no apologies for his blatant boosterism of University of Washington athletics. Nor does he hide his contempt for all things Washington State.

8. Pullman ain't Chapel Hill. Talk to Cougs fans about basketball before 2006 and their eyes glaze over like dogs that want to please but can't comprehend what you're saying. Listen to Cougs fans since 2006 and you'll walk away convinced that Dr. James Naismith thought the game up on a beer bender at Pete's.

7. One date: November 22, 1997. The Boogers came to Husky Stadium looking for their first Rose Bowl berth in 67 years. They beat Washington 41–35, and after the game an intoxicated band of Neanderthals climbed the east-end goalpost underneath the scoreboard. Witnessing that was like watching a pig climb into a Ferrari.

6. Learn how to win. A little tip: When you win, all that should matter in the universe is what YOUR team is doing. In 2008, the WSU basketball team made the NCAA Sweet 16. However, no Cougars fan was aware of this event because they were all taking joy in the fact that Washington had lost to Valparaiso in the CBI tournament. I guess that's what happens when you're used to being a loser. You tend to gravitate toward the most comfortable situation.

5. You call that media friendly? Ever been inside a shanty? Then you know what it's like inside the Martin Stadium press box. Small, cold and reminiscent of the tree house you built when you were seven. By far, the worst football press area in the Pac-10. If the WSU media relations office tried any less to placate the journalists who cover the game, they'd be standing outside The Coug, waiting for drunk Betas to puke game reports onto their laptops.

4. But you didn't even go there! If I had a dollar for every time I heard that, I'd be able to afford tuition on a standard seven-year degree at WSU. I didn't attend the UW, so using Cougs logic, I am prohibited from any display of loyalty to their athletic programs. So you need to attend a university to be a fan? No wonder they made it so easy to get into Washington State.

3. Don't get cocky. After the 2003 Rose Bowl, the Cougars' second in five years, I actually heard someone refer to the WSU football team as a "powerhouse." If going to Pasadena twice in 71 years constitutes a powerhouse football program, then I guess Purdue should compare themselves to the Dallas Cowboys. They went twice in 34 years. You can always count on WSU to raise the bar for everyone, eh?

2. To Coug it. Losing has become such a tradition at WSU that it has developed new ways to describe achievements (or lack thereof). WSU's losing is so legendary that there is an official verb to describe it: to coug it—1. (U.S., idiomatic, slang) To suddenly lose a contest through reversal of fortune, mistakes or bad judgment. The phrase is analogous to "blow it," or "snatch defeat from the jaws of victory." Are you kidding me?

1. Go2Guy. They have infiltrated the media with their very own "GoCougGuy," Jim Moore, *Seattle Post-Intelligencer* columnist. This has got to be one of the most irritating examples of what happens when your stupid little brother wins a few games of H-O-R-S-E. This moron has two shticks. 1. Coug-deprecating humor is actually funny to the Cougs nation. 2. His greatest days are when the Huskies lose. He gets page 1 columns and has a radio show on KJR, but in typical Coug fashion, Go2Guy manages to be just good enough to make the Cougs happy, without actually being talented at all.

For the *Seattle Post-Intelligencer* columnist and shameless Cougar honk, not a day goes by when he doesn't see purple and chuckle.

8. Criminal element. If you're scoring at home, the number of crooks the UW football team has produced vs. the number of Heisman Trophy winners: Somewhere in the neighborhood of 275–0. Okay, I'm exaggerating. It might be 475–0. You can't call yourself a true Husky without having a scrape with the law. And if you really want to be one of the all-time greats, all you have to do is sign your letter of intent, get drunk and bash windshields with your fists or drive into a rest home, and you're in as a Husky who will be revered forever! If you're not drunk enough to bash windshields, that's okay, you can make like center Olin Kreutz and just sucker-punch a teammate. At Washington, you're allowed to be criminally creative.

7. Ah, women's hoops. Let's not forget this wonderful program. When coach June Daugherty was fired at the end of the 2006–07 season following another NCAA Tournament appearance, athletic director Todd Turner said there just wasn't enough "buzz" about the women's basketball team. So he canned Daugherty and hired Tia Jackson. Turns out that Turner was right—there's more buzz now. Four players and an assistant coach left the team since the end of the 2007–08 season, probably more by the time this book is published. Everybody's wondering what's going on. I guess that's buzz.

6. Dave "Softy" Mahler. This blabbermouth hosts a weekly show during the football season called "Husky Honks" in which he and former player Hugh Millen and ex-coach Dick Baird somehow fill an hour with drip, drip, drip, homer-filled drivel. I'm amazed that Mahler has not been inducted into the Broadcasting Hall of Fame for his work on "Husky Honks," but that must be an oversight that will be corrected soon. It's interesting to note Mahler never attended Washington, but he did go to Bellevue High, which is perfect because it, too, is loaded with jock-sniffing boosters, ideal for cultivating future U-Dub fans.

5. Speaking of Don James. I don't hate the man, never have. He was a terrific coach who in retirement plays a lot of golf. But Husky fans forget that their god of all things football resigned in protest over Pac-10 sanctions. He quit on his team. This was like the captain of a sinking ship taking the first lifeboat, though I didn't blame him for that—if I were associated with Husky football, I'd want to get the hell out of there, too.

4. Even the men's hoopsters. I loved it in 2006 when Quincy Pondexter told a reporter after his freshman season that he would not declare for the NBA draft. This was after he averaged about three points a game. In his defense, he was just being a Husky, having an inflated opinion of himself.

3. Delusional Dawgs. UW fans always think the Dawgs are something special even when they're not. As proof, the Huskies actually held a big whoop-tee-doo in 2007, paying tribute to the 1960 team by declaring it the national champion. One problem: they weren't the national champions that year. But when you're from Washington, you just make things up and pretend you're great.

2. Living in the past. That's where all of their fans are, back in the James era when the Huskies miraculously won more games than they lost, year after year. They should be celebrating the true tradition of Husky football, which started this century with Pac-10 violations and continued with second-division finishes.

1. Over-the-top boosters. Ed Hansen is a prominent businessman and former mayor of Everett, 20 miles north of Seattle. By most accounts, he's a good man. But he's also a goof, consumed by his passion for the Huskies. In a 2007 e-mail to UW President Mark Emmert, Hansen wrote he would donate $100,000 for the dismissal of football coach Tyrone Willingham and another 100K for the dismissal of athletic director Todd Turner. Hansen wrote he was embarrassed to be a Husky and can't wear the school colors in public. Rumor is he still sleeps with his purple pacifier and gold blankie, dreaming of better years to come.

Best Apple Cup Gum Flaps

Verbal pre-game decorum rarely prevails in the Apple Cup rivalry, regardless of whether Washington and Washington State are ranked or wretched or both. For more than 100 years, the Huskies and the Cougars have traded zings, barbs and insults, with the Golden Age of Apple Cup gum flapping starting in the 1980s. The Best Apple Cup smack:

"Everybody needs something to hate. The Huskies make it nice.'"

Jim Walden, WSU coach, before the 1986 Apple Cup.

"They've got a lot of great dancers on their team. Too bad they can't hit as well as they dance."

Timm Rosenbach, WSU quarterback, after LOSING the game in 1987, 34–19.

"Nothing in my job—not the Rose Bowl, not the Holiday Bowl, nothing—is more important than beating the University of Washington."

Jim Walden, WSU coach, before the 1982 Apple Cup.

"It doesn't matter if you have a 1–10 season. Beating the Huskies is everything."

Will Derting, WSU linebacker, after the Cougars defeated the Huskies 26–22 in the 2005 Apple Cup.

"No matter what happens, they have to go back to Pullman, and I feel sorry for them."

Chris Chandler, UW quarterback, before the 1987 Apple Cup.

"The Huskies either win and they're obnoxious about it, or they lose and have excuses."

Robbie Tobeck, former Cougar offensive lineman, before the 2000 Apple Cup.

"I'll count every one of them. I'm going to ask myself, 'What did I do as a football coach today to beat the Huskies?'"

Dennis Erickson, WSU coach, after the 1987 Apple Cup, referring to the 365 days before the next Apple Cup.

"One game doesn't make a season, but the people who say that haven't participated in the Apple Cup."

Mike Price, WSU coach, before the 1991 Apple Cup.

"I'm a 2,000-word underdog."

Don James, UW coach, on his loquacious counterpart, Jim Walden, in 1985.

"None of my kids are going to be at WSU, because I want them to be able to get a job some day."

Jordan Reffert, UW defensive tackle, before the 2007 Apple Cup.

"This is the potatoes, gravy, stuffing, peas and everything."

Marlin Brown, WSU defensive end, after the Cougars' 32–31 victory over the UW in 1988.

"I've always felt that being a Cougar prepares you well for life. You learn not to expect too much."

Don James, UW coach, before the 1983 Apple Cup.

"There are four important stages in your life. You're born, you play the Huskies, you get married and you die."

Dan Lynch, WSU offensive lineman, explaining his view of the rivalry in 1984.

More than 40 years after his Seattle arrival, Sonny Sixkiller remains a Huskies quarterback icon. Unlike his WSU counterpart, Jack Thompson, he left himself off his own list. He is, however, from Ashland, OR, which is useful in reading this list.

10. Paul Sicuro. Led the Huskies to the Orange Bowl in 1985. He was the second-best quarterback from Ashland, OR.

9. Gene Willis. He's the only guy to ever quarterback the wishbone at UW. And he's the third-best quarterback from Ashland, OR.

8. Mark Brunell. Extremely composed quarterback with a highly accurate arm (even though he threw from the wrong side.)

7. Billy Joe Hobert. UW won every game he ever started at quarterback. He led the Dawgs to a huge win at Nebraska in 1991 and to the 1991 co-national championship.

6. Steve Pelluer. A very athletic quarterback who led the Huskies to a big win over Michigan at Husky Stadium in 1983.

5. Cary Conklin. Big kid from eastern Washington (it's always great to get the good ones away from Pullman!) Set a season mark for yardage in 1989.

4. Chris Chandler. Very gifted. Started it all off with a great win over USC in his sophomore year.

3. Marques Tuiasosopo. Great leader, very competitive and led the Dawgs back to the Rose Bowl in 2001.

2. Bob Schloredt. Won two Rose Bowls while playing both QB and DB.

1. Warren Moon. Led the Dawgs to the 1978 Rose Bowl and made the NFL Hall of Fame.

The "Throwin' Samoan" came out of Seattle's Evergreen High in 1975 to Washington State, where he ended his college career as the then-leading passer in NCAA history with 7,818 yards. His name remains thick in the WSU record book.

10. Clete Casper (1980–82). Casper would have flourished even more in a pass-oriented offense. He led the Cougs to a big upset win over the Huskies in the 1982 Apple Cup.

9. Matt Kegel (2003). Had one terrific season as a starter with 10 wins and a big-time Holiday Bowl victory over the No. 5 Texas Longhorns. Showed tremendous class as Jason Gesser's back up.

8. Alex Brink (2004–07). Shattered nearly every school quarterback record. If only he had better defenses to match his offense.

7. Ty Paine (1970–72). Only other college QB I idolized outside of Sonny Sixkiller. Ty epitomized, for me, what it was to be a Cougar QB. He is why I wore No. 14.

6. Mark Rypien (1983–85). Great athlete who had a gun for an arm but played for mostly run-oriented offenses under coach Jim Walden. Best golfer of the bunch, by far.

5. Timm Rosenbach (1986–88). Tough, strong-willed QB who led his 1988 team to the Aloha Bowl. Helped set stage for the Mike Price years and their bowl appearances.

4. Drew Bledsoe (1990–92). Best pure passer of them all. The 1992 Apple Cup game was one for the ages. First pick in the 1993 NFL draft.

3. Ryan Leaf (1995–97). Boldly took the Cougs to a new frontier (first Rose Bowl in 67 years). In 1997, he had the best single-season performance of any Cougar QB in history.

2. Jason Gesser (1999–02). Took us to a Rose Bowl and a Sun Bowl with 20 wins his last two seasons. Broke all the long-standing QB career records along the way. After suffering a severe high-ankle sprain vs. UW, he played the UCLA game (which WSU had to win to go to the Rose Bowl) with his ankle in a soft cast. Gutsiest Cougar QB performance ever.

1. Jack Thompson (1975–78). Hey it's my list, who else did you think I was going to put No. 1?

Sometimes you make history. Sometimes history makes you. Seattle teams have been posterized in original and startling ways by famous and not-so-famous athletes.

11. Earl Boykins' 15 Overtime Points, January 18, 2005. The 5–5 Boykins entered an overtime session against the Sonics having scored just three points. Then he exploded for 15, breaking the NBA record for most points in overtime, as the Nuggets beat the Sonics 116–110. Butch Carter of Indiana had held the record, 14 against Boston on March 20, 1984.

10. Kobe drains a dozen treys against Sonics, January 7, 2003. Bryant established an NBA record by making 12 3-point shots in Los Angeles' 119–98 victory over the Sonics at the Staples Center. He beat by one the mark set by Orlando's Dennis Scott on April 18, 1996.

9. Mariano Rivera's 3-pitch inning, October 21, 2001. In the top of the ninth of Game 4 of the ALCS, with the Yankees ahead 3–1 and the Mariners desperate for a win to even the series, New York closer Mariano Rivera retired John Olerud on a first-pitch groundout, Stan Javier on a first-pitch bunt groundout, and Mike Cameron on a first-pitch pop fly. The Mariners became the first team since World War II to go down on three pitches in a postseason inning.

8. Moses Malone's 21 offensive rebounds, February 11, 1982. In a 117–110 Houston victory over the Sonics, the Rockets' center broke his own NBA single-game record of 19, set against the New Orleans Jazz in 1979. The record still stood entering 2008–2009, and the Sonics still haven't blocked him out.

7. Glyn Milburn runs all over the Seahawks, December 10, 1995. Milburn nearly ran the Seahawks out of Mile High Stadium, compiling an NFL-record 404 all-purpose yards. The five-foot-eight, 177-pound Milburn rushed 18 times for 131 yards, caught five passes for 45, returned five kickoffs for 133, and five punts for 95. Milburn's performance broke a 34-year-old NFL record held by Billy Cannon of the Houston Oilers, who compiled 373 yards against the New York Titans on December 10, 1961.

6. John Valentin's unassisted triple play, July 8, 1994. The story of the day was supposed to be the major league debut of Seattle's 18-year-old shortstop, Alex Rodriguez. But in the sixth inning, the Boston shortstop turned the 10th unassisted triple play in major league history. After Mike Blowers singled and Kevin Mitchell walked, Marc Newfield cracked a line drive that Valentin snagged. He tagged out Blowers near second base and got Mitchell coming down from first.

5. Willie Parker's 75-yard Super Bowl run, February 5, 2006. Two snaps into the second half of Super Bowl XL, Parker turned one of the Steelers' bread-and-butter plays—a right counter off guard Alan Faneca—into the longest run in Super Bowl history. Parker's 75-yard score was the key play in Pittsburgh's 21–10 victory.

4. Mark McGwire's 538-foot homer, June 24, 1997. The instant it left his bat, everyone knew it was not only a long home run, it was a threat to rip a gash in the time-space continuum. The pitch from Mariners ace Randy Johnson reached McGwire at 97 mph. According to Mariners officials, when it left McGwire's bat, it was going 105 mph. It traveled on a rising liner, finally crashing eight rows up into the third deck, an estimated 538 feet away. The longest home run in Northwest history was the most talked-about play of a night that also included Johnson becoming the first AL left-hander to whiff 19 batters in a game, including McGwire twice.

3. Francisco Rodriguez's 58th Save, September 13, 2008. The Angels closer, who had tied Bobby Thigpen's major league saves record two nights earlier against Seattle, took the record for his own when he fanned Raul Ibanez to end a 5–2 victory over the Mariners in Anaheim.

2. Derrick Thomas's seven sacks, November 11, 1990. The Kansas City linebacker spent the entire game in the Seahawks backfield, setting an NFL record by sacking Seattle quarterback Dave Krieg seven times. The Seahawks still won.

1. Roger Clemens fans 20 Mariners, April 29, 1986. A 23-year-old Clemens, in his first full season as a starter that would produce a 24–4 record, struck out a major league record 20 batters in Boston's 3–1 victory at Fenway Park. Short-stop Spike Owen became Clemens' 19th victim to open the ninth, and Phil Bradley whiffed a fourth time to become the 20th when he took a called third strike.

Dan Raley, a Roosevelt High and Western Washington University grad, has local roots as deep as anyone in Washington sports media. A staffer at the *Seattle Post-Intelligencer* since 1980, his popular "Where Are They Now?" feature has made him the personality curator of local sports figures. The University of Washington's long tradition of football is Raley's motherlode. Here's his list of five of the most intriguing football characters and episodes.

5. Ralph Bayard, Gregg Alex, Lamar Mills and Harvey Blanks, 1969.

The African-Americans were banished from the team during the upheaval surrounding civil rights and race issues that were consuming the UW as well as campuses across America. The dismissals were said to be because each failed to give a loyalty oath to coach Jim Owens. They thought otherwise. Some received death threats. All were labeled outlaws to some degree. The turmoil helped create one of the worst seasons (1–9) in UW history. But the bad-guy labels didn't stick. In order, they became a UW assistant athletic director, minister, public defender and actor.

4. George Jugum, 1966–68.

A tough guy with an unbridled temper, he was complimented for his fearless play at linebacker by USC running back O.J. Simpson in 1968 after a particularly brutal game won 14–7 by the Trojans in Los Angeles. Within the decade, Jugum would be imprisoned after losing control and killing a high school kid who gave him the finger. Twenty years following that ordeal, Simpson would find himself in a similar position, accused of rage-inspired murder—yet acquitted of the stabbing deaths of his wife and her friend.

3. Donnie Moore, 1965–66.

A powerful running back from Tacoma with calves the size of toddlers and the strength of two men, Moore had enough talent to carry the Huskies to the Rose Bowl. In 1966, he had the nation buzzing when he went into Ohio State and smashed records by churning out 221 yards on 30 carries and scoring twice in a startling 38–22 whipping of the Buckeyes. One of Moore's virtues was loyalty. He wore his letterman's jacket everywhere. One of his liabilities was he couldn't help himself when it came to personal indulgences. He was a first-time father at 15 and dad to three when he left high school. Two weeks after wowing everyone in Ohio, Moore and teammates showed up in a tavern after being told it was taboo. Moore was the only one wearing his jacket. He was suspended indefinitely. Curiously, Moore showed great discipline after his football banishment. He was drafted and worked his way up to Army sergeant in 11 months and became a leader. Feeling disgraced, if not treated in a prejudicial manner, Moore didn't attend another UW game or practice until more than three decades later, when he showed unannounced at a preseason practice in Olympia and was welcomed enthusiastically.

2. Hugh McElhenny, 1949–51. "The King" was arguably the greatest player in Husky football history, if not the highest paid. The fleet, shifty running back from Los Angeles turned up after leaving USC because the school reneged on a promised $65 monthly stipend for the arduous chore of watering the grass around the Tommy Trojan statue. Washington made his stay in Seattle so profitable, people used to joke that McElhenny took a pay cut when he moved to the NFL and the San Francisco 49ers, and McElhenny used to laugh because it was true. He received a combined $10,000 per year from the Huskies, counting his $75 monthly scholarship, an insurance company job for his wife, Peggy, and an extra $300 monthly payout. That didn't include a Palm Springs honeymoon, airline tickets and hotel stay that were funded when he first arrived, or the cars, clothes, furniture and extra cash. As a 49ers rookie in 1952, the first-round draft pick received a modest $7,000 salary. Years later, McElhenny was asked to play in a Seahawks golf charity event. His flight and hotel would be covered, not his meals. He declined over the absence of meal money. The King was used to getting everything paid for. He asked, "Was that bad of me?"

1. Robert "Spider" Gaines 1977–79. A Rose Bowl hero and Warren Moon's favorite wide receiver, Gaines was supposed to be a first-round NFL draft pick in 1979. A world-class hurdler, he was seeking a spot on the Olympic team before the boycott of the Moscow Games. By the mid-1980s, after blowing out a knee and exhausting his chances in the Canadian Football League, Gaines became a pimp in Vancouver, B.C. Answering to the street name "Slam," Gaines rode around in a limo wearing a boa. Canadian authorities interceded and deported him. "Don't use the word P-I-M-P," Gaines suggested when describing his career move. "Make it gigolo."

For every sports idea that makes it, there's a bunch that don't. Here's a sampling of Seattle's best, or worst, depending on your perspective.

10. A Rival For Longacres, 1984. Washington National would have been Western Washington's second thoroughbred track, following Longacres. It would have opened in 1985–86, cost about $40 million, and would have been located in Sumner. It would have featured five days of racing per week during the winter. Not a shovel of dirt was ever turned to make it happen.

9. Harness racing gets the whip, 1982. For a brief period in the early 1980s, when Longacres was prospering and before the introduction of the state lottery, several groups wanted to build a harness racetrack in the Puget Sound area and conduct winter racing. The brains behind the proposed $25 million Auburn Downs project was sure of the market desires. But despite months of labor over financing and location, the project died.

8. The Seattle Nyets, 1989. In advance of the 1990 Goodwill Games, a mini-Olympics featuring athletes from the U.S. and then-Soviet Union, a Seattle sports-event firm, Bob Walsh & Associates, proposed to the National Hockey League that it grant a franchise to Seattle stocked exclusively with players from the Soviet Union. The NHL nixed the idea, commissioner John Ziegler calling it "unworkable."

7. Pacific Rim sports summit, 2004. This was supposed to be an Olympics-style competition for two weeks in 2006 that would have attracted world-caliber athletes from 10 Pacific Rim nations, plus Russia. The event was scotched in just six months when the U.S. Olympic Committee, which originally proposed it, ultimately refused to fund the competitions or fulfill any contractual obligations with the local Seattle Organizing Committee. The SOC wound up suing the USOC and won a $3.5 million arbitration award.

6. Cable-TV ahead of its time, 1981. Walsh & Associates proposed a first in national-cable sportscasts to the Sonics: A subscription for all 82 games for one price. Implemented largely by the firm's vice president, Rick Welts, the SuperChannel was initially profitable. But team owner Sam Schulman sold SuperChannel to Group W as soon as fans discovered that it was easier and cheaper to watch on TV than to attend games in person. Fifteen years later, NBA and MLB games were all over paid cable (albeit on regional or national networks), and attendance was enhanced, not hurt.

5. Challenge Bowl, 1978–79; Seattle Bowl, 2001–02. Post-season college games don't quite cut it here, mostly because December is no time to be outdoors in this neighborhood. The Challenge Bowl was an all-star gig featuring seniors from the Big 10 and Pac-10 conferences at the Kingdome, and lured a number of future NFL stars, but not fans. Attendance never exceeded 21,000 for either game, and it was canceled. In 2001, Safeco Field hosted Stanford and Georgia Tech in the first Seattle Bowl. Next season at Qwest Field, it was Wake Forest and Oregon. There was no third game.

4. 2012 Olympic Games, 1996. Based on its successful staging of three NCAA Final Fours (1984, 1989, 1995) and the 1990 Goodwill Games, the Seattle Organizing Committee behind those events learned that, with a proper presentation, it stood a chance of becoming the U.S. bid city for the 2012 Summer Olympic Games. SOC worked for nearly two years and spent nearly $500,000 mounting the presentation. It needed only authorization from the City Council before making its pitch to U.S. Olympic officials. But the council voted 8–1 against, saying Seattle didn't need the hassle of an Olympics.

3. Stadium dreams, 1990s. Former Sonics owner Barry Ackerley desired to construct a palatial new basketball/hockey arena on a lot he owned south of the Kingdome. A lack of suitable financing, as well as no owner for an NHL team, derailed the sportswriter-dubbed "Ack-Dome." "Stardome" was the brainchild of real estate maven John Torrance, whose idea was to build a baseball stadium with a retractable roof in the north parking lot of the Kingdome. That didn't fly, either. But . . . a baseball stadium with a retractable roof (Safeco Field) was built on the once-proposed site of the Ack-Dome, and an exhibition center and football stadium went up on the site of the old Kingdome.

2. A bullfight at the Coliseum, 1967. Two Seattle-area promoters, William Leopold and Don Nicholson, sought the City Council's approval to stage a bullfight in the Coliseum as part of the Seafair celebration. But the city's license chiefs turned them down, ruling that a bullfight ran contrary to a state law, originally enacted in 1901 to halt cock fighting, that prohibited cruelty to animals. The promoters threatened a $200,000 lawsuit, but nothing came of it.

1. A floater, 1960. During the planning for the 1962 World's Fair, Century 21 Exposition organizers briefly considered the idea of building a floating stadium on Elliott Bay, at the foot of Harrison Street, as a way to attract a professional football franchise. A group of Seattle architects and contractors pushed the idea, and Seattleites seemed to like it. But they didn't like the idea of paying for it. Nevertheless, discussions on how to build a stadium, its location and how to pay for it evolved over the years. Finally, a 1968 bond measure won voter approval, creating a land-based domed stadium, the Kingdome.

Compared to some bigger markets, Seattle hasn't had quite the same load of compost piled upon its sports outfits. Which is not to say that the *National Enquirer* couldn't justify establishment of a sports bureau in the area.

10. Maury Wills and cocaine. After his dubious, brief career as Mariners manager ended with his midseason firing in 1981, Wills was arrested in December 1983 in Los Angeles on a car-theft charge. The car turned out to be borrowed, but the cops found cocaine on him, confirming the worst fears of Don Newcombe, the Los Angeles Dodgers coordinator of alcohol and drug programs who said, "I took him to the Care Unit in May or June and admitted him. He walked out two weeks later, on his own, before being released. I asked him why he left and he said he didn't think he had a problem."

9. Ken Behring and disgruntled women, 1996. The Seahawks owner's misguided attempt to relocate the franchise to Los Angeles in February 1996 created the bigger headlines, but a smaller one actually summarized the essence of Behring. He asked his chief financial officer to prepare forms that would require Behring's extramarital sexual partners not to sue him or ask him for money, according to court filings in a sexual harassment suit against him by Patricia Parker, the former CFO of Behring's Blackhawk real estate firm. According to Parker, Behring wanted legal protection from female traveling companions who may end up unhappy.

8. High times at Montlake, 2003. In April, the UW released a report detailing the activities of Dr. William Scheyer, a former consulting physician to the school's softball program. In disturbing detail, it described how Dr. Scheyer and athletic department trainers dispensed thousands of doses of prescription drugs to players, often placing the athletes' health at risk. Before long, the UW was aswarm with DEA agents and State Patrol detectives. One player, not identified by name, stated that she was so high from medication that she was "giggly, loopy and laughing on the dugout floor." Another told a trainer that she had taken so many pills that she felt woozy and worried that she might get hit in the face with a ball. A trainer responded by telling the player to take a "focus pill" (said to be the stimulant Ritalin). Players were issued drugs to get up, drugs to stay on the field, and drugs to get down. In a two-year period, 3,100 doses of controlled substances were issued in the name of a single player. No one in charge at UW claimed to know anything. Athletic director Barbara Hedges, who had just presided over a gambling-rules fiasco with the football team, later characterized the myriad problems at the UW as "glitches." She eventually was urged to retire.

7. Seattle U.'s illegal aid, 1958. Just a month after the Chieftains lost the NCAA basketball championship game to Kentucky, head coach John Castellani resigned amid allegations that he offered illegal aid to recruits. The NCAA placed Seattle U. on probation.

6. Huskies football's first big bust by the NCAA, 1956. A slush fund set up by a downtown booster group, the Washington Advertising Association, came to light when fired head coach John Cherberg spilled the beans. In the wake of revelations that football players were receiving more money—$75 per month instead of the NCAA-allowable $60—than was permitted, the NCAA fined Washington $52,000, athletic director Harvey Cassill resigned and all UW athletic programs went on probation for two years.

5. Seattle U. point shaving, 1965. Seattle U. players "Sweet" Charlie Williams, the team captain and leading scorer, and Peller Phillips were arrested and accused of point shaving in a game against Idaho. They were kicked off the team.

4. Disarray in the Dawghouse, 2003. It started with a cell phone call in which UW football coach Rick Neuheisel was overheard—by *Post-Intelligencer* columnist John Levesque—expressing interest in becoming head coach of the San Francisco 49ers. Confronted about it, Neuheisel lied, saying he had no interest. By the time the story climaxed months later, Neuheisel had apologized for lying, but had also been caught participating in a high-stakes basketball betting pool. That was only part of it. The Pac-10 reprimanded the men's basketball program for secondary recruiting violations. An attempt to honor a former football coach, Jim Owens, also backfired when the athletic department failed to adequately review the program's racial history during his tenure. Among the numerous heads that rolled was Neuheisel's, who was fired, yet won a lawsuit against the UW and NCAA in which he claimed to have been fired unfairly. Three-quarters of the way through the serial messes, athletic director Barbara Hedges told the *Post-Intelligencer*, "Sometimes I wish I could put a bag over my head."

3. Clay Bennett and David Stern, April 2008. As part of legal discovery in the city's lawsuit against the Sonics to keep the team in Seattle (it obviously didn't work), an e-mail from August 2007 was made public from owner Clay Bennett to NBA Commissioner David Stern, which read in part: "David you know how I feel about our relationship both personally and professionally. You are among a very few, notwithstanding our relative brief actual physical time together, that have significantly affected my life. I view you as a role model and as an extraordinarily gifted executive, a deep and compassionate thinker, and a person with a rare and unique charisma that brings out the best in everyone you touch. You are just one of my favorite people on earth and I so cherish our relationship." To which any teenage girl writing in Facebook would respond: Ewwwww!

2. Huskies football mutiny, 1969. On October 30, UW football coach Jim Owens suspended four African American players—Gregg Alex, Ralph Bayard, Harvey Blanks and LaMar Mills—for "a lack of commitment to the team." In response, all of the team's other African American players refused to travel to Los Angeles to play UCLA. Under pressure from the university's administration, Owens reinstated all but Blanks less than two weeks later.

1. UW football's second big bust by the NCAA, 1992. After Billy Joe Hobert, who had quarterbacked the Huskies to the 1991 co-national championship, was discovered to have accepted an improper $50,000 loan from an Idaho man, his eligibility was revoked. Subsequent investigation discovered a no-work jobs program and other improper benefits to players. After three consecutive Rose Bowl appearances, UW went on NCAA probation (no TV, no bowl games) for two years. In the furor over additional Pac-10 sanctions, Don James resigned after 18 years as head coach 12 days before the 1993 season. The Huskies subsequently had four head coaches in the next 12 years, but only one more Rose Bowl appearance.

If you build it, they will come. But when you give something away, they'll knock down the doors to get in, evidenced by this list of Seattle's most unusual sports promotions.

5. Sue Bird broken-nose bandage night, October 10, 2004. It wasn't a team-sanctioned idea, but it was fun. To acknowledge the Storm guard's pancaked proboscis, many of the 17,072 fans on hand for the Storm's 67–65 victory over the Connecticut Sun in Game 2 of the WNBA finals, including team mascot Doppler, most every pre-teen girl and a few shameless grown-up men, wore strips of yellow tape on their noses as a sign of solidarity with Bird, who had played much of the postseason with a broken nose. A few fans even did the full Monty, sporting sweat-inducing facial transparent plastic masks – just like Bird.

4. Dave Valle Days, August 1991. During the dog days of the season, with Mariners catcher Dave Valle batting a myopic .136, a restaurant and bar near the Kingdome, Swannie's, launched a special promotion titled "Dave Valle Days." It worked like this: The price of well drinks or beers at the bar cost whatever Valle's batting average was. So if Valle had a .136 average, a drink cost $1.36. The promotion, which ran for six weeks, during which drinks (and Valle's average) fluctuated between $1.27 and $1.57, didn't elate Valle, but Swannie's proprietor, Jim Swanson, told reporters he wasn't worried about it. "If Dave Valle ever got mad and walked in the bar to confront me," he said, "I told my doorman to just give him a bat. That way I know I won't get hurt."

3. Buhner Buzz Cut Nights, 1994–01. During the first-ever "Jay Buhner Buzz Cut Night," held in 1994 near Gate D at the Kingdome, 512 fans happily had their locks, curls and cowlicks removed in the fashion of the Mariners' cueballed rightfielder, with Seattle resident Lori Hanson, a redhead, becoming the first woman to have her head buzzed. In all, seven Buhner Buzz Cut nights drew 22,302, including 298 women. The last one, in 2001, drew a record 6,246, including 112 women.

2. Dunk the owner, May 27, 1983. Sounders owner Bruce Anderson, who had riled local soccer fans for his systematic dismantling of what had been a championship-caliber team (he wanted to save money), decided to allow fans to vent at his expense. So Anderson climbed up on a chair suspended over a huge water tank. Fans fired soccer balls at a target. Every time their aim was accurate, Anderson's chair collapsed and he plunged into the drink. Perhaps the most appropriate remark about this buffoonery was that it enabled Anderson to emerge with a clean foot to stick in his mouth. Anderson wound up selling his portion of the Sounders for $1 to a previous owner.

1. Funny nose and glasses night, May 8, 1982. Two nights after Gaylord Perry won his 300th game, in front of a Kingdome throng of 27,369, a Funny Nose and Glasses Night Promotion at the Kingdome attracted a crowd of 36,716. Owner George Argyros and his wife, Julie, wore the glasses, as did many players. The relief pitchers wore them on their way to the bullpen. Manager Rene Lachemann wore them to home plate for the pregame meeting with umpires, one of whom, Tom Haller, took one look at Lachemann and said, "No wonder you guys are in last place." Haller had a point. That the promotion outdrew Perry's milestone was cited by baseball columnists and commentators for years as evidence that Seattle did not have the makings of a major league city.

George Karl coached the Sonics during the best period of sustained excellence in the history of Seattle's first (and now departed) pro sports franchise. From January 1992, until his contract was not renewed after 1998, the Sonics won 72 percent of their regular-season games and made the 1996 NBA Finals against the 72-win Chicago Bulls. Tumultuous players, led by Gary Payton and Shawn Kemp, preposterous outcomes of games and seasons and tense battles with management were hallmarks of the wildest times in Sonics annals. Karl offered up five stories of his Sonics days you may not have heard.

5. How to unload a stiff. In my first full season (1992–93), Bob Whitsitt (president and GM) knew I was a young coach being driven crazy by (lazy center) Benoit Benjamin. Bob said, "From November to February, you gotta play Benoit for me, then I'll get rid of him" at the trade deadline. Instead of a confrontation about a player I didn't want, he walked me through his plan. He wanted to showcase Benoit, but he would support me on the decision to play him with players and media. (On February 22, 1993) Bob traded Benoit (and the rights to unsigned draftee Doug Christie) to the Lakers for Sam Perkins. It was a tossup whether acquiring Perkins or Detlef Schrempf (in the fall) was the better trade, but Sam was huge for us. It was the first time a GM helped me with my career in something like that. He helped me be a better coach. I really enjoyed that relationship.

4. Rage against the machine, June 5, 1993. (Seventh game of the Western Conference finals in Phoenix; winner to go the Finals against Chicago and Michael Jordan.) The Suns, led by newcomer Charles Barkley, won 123–110, the most points given up by the Sonics all season, thanks mostly to 64 free throw attempts by the Suns, the most by a playoff team in 40 years. I remember the coaching staff talking me into staying in the game, because I wanted to get thrown out to protest the lopsided officiating. I was so angry. I told assistant coach Tim Grgurich, "I gotta get thrown out. This is ridiculous." Ninety percent of the time in that situation, I would have gotten myself thrown. But this was Game 7. What also pissed me off about that game was that legendary Washington fan/heckler Robin Ficker was flown in to sit behind our bench—such a classless thing to do. Everyone brings up the conspiracy theory that the NBA wanted Barkley and Jordan in the Finals. They didn't want us.

3. 1996 Finals Game 3. Lost to a traveling violation? In the 1996 Finals, Sonics met Chicago, perhaps the best of the Bulls six championship teams. Chicago won the first two at home and the first one in Seattle, but the Sonics won the next two to force a return to Chicago, where the Bulls won 87–75. Phil Jackson told my son (Coby Karl, who played for the Lakers in 2008) that a big reason we lost Game 3 so bad (108–86) was not a tactical error, but a travel error. After Game 2 ended late in Chicago, we flew right after the game, had to stop in Billings to refuel and got to Seattle maybe around 6 a.m. Saturday for a noon tip on Sunday. We never re-energized. We were dead in Game 3. The Bulls stayed in Chicago Friday night, then Saturday flew instead of practiced. Phil knew what we had done. That was maybe my inexperience in traveling in those circumstances. Game 3 was the only one in the series where I thought they dominated.

2. No Glove love, even at Christmas. Probably the ugliest confrontation Gary Payton and I had ruined Christmas one year. We played Phoenix (December 23, 1993, losing 87–86 to drop the Sonics record to 20–3). Gary had this individual challenge going with (Suns guard) Kevin Johnson that took away from the game plan—too much one-on-one. This is when he was trying to become an All-Star, and KJ was in front of him. Gary's a rough guy to confront during the game. So it boiled over afterward. We had a huge confrontation in the coaches' room. I threw things, he threw things. He yelled. I yelled. I remember him saying, "You're not my fucking father! I have a father!" I said, "I don't want to be your fucking father!" and Tim Grgurich is there, holding us apart. We tried to "kiss and make up" on Christmas Day, but I was miserable the rest of the week through New Year's Eve.

1. Shawn Kemp. What could have been. I realized early Shawn Kemp was very good on the court, and you worried about him off the court. On the court, no problem—he was coachable, workable. Getting him there in the right frame of mind, keeping him there, was always a tug of war. He taught me then that was the way the game was going. There are a lot of players like Shawn now. There are a lot of players who could be a little more professional, a little more coachable, a little more respectful. Getting Shawn to accept that was frustrating. One on one, he was great. It's when he got around others . . . was he a leader, a follower? We heard all the stories, but we never really knew. Deep down inside, he's got a great heart. There's no question he was the best player on the court for six games in the 1996 Finals. No question.

As sports grow ever more serious, it's important to remember those moments that establish that little boys lurk in adult clothing.

9. Pilfering the Rose Bowl trophy, February 3, 1992.
Burglars entered the lobby of the Tubby Graves building, home of the UW's athletic department, shattered a glass trophy case and made off with the 30-inch high, 50-pound trophy that the football team had been awarded for defeating Michigan in the Rose Bowl on New Year's Day. The trophy, valued at $3,000, was subsequently recovered at the University of British Columbia in a campus hangout known as the Cheese Factory. It had been swiped as part of an Engineering Week prank. "This is a pretty good stunt," one of the culprits told the *Vancouver Sun*. "It's one of my favorites—right next to the one in 1988 when we had the lights on the Lions Gate Bridge blinking in Morse code."

8. Jell-O Gate, 1982.
After arriving in Chicago to start a road trip, Larry Andersen, Richie Zisk and Joe Simpson of the Mariners went to a grocery store and purchased 16 boxes of Jell-O. After finagling their way into manager Rene Lachemann's hotel room, they poured the Jell-O into the toilet, sink and bathtub and then stuffed all of the furniture into the bathroom. According to an interview Andersen gave years later to http://www.astrosdaily.com, the players also unscrewed the telephone, removed all the light bulbs, and strung toilet paper all over the room. When Lachemann returned, he threatened to call police, so determined was he to find out the identity of the culprits. That wasn't the end of it. Jell-O pranks followed Lachemann all season (once, when he went to take a swig of beer, he discovered that someone had poured the beer out of the can and replaced it with Jell-0), and it wasn't until the end of the year that Andersen, Zisk and Simpson revealed themselves—by showing up at a team party wearing giant Jell-O boxes over their heads.

7. Brian Bosworth's T-shirt scam, 1987.
In the days before his first NFL game at Denver's Mile High Stadium, Bosworth told reporters he was looking forward to playing against Elway, whom he repeatedly characterized as "Mr. Ed," of sitcom notoriety. Said Bosworth, "You very rarely get a chance to get a shot on somebody like that. I'm going to take as many hard shots as I can get on him." Asked if wanted to hurt Elway, Bosworth replied, "Yeah, that's just the way I approach the game. It might cost us 15 yards for roughing, but I'm not going to pull off on him." Having enraged Denver fans with his trash talk, Bosworth (and his agent) secretly printed up dozens of "Boz-Buster" t-shirts bearing his image, and made a tidy sum selling them to duped Broncos' fans.

6. Terrell Owens and his Sharpie, December 1, 2002.
After scoring a touchdown during a Monday Night game against the Seahawks, the San Francisco receiver took a marker out of his uniform pants and signed the football while standing in the end zone. Then he presented it to his manager, who was sitting in the stands. Since it wasn't technically a celebration, the league had to get creative, so it slapped T.O. with a $5,000 fine for having his jersey untucked.

5. Mike Price's motivational tricks, 1989. Before Washington State's football game against Arizona State, the Cougars coach showed up on the sidelines looking like a daffy version of the ASU mascot, Sparky The Devil. Clad in pink tights and a cape and sporting horns, Price brandished a pitchfork as he urged the Cougars to beat the Sun Devils. Price's routine didn't work as WSU lost 44–39. Later that year, in preparation for a game against USC, Price hired an actor to portray the USC Trojan and gallop onto the WSU practice field astride a white horse. As his team watched, Price whipped out a starter's pistol loaded with blanks and blazed away at the interloper, who slumped in the saddle and rode away "mortally" wounded. Didn't work, either, as WSU lost 18–17. Before a game against the Oregon Ducks, Price disguised himself as a duck hunter. He wore a hunting outfit and waders and stalked the sidelines carrying a shotgun and a bagful of dead ducks. Didn't work, again.

4. Marv Harshman's whammies, 1972, 1976. When Harshman made his first trip back to Pullman (he'd coached the Cougars for 13 years) as the new UW basketball coach, he knew he would take some heckling. So when Harshman came out on Friel Court before the start of the game, he wore a woman's wig and dark glasses. Harshman's Huskies won 96–63. Four years later, Washington traveled to Oregon to play the Ducks, who liked to intimidate visiting players by standing at midcourt during pre-game warmups, crossing their arms and "staring down" their opponents. When Oregon started its menacing staredown on the Huskies, Harshman had some of his players stare back at the Ducks—while wearing Groucho Marx glasses.

3. Cliff McCrath's Space Needle crawl, 1978, 1983. Before the Seattle Pacific Falcons entered the NCAA Division II soccer tournament in 1978, McCrath vowed if his team won, he would crawl on his knees from the SPU campus to the Space Needle. They did, and he did—a distance of more than two miles. In anticipation of another NCAA title in 1983, McCrath flopped face first into a pool of Jell-O (McCrath, also an ordained Presbyterian minister, also performed many weddings, including one in which he ran backwards across a floating bridge during a marathon).

2. The Griffey-Piniella wager, 1995. During spring training, Mariners manager Lou Piniella made a bet with outfielder Ken Griffey Jr. that he couldn't hit a home run to each field on three swings. The wager: a steak dinner. Griffey hit one to right and then one to center, but missed the one to left. The next day, Piniella arrived at the ballpark to find that a live 1,200-pound Hereford cow had been placed in his office. "There's his steak," Griffey said, laughing. The cow had slobbered all over and left another "present" for Piniella that almost made him gag.

1. Rose Bowl card stunt, January 2, 1961. A plot hatched just before Christmas perplexed TV viewers who were watching the halftime show of the 1961 Rose Bowl between Washington and Minnesota. Students from Cal Tech managed to replace the 2,232 flash cards in the Huskies' rooting section, a piece of subterfuge that involved changing every card as well as all the instructions without being discovered. At halftime, as NBC cameras showed the stunts to a national audience, the first 11 displays went off without a hitch. But display No. 12, intended to depict the Husky mascot, instead turned out to be the Cal Tech Beaver. Next, the word "Washington" came up spelled backward. Display No. 14 was supposed to form HUSKIES in block letters. Instead, it came up CAL TECH. Washington's cheerleaders were so bewildered that they aborted the remaining card displays, and the Washington band marched off the field. One of the card-stunt perps confessed that it took 170 hours of work to make the prank work.

In addition to being a part of every Mariners team that won the AL West (you could look it up), relief pitcher-turned-bullpen coach Norm Charlton is an acknowledged master of the ancient baseball art of the prank.

8. You may have been a victim. In the Kingdome, the entrance to the dugout from the locker room is right under the metal stands. When it was quiet during the national anthem, we'd take the big metal thing they use to tap down the mound after the game, turn it over, and slam it against the stands. It made a huge noise, and people would spill beer and coffee, women and kids would be screaming.

7. Can you pitch with a dunce cap? At San Diego's old ballpark, the Padres bullpen was on the left-field line and the visitors' bullpen on the right-field line. You could go either way from the tunnel under the stadium. We'd send guys who hadn't been there before the wrong way. Five minutes before game time they'd walk into the wrong bullpen and San Diego guys would say, "Ah, you must be the new guy."

6. The 'pen can be boring, so . . . The door at Yankee Stadium to the bullpen opens in, so we'd always wedge it open a bit and put a big cup of water on top. First guy in gets soaked. Not that big a deal, and sometimes refreshing in the middle of summer. But you're way out in the bullpen for the rest of the game, so unless you want to sit there soaked on a cold day, you had to go back to the locker room and change.

5. The real meaning of painting the black. We always had binoculars in the bullpen. Now, of course, the ONLY thing we were looking at was trying to see how the ump was calling balls and strikes. We'd take eye black and line the eyepieces on the binoculars and say, "Hey, look over there!" A guy would grab 'em and look and have raccoon eyes.

4. The principal's office for you! The problem with the eye-blacking or shave-creaming the bullpen phone is that if you screw it up and the pitching coach can't get through, you can end up losing a ballgame.

3. Before they were Nasty Boys, they were silly boys. In Philly at the Vet, there was an electric garage door in the bullpen. It was about 25 feet tall. When it went all the way up, it stayed for a bit and then automatically cames down. One of us— Rob Dibble, Randy Myers and me—hit the up button and all three grabbed the door to see who would be the last to let go. None of us let go. The three of us were hanging up there off the concrete in our spikes. It seemed like an hour, but it took 15 or 20 seconds to get all the way up. (Reds pitching coach Larry Rothschild) was having a coronary. He was screaming, "You guys get down, get down from there!" But if we came down on our spikes our legs were going right out from under us. It would have been a disaster. We were up there for a minute or so before Rothschild calmed down and pushed the down button.

2. Hydro injuries don't just happen on the lake. Kazuhiro Sasaki and Ryan Franklin used to bet a head slap on which boat would win the video hydro race on the scoreboard screen. Winner got to slap the loser. Well, Kaz would have his interpreter call upstairs and find out who was going to win the race. He won all the time, and was beating the piss out of Frankie on a regular basis. One day I figure I've seen enough. I called up there and found out who was going to win and told Frankie, "See if you can pick first and pick the blue one." And he said, "Why?" And I said, "Just trust me on this, pick the blue one." Frankie picked the blue one. He won. I stood behind Kaz and Frankie acted like he was gonna slap him and instead I slapped the tar out of his neck. Kaz didn't speak to me for three or four days.

1. Possible source of the Nasty Boys nickname. In Cincinnati right before a game, Lou came out of his office. Rob, Randy and I were standing there and Randy had a stun gun. Lou wanted to know how it worked. Randy told him. "You just hit the button and it arcs and it shocks you." So Randy hit it and the blue flame arcs across. Lou said, "Ah, you're not shocking anyone with that." So I offered to have Randy shock me with it. Randy put it up behind my leg and hits it. He wasn't touching me, but I acted like I was being shocked. Eventually we talked Lou into letting Randy try it on him. Randy shocked the hell out of him. Lou ended up on the ground, screaming mad. He yelled at us after peeling himself off the ground, "You guys will never pitch for me again!"

Foolishness and error in sports is hardly the province of players and coaches. The guys in ties are just as capable of stepping on rakes.

10. Huskies poorly choose their Rose Bowl opponent, 1936. After receiving an invitation to play in the 1937 Rose Bowl, Washington was allowed to select its opponent for the Pasadena classic. Passing over powerhouse LSU, the Huskies picked Pittsburgh after assessing the Panthers as softies. A huge underdog, Pittsburgh clobbered Washington 21–0.

9. Sounders fire Alan Hinton, 1983. At a January 13 press conference at the Seattle Sheraton to explain details of the transfer of majority ownership of the club from Vince and Frank Coluccio to Bruce Anderson and Jerry Horn, the announcement that Hinton was out as coach was so subtle it hardly amounted to an announcement. Hinton's ouster came to light midway through Anderson's statement on policy and, when it did, Anderson was merely responding to a reporter's question. "The current coach," Anderson said, "is no longer the coach. I thought that would have been the first question you asked." Hinton's wife, Joy, was in the room and didn't have a clue that her husband had been canned. Hinton had been informed an hour earlier and had already left the building.

8. Dana's dumbfounding e-mail, 2003. On March 13, UW athletic compliance director Dana Richardson wrote an e-mail to staff that incorrectly sanctioned football coach Rick Neuheisel's participation in an NCAA basketball betting pool. The compliance director was so clueless about NCAA rules that she joined a different, smaller pool herself.

7. Owner fires manager over bonus, 1937. Bill Klepper, who owned the Rainiers before Emil Sick purchased them in 1938, fired manager Johnny Bassler for allowing pitcher "Kewpie" Dick Barrett to try to earn a $250 bonus. Barrett had a clause in his contract providing the extra cash if he won 20 games. Barrett entered the last day of the season with 18 victories and pitched a 4–1 victory over the Sacramento Senators in the first game of a doubleheader. When Bassler sent Barrett to the mound in the nightcap for a try at 20, Klepper ordered Bassler to keep Barrett on the bench. Bassler's answer, published in the *Seattle Post-Intelligencer*, "I'm running this ball club and Barrett is going to pitch!" Klepper's reply, "This will cost you plenty!" After Barrett beat Sacramento 11–2 for his 20th victory, it did. Klepper fired his manager.

6. Seahawks cut union leader, 1982. Prior to the NFL season, amid speculation that a labor strike was imminent, the Seahawks waived Sam McCullum, the club's second-best receiver behind Steve Largent. Although ownership had already fined team members for participating in an August 13 "solidarity handshake" with St. Louis Cardinals players, the club explained the subsequent McCullum cutting as a "football decision." McCullum's teammates saw it otherwise and signed a petition accusing management of cutting McCullum because he was the team's union rep. The case wound up before the National Labor Relations Board. A federal judge held that the Seahawks had unlawfully cut McCullum because of his union activities and ordered him reinstated with full back pay. But by that time, he'd signed with Minnesota.

5. Seahawks botch Steve Hutchinson free agency, 2006. When the Seahawks tried to save money by keeping their All-Pro guard with a "transition" tag instead of a "franchise" tag, it paved the way for the 28-year-old Hutchinson to sign with the Minnesota Vikings without compensation. Hutchinson's loss, coming just a month after the Seahawks' appearance in Super Bowl XL, factored heavily in the team's offensive decline over the next few seasons.

4. No love for George anywhere, March 27, 1987. After years of lousy franchise stewardship, Mariners owner George Argyros announced he intended to purchase the San Diego Padres and sell the Mariners (the ownership of the club was placed in trust). But Argyros bungled the negotiations by insisting on an escape clause in his San Diego stadium lease as he had in Seattle. Worse, he was forced to drop his bid when it came out that National League owners were prepared to vote 11–0 against admitting him as an owner. "We want nothing to do with that guy," one National League owner told the *Seattle Post-Intelligencer.*

3. Mike Blatt and the "crossbow trial," 1989. Blatt, a one-time player agent who helped broker the 1988 sale of the Seahawks from the Nordstrom family to California real estate developers Ken Behring and Ken Hoffman, served as the club's interim GM for three weeks after the new owners dismissed Mike McCormack. Blatt lobbied to become the full-time GM (his plan was to fire coach Chuck Knox and replace him with Bruce Coslet). When he didn't get the job, he hired, according to police charges filed against him, two men to kill a Stockton, Calif., business rival, Laurence Carnegie, whom Blatt blamed in part for his failure to head up the Seahawks. According to prosecutors, Carnegie died when either James Mackey or Carl Hancock, two former University of Pacific football players, shot him with a crossbow on February 28, 1989. Some months later, Mackey was arrested, eventually fingering Blatt as the man who hired him for the hit. Blatt's first trial, which lasted five months, ended in a mistrial. The second trial resulted in Blatt's acquittal, jury members saying they could not trust Mackey's credibility.

2. Feds raid the ballpark for back taxes, 1937. On September 19, after the Seattle Indians won both games of a doubleheader against Sacramento, a phalanx of federal agents from the Treasury Department swooped down on the Civic Stadium box office and demanded that ticket sellers produce the gate receipts, charging the club was thousands of dollars behind in admission taxes. As agents threatened to batter down the box office door, a squad of state patrolmen rushed to get the state tax commission's share of the proceeds. But Wee Willie Coyle, manager of Civic Stadium and a quarterback under Gil Dobie at Washington (1908–11), got to the till first and grabbed a handful of cash. "The city's got the rent money now," he shouted. "Now you fellows can fight over the rest."

1. Mariners practice vs. the Final Four, 1978. Mariners executive vice president Kip Horsburgh created a public uproar when he said the club would not make the Kingdome available for the 1984 NCAA Final Four. "We have things we want to do in that building." By agreement between the Mariners and King County, owner of the Kingdome, the team had exclusive scheduling rights to the facility after March 15, and Horsburg determined that the team might want to use the Kingdome for a public practice, exhibition game, or both on March 31 and April 2, the Final Four dates. Kingdome officials also reported that Horsburgh felt that the Final Four would cut into attention and revenue for the Mariners' opener. Media and fans pounced upon Horsburgh so forcefully that he quickly reversed his decision.

Longtime rock station KJR–AM 950 began the move to a sports talk format in the late 1980s when Sonics voice Kevin Calabro teamed with Rick Dupree to host "Calling All Sports." Full commitment to sports began October 14, 1991. The day after popular local morning DJ Gary Lockwood was fired, fans could call to talk sports from 6 a.m. to 7 p.m. The format was extended to 10 p.m. nightly. Here's some benchmark days for Seattle's first sports-talk outlet.

5. August 31, 2002. The station took away the broadcast rights for University of Washington sports, and play-by-play voice Bob Rondeau, from KOMO-AM, and began with the football opener at Michigan. To celebrate, Mike Gastineau hosted an all-night broadcast at the Ram in University Village that led into KJR's first pre-game show. The Huskies lost after a 12th-man penalty gave Michigan's Phillip Brabbs a chance at a 44-yard field goal, which was the difference in a 31–29 win. A lengthy slide was underway for UW football.

4. May 17, 1996. KJR brought Dave Grosby back from KIRO. Part of his new job was to co-host a show with Mike Gastineau (Groz with Gas). An early topic on the eve of a Sonics-Jazz playoff series was how fun it would be if the KeyArena crowd counted backward from 10 each time Utah's Karl Malone, a notoriously slow free throw shooter, stepped to the foul line. By rule, players have 10 seconds. Malone's first three throw in Game 1 was greeted with "10! 9! 8! . . . " Zero brought a huge roar. Malone had a miserable series from the line, including two huge free-throw misses in the final minute of Game 7.

3. February 22, 2008. KJR devoted an entire broadcast day to interviews and discussion about the Sonics history in Seattle, with emphasis on the glorious 1990s run the team enjoyed under George Karl. The goal was to remind fans, politicians, and maybe even the NBA, that there was indeed a great history to this franchise.

2. November 7, 1991. Magic Johnson announced he had HIV. Listeners packed the phone lines for hours to share their feelings—compassion, rage, sympathy, ignorance and acceptance. Several HIV-positive callers reassured other listeners (and hosts) that this wasn't necessarily a death sentence. By the end of the day, all who worked and listened realized "all sports" was going to be about much more than just games.

1. January 21–23, 2006. KJR's coverage of the run-up to the first NFL conference championship game in Seattle included an all-night pre-game show at The Fenix in Pioneer Square. Due to a scheduling mix-up, it began during a party held by Seattle's Girl4Girl club. For two hours, hundreds of lesbians danced the night away while Gastineau and Mitch Levy previewed the game. Coverage continued next day to up to kickoff. After the victory over Carolina that launched the Super Bowl hype, the post game show ended at 11 p.m. But night host David Locke didn't want to quit. He announced he would take calls as long as anyone wanted to talk Hawks. Seven hours and hundreds of calls later, Locke handed off the mike to Mitch Levy, who began his Monday morning show.

As sports markets go, we're about as genial a group as can be found. Too nice, many East Coasters say. And it's true that spectator sports aren't felt as intensely by most people here, not when the easy alternatives are a hike in the Cascades or a boat cruise on the Sound. Still, we can be pissed off.

10. Shaun Alexander, Seahawks. Nobody hated Alexander personally, but Seahawks fans sure hated the way he didn't run hard, hated the way he fell down too easily, and hated the fact he wouldn't block or catch passes. He had to be the most unloved 100-touchdown scorer in NFL history.

9. Barry Ackerley, Sonics. He owned the Sonics from 1983–2000 and, compared to the dirty deeds of the last two regimes, Ol' Bear isn't looking so bad. But this one gets a little personal for scribe Art Thiel, who once was ordered arrested by Ackerley if he entered a private area of a hotel ballroom reserved for media at a Sonics draft-day function. Seems Ackerley was upset with him for a line in a column in which he wrote, "I'd rather sleep in a bed of broken light bulbs than make a business deal with Ackerley." As a billboard baron, Ackerley proved surprisingly prickly when dealing with media he couldn't control. He also had a well-earned reputation for treating employees shabbily and was often impulsive in basketball decisions. His 1994 firing of Bob Whitsitt, in which the GM found his stuff on the floor outside his locked office, was a classic.

8. Wally Walker, Sonics. As Whitsitt's replacement, Walker, who played on the Sonics 1979 title team, inherited a good team with a volatile coach, George Karl, and rode them to five post-season berths, including the 1996 Finals. But after he didn't re-hire Karl following the 1998 season, Walker's reputation went south. The hires of Jim McIlvaine, Calvin Booth, Patrick Ewing and Vin Baker, the drafting of Robert Swift, Johan Petro and Mohammed Sene and the replacement of Karl with Paul Westphal, were collectively disastrous. Walker also organized the Howard Schultz-led group that bought the club from Ackerley, but ultimately sold it in 2006 to Clay Bennett, prompting a bitter fight to jerk the team to Oklahoma City. The fans are not in a forgiving mood.

7. Alex Rodriguez, Mariners. Fans adored A-Rod when he played in Seattle (1994–2000), which is why he isn't higher on this list. When he jilted Seattle by accepting a record 10-year, $252 million free-agent contract from Texas, they turned against him, citing his phoniness, even though anyone in his position would have done what he did. Upon his every return to the plate at Safeco Field, he is booed, which has become a Seattle tradition of remarkable emptiness.

6. Brian Bosworth, Seahawks. Teammates claimed the private Bosworth was really a likeable guy. But the bejeweled "Boz" was an insufferable, steroid-bloated publicity hound forever in search of a camera. Teammates never forgave him for making the TV talk show circuit while they walked the picket line in the 1987 strike, and fans never forgave him for failing to live up to the hype.

5. Rick Neuheisel, Huskies. Some fans considered him sophisticated, glib and a good recruiter, but more found Neuheisel—whose contract put him in the top 10 nationally—sleazy, political and phony. The NCAA confirmed Slick Rick to be a corner cutter, and the UW determined he was a liar. But he did get the Huskies to the 2001 Rose Bowl, although critics will say that was more quarterback Marques Tuiasosopo than the coach. Neuheisel's controversial hiring, firing and subsequent trial sent the program into free fall, from which its reputation has yet to recover.

4. Howard Schultz-Clay Bennett, Sonics. It's hard to separate these two, because each had such a large hand in orchestrating the Sonics' move to Oklahoma City. While Bennett is easy to demonize as the out-of-town carpetbagger with a hopeless arena plan—his e-mails disclosed his agenda to move the team—it was Schultz who lacked the will to see the Sonics through their arena headache and jumped at Bennett's way-over-the-top offer of $350 million. He soured on the NBA and its players, too, disappointed that his personal charm had none of the effect it did in the coffee business. His overly demonstrative, sometimes pouty behavior from his courtside seat won him no respect among players or fans. And hey, Bennett and Schultz don't even like each other. What does that tell you?

3. Bobby Ayala, Mariners. The only man in Seattle who could light a fire without a match, the incendiary relief pitcher had a remarkable knack for turning sure Mariners victories into crushing defeats. He blew 43 saves during his Seattle tenure, nine alone in 1998 when fans booed him as soon as he started to warm up.

2. George Argyros, Mariners. The Newport Beach, Calif., real estate mogul bought the club in 1981, refused to put a competitive, watchable product on the field (no winning record during his ownership), squabbled for years with King County over the terms of his Kingdome lease, and had an ego that he could barely wedge inside the Dome. "Patience is for losers," was his famous saying. Must have been a patient man.

1. Ken Behring, Seahawks. By making horrendous front-office hires and overseeing disastrous draft picks (he personally selected quarterback bust Dan McGwire in 1991), the California real estate developer quickly erased a Nordstrom-era fan base that had 20,000 more customers than the Kingdome had seats. "Bubba" cost Seattle a chance to host the 1992 Super Bowl (NFL owners didn't like him) and tried to hijack the Seahawks to Los Angeles by ludicrously arguing that the Kingdome was susceptible to earthquakes. A loathsome fellow.

Most Significant—and Amusing—Lawsuits

Not sure if national records are kept on such things, but jeez, we have a lot of sports-related litigation. Can't we all just get along by playing ball?

15. Most frivolous suit in state sports history, January 6, 1936. The Seattle Indians (PCL) were sued for $254 over an unpaid lumber bill. The team had purchased the lumber to repair the outfield fence at Civic Stadium.

14. Biggest lawsuit over a press table, April 9, 1980. Seattle attorney Fred Smart filed suit against the Sonics in King County Superior Court because the Coliseum press table partially obstructed his view of the action. Smart wanted a temporary injunction to move press row out of the way. He didn't get it.

13. Biggest lawsuit by an athlete against the city, 1972. Spencer Haywood and the Sonics filed claims against the city totaling $441,100 for a knee injury Haywood suffered when he slipped on the wet Coliseum floor March 5. Claims by Haywood totaled $278,325 and those by the Sonics came to $162,725. The sides settled.

12. Mariners sue Seahawks, September 2, 1984. The Mariners filed a lawsuit against the Seahawks and King County in Kittitas County Superior Court in Ellensburg over use of the Kingdome on September 2. The Mariners had a game scheduled against the Baltimore Orioles in the Dome that day, while the Seahawks were slated to open their season in the Dome against Cleveland. The Mariners prevailed in the argument, but blew the day by losing to the Orioles 4–3. The Seahawks were forced to move their home opener to September 3. They defeated Cleveland 33–0, but lost running back Curt Warner for the season with a knee injury. Ironically, the King County attorney hired to argue on behalf of the Seahawks was Bill Dwyer, who worked the county's suit against the American League that brought the Mariners to Seattle.

11. Longest lawsuit, 1976. Vince Abbey, Seattle owner of the minor league Totems, tried to position himself to gain either an expansion NHL franchise or a team from the now-defunct World Hockey Association. When his efforts failed, the Totems were out of business and Abbey sued the NHL in federal court over anti-trust violations. Abbey doggedly pursued the case until 1986, when the Ninth Circuit Court of Appeals, in the longest-lasting case in the court's history, finally threw it out.

10. Longest-running feud born of a lawsuit, 1980–89. On March 19, the Mariners charged that the club had lost between $6 million and $8 million, as well as games, because the Kingdome field was too small, its ushers ill-trained, its lights too dim and office facilities non-existent. In a countersuit, King County alleged the Mariners were $140,000 behind in their rent. The suit dragged on for more than two years before a settlement was reached that not only favored the Mariners, but ultimately put owner George Argyros in position to extract over the next nine years $19 million in lease concessions from the county by virtue of an escape clause in the lease tied to paid attendance.

9. Only lawsuit in which we sued ourselves, December 4, 1984. A

$200,000 lawsuit filed by King County had this amusing twist: In essence, the people, represented by King County, sued the SuperSonics because not enough people were attending games at the county-owned Kingdome. The county filed the suit against Ackerley Communications (owners of the Sonics), claiming that it had lost substantial ticket, parking and concession revenue as a result of games televised on the Sonics' SuperChannel, a pay station (it ultimately flopped), which discouraged fans from attending.

8. Biggest lawsuit by a coach vs. his former team, 1973. When the Son-

ics fired Tom Nissalke halfway through the first year of a three-year contract, they were on the hook for the balance of his contract, worth nearly $135,000. The Sonics offered a $50,000 settlement, and Nissalke accepted it. Then Nissalke hired a lawyer, who told him not to accept it, and instead sued the Sonics for $1.2 million. Eventually, the parties settled for an undisclosed sum.

7. Biggest lawsuit by a player against his former team, 1989. Five-time

All-Pro safety Kenny Easley sued the Seahawks and their trainers, doctors and Advil, blaming them for the degenerative kidney condition he developed while taking pain medication and not making him aware of the risk. One year after receiving a kidney transplant, Easley accepted a settlement from team doctors and the New York lab that distributed the painkiller to the Seahawks.

6. Most profitable lawsuit filed by a coach, 2003. If former WSU football

coach Mike Price hadn't gone to Arety's Angels, a Pensacola, FL topless club, and then taken a stripper (or strippers) back to his hotel room, he wouldn't have lost his job as head coach at Alabama. On the other hand, the episode turned into a wonderful primer on how to profit from one's mistakes. If *Sports Illustrated* hadn't written a shoddily researched story about Price's night of carousing, Price wouldn't have been able to sue Time Inc. for $20 million and ultimately receive a handsome settlement.

5. Only time a team sued itself, 1973. Shareholders in First Northwest In-

dustries, parent company of the Sonics, sued club owner Sam Schulman, alleging that more than $2 million in corporate funds had been misspent on ill-advised player acquisitions. The complaint said Schulman had embarked on "an extensive course of unauthorized conduct" in the acquisitions of Spencer Haywood, Jim McDaniels and John Brisker, "recklessness" that cost the shareholders $1.52 million. Shareholders also said Schulman executed a series of trades that caused "corporate waste" exceeding $500,000. The suit asked that Schulman repay shareholders out of his own pocket.

4. Old owner vs. new owner, April 23, 2008. When Howard Schultz, for-

mer owner of the Sonics, filed suit against current owner Clay Bennett, it marked the first time in Seattle pro sports history that an ex-owner sued a current one to rescind the sale of a franchise. Filed in U.S. District Court, the suit asked that the franchise be taken away from Bennett because he lied about his intentions. Schultz sought to have the club placed in trust and made available to a local buyer.

3. Lawsuit in which everyone looked bad, 2003. Former football coach Rick Neuheisel's lawsuit against Washington for wrongful termination resulted in a highly entertaining five-week trial. Neuheisel teared up on the stand as he tried to explain why he had layered lie upon lie about pursuing the 49ers' head coach vacancy and his involvement in a college basketball betting pool. On another occasion, his cell phone went off while he was on the witness stand, and he answered. UW compliance director Dana Richardson tried to explain how she could have been out of compliance with long-established NCAA rules on gambling. The judge discovered the NCAA didn't know or follow its own rules. And the NCAA and Washington lost—but not before Neuheisel's sister gave KJR reporter Hugh Millen the finger.

2. Lawsuit with greatest local impact, 1976. The city of Seattle, King County and Washington state sued the American League for $32 million in damages resulting from the move of the Seattle Pilots in 1970 to Milwaukee. The trial in Everett lasted 18 days before AL owners sued for peace, awarding Seattle an expansion team that in 1977 started play as the Mariners.

1. Lawsuit with greatest national impact, 1970. When 20-year-old Spencer Haywood made the jump from the ABA's Denver Rockets to the Sonics, the NBA sued to keep Haywood out of the league, arguing he was ineligible because he was not four years removed from high school. Arguing that he was a "hardship" case, Haywood countersued, ultimately winning the right to play, in a 7–2 Supreme Court decision in March 1971. Haywood's success paved the way for high school graduates and college attendees to become eligible for the NBA draft.

Coincidence, preposterousness, randomness . . . some sports things defy categorization. That doesn't mean they defy an appearance in this book.

15. 1973—74. A 58-0 loser to Oregon in 1973, the UW football team turned around a year later and shellacked the Ducks 66–0, the greatest swing in points against a conference rival from one year to the next in school history.

14. April 27, 1979. Mariners catcher Bob Stinson, pinch hitting for Larry Cox, hit an eighth-inning home run off New York's Dick Tidrow. Dan Meyer, pinch hitting for Mario Mendoza, followed with another home run off Tidrow, marking the only time in Mariners history that they had two pinch-hit homers in the same inning.

13. September 30, 1987. Harold Reynolds not only won the American League stolen base crown with 60 thefts, he became the first player to lead the league in steals while batting ninth in the order.

12. September 11, 1992. In Seattle's 4–3 loss to the Athletics at Oakland-Alameda Coliseum, the Mariners set a major league record by using five left fielders. Two weeks later, on September 25, in a 4–3, 16-inning win over Texas, the Mariners set a major league record by using 11 pitchers.

11. July 15, 1978. Larry Milbourne of the Mariners hit homers batting right-handed and left-handed. They were Milbourne's only homers all season.

10. September 11, 2005. To open the NFL season, Jacksonville's Josh Scobee kicked off to Seattle's Josh Scobey.

9. May 14, 2004. The Yankees scored six runs against the Mariners without the benefit of an official at-bat (Mariners pitchers issued 10 walks, including four with the bases loaded).

8. December 7, 1935. Washington's Byron Haines scored every point in the UW's 6–2 football victory over USC. He was tackled in the end zone for a safety in the first quarter, giving the Trojans a 2–0 lead. In the second quarter, he ran 25 yards for a TD, accounting for all eight points.

7. June 22, 1992. In a 7–2 loss to Oakland, Dave Cochrane of the Mariners tied a club record for most outfield assists in a game with two, and set a club record for most errors in a game by an outfielder with three.

6. January 28, 2003. While on a corporate outing at Whiteface Mountain at Lake Placid, N.Y., identical twins Phil and Steve Mahre (long retired from competitive skiing) both clocked 23.64 seconds in a special slalom race.

5. September 25, 1971. The UW football team defeated Texas Christian, 44–26. Notable is that TCU ran back a kickoff for a touchdown. Then Jim Krieg of the Huskies turned right around and ran a TCU kickoff all the way back.

4. 1998–99. The UW football team went 6–6, the Seahawks 8–8 and the Sonics 25–25 (strike-shortened season).

3. June 4, 2003. In a 7–2 win over the Philadelphia Phillies, the Mariners turned a 6–4–3 (SS Carlos Guillen, 2B Bret Boone, 1B John Olerud) double play against Jimmy Rollins, marking the only 6–4–3 double play ever turned on June 4, 2003.

2. September 24, 1995 and December 19, 2004. Former UW star Chris Chandler is the only quarterback in NFL history to play a game in which he had a perfect (158.3) passer rating (September 24, 1995, for Houston) and also play a game in which he had a 0.0 passer rating (December 19, 2004, for St. Louis), the lowest score possible.

1. February 5, 2006. The Seahawks became the only team in the 40-year history of the Super Bowl to rush for more yards and commit fewer turnovers than their Super Bowl opponent—and still lose.

Pat O'Day has lived many lives: Pioneering radio DJ, Rock and Roll Hall of Fame member, concert promoter in the 1960s and 1970s (he worked with Jimi Hendrix, Led Zeppelin, Three Dog Night and others) and rehab spokesman. But the biggest noise he created was as a broadcaster and promoter of unlimited hydroplane racing.

10. High rollers. No sport had a more interesting cast of owners. Automobile czar Horace Dodge; band leader Guy Lombardo; Bill Harrah of Harrah's; Bill Bennett of Circus Circus; Ole Bardahl, creator of the famous Seattle oil additive; Thriftway founder Willard Rhodes; Bob Stiel, owner of the Squire Shop men's stores; Steve Woomer, who founded Competition Specialty; Bill Boeing; Dave Heerensperger of Pay N Pak and Eagle Hardware, and the incredible Bernie Little.

9. Curse of the turbine. Hyrdoplane racing was once a giant rock festival with ear-shattering engines. Today's hydros sound like hairdryers. Who's to blame? I'm guilty! In 1972 I convinced Jim Clapp he could install turbine engines in a hydroplane and be instantly competitive. Little did I know we were wrecking the sport. Turbines turned an exciting spectacle powered by loud gasoline and piston aircraft engines into faster but sadly neutered events. I regret having played any role in this development.

8. Fred Leland. A Seattle contractor who became obsessed with owning and racing boats. Usually underfunded, he hit the jackpot with Pico Manufacturing of Detroit as his sponsor, and with driver Dave Villwock. They won the 1996 national championship.

7. Fred Farley. Official historian of the sport, he's witnessed more than 1,400 heats of unlimited racing. He's a walking encyclopedia of boat racing.

6. Bill Doner. Bill took over the sport when it was crumbling and built it into a 12-race circuit. He also stepped on numerous toes. You either traveled with him or got run over. Once in Detroit on a windy day when drivers complained that races should be canceled, Doner quieted the group with a legendary command: "Carmen was announced; and at 5 p.m. Carmen will be sung."

5. Tragedy leads to safety. The first unlimited race on Lake Washington (1951) produced two fatalities. In the next 15 years, there were none. A false sense of security prevailed in 1966 at the President's Cup on the Potomac in Washington D.C. Ronnie Musson, Rex Manchester and Donnie Wilson all were killed. As a result, Bernie Little and Jim Lucero developed the fighter plane canopy allowing the driver to remain belted in the boat rather than pitched violently into the water. Only one driver has lost his life since the canopy became a requirement.

4. Seattle vs. Detroit. In the 1950s, Seattle had nothing major league but Boeing. Detroit was a big-league town. They had the Tigers, Pistons, Red Wings, Lions and the nation's biggest boat race, The Gold Cup. When Seattleite Ted Jones and Slo Mo Shun IV won that cup and brought the race to Seattle, we were ecstatic. However, along with that trophy came those hated boats and drivers from Michigan. How we despised those Motor City mouths as they rained insults down upon us. How thrilled we were as we defeated them year after year. Hydros brought new and needed self-respect to our area.

3. Bill Muncey. The winningest driver with 62 career victories, he also made more waves than a battleship. Accurately described as warm, hostile, kind, angry, giving, selfish, fair, unfair, cooperative, inflexible, loyal, generous, happy, volatile, forgiving, nasty, clever, persistent and totally lovable. Muncey was the poorest loser, but the happiest winner, the sport ever knew.

2. Bernie Little. One of a kind. Brilliant. Charming. Flamboyant. Arrogant. Fierce competitor. Unlimited racing would have fallen by the wayside without his passion. Bernie arrived at races in his Lear jet. Already waiting was his ostentatious, customized Budweiser bus trimmed in gold. His racing equipment was immaculate, as was his traditional attire: bright red slacks, a perfectly pressed white shirt, white shoes, and loads of gold chains, rings, and watches that were the finishing touch to the message he sent to all when he said, "I'm Bernie Little. And you're not!"

1. Ted Jones. Nothing equals the innovation in design created by this Seattleite in 1950. His notion that a boat could fly across the water instead of through it found him setting world speed records. His Gold Cup win in 1950 helped create our annual Seafair race.

Accidents and Tragedies

Even though sports is said to be an escape, there is no running from real life, or death. Any compendium of sports history would not be complete without a history of sadness. Listed chronologically:

Spokane Indians baseball, June 24, 1946. In one of the worst accidents in American sports history, a bus carrying 16 members of the minor league baseball team to a game in Bremerton crashed on U.S. 10, which carried traffic over Snoqualmie Pass. The bus swerved to avoid a car that crossed the centerline. Nine members of the team died and six were injured. Jack Lohrke, a Spokane infielder, was on the trip but received word when the team stopped for lunch in Ellensburg that the San Diego Padres of the Pacific Coast League had recalled him. Lohrke did not re-board the bus, and instead hitched back to Spokane.

Seattle's first Gold Cup race, August 4, 1951. In the third heat of a race that ushered in the city's unlimited hydroplane tradition, Orth Mathiot, 56, and his mechanic, Thompson Whitaker, 27, were riding in Quicksilver, a Rolls-powered hydro from Portland, OR. To the horror of 250,000 Lake Washington witnesses, the Quicksilver suddenly nosed down, flipped and sank to the bottom of the lake, taking both Mathiot and Whitaker to their deaths.

Brian Sternberg, pole vaulter, July 2, 1963. One month after he set the world record in the pole vault for the third time during the year, the UW sophomore was paralyzed from the neck down in a trampoline accident. Sternberg sustained the injury while attempting a double-back somersault with a twist.

Hydro drivers Bill Muncey, October 18, 1981, and Dean Chenoweth, July 31, 1982. Two unlimited hydroplane legends died in less than a year of each other. Muncey was leading the final heat of a world championship race in the Atlas Van Lines at Acapulco, Mexico, when he died in a blowover while traveling at 175 mph. Chenoweth, a four-time national champion, also died in a blowover while racing the Miss Budweiser in a qualifying heat on the Columbia River near Pasco.

Mike Utley, football, November 17, 1991. A Kennedy High (Burien) and Washington State graduate, Utley's NFL career came to an end when, playing for the Detroit Lions, he was paralyzed from the chest down during a game against the Los Angeles Rams. Utley offered a memorable "thumbs up" sign as he was removed from the field.

Mike Frier, football, December 1, 1994. A car driven by Seahawks rookie running back Lamar Smith crashed in Kirkland, leaving teammate Frier paralyzed and running back Chris Warren with cracked ribs. Smith, who originally denied that he had been the driver, settled with Frier after the King County prosecutor alleged Smith drank at least five beers and six ounces of Scotch shortly before his car piled into a utility pole. In 1997, Smith agreed to pay Frier $4 million over a seven-year period.

Charles and Brian Blades, football, July 5, 1995. The cousin of Seahawks wide receiver Brian Blades, who caught 77 passes for 1,001 yards the previous season, died of a gunshot wound as the pair struggled for possession of a gun in Blades' Plantation, FL, home. A jury convicted Blades of manslaughter in 1996, but 72 hours later a judge overturned the verdict and acquitted Blades, stating that the prosecutor had not proved that Blades acted negligently.

Huskies football boosters, September 12, 2001. One day after the terrorist attacks on the World Trade Center's twin towers in New York and on the Pentagon, 16 Husky football fans (along with three others) died in a plane crash in a corn field on Mexico's Yucatan Peninsula. The fans were on a Caribbean cruise that was to culminate with attendance at the Washington-Miami game in the Orange Bowl on September 15. Cause of crash: engine failure.

Curtis Williams, May 6, 2002. The former UW safety died in Fresno, CA, two years after he was paralyzed from the neck down as the result of a helmet-to-helmet collision at Stanford on October 28, 2000. Williams and Cardinal running back Kerry Carter collided in the third quarter of the UW's 31–28 victory, with Williams suffering an injury to the C-2 vertebrae. Williams made a much-publicized trip to Seattle to watch the 2002 UW spring game, but died suddenly a month later, two days after his 24th birthday.

Sometimes the best thing about sports is doing the same thing over and over again, year after year, generation after generation. What else but sports in our culture can pull so many off couches at once? Note that three of our greatest traditions involve dampness. Whoda thunk?

10. "Louie, Louie" at the yard, 1990. The Mariners began playing the goofy pop song during the seventh-inning stretch. But the idea really took off June 2, when the Kingsmen, the local band that long ago made a national hit out of the ditty, played it live, in advance of their post-game concert. Two innings later, Mariners pitcher Randy Johnson completed a no-hitter.

9. Thanksgiving football, 1929. This high school tradition lasted for 45 years until it was discontinued in 1974 due to the advent of a state playoff system. In the final game at Memorial Stadium, Shoreline defeated Ingraham, 20–14, for the Metro League title in front of 10,500 fans.

8. The Hutch Award, 1965. Honoring Seattle native Fred Hutchinson, major league pitcher and manager who died of cancer on November 12, 1964, at age 45, the award was created by longtime friends Bob Prince, broadcaster of the Pittsburgh Pirates; Jim Enright, Chicago sportswriter; and Ritter Collett, sports editor of the Dayton Journal Herald. The award honors baseball players for outstanding community service. The inaugural recipient was Mickey Mantle.

7. P-I Star of the Year Banquet, 1936. Created by former *Seattle Post-Intelligencer* sports editor Royal Brougham as "a little clambake," the annual banquet, one of the nation's longest-running sports celebrations, honors the best male and female athletes from the previous year.

6. Boating to Huskies football games, 1920s. Long considered among the greatest locations in national sports, Husky Stadium's perch on the west edge of Lake Washington invites hundreds of boat-mad Seattleites to motor up to the dock on game-day Saturdays. Every year, it seems an out-of-town or national reporter will jump aboard and write an awed account.

5. Seahawks 12th man, 1984. Before the final game of the 1984 season, the Seahawks became the first team in professional sports to retire a number in honor of their fans. A fan, Randy Ford, proposed the idea. After many seasons of mediocrity, the Seahawks' five consecutive playoff appearances helped revive the tradition under CEO Tod Leiweke. Before each game, former players or local celebrities raise the 12th man flag at Qwest Field's south end concourse.

4. Opening Day Regatta, 1970. Combined with the Seattle Yacht Club's Opening Day Boat Parade, the UW-hosted crew regatta marks the beginning of the region's boating season. Since being renamed the Windemere Cup in 1987, the regatta has featured national crews from the Soviet Union (1987), People's Republic of China (1990), Czechoslovakia (1991), The Netherlands (1994), South Africa (1995), Australia (1997) and Egypt (2000), as well as teams representing Cambridge University (1992) and Nottinghamshire County, England (1998).

3. Seafair Trophy Race, 1951. Seattle hasn't been much for motor sports except for this one, the unlimited hydroplane race that is the marquee conclusion to Seafair, Seattle's annual summer festival. The race annually attracts hundreds of thousands of land- and water-borne party hounds to the shores of Lake Washington, some of whom actually see the race.

2. Longacres Mile, 1935. Track founder Joe Gottstein inaugurated The Mile with a $10,000-added purse, and for more than four decades it was the biggest horse race in the Northwest and the richest stakes event in the country at the mile distance. Now contested every August at Emerald Downs in Auburn, it still carries Grade III status.

1. Apple Cup, 1900. The state's most heated sports rivalry, the Washington-Washington State football game, with its subplot clashes of geography and campus cultures, is the longest-running tradition of any kind in the state. Choose purple or crimson; otherwise stand back and listen to the smack.

America's online video library soon will contain embarrassing moments on everyone. Before you look for your own, here are five dubious Seattle sports moments caught on tape.

5. Bo bombs Boz, November 30, 1987. During a media briefing prior to the Oakland-Seattle Monday Night Football game at the Kingdome, Seattle's mouthy rookie linebacker Brian Bosworth promised to contain the former Heisman winner. Didn't happen. Jackson rushed for 221 yards, still an opponent record against the Seahawks. He scored three touchdowns, one on a 91-yard jaunt. But what everybody recalls occurred in the third quarter when Jackson literally ran over Bosworth, who described it thusly in his own biography: "He freight-trained my ass."

4. Lighting up the scoreboard for real, December 2, 2007. KeyArena looked every bit its 45 years during the first quarter of a Sonics game against Golden State when a faulty spotlight caused a fire in the huge scoreboard directly above the court. Flames and smoke were visible as the game was halted and the scoreboard lowered to remove the offending object. No one was hurt, but the bad news was, given the Sonics' road to a franchise-worst 20–62 season, the game continued.

3. Moose goes loco over Coco, August 5, 2007. Before the bottom of the fifth inning in a Mariners game against the Red Sox at Safeco Field, Boston's Coco Crisp jogged out of the dugout to take his position in center field. The Mariners' mascot, the Moose, driving an ATV around the field on the warning track, drove the vehicle straight into Crisp's knee, nearly knocking him down. He was uninjured, but it marked the second time the Moose had witlessly interacted with a player. On April 15, 1991, Seattle pitcher Randy Johnson committed a balk when the Moose threw a bag of peanuts onto the Kingdome carpet in the fourth inning.

2. Sooner Schooner boner, January 1, 1985. Early in the fourth quarter of the Orange Bowl, Washington was involved in one of the strangest spectacles in college football history. After Tim Lashar kicked a 22-yard field goal to give Oklahoma a 17–14 lead, a penalty was called on the Sooners that nullified the score. Rex Harris, driver of the Sooner Schooner, a Conestoga wagon pulled by two ponies, immediately charged on the field for a brief celebration, apparently not realizing that a flag had been thrown. Officials promptly called a 15-yard unsportsmanlike penalty on the cheer squad and tacked it on the first penalty. The 20-yard setback made Lashar's next attempt a 42-yarder, which was blocked by Washington's Tim Peoples. Inspired by the momentum swing, the Huskies scored two TDs in less than 60 seconds and won the game 28–17.

1. Taking a hit for the team, October 26, 2007. Cheerleader Cali Kaltschmidt of Auburn High School was holding up a long paper banner on the field through which her football team would burst as it returned from the locker room for the start of the second half. Neither, however, knew the other was there. The collision knocked Kaltschmidt through the air backward and left her underfoot as the team stumbled over her. Somehow, she emerged with only minor injuries, but became a major entertainment for millions of YouTubers.

Moments We Wish Were On *YouTube*

It's a shame there's no video record of these delightful little absurdities.

5. End zone mayhem, October 27, 1962. Washington and Oregon were tied at 21 with six seconds to play. The Ducks had the ball on the 50-yard line, and quarterback Bob Berry's only option was a Hail Mary into the end zone at the east end of Husky Stadium. As Berry drifted back to throw, Larry Hill ran deep with Washington's Kim Stiger covering him. As the ball came down, Hill got his hand on it, and so did Stiger. But at that moment, a horde of youngsters flooded into the end zone and surrounded Hill, denying him any opportunity to make the catch. The officials did nothing on Oregon's behalf and the game ended in a tie.

4. A game-free teardown of goal posts, November 13, 1982. Because Washington's football game at Arizona State would not be carried on local TV, UW officials decided it should be televised back to Seattle via closed circuit and shown on a giant screen at the basketball gym. Demand to see the game was such that Hec Ed could not accommodate the crowd, and so an overflow of 3,000 fans parked themselves in front of a second screen in Husky Stadium. After Washington's 17–13 victory over the No. 3-ranked Sun Devils, fans were so thrilled that they stormed into the end zone in a dark and otherwise deserted stadium and ripped down the goalposts.

3. Cheerleader catches on fire, November 23, 1985. More than a foot of snow fell on Seattle during the week preceding the 1985 Apple Cup at Husky Stadium. So cold was it that UW officials were forced to fill the toilets with antifreeze to keep them working. On game day, it was still so cold that portable heaters had to be placed along the sidelines to keep players from freezing. While the hottest person on the turf was WSU running back Rueben Mayes, the hottest person on the sideline was UW cheerleader Marilou Franco. She got too near one of the portable heaters and caught on fire. One of Washington's players picked her up and dumped her in a snow bank, dousing the flames that burned a hole in Franco's warm-ups.

2. There's no (deleted) in baseball! May 15, 1990. Fans attending a Blue Jays-Mariners game in Toronto got an eyeful in the seventh inning. Those with binoculars who looked above the scoreboard saw a naked man and a towel-clad woman in the window of their room at the SkyDome Hotel in an intimate interlude. The lights were off in the $800 room overlooking the baseball diamond, but the ballpark lights revealed, well, everything. Said Blue Jays president Paul Beeston, "I never suspected in my wildest dreams that someone would be doing it right in front of the window."

1. Disorder in the court, February 3, 2006. Two days before Super Bowl XL between the Seahawks and Pittsburgh Steelers, Pierce County Superior Court judge Beverly Grant opened a first-degree manslaughter sentencing hearing by urging everyone in her courtroom to yell "Go Seahawks!" When the response was tepid, she demanded that onlookers shout it out again. Said the prosecutor, "One family is seeing a son go off to prison, and one family is here to find justice for a murdered loved one. Do you think they want to root for the Seahawks?" After newspapers across the country ran stories about the incident, Grant issued an apology.

Issues that Became Talk Show Fodder

Seattle's only sports-talk station since 1991, KJR-AM has been the local forum for the instant sports vent. But when it comes to controversy, instant doesn't imply that these hot buttons had just a push or two. These topics went on for days, weeks, months, years, with much gnashing of teeth and spilling of bile.

10. Trading Griffey, 1999–2000. The greatest figure in Seattle sports history, Ken Griffey Jr. was hugely popular but also began to wear down fans with complaints and moodiness. He had the right to ask for a trade, and did so in November 1999. By the time he was dealt to his hometown of Cincinnati on February 10, 2000 for what he claimed were family reasons, the deal had been long anticipated, generating more listener sadness than anger. The controversy became more about how little the Mariners received for a 28-year-old superstar. Some of the sting went away with the emergence of the ebullient Mike Cameron in CF. From about 2004 on, the debate regarding Junior turned towards if, how, and when the M's could get him back.

9. A-Rod leaves in free agency, December 2000. Last of the three superstars of the 1990s to leave Seattle, Rodriguez helped the Mariners to the 2000 ALCS and finished third in the MVP voting. Then he turned his back on his original team, which had agreed in spring to let him enter free agency as long as it had a fair shot to bid for him. Turns out they had no shot, with the Rangers agreeing to pay him $252 million, double the largest previous contract (Kevin Garnett) in sports history. Callers overwhelmingly ripped him as a greedy liar to whom only money mattered. A small minority was willing to admit they would have taken the deal, too.

8. The Big Unit—to sign or not to sign, 1998. Seattle split over the issue. One side contended that the Big Unit, in his walk year, was 34 years old, likely near the end of his career, had a bad back, and a trade could reap top-of-the line younger players. The other argued that Johnson, coming off a 20–4 season, was irreplaceable and a must-sign. Johnson wanted out, and helped his cause with a terrible first half. He was traded to Houston for three good prospects and then defied critics starting in 1999 with four Cy Young awards in four years with the Arizona Diamondbacks.

7. The Lockhorns: Wally Walker and George Karl, 1994–1998. Whether it was because Walker was a Virginia graduate and Karl was from North Carolina, the Sonics president and Sonics coach never really got along. Many callers wanted Walker to fire Karl after the Sonics lost in the first round of the playoffs for the second straight year in 1995. Walker didn't do it and the Sonics made it to the NBA Finals the next year. But the two constantly clashed over big and little things. The debate fell along classic American work lines. Those who identified with the challenges faced in managing a business sided with Walker. Others found a kindred soul in the free spirited anti-management rants of Karl. A sensational five-year debate.

6. The Rick Neuheisel circus, 2003–04. Among the prevarications and lamentations surrounding the University of Washington football coach, nothing was more astonishing than when, in a live KJR interview, which he had personally arranged in an effort to "set the record straight," he lied to the audience about his interest in the vacant head coaching job with the 49ers, just as he earlier lied to the P-I.

5. The hijacking of the Sonics, 2006–08. No shortage of people taking heat from callers in this melodrama. Clay Bennett said repeatedly the Sonics belonged in the Northwest, and that he would make a good-faith effort to keep them there. But after his long-shot bid for public money for a $500 million arena in Renton died, disclosure of subsequent e-mails suggested Bennett and partners wanted all along to abscond with the team to his hometown of Oklahoma City. He was villainized as the man who stole the Sonics, although previous owner Howard Schultz came in for his own bashing as did local politicians and NBA commissioner David Stern.

4. Japanese baron buys Mariners, 1991–1992. The Mariners under owner Jeff Smulyan seemed gone to Tampa until the owner of video-game maker Nintendo of Japan, Hiroshi Yamauchi, unexpectedly was persuaded by Sen. Slade Gorton to buy the team to keep it in Seattle, Nintendo's North American headquarters. Because of his nationality, major league baseball owners fought the purchase, making it a national controversy. Locally, nearly everyone was thrilled someone stepped up, and resented MLB's xenophobic resistance.

3. The new ballpark debate, 1994–1996. Replacing the Kingdome, where ceiling tiles fell in 1994, with an open-air, baseball-only park funded mostly with tax dollars became a civic debate that roared for three years through several controversies. It actually resonates to this day as anti-stadium callers will still occasionally complain, "We voted that stadium down and they built it anyway."

2. Don James resigns, August 1993. One of the great shockers in Seattle sports history, the legendary UW football coach suddenly quit after the Pac-10 Conference concluded an investigation by giving the Huskies a two-year bowl ban instead of an expected one-year penalty. Local columnists and called him a quitter, while many fans defended him and railed against the Pac-10, the NCAA and jealous Pac-10 rivals. Three weeks after he quit he began a new career—as a KJR talk show host. He did a weekly college football show for three years.

1. Controversial Super Bowl calls, February 2006. The outrage was intense, relentless and unresolved. In the view of nearly every Seattle fan, the Seahawks, in their first appearance in the Super Bowl, were given an XL screw job by officials in the 21–10 loss to Pittsburgh in Detroit. Charges of fix, conspiracy and reckless incompetence were some of the nicer things said.

The coulda-woulda-shoulda syndrome runs strong here. Let the imagination fly with these possibilities.

10. Seabiscuit could have run at Longacres, September 11, 1938. The legendary thoroughbred was supposed to run in the Longacres Mile, but his trainer, Tom Smith, thought the weight assigned his horse was unfair and opted out. How much weight did the stewards demand? A preposterous 142 pounds! Next highest was 113. Lost was the only chance Washington fans had to see one of the most celebrated horses in racing history.

9. Any of three legends could have coached Huskies football, 1956. Following the ouster of John Cherberg as UW football coach in the wake of a slush-fund scandal, athletic director George Briggs offered the Husky vacancy to Bear Bryant of Texas A&M, Bud Wilkinson of Oklahoma and Duffy Daugherty of Michigan State. Predictably, all turned Briggs down, but Wilkinson suggested that the Huskies hire Darrell Royal, his former quarterback then coaching Mississippi State. Briggs hired Royal, who coached for one year and then bolted for Texas, endorsing his former teammate at Oklahoma, Jim Owens, as his successor. Owens spent 18 years at Washington.

8. The Cleveland Indians could have moved to Seattle, 1964. Cleveland owner William R. Daley would have relocated his franchise if he had been able to convince Seattle political leaders to replace an aging Sicks' Stadium with a new ballpark. He couldn't, so the Indians stayed put, delaying Seattle's entry into the major leagues by four years until the 1969 expansion Pilots.

7. Muhammad Ali could have fought in Seattle—twice, 1971. Seattle was seriously considered as the site of an Ali-Joe Frazier fight in 1971 that was ultimately held in New York's Madison Square Garden (Ali-Frazier I). Ali also once had a fight scheduled against Jimmy Ellis at the Seattle Coliseum. The pair eventually fought in Houston, which offered a bigger purse.

6. Seattle could have had an NHL franchise, 1974. In April, the National Hockey League announced Seattle and Denver had been awarded franchises, to begin play in the 1976–77 season. That spelled the end of the Western Hockey League following the 1973–74 season, forcing the move of the Seattle Totems from the WHL to the Central Hockey League. When Totems owner Vince Abbey couldn't come up with the money required by the NHL for an expansion franchise, he tried to buy both the San Francisco and the Pittsburgh franchises so that he could move them to Seattle for the 1975–76 season. He couldn't close either deal. Eventually the Seattle and Denver expansion deals fell apart, Denver joined the new World Hockey Association, Seattle got nothing, the money-losing Totems folded, and Abbey sued the NHL for a decade, to no avail.

5. The White Sox could have moved to Seattle, 1974. And they probably would have if Oakland A's owner Charles O. Finely had gotten his way. Finley's plan: The poorly supported White Sox would move to Seattle (which had yet to be awarded the Mariners), and Finley would take his poorly supported A's to Chicago, taking the place of the White Sox in Comiskey Park. The shuffle, Finley believed, would benefit both franchises and also place him closer to his home in LaPorte, Ind. Finley's plan came apart when Bill Veeck jumped in and bought the White Sox from Arthur Allyn. Veeck had no intention of leaving Chicago.

4. Bob Robertson could have been the voice of the Mariners, 1976. In fact, Bill Schonley, the voice of the Totems and Pilots, also could have been the voice of the Mariners. They, along with local radio/TV personalities Ray McMackin and Wayne Cody, were among the candidates for the job that ultimately went to 41-year-old Dave Niehaus.

3. Nelson Skalbania could have owned the Mariners, 1980. The Canadian real estate entrepreneur at various times owned the NHL's Edmonton Oilers, the WHA's Indianapolis Racers (Skalbania signed Wayne Gretzky) and the NASL's Memphis Rogues. In 1980, Skalbania made a $12 million pitch to purchase the Mariners from a Seattle ownership group headed by comedian Danny Kaye. The offer was turned down, but a year later Kaye et al sold to George Argyros (for $13 million), who went on to savage the franchise in a brutal nine-year reign of error. Skalbania went on to purchase the-then highly successful Montreal Alouettes of the Canadian Football League. After changing the team's name to "Concordes" and driving the franchise into bankruptcy, Skalbania infuriated fans with his infamous comment, "It's not like I raped a nun."

2. Seattle could have hosted the Super Bowl, 1988. When the NFL decided to award the 1992 Super Bowl to a northern city, Seattle, Indianapolis and Minneapolis quickly emerged as the leading candidates to host the event. The Seattle Bid Committee, led by Seahawks owner John Nordstrom, were all but assured of winning by Commissioner Pete Rozelle. But two problems wrecked the effort. The Nordstrom family sold the Seahawks to California real estate developer Ken Behring, whom most NFL executives quickly came to loathe. Then King County Executive Tim Hill and Chamber of Commerce President George Duff formed a rival Seattle bid committee. The NFL did not look favorably on the second group, but rather than sort out which bid committee was the official one, it simply awarded the 1992 Super Bowl to Minneapolis.

1. The Mariners could have lost the coin flip, 1995. The famous one-game playoff between the Mariners and Angels on October 1, 1995, to decide the AL West title could have been played in Anaheim instead of in the Kingdome. On September 18, per league custom, the Mariners and Angels participated in a coin flip to determine which team would host a one-game playoff if the clubs finished the regular season in a tie. The Mariners called tails, and won. The Mariners won 9–1 in front of 52,326 fans.

Howard's Froot-Loop Hoops

For parts of three years at the start of the century, local sports fans were treated to the thoughts of a new guest columnist in the pages of the *Seattle Times*. New Sonics owner and Starbucks inventor Howard Schultz wrote periodically about his hoops thoughts, dreams, and goals, which suddenly went poof when he sold the team to owners who lived in sports-starved Oklahoma City. Here are the ten biggest piles of compost extracted from those columns, and our post-debacle analysis.

10. October 28, 2001. "With the success of the Seattle Mariners, we were all reminded that Seattle is home to some of the best fans in sports. It's our intention to keep alive, throughout the basketball season, that civic pride the Mariners resurrected with their enthusiasm this year. And like the M's, we'll do it with dignity and by putting our fans first. It's all out of respect for the game."

What is most galling about this remark is the fact that the "best fans" were also part of the huge Sonics following, most of whom who were pleased, along with the NBA, with the team and the newly remodeled KeyArena. When it came to new buildings, the Mariners combined an exciting team with a shrewd, tough set of lobbyists and political allies in Olympia that still took five years to seal the deal to replace the dreary Kingdome with Safeco Field. Schultz & Co. didn't field the same caliber of teams on the floor or in Olympia, then sold out when the going was tough. Dignity? Where?

9. August 12, 2001. "I've spent a lot of time with Vin (Baker) in the past several weeks, getting to know him as a person. I invited him to spend time at my home, and we talked. He told me about his goals, his dreams, his family and his faith. He gave me some glimpses into his reactions to fans, his analysis of his own play and his plan for a comeback."

If that demonstrates Schultz's keen insight into human behavior, we're all grateful that Schultz picked coffee as his way of dominating the world (instead of, say, becoming Secretary of Defense).

8. September 22, 2002. "If there's one thing I've learned in the world of business over the years, it's the importance of having a plan. After our ownership group bought the Sonics last year, we quickly constructed a strategic plan that would reflect our values, put our fans and the community first and keep the franchise moving in the right direction. Simply put, the coming excitement is all part of the long-term plan. A plan we're committed to. A plan that's working."

What, exactly, were the values reflected in selling the team to out-of-towners for the inflated price of $350 million six years after buying it for $200 million? Apparently the values committed to was profit on sale. He was right. The plan worked.

7. July 8, 2001. "I believe that securing (Vladimir) Radmanovic will be viewed as a key step in leading the Sonics back to the ranks of the NBA's elite."

No, I meant Robert Swift. Uh, wait—Danny Fortson. Hold it—Mouhamed Sene. Oh yeah—Johan Petro . . .

6. September 22, 2002. "Included in our blueprint for returning the team to the NBA's elite involved five major goals that we accomplished this summer: re-signing Rashard Lewis, Jerome James and Ansu Sesay; bringing Calvin Booth back from injury; and trading Vin Baker."

Obviously, the little chat at Howard's house didn't work so well for Baker. Probably spilled some coffee. Re-signing Lewis was a no-brainer. But somehow, the names Ansu Sesay and Calvin Booth never made anyone else's blueprint for returning to the NBA's elite.

5. September 22, 2001. "Another player I've gotten to know is Calvin Booth. The Sonics' coaching and player-personnel staffs spent weeks evaluating free agents. We reached a consensus that the guy we wanted was Calvin. I spent a lot of time with Calvin and learned much about him. We flew to Cleveland and invited him and his fiancée to dinner."

Got to admire that kind of dedication and keen eye by Schultz. Booth apparently demonstrated sufficient dinner dexterity with a knife and fork to get a six-year, $34 million guaranteed deal. It was the damn basketball, all round and smooth, that Booth couldn't handle (50 starts in three seasons, four points a game).

4. April 8, 2001. "Howard, don't do this," my friends said. Buying the Sonics could only lead to disappointment and disillusion, they told me. When I went ahead anyway, making the biggest investment of my life, they warned me not to expect to be able to change much. "You're naïve," they said when they heard my lofty plans. "Don't aim too high." But I want to aim high. I believe we can bring an NBA championship to Seattle. I believe we can fill KeyArena every game and renew its reputation for being one of the loudest buildings in the league."

Disappointment? Check. Disillusion? Check. Can't change much? Check. Naïve? Check. Aim too high? Check. Championship in a loud, filled KeyArena? Not so much. Howard, you have good friends. Um, make that had good friends.

3. September 22, 2002. "Like everyone else, our organization would like to see Gary (Payton) finish his career as a Sonic just like Nate (McMillan)."

Quoting the late, great Sam Kinison: "AAAAAAAAAAAHHHHHH!"

2. April 8, 2001. "This is an exciting moment in the history of the Sonics, an opportunity to reinvent the experience. This is the start of a journey to make Seattle a basketball town once again, a place where fans are proud of their team. If I succeed, even partially, they—and the game of basketball—will be the winners."

What a bloviating, supercilious twit. The single biggest WTF moment of his column career came in his first one. What needed reinventing? The previous owner, Barry Ackerley, had the Sonics in the playoffs 13 times in his 17 years, which included three trips to the Western Conference finals and a trip to the NBA Finals. The regular-season record during the Ackerley years was 218 games above .500. Killing pro hoops in Seattle was the greatest reinvention since the adobe submarine.

1. February 23, 2003. "It's always been my feeling that sports teams are a public trust."

It's always been our feeling that when an owner says sports teams are a public trust, don't trust anything he says.

Much as we wish it were otherwise, sports provides us only temporary escape from the realities of the world. There is only one permanent escape. The escape routes taken by these state sports figures were noteworthy (listed chronologically).

Hiram Conibear, September 10, 1917. A former trainer for the Chicago White Sox and Washington's crew coach from 1907–17, Conibear died instantly when he fell from a tree in his backyard while harvesting plums. He was 46 years old.

Warren Grimm, November 11, 1919. A receiver on the Washington football team from 1908–11, Grimm was killed by gunfire from members of the Industrial Workers of the World while marching in an Armistice Day parade in his hometown of Centralia.

Enoch Bagshaw, October 3, 1930. The former UW football (1921–29) coach, serving as the supervisor of the Washington State transportation department, died of a heart attack at the age of 46 shortly after eating a cucumber salad in the State Capitol cafeteria. He was discovered lying face down on the floor of the Capitol building.

Dan Dugdale, March 9, 1934. A City Light truck struck and killed Seattle's original baseball pioneer (owner of the Seattle Klondikers, Clamdiggers and Giants and built two ballparks in the city) when Dugdale attempted to cross Fourth Avenue near Atlantic Street in downtown Seattle, just outside today's Safeco Field. Dugdale died of internal injuries at Providence Hospital three hours later.

Jack Stevens, March 1, 1940. A referee, Stevens died at Civic Auditorium (now the location of McCaw Hall at Seattle Center) after he was hurled into the ropes by wrestler Verne Baxter of Monroe, a loser to Montreal's John Katan. Stevens slipped through the ropes, cracked his head on a steel support and fell out of the ring to the floor. Stevens, who had a pre-existing heart condition, died minutes later in a dressing room. Seattle police held Baxter until it was determined Stevens likely died from his heart condition.

Jack Lelivelt, January 20, 1941. Lelivelt, who managed the Seattle Rainiers to Pacific Coast League baseball championships in 1939 and 1940, suffered a heart attack while watching a Harlem Globetrotters basketball game at Seattle's Civic Auditorium, and died about an hour later at Maynard Hospital.

Royal Brougham, October 29, 1978. A 68-year newspaper veteran and the *Post-Intelligencer's* sports editor for more than 50 years, Brougham suffered a ruptured aorta after eating half a dozen hotdogs in the Kingdome press box during the closing minutes of a Seahawks-Broncos football game, and died several hours later at Swedish Hospital.

Curtis Williams, May 6, 2002. On October 28, 2000, in Palo Alto, Calif., Williams, a UW cornerback, tackled Stanford running back Kerry Carter in a helmet-to-helmet collision, suffering a spinal cord injury between the C1 and C2 vertebrae that left him paralyzed below the neck. A little more than two years later, Williams died of natural causes at the home of his brother in Fresno, CA, the first death of a student-athlete in UW history due to a sports-related injury.

Anthony Vontoure, May 31, 2002. The former UW cornerback died during a violent struggle with sheriff's deputies while being taken into custody in Sacramento, CA. Dismissed from the Huskies by coach Rick Neuheisel in February 2001 after a series of disciplinary problems, Vontoure had been placed in a patrol car when his breathing became labored. He died shortly thereafter.

Craig Kelly, January 20, 2003. A world-class snowboarder from Mount Vernon, Kelly died with six others in an avalanche near the Durrand Glacier in British Columbia. Kelly, 36, a Mount Vernon High graduate and honors student at the UW, was one of the first professionals in the sport.

Ivan Calderon, December 27, 2003. A Mariners outfielder from 1984–86, Calderon was shot to death in Loiza, Puerto Rico. Witnesses said that Calderon was in a store when two people entered and, without a word, shot the former player multiple times.

Tony Harris, November 17, 2007. The body of Harris, a Garfield High grad who helped lead the Washington State University basketball team to an NCAA tournament berth in 1994, was found in central Brazil two weeks after he was reported missing. He may have committed suicide, or maybe not. Harris left the U.S. October 31 to play for the Universo team in Brasilia, and shortly thereafter began telling people, including his wife via phone calls and e-mails, that he feared for his life. When his body was discovered in a heavily wooded area, it had no bullet holes or stab wounds, no broken bones or tissue under fingernails—and its exposure to the elements had erased significant forensic clues.

Steve Raible played wide receiver for the Seahawks from 1976–81, then joined KIRO in 1982, becoming part of the Seahawks' radio broadcast team with Pete Gross and Wayne Cody. Gross died in 1992 and Cody in 2002. Before they departed, Raible had way too much fun with these guys.

"I know a shortcut." Leaving Kansas City's Arrowhead Stadium in the 1980s after another loss to the Chiefs, Wayne, Pete, Norm Graham (broadcast engineer), and I climbed into our rental car for the long drive to the airport. In those days, the by-pass hadn't been constructed around K.C., so you had to drive back into town, then to the airport. Wayne said he knew a shortcut through unending cornfields to the airport. Big mistake. An hour later, we're lost. I'm driving, Wayne's riding shotgun giving directions, and Pete, livid, is in the back seat. Finally, on the horizon, I see a speck of a plane. We follow it, knowing the team plane we're trying make is probably long gone. Eventually, we arrived at the airport. I drove two wheels up on the curb in front of our departure gate and tossed the keys to a confused skycap. Wayne gave him $20, told him to return the car to Hertz, and ran (or as close to running as Wayne could come) into the airport. To our eternal surprise the plane was still there, waiting for us. Chuck Knox wanted to strangle us and was two minutes from leaving. But team VP Gary Wright, I learned later, convinced Chuck to wait. No problem for Wayne though. He went right to sleep and snored all the way back to Seattle.

"What the hell was that noise?" In 1976, Wayne did the sideline reports for the Hawks radio broadcasts. He also did some Husky games on TV. So he called the Husky home game on Saturday, jumped on a red-eye, and arrived in Tampa Bay about 90 minutes before kickoff. He got to the stadium during pre-game warm-ups, sat on the end of the Seahawks bench and promptly nodded off. In slow motion, he teetered, and then fell off the end of the bench, landing on his side with an audible thud. From 40 yards away, you could hear the sort of sound a hot air balloon makes when the air releases. He lay there on his side for a moment, like an upturned turtle, unable to breathe, when defensive tackle and team funnyman Bob Lurtsema walked over and said loud enough for everyone around to hear, "No more drinks for you on the trip home, Cody."

"Hello, 911? We're gonna need the 'Jaws Of Life.'" Wayne, Pete and I were returning from a big dinner on the road in L.A. Cody laid on the back seat while I drove with Pete in the passenger seat. In a flash, a van swerved into my lane and I jumped on the brakes. Wayne rolled off the back seat, landing face down on the floor of the car, pinned between his seat and ours—a Town Car straitjacket. He was wedged tighter than two coats of paint. When Pete stopped laughing, he reached back and tried to pull out Wayne, who was yelling, cursing and losing the feeling in his arms. For Pete, it was like trying to lift a 55-gallon drum of ball bearings. Eventually we pried him out, returned to the hotel, and laughed about it for the next 10 years.

"Great game, fellas, tell me all about it." Wayne's favorite part of Seahawks trips was enjoying a fine meal or two (or five) at some great restaurants. His No. 1 one choice was Anthony's Star of the Sea in San Diego. He liked it so much that after having a wonderful meal on Saturday night, he went Sunday morning to Jack Murphy Stadium, did his pre-game show, and then left for the restaurant. He returned midway through the third quarter with two huge orders of garlic scampi, pulled into the parking lot and listened to the game on the car radio, eating scampi and pumpernickel crackers like a condemned man savoring his last meal. He threw the shrimp skins out the window and under the car until the skies over the stadium parking lot were darkened by the seagulls that were coming from as far away as Cabo San Lucas to enjoy the leftovers. Never missing a beat, Wayne headed into the locker room to interview the players as though he's seen every play. To this day, I've never been in a car so thoroughly saturated in garlic. It was a delightful ride to the airport.

Goodbye to a friend. My lasting memory of Wayne is one all long-time Seahawks fans remember, Monday night, November 30, 1992. The Seahawks were playing the Denver Broncos in the Kingdome. Before the game, Pete was inducted into the Seahawks Ring of Honor. He was also dying of cancer. Wayne and I were positioned in the 300 level. Frail and weak, Pete was driven to mid-field. He made a short speech of thanks. Then Wayne and I pulled the covering to reveal Pete's name in the Ring. We walked back to the broadcast booth crying. Wayne said, "I love that little guy and I'm going to miss him." Pete died two days later.

Hard to tell whether the team or the player was more desperate, but some nationally renowned pro athletes passed through Seattle on the way to the door—but only barely, because they were on fumes. (Ranked by stature and accomplishments before coming to Seattle.)

11. Patrick Ewing (2000–01), John Lucas (1988–89), Maurice Lucas (1986–87), Dennis Martinez (1997), Gaylord Perry (1983). Although all seemed spent when they got here, each legend went on to play at least part of another season elsewhere.

10. Harold Jackson, Seahawks 1983. Jackson played 15 seasons with the Rams, Eagles and Patriots before joining the Seahawks at 37. Playing sparingly in 15 games, the wide receiver caught eight passes for 126 yards and one touchdown, and then retired.

9. Willie Horton, Mariners 1979–80. The 36-year-old Horton, who signed with the Mariners after a long career in Detroit, had one good season left. In 1979, he hit 29 home runs and drove in 106 as the team's designated hitter. A year later, he had a .221 batting average with eight homers when the Mariners made him part of an 11-player trade with the Texas Rangers, where he did not play.

8. Bob Love, Sonics 1976–77. A three-time All-Star who had spent the majority of his 11-year career with the Chicago Bulls, Love played part of his final season with the Sonics, appearing in 32 games and averaging 4.1 points.

7. Bobby Moore, Sounders 1978. No, not the Mount Tahoma/Oregon/Minnesota receiver and Michael Jordan valet (now Ahmad Rashad). This Bobby Moore participated in more than 1,000 soccer matches over a 20-year career in the English First Division. The high point was 1966 when he led England to a 4–2 victory over West Germany in the World Cup final at Wembley Stadium. As a result, Moore, a defender, was awarded the Order of the British Empire. With the Sounders, the 37-year-old played seven games, took three shots and recorded one assist.

6. Ken Griffey Sr., Mariners 1990–91. At 41, Dad played in just 30 games in 1990 but they were memorable—the only father-son tandem in history on the same MLB team. His only home run was part of a back-to-back with his son, of whom you may have heard. Injuries in a spring training auto accident curtailed a return in 1991.

5. Rich Gossage, Mariners 1994. The 42-year-old closer and 2008 Hall of Fame inductee pitched 47 innings, had a 3–0 record and saved a game in his only season with the Mariners.

4. Carl Eller, Seahawks 1978. After 15 years with the Vikings, the former All-Pro defensive end signed with the Seahawks at 37 for his final 16 NFL games. Eller led the Seahawks in an official (and self-explanatory) coaches' statistic called "loafs."

3. Warren Moon, Seahawkes, 1997-98. Following a near Hall of Fame career with the Oilers and Vikings, Moon, a former UW quarterback, came back to Seattle and sealed the deal in a two-year stint with the team. In 1997, he threw for 3,678 yards and 25 TDs as a 41-year-old and made his ninth Pro Bowl. Moon went to the Pro Football Hall of Fame in 2006.

2. Franco Harris, Seahawks 1984. After 12 years with the Pittsburgh Steelers, the 34-year-old future Hall of Famer played eight lamentable games for the Seahawks, gaining 170 yards, mostly heading in the direction of the sideline, in 68 attempts with no touchdowns.

1. Jerry Rice, Seahawks 2004. Signed at 42, the 13-time Pro Bowler and leading receiver in pro football history, played in 11 games, starting nine. He caught 25 passes for 362 yards and scored three of his 197 receiving touchdowns. He left largely with dignity intact.

Sports fans are used to all manner of pulled hammies, turf toes, back spasms and hangovers compromising their heroes. But sometimes things happen that defy the odds or common sense or any legit explanation. Or all of the above.

10. Bobby Ayala, Mariners pitcher, 1996. On April 23, a Mariners' off-day, Ayala punched out a Chicago hotel window, cut his hand, and went on disabled list for a couple months.

9. Steve Trout, Mariners pitcher, 1988. "Rainbow" not only had a dismal year on the mound—he went 4–7 with a 7.83 ERA—he injured himself when he fell off an exercise bike in the Kingdome clubhouse.

8. Byron McLaughlin, Mariners pitcher, 1980. The Mariners left-hander cut his right hand on a bathroom mirror while he was practicing his windup in his hotel room during a road trip.

7. Kazuhiro Sasaki, Mariners pitcher, 2003. Sasaki spent 68 days on the disabled list with fractured ribs after the club said he slipped while carrying his suitcase up a flight of stairs after returning from a road trip. Closer to the truth was word from Japan that a drunken Sasaki was engaged in play wrestling with friends when he fell on a table.

6. John Moses, Mariners outfielder, 1986. Moses sustained deep bruises to his elbow and hip, forcing him to miss five games, after teammate Mark Langston flipped their cart at the Glen Abbey Golf Course during a road trip in Toronto.

5. Rufus Porter, Seahawks linebacker, 1992. Missed two games when he burned himself frying catfish. Porter suffered second-degree burns after throwing water on the flaming fish he was frying. "It just blew up in my face," he said.

4. Dave Valle, Mariners catcher, 1991. On August 5, the Mariners catcher was taking a muscle relaxant to ease the pain in his back after a game in Oakland. Valle washed it down with a cup of coffee, which went down the wrong pipe. Valle began coughing and dropped to the floor. The coughing caused muscle spasms, and Valle had to be rolled out of the Oakland Coliseum in a wheelchair.

3. Kevin Mitchell, Mariners outfielder, 1992. While sitting in the dugout before a game in Anaheim, the portly Mitchell, a relentless eater, suddenly began to vomit. The spasm was so severe that Mitchell tore a muscle in his rib cage, forcing him to miss two games.

2. Ibar "The Sailor Man" Arrington, boxer, 1978. A heavyweight contender who compiled a 29–7–2 record from 1974–82, including a close loss to eventual champion Larry Holmes in Las Vegas in 1977, Arrington was legendary for his ability to take a big punch and stay on his feet. Once, when a backhoe dumped its bucket contents on his head, Arrington, a graduate of Monroe High outside Seattle, never lost consciousness. Perhaps the only time he keeled over was during a workout when, to strengthen his arms and shoulders, he pounded a tractor tire with a sledgehammer. He swung too hard and the hammer bounced off the tire and smashed into Arrington's head, knocking him cold.

1. Glen "Turk" Edwards, Washington Redskins lineman, 1940. On September 22, the former Washington State star from Mold, in north central Washington, became the only player in pro football history to suffer an injury during the pre-game coin toss. Before his team faced the New York Giants, the six-foot-two, 255-pound lineman walked to midfield where he met the opposing captain, former WSU teammate and fellow All-America Mel Hein. The official flipped the coin and Hein called heads. It came up tails. Edwards pivoted for the sidelines and toppled over. His cleats had caught in the turf, wrenching his knee so seriously he had to be carted off the field. The injury ended a nine-year career that made the NFL Hall of Fame.

The Mariners had a chance to draft two pitchers, Roger Clemens and Randy Johnson, who would combine to win 12 Cy Young awards. They had shots at drafting Tony Gwynn and Rafael Palmeiro, both members of the 3,000-hit club. Recognizing that every team counts some successes and many failures among its draft choices, the following represents a team by position the Mariners could have assembled via the draft—if they had known then what everyone knows now.

11. 1B: Rafael Palmeiro

Pick: 189th, 1982

M's: With the No. 6 pick overall, Seattle selected SS Spike Owen, who served as the club's starter from 1983 until mid-1986. Palmeiro went on to collect more than 3,000 hits and smack 52 long balls against the Mariners. In the same draft, the M's also could have snatched Mike Greenwell with the 72nd pick, Randy Johnson with the 89th or Jose Canseco with the 391st.

Slap forehead here: M's used the No. 1 overall in 1979 on future OF bust Al Chambers when Don Mattingly was there for the plucking. In 1992, when the M's went for LHP Ron Villone with the 14th pick, Jason Giambi lasted until the 58th pick.

10. 2B: Ryne Sandberg

Pick: 511th, 1978

M's: Used sixth pick overall on OF Tito Nanni, who never reached the majors. Sandberg won nine Gold Gloves, seven Silver Slugger awards and entered the Hall of Fame in 2005.

Slap forehead here: M's used No. 3 overall in 1989 on RHP Roger Salkeld with Chuck Knoblauch still on the board. M's drafted C Ryan Christianson No. 11 overall in 1999 with Brian Roberts on the board.

9. 3B: Albert Pujols

Pick: 402nd, 1999

M's: With the 395th pick in the 13th round, the Mariners took a flyer on Justin Leone, an infielder who played briefly for Seattle in its dismal 2004 season and otherwise languished in the minors. Albert Pujols was still on the draft board.

Slap forehead here: M's used 86th pick in 1982 on cup-of-coffee pitcher Terry Taylor while multiple Gold Glover Terry Pendleton lasted until 179th pick; M's used 1984 No. 1 on RHP Bill Swift, then took Ps Mike Christ (30th) and Ken Spratke (56th) with Ken Caminiti still available.

8. SS: Ozzie Smith

Pick: 68th, 1977

M's: Used first-round pick on OF Dave Henderson (26th overall). Henderson became an outfield regular, but the M's traded him in 1986. With Smith, a future 13-time Gold Glover, still on draft board, the M's took nogoodnik OF Henry Bender at No. 52.

Slap forehead here: Cal Ripken was available when M's selected Tito Nanni No. 3 overall and C Dave Valle No. 32 overall. In 1982, instead of drafting Spike Owen to play SS, they could have drafted Barry Larkin.

7. C: Mike Piazza

Pick: 1,390th, 1988

M's: Used first-round pick on Tino Martinez, a fine player whom they ultimately traded (1995) to save on payroll. Later in the 1988 draft, M's plucked sub-luminaries Greg Pirkl, Jim Campanis and Lee Hancock while Piazza, a 12-time All-Star with more than 400 homers, went unclaimed.

Slap forehead here: In 1991, M's took Tommy Adams (54th), Jim Mecir (85th) and Desi Relaford (111th), leaving future four-time Gold Glover Mike Matheny still on the board.

6. OF: Barry Bonds

Pick: 39th, 1982

M's: After taking SS Spike Owen, Seattle had another crack at Bonds when it selected 34th, but opted for pitcher Mike Wishnevski, who never reached the majors. Bonds won three MVPs before becoming scientific experiment.

Slap forehead here: In 1987, M's could have taken Albert Belle, but grabbed RHP Dave Burba, whom they traded in 1991 for declining Kevin Mitchell. FYI: Bonds out-homered Owen 762–11.

5. OF: Manny Ramirez

Pick: 13th, 1991

M's: Drafted LHP Shawn Estes 11th overall. Seattle traded then-minor leaguer Estes to the Giants in disastrous Salomon Torres deal in 1995. Nine-time All-Star Ramirez has whacked more than 450 homers.

Slap forehead here: In 1977, the M's drafted SS Kyle Koke, who never reached majors, two picks ahead of Tim Raines.

4. OF: Tony Gwynn

Pick: 58th, 1981

M's: Spent No. 1 overall on RHP Mike Moore, who became winningest (66 wins) and losingest (96 losses) pitcher in club history. Gwynn made 15 All-Star teams and won eight batting titles. (In taking Moore, M's also overlooked OFs Joe Carter, Fred McGriff and RHP David Cone).

Slap forehead here: M's selected Darnell Coles sixth overall in 1980, leaving Kelly Gruber and Tim Teufel on the board.

3. DH: Mark McGwire

Pick: 10th, 1984

M's: After Shawn Abner went first overall to the Mets, Seattle used the No. 2 on Bill Swift, who wound up completing two journeymen stints with the club. McGwire pounded 583 home runs.

Slap forehead here: M's used first-round pick in 1985 on RHP Mike Campbell, who won eight games in three years. Then they deemed SS Nezi Balelo (87th pick) more valuable than David Justice (89th).

2. RHP: Roger Clemens

Pick: 19th, 1983

M's: With the No. 7 overall, M's drafted RHP Darrel Akerfelds, who never pitched for Seattle and won just nine games between 1986–91.

Slap forehead here: One year after not drafting Clemens (1983), the Mariners did not draft Greg Maddux, Tom Glavine or Chuck Finley.

1. LHP: Randy Johnson

Pick: 36th, 1985

M's: After using No. 7 overall on RHP Mike Campbell, M's spent 35th overall on Mike Schooler, who became "epitome of grand slamness" in 1992 when he tied MLB record by yielding four salamis. Expos took the Big Unit one pick later, and M's ultimately traded Mark Langston to acquire him.

Slap forehead here: With 116th pick in 2000, M's selected LHP Sam Hays. Marlins took Dontrelle Willis 100+ picks later.

If you have gone this far in the book, you should know most everything worthwhile in Seattle-area sports. But you don't. Not until you read this list.

12. First Washington athlete to appear on a box of Wheaties. Earl Averill of Snohomish, inducted into baseball's Hall of Fame in 1975, made the Wheaties box in 1937 (Ken Griffey made four Wheaties boxes, a record for a Seattle athlete).

11. Most aptly named manager. Cliff Ditto managed the 1977 Walla Walla Padres, an affiliate of the San Diego Padres.

10. Shortest Seattle career by a Hall of Famer. On June 1, 1978, NBA Hall of Famer Wilt Chamberlain, the ostensible International Volleyball Association "commissioner," played his only game in a local uniform when he suited up for the Seattle Smashers against the Tucson Sky at the Seattle Center Arena. Only 1,415 fans witnessed Chamberlain's three-match stint.

9. Only one-time Seattle athlete to become one of the "Eight Men Out." Fred McMullen, who played for the 1912 Seattle Giants of the Northwest League, was eventually banned from baseball as one of the "Eight Men Out" Chicago Black Sox who threw the 1919 World Series.

8. Lowest-attended Mariners' game. On April 17, 1979, the Mariners and Oakland A's played before just 653 fans in the Oakland Coliseum. The A's won 6–5.

7. First (and only) Seattle athlete to play a game wearing just half a beard. Between innings of a 1983 contest against Toronto, Seattle closer Bill Caudill shaved off half his beard. After pitching the next half-inning half-bearded, during which he took a line drive to the chest off the bat of Barry Bonnell, Caudill shaved off the remaining whiskers.

6. Worst-attended Kingdome event. Only 11 fans showed up to watch the Museum of Flight Paper Airplane Contest on May 22, 1985.

5. $1 Million Salmon Derby, 1987. Credit—or blame—eccentric Seattle promoter Bob Walsh for this one: a lone coho salmon, implanted with a wire tag bearing the code C36 just aft of its left eye, swam somewhere in Puget Sound. The prize for catching it: $1 million. No one snared the elusive fish, but 7,000 stymied anglers collaborated to set a world record in simultaneous skunkings.

4. The first (and only) Seattle athlete to appear on a postage stamp.

"Queen Helene," Helene Madison, who won three Olympic gold swimming medals in 1932, appeared on a U.S. postage stamp in 1990, the only athlete from the state of Washington to do so.

3. The only Seattle athlete to end his playing career hawking peanuts.

Mariners pitcher Jim Colborn spent part of his last day in the major leagues—October 1, 1978—selling peanuts in the Kingdome stands.

2. Worst Pioneer Square postgame brawl.

Following the Seahawks' 42–10 win over the Houston Texans at Safeco Field on October 16, 2005, Seattle DB Ken Hamlin suffered a fractured skull during an altercation outside a nightclub. His assailant was found murdered hours later.

1. Only Seattle athlete to appear in a "Simpsons" episode.

Ken Griffey Jr., the Mariners center fielder from 1989–99, is the only Seattle athlete to appear on TV's long-running animated hilarity. Along with Wade Boggs, Jose Canseco, Roger Clemens, Don Mattingly, Steve Sax, Mike Scioscia, Ozzie Smith and Darryl Strawberry, Griffey had a cameo in the February 20, 1992, episode titled "Homer at the Bat."

Seattle's Grammy Award-winning hip-hop artist is best known for the 1992 smash "Baby Got Back." He's a big-time sports fan and also a successful producer who scours the Seattle scene looking for the next big act. He's the kind of dude of whom many guys would say, "I'd like to be HIM for a day." So what sports stars elicit that same feeling from Mix?

Alex Rodriguez. Because every woman I have ever dated has uttered these words: "If he asked, of course I would." Even men call this dude good looking. At least he has Derek Jeter to give him competition in NYC. $250 mil, good looks, young, single (when he was in Seattle) and looking to be a He-Whore!

Gary Payton. I would have loved to be Gary Payton on this particular day: Seattle vs. Chicago in Game 3 of the 1996 Finals. Chicago had the game won and they were shooting free throws when Michael Jordan said something to Gary and Gary WENT NUTZ! He got in Michael's face and not only tore him a new one, he also destroyed the old one. He cussed Mike out and got away with it. AWESOME!

Lenny Wilkens. Who wouldn't have loved to be Lenny when the Sonics won the championship after going to the NBA Finals back-to-back? I was fortunate enough to be at the parade and it's something that has not been seen in this city since. Lenny is still the man.

Jack Sikma. Picture this: You're a seven-foot center, you can leap out of the building, you block shots and you have dominated just about every center in the NBA. Then you hit the court in the old Coliseum and you are looking at this slow, no-jumping center who has not one dunk on his highlight reel. You're on defense, he turns his back on you, and you know you will block his shot. But he slowly turns into your face (yes, your face) and shoots what looks to be the most basic set shot on earth. Swish. The crowd yells and you are PISSED! After your sixth foul and Jack's 30th point, you realize you just got your ass handed to you by Frankenstein. I would love to have been Jack for a day back then. I can only imagine the four-letter outburst he heard after each one of those slow-motion set shots.

Mike Holmgren. We all wanted to run this man out of town. I would love to have been Mike for a day over the last couple of years. I would have been able to drive down the street and listen to Softy (Mahler, KJR host) kiss my ass over and over. All the sports radio callers begging me to stay and telling Paul Allen to give me whatever I want because now I am the MAN! I would have done the same thing: Tell you all I am talking to my wife about it, then my wife and I would sit back and laugh as you Seahawk fans begged for me to stay. Success is the sweetest revenge! Mike is a BAD MOFO.

These are guys who told good stories, and were good stories. They are sports people who hardly ever had to buy a drink for themselves (of course, a couple of them never drank) but would be happy to buy the house a round. They would have great fun with this book, because all of them would swear they could have done it better. Listed alphabetically.

Royal Brougham (1978). The P-I sports editor and columnist, as well as a legendary promoter of city and self, covered the Seattle Metropolitans victory in the 1917 Stanley Cup, and was in the Kingdome covering a Seahawks game in 1978 when the aid crew carried him past Steve Rudman. That would be one degree of separation between the beginning of major sports in Seattle, and now.

Wayne Cody (2002). You know how long people have lived in Seattle by the number of Wayne Cody stories they tell about the rotund bon vivant who dabbled in sports broadcasting. One favorite: Back when he was doing Sonics play-by-play on TV, a panicked producer ran into a Seattle writer before a game in Phoenix and said, "Have you seen Wayne? We're on the air in five!" Seconds before the broadcast, Cody casually strolled into the arena, grabbed the mike and stood in front of the camera. "Hi everybody, welcome to Phoenix. I'm Wayne Cody. Back with the lineups in a minute." Asked during the break where he had been, Cody said, "I took a flight from Seattle that stopped in Vegas, and I was hot at the tables. Did I miss anything?"

Dick Erickson (2001). A legendary crew coach, Erickson spent nearly 50 years at the University of Washington as an athlete, coach and administrator. He was especially adept at telling stories and loved to regale listeners (off-the-record, of course) with yarns involving the crew team's legendary pranks (we especially liked the one about a huge Gilby's Gin banner draped across the Tower of London during the 1977 Henley Royal Regatta).

Pete Gross (1992). The Seahawks radio voice and a member of the franchise's Ring of Honor, Gross may have been the most upbeat, funny, sincere guy in the history of the mammalian species. They will find weapons of mass destruction in Iraq before they find the first person to say a bad thing about this guy.

Mike Kahn (2008). A sportwriter and editor for more than 30 years, the 54-year-old Kahn toiled at the Tacoma News Tribune, had a fling with CBS Sportsline and ended his career as a digital reporter with the Seattle Seahawkes. The guy knew more about the NBA than practically anyone on the planet and talked sports 24/7. Lung cancer got him after a long battle.

Mark Kauffman (1995). No man in Seattle sports history loved to talk horses more than Kauffman, who served as public relations director at Longacres race track until his death in 1995. He had an infectious sense of humor and departed way too soon. At least he did it while attending the Kentucky Derby.

Bernie Little (2003). A Florida guy, he nevertheless was a blustery fixture on the shores of Lake Washington for more than 30 years as the owner of the always dominant Budweiser unlimited hydroplane race team. Pompous, obnoxious, cantankerous and an over-the-top hoot, Little's wardrobe of gold chains, white shoes and red pants barely began to tell the story. He once said to Art Thiel after a race that, because of what he had written in the *P-I*, if he could get his leg that high, he'd kick Art in the nuts. Now that's how to talk back to a sports columnist.

Earl Luebker (2001). The garrulous *Tacoma News Tribune* sports editor and columnist would always answer the question, "howareya?" with, "Old, tired and confused." He was none of the above the time he was asked whether he kept an "evergreen" column on file, to fill the space on days when nothing came to mind for a topic. "No," Leubker said. "If I died that day, the company would get a free one."

Georg Meyers (2007). One of the most literate sportswriters in America, Meyers started at the *Seattle Times* in 1949 and retired after the 1984 Olympics, having earned the respect of everyone who read his words or met him in person. Sufficiently fastidious and punctual to drive many in a slovenly profession crazy, no one had the heart to mess the hair or wrinkle the shirt of such a warm, considerate guy.

Bill "The Beerman" Scott (2007). A beer salesman with a bass voice that cracked concrete (is that what did in the Kingdome?), Scott made himself famous for starting college-like chants from one side of the stadium to the other. The man who launched a thousand "waves" liked to call it "synergy facilitation," but it was cheerleading from a sports fan's heart that filled much of his barrel chest. You couldn't call yourself a Seattle sports fan without knowing his signature vendor pitch: "Freeze your teeth and give your tongue a sleigh ride—cold beer!"

Torchy Torrance (1990). As you can read elsewhere in these pages, Torrance had a hand in just about everything to do with Seattle sports, good and bad, from the 1920s through the 1970s. He was in on the creation of the original Husky Stadium as well as Longacres race track, helped found the Washington Athletic Club and worked for the Triple A Rainiers baseball team. He even helped put his beloved Huskies football team on NCAA probation, creating another Seattle tradition. There will never be another like Roscoe Conkling Torrance.

As has often been said in sports, ya gotta believe. Until proven otherwise, of course. Here's the best collection of proofs otherwise.

"We'll win by 30 points."

William Allen, Washington State football coach, predicting the outcome of the first contest between WSU and Washington in 1900 (the two teams played to a 5–5 tie).

"I want to assure the baseball world and Pacific Northwest fans that this will be a stable organization and we can expect to see major league baseball here for many years to come."

Marvin Milkes, Seattle Pilots general manager, during a press conference after the American League awarded Seattle a franchise for the 1969 major league baseball season (the Pilots lasted just one year in Seattle, went bankrupt, and moved to Milwaukee, becoming the Brewers).

"We feel Steve Niehaus will be as valuable to us as a quarterback. He can be an anchor for our defense, and he will be here for 10 years."

Jack Patera, Seahawks coach, after the team made the Notre Dame lineman the team's No. 1 pick in the 1976 NFL draft (Niehaus lasted three years before the Seahawks sent him to Minnesota for an over-the-hill Carl Eller).

"I plan to be a Sonic for the rest of my career."

Dennis Johnson, Sonics guard, after he signed a five-year, $400,000 contract on October 11, 1979 (Johnson was traded less than a year later. Coach Lenny Wilkens called him a "cancer" on the team).

"I am totally prepared for this chance, mentally, emotionally and physically. Playing .500 will be easy."

Maury Wills, new Mariners manager, at his first press conference in 1980 (Wills became the worst coach or manager in Seattle pro sports history and the club never played .500 on his watch).

"This is a great deal for our future."

Bernie Bickerstaff, Sonics coach, after the team traded its No. 1 pick in the 1987 NBA draft, Scottie Pippen, for Chicago's No. 1, Olden Polynice (Pippen became one of the 50 greatest players in NBA history and was a member of six title teams in Chicago. Polynice went on to a sideline career of impersonating police officers).

"We think he'll be the quarterback of the future."

Mike McCormack, Seahawks president, speaking to reporters on April 22, 1988, when the club signed quarterback Kelly Stouffer (Stouffer started just 16 games in five years and was gone after 1992, when he led one of the worst offenses in NFL history).

"You sure would not take a team out of a place where they sell the stadium out every week. The fans would kill you, and I wouldn't blame them. I think Seattle is the greatest football city in the country. I would not even consider buying the team if for some reason they had to be moved."

Ken Behring, Seahawks owner, after he purchased the franchise in 1988 from the Nordstrom family (Behring relocated the team to California in February 1996, but was ordered to take it back to Seattle by NFL Commissioner Paul Tagliabue).

"That's absolutely and totally preposterous. We have no interest in selling this team."

Jeff Smulyan, Mariners owner, telling the media in 1990 that he would not sell the club to buyers from Japan (two years later, the Mariners were sold to a Japanese businessman).

"He's a very competitive guy and is going to do great things in this league. He has a tremendous arm and great vision."

Tom Flores, Seahawks president, after the team selected San Diego quarterback Dan McGwire with its first pick in the 1991 NFL draft (McGwire started just five games in four years, retiring with a passer rating of 52.3).

"Rick has all the intangibles, the fearless ability to do whatever it takes to make the play."

Tom Flores, Seahawks president, after the club selected Rick Mirer of Notre Dame with the No. 2 overall pick in the 1993 NFL draft (Mirer had a decent rookie year, then bombed).

"The Mariners are going to love him."

Billy Connors, Mariners pitching coach, after the club signed free agent Greg Hibbard for the 1994 season (Hibbard went 1–5 with a 4.90 ERA, suffered a shoulder injury, and set a Mariners record for allowing 15 hits in a game against Oakland on May 24).

"He has a lot of potential that's untapped. He keeps getting better and better."

Wally Walker, Sonics president, after giving free agent center Jim McIlvaine a seven-year, $31 million contract on July 22, 1996 (McIlvaine lasted two years, averaged 3.5 points per game; his contract so alienated Shawn Kemp that he forced a trade).

"You'd have to be nuts to want to leave here. Especially if you like living in Pullman, which I do."

Mike Price, Washington State football coach, after signing an eight-year contract in 1998 worth $469,000 per year (by 2003, Price had taken a job at Alabama, which lasted only a matter of weeks).

"He's got a great arm and has shown the ability to pitch in the set-up role and close games."

Lee Pelekoudas, Mariners senior director of baseball administration, after the club signed reliever Bobby Ayala to a two-year, $3.3 million contract in 1998 (Ayala went 1–10 with a 7.29 ERA and was released).

"I think he's one of the best young centers in the league. He's a legitimate center. He has a bright future."

Nate McMillan, Sonics coach, after the club signed Calvin Booth to a six-year, $34 million contract in August 2001 (Booth never averaged more than 6.2 points per game in Seattle and lasted just three years).

"Let me interject one thing. We'll be back here to play Game 6! I've got confidence in my baseball club. We've gone to New York and beaten them five of six times. We'll do it again!"

Lou Piniella, Mariners manger, after his team fell behind the Yankees 2–0 in the 2001 ALCS (The Mariners did not go back to New York, losing the series 4–1).

"This was a great move by the Seahawks."

Mike Price, WSU football coach, on May 21, 2002 after the Seahawks signed former Cougar quarterback Ryan Leaf to a one-year contract (Leaf quit three weeks after signing).

"It's an adjustment coming to a new team. He's going to fit in fine here. And we know he's going to hit. We know that. He's always hit."

Lou Piniella, Mariners manager, talking about newly acquired Jeff Cirillo during spring training in 2002 (Cirillo never did hit and was traded to the San Diego Padres).

"I'll be back. I have another year on my contract."

Lou Piniella, Mariners manager, talking to Seattle reporters about his contract situation in September 2002 (Piniella left the Mariners two months later to become manager of the Tampa Bay Devil Rays).

"Things turn around quickly. I'm fine."

Bob Bender, UW hoop coach, when asked about his job security in 2002 (he was fired six weeks later).

"When you have a few bad years, people get down on you. But I certainly haven't gotten down on myself. My confidence is at an all-time high. I feel like I can still be one of the premier forwards in this league."

Vin Baker, Boston Celtics, following his trade from the Sonics in 2002 (Baker never again averaged in double figures and was out of the league three years later).

"I think good things are coming. We're about to turn a corner."

Bob Melvin, Mariners manager, on April 25, 2004 (the Mariners wound up last in the league in runs scored and lost 99 games).

"He's our horse and we're riding him all the way."

Howard Lincoln, Mariners CEO, after extending manager Bob Melvin's contract for one year on May 4, 2004 (Lincoln fired Melvin five months later).

"We want the ball. We're gonna score."

Matt Hasselbeck, Seahawks quarterback, calling heads on a coin flip heading into OT in a playoff game at Green Bay on January 4, 2004 (the Seahawks did not score as Hasselbeck threw the game-losing interception when receiver Alex Bannister ran the wrong route).

"I'm a 40-home run guy for sure. If I have a great year, it'd be more than that. A poor year would be in the high 20s to 30s."

Bucky Jacobsen, Mariners slugger, during the Mariners Winter Caravan tour on January 12, 2005 (Jacobsen didn't make the team coming out of spring training and never returned to the majors).

"I did not interview with the 49ers."

Rick Neuheisel, UW football coach, denying that he had a job talk with the NFL team (he later admitted to interviewing with the 49ers and issued an apology for lying).

"I feel real good about the direction this program is going. I don't care what anyone says. This program is going to turn around and we're going to get it done."

J.R. Hasty, Bellevue High running back, after making an oral commitment to play football at the University of Washington (Hasty never had any kind of career at the UW, which didn't turn it around).

"See you in a month. I'm going to come out there and pummel Joel Pineiro."

Bret Boone, after his trade to Minnesota in mid-2005, talking about a return to Safeco Field with the Twins (Boone was released by the Twins three weeks later).

"I really like this signing. Jeff not only gives us another quality starter that we can count on, but he helps us by creating depth in our pitching staff both in the rotation and the bullpen."

Mike Hargrove, Mariners manger, after the club signed Jeff Weaver to a one-year, $8.3 million contract on January 29, 2007 (Weaver started out 0–6 with a 14.32 ERA, finished 7–13 with a 6.20 ERA, and was not invited to return in 2008).

"I am ever encouraged each time I'm here and as the meetings progress and as we continue to begin to frame up our team and ideas about the future I continue to see a successful conclusion."

Clay Bennett, Sonics owner, after purchasing the club from Howard Schultz in 2006 (e-mails later proved that Bennett's intention was to move the Sonics to Oklahoma City all along).

Only after this list is studied will the breadth and depth of sports achievement in this corner of the woods be understood. A century's worth of Olympians, world champions, collegiate heroes, pro sports kingpins, record-makers and thrill-producers have done themselves and the state proud. We did our best to rank by impact and sustained quality. Let the arguments begin, but let the appreciation never end.

100. Billy Joe Hobert. We still don't know whether to love the Puyallup kid for quarterbacking the UW to a co-national championship in 1991, or loathe him for accepting a $50,000 loan that started the fall of the House of (Don) James.

99. Steve Mahre. Two-time national slalom champion, silver medalist at the 1984 Winter Olympics, and a gold medalist (giant slalom) at the 1983 World Championships, Steve was nearly as good as twin brother Phil.

98. Don McKeta. He captained the 1959 and 1960 Rose Bowl teams and is one of two players (Tom Wand in 1911–12) in UW football history to win the Guy Flaherty award as the team's most inspirational player twice (not even Guy Flaherty won twice).

97. Jack Thompson. "Throwin' Samoan" from Seattle's Evergreen High established numerous passing records during his WSU career (1976–78), including an NCAA record 7,818 yards, and is one of only two players in school history to have his number (14) retired.

96. Sonny Sixkiller. Native American from Oregon revived a moribund UW football program between 1970–73 when he established 15 school passing records, landed on the cover of *Sports Illustrated* (October 4, 1971), and remains one of the most popular players in school history.

95. Rebecca Twigg. Seattle's most decorated cyclist: six world and 15 national titles in individual pursuit, plus two Olympic medals (silver in the 1984 road race in Los Angeles, bronze in the 1992 pursuit in Barcelona).

94. Alvin Davis. AL Rookie of the Year and an All-Star in 1984, "Mr. Mariner" brought respect to a franchise during an eight-year span (1984–91) that ranks among its darkest periods. He hit 29 home runs in 1987 and batted .305 in 1989.

93. Steve Hawes. A star at Mercer Island High and an All-America pick at UW (1971–72), Hawes spent 10 productive seasons in the NBA with the Rockets, Trail Blazers and Sonics, retiring in 1984 after scoring 5,768 points.

92. Brad Walker. Despite his flameout in the Beijing Olympics when he no-heighted as the favorite to win the pole vault (a mechanical problem with the vault standard caused several athletes to no-height), Walker remains one of the most successful track and field athletes in state history. He set an American record of 19-9¾ at the Prefontaine Classic in June of 2008, won gold at the 2007 IAAF World Championships (19-2½) and 2007 U.S. Track and Field Championships (18-8¾), and is just one of 15 men in history to make the "Six Meter Club," an organization reserved for vaulters who cleared 19-8¼.

91. Joe Steele. Prep sensation at Blanchet and an honorable mention All-America, Steele ended his career (1976–79) as Washington's single-season (1,111 yards) and all-time leading rusher (3,091 yards), breaking Hugh McElhenny records that stood for 28 years.

90. Anna (Mickelson) Cummins and Mary Whipple. University of Washington graduates won a gold medal in eight at the 2008 Olympic Games in Beijing to become the first state women to win rowing medals in two Olympics. They also won a silver in eight in Athens in 2004. In their nine years together, at Washington and on the U.S. National Team, Cummins (No. 5 seat) and Whipple (cox) won numerous national and international races, including gold medals at the 2006 and 2007 World Rowing Championships.

89. Dave Krieg. "Mudbone" spent 12 years with the Seahawks, becoming the franchise's all-time leader in 31 career, season and single-game passing categories. A three-time Pro Bowler (1984, 1988–89), Krieg directed the Seahawks to the AFC Championship game in 1983 and to a 12–4 season in 1984.

88. Rueben Mayes. A 2008 College Football Hall of Fame inductee, Mayes, a native of Saskatchewan, set single season (1,632 yards) and career (3,519) rushing records while playing for Washington State from 1982–85. Selected by New Orleans in the third round of the 1986 NFL Draft, Mayes was the NFL's Offensive Rookie of the Year in 1986.

87. Jason Terry. A 1995 graduate of Franklin High, which he led to consecutive state championships, Terry became Pac-10 Player of the Year in 1999 at Arizona and the No. 10 overall choice in the NBA draft by the Atlanta Hawks, with whom he played his first five seasons before moving to the Dallas Mavericks.

86. Reggie Williams. A consensus All-America from Tacoma's Lakes High, the former UW receiver (2001–03) obliterated Husky records for career receptions (243) and yards (3,598). His 2002–03 combined marks of 183 catches and 2,563 yards remain the best two-year total in Pac-10 history.

85. Gerry Lindgren. Pint-size runner from Spokane's Rogers High gained national attention during his senior year (1964) when he ran 5,000 meters in 13:44.0, setting a U.S. high school record that lasted more than 40 years. Lindgren gained international acclaim when the 17-year-old defeated the heavily favored Russians in the 10,000 meters at the USA-USSR Track and Field meet at Los Angeles. Lindgren subsequently starred at WSU, where he won 11 NCAA indoor and outdoor championships.

84. Arnie Weinmeister. A two-way tackle, fullback and end during his career at the UW (1941–42, 1946), Weinmeister played six seasons in the NFL, earning All-Pro honors four times (1950–53) with the New York Giants. Inducted into the Pro Football Hall of Fame in 1984.

83. Gretchen Fraser. A Tacoma native and University of Puget Sound product, Fraser in 1948 became the first American skier to win a gold medal in the Olympics when she captured the slalom at St. Moritz. Inducted into the National Skiing Hall of Fame in 1960.

82. Lincoln Kennedy. The main operative on an offensive line that helped Washington average 387 rushing yards per game in 1992, the Husky tackle earned unanimous All-America honors and was a finalist for the Lombardi Award. The San Diego native had an 11-year NFL career that included three Pro Bowl selections.

81. Benji Olson. The first two-time All-America offensive lineman in UW history (1996–97), Olson as a sophomore helped spring Corey Dillon for 1,555 yards and 22 TDs. As a junior, he anchored a Husky line that allowed the fewest sacks in the Pac-10. The Bremerton native had a 10-year NFL career, all with Tennessee, where he started 140 of 152 games, and played in the 2000 Super Bowl.

80. Reggie Rogers. Played forward on two of Marv Harshman's Pac-10 basketball title teams at Washington, then switched to football and became the Pac-10's top defensive player (Morris Trophy winner, 1986). In his final season, he anchored a UW defense that allowed 88.9 yards rushing yards per game. The Detroit Lions made the native of Sacramento the No. 7 overall pick in the 1986 NFL draft.

79. Apolo Anton Ohno. Federal Way short-track speed skater won five medals, including two gold, at the 2002 and 2006 Winter Olympics, and 13 additional medals at various world championship competitions. He also won the reality TV show, *Dancing With The Stars*, in 2007.

78. Lauren Jackson. Australian import made eight WNBA All-Star teams, won MVP awards in 2002 and 2007, led the Storm to the 2004 title, and is the franchise's all-time leader in points, rebounds and blocked shots.

77. Chris Chandler. A two-time bowl MVP, Chandler threw 32 TD passes during three seasons with the Huskies (1983–86) before embarking on a 17-year career in the NFL in which the Everett native became the only quarterback in history to start for eight teams, including the Atlanta Falcons, whom he quarterbacked to the Super Bowl in 1998.

76. Ron Santo. A Franklin High graduate and a onetime Sicks' Stadium ballboy, Santo spent most his major league career with the Chicago Cubs. A National League All-Star nine times, Santo won five consecutive Gold Gloves at third base from 1964–68, and hit 342 home runs.

75. Jacob Green. The NFL's third-most productive sack artist during his Seahawks tenure (1980–91), trailing only Lawrence Taylor and Reggie White, Green made the Pro Bowl twice (1986–87), played the third-most games (218), had the second-most starts (176), and most sacks (116) in franchise history.

74. James Edwards. The seven-foot-one center won a state championship at Roosevelt (1973), became an All-America at the UW in 1976 and earned three NBA championship rings in a 21-year pro career.

73. Ahmad Rashad. Known as Bobby Moore when he prepped at Tacoma's Mount Tahoma High, Rashad developed into an incredibly versatile athlete. He was All-State in football and basketball in high school and set a state record in the high jump. At the University of Oregon, he made All-Pac-8 (forerunner of the Pac-10) as both a runner and a receiver. During his 10-year NFL career with the Cardinals, Bills, Seahawks and Vikings, he made All-Pro five times. Rashad entered the College Football Hall of Fame in 2007.

72. Pete Rademacher. The only man to fight for the world heavyweight title (lost to Floyd Patterson) in his first pro bout, Rademacher, who grew up near Yakima, started his athletic career as a football player at WSU, went on win the light heavyweight gold medal at the 1956 Olympics, and later fought Zora Foley, George Chuvalo and Archie Moore, compiling a record of 15–7–1 with eight knockouts.

71. Anne Sander. One of the two greatest women golfers to come out of the Northwest along with JoAnne Carner, Sander was U.S. Amateur champion in 1958, 1961 and 1963, an eight-time member of the Curtis Cup team and British Amateur champion in 1980.

70. Lawyer Milloy. A 1995 All-America, Milloy that year became the first UW defensive back to lead the team in tackles in back-to-back seasons. A graduate of Tacoma's Lincoln High, Milloy had a 12-year NFL career with three teams that included four Pro Bowls and a Super Bowl win with the New England Patriots.

69. Al Hostak. A tough kid who grew up in Seattle's Georgetown neighborhood, he won the world middleweight title in 1938, lost it, and won it again in 1939. Hostak had 63 wins—42 by KO—against nine losses and 12 draws. In 2003, *Ring Magazine* named Hostak to its list of "The 100 Greatest Punchers of All Time."

68. Jay Buhner. He mashed more than 300 home runs during his Mariners career (1987–01), played Gold Glove-caliber defense, and was at the heart of the 1995 team that rallied from 13 games down in August to make the playoffs for the first time.

67. Todd MacCulloch. A three-time NCAA field-goal percentage leader (1996–99), the seven-footer and native of Winnipeg averaged 19 points and 12 rebounds his senior year at Washington. He scored 1,743 career points, a total exceeded only by Chris Welp (1984–87) and Bob Houbregs (1951–53). He played four years in the NBA.

66. Jack Medica. Seattle native won nine national collegiate championships and set 11 world records during his four years at the UW (1933–36). At the 1936 Olympics in Berlin, Medica won gold in the 400 meters and silver in the 1,500.

65. Fred Brown. "Downtown" played more games (963), scored more points (14,018) and had more steals (1,149) than any player in Sonics history. He delivered a team-record 58 points against Golden State on March 23, 1974, and captained the 1978–79 world champions.

64. Debbie Armstrong. A star at Garfield High in basketball and soccer (1976–80), Armstrong became a world-class skier. In 1984 at Sarajevo, Yugoslavia, Armstrong became the first U.S. woman to win Olympic gold in the giant slalom.

63. Nate Robinson. A star at Rainier Beach High (3A player of the year in football and basketball; state record holder in the 110 high hurdles), Robinson played a season at cornerback for the UW football team. He switched to basketball, becoming an Associated Press All-America in 2005 while leading the Huskies to the NCAA Tournament. A first-round pick of the Phoenix Suns in the 2005 NBA draft, he won the 2006 NBA dunk contest.

62. Earl Averill. The "Earl of Snohomish" hit .318 in 13 seasons with the Cleveland Indians, Detroit Tigers and Boston Braves (1929–41), was a six-time All-Star, and enjoyed his best year in 1936 when he hit .378 with 28 home runs and 126 RBIs. Inducted into the Baseball Hall of Fame in 1975.

61. Marques Tuiasosopo. The 2000 Pac-10 Offensive Player of the Year and 2001 Rose Bowl MVP, Tuiasosopo set a UW career record for total offense between 1997–00 while becoming one of the most popular quarterbacks in Husky history. In 1999, against Stanford, Tuiasosopo, of Woodinville, became the only player in college history to rush for 200 yards and pass for 300 in the same game.

60. Scott Nielson. British Columbia weight man took part in 40 competitions while at the UW (1976–79) and never lost. Nielson won seven NCAA titles in the hammer and 35-pound weight throw. His four hammer titles in a row enabled him to join Steve Prefontaine as the only collegians to win four national championships in the same event.

59. Tom Gorman. The Seattle Prep/Seattle U. alum climbed as high as No. 10 on the ATP rankings (May 1, 1974), reached the semifinal rounds in singles at Wimbledon (1971), the U.S. Open (1972) and French Open (1973), and was a member of the winning U.S. Davis Cup team (1972).

58. Charlie Greene. An outstanding sprinter at O'Dea High (9.5 seconds for 100 yards in 1963), Greene became a six-time NCAA champion at the University of Nebraska and a world record holder at both 100 yards and 100 meters, setting the mark in the latter by running 9.90 on June 20, 1968. At the 1968 Mexico City Olympics, Greene won a bronze in the 100 and led the U.S. 4x100 relay team to a world record and gold medal.

57. Lenny Wilkens. Hall of Famer spent four (1968–72) years with the Sonics as a player and player-coach, making three All-Star teams and winning the MVP award at the 1971 All-Star Game. Following a controversial trade to Cleveland in 1972, Wilkens returned to Seattle six years later and coached the club to back-to-back appearances in the NBA Finals and its only NBA championship (1979).

56. Napoleon Kaufman. Kaufman, from Lompoc, CA, is the only runner in UW history with three 1,000-yard seasons (high of 1,480 in 1994), and the only one with four 200-yard games, topped by a 254-yard dazzler against San Jose State in 1994. Kaufman played six years in the NFL with the Oakland Raiders, averaging 4.9 yards per carry.

55. Don Heinrich. A two-time (1950, 1952) All-America quarterback at the UW, Heinrich teamed with Hugh McElhenny to form one of the greatest backfields in Husky history. He twice led the NCAA in passing and was inducted into the College Football Hall of Fame in 1987.

54. Joyce Walker. A graduate of Garfield High, where as a senior in 1980 she averaged 35 points per game, Walker became a two-time All-America and at Louisiana State, leading her Lady Tiger teams in scoring all four seasons. After playing professionally in Italy and Germany, Walker became the third woman to play for the Harlem Globetrotters, following Lynette Woodward and Jackie White.

53. Rick Redman. A two-time All-America guard/linebacker at the UW (1963–64), Redman had a nine-year pro career with the San Diego Chargers and earned induction into the College Football Hall of Fame in 1995.

52. Chip Hanauer. Winner of seven unlimited hydroplane season championships and the APBA Gold Cup a record 12 times, Hanauer posted 61 victories in 15 seasons while winning 37.6 percent of his races, the highest in unlimited history. In 1995, Hanauer became the youngest individual inducted into the Motorsports Hall of Fame.

51. Mark Rypien. After starring at Shadle Park High in Spokane, Rypien threw for 4,573 yards and 28 TDs during his WSU career (1981–85), then went on to play for six NFL teams. His best season was 1991, when he led the Redskins to victory in Super Bowl XXVII and was named Most Valuable Player.

50. Kaye Hall (Greff). The Wilson High (Tacoma) product set six world records during her swimming career, which she capped by winning two gold medals and a bronze at the 1968 Olympic Games. Hall entered the International Swimming Hall of Fame in 1979.

49. Mark Langston. As a Mariners rookie in 1984, the California native went 17–10 and finished second to teammate Alvin Davis in the Rookie of the Year voting. He led the American League in strikeouts three times (1984, 1986, 1987) and won a pair of Gold Gloves in a 16-year career that included 179 wins and four All-Star games.

48. Terry Metcalf. A star at Franklin High, Metcalf played at Long Beach State before becoming a three-time All-Pro running back for the St. Louis Cardinals (1974, 1975, 1977). Metcalf scored 33 TDs in his 81-game NFL career.

47. Matt Hasselbeck. The highest-rated passer in franchise history, Hasselbeck joined the Seahawks via a trade with Green Bay and quarterbacked the club to five consecutive playoff appearances, including the Super Bowl between 2003–07, a span in which he made three Pro Bowl appearances.

46. Tom Sneva. Sneva, of Spokane, became the first man to qualify for the Indy 500 at more than 200 mph, a feat he achieved in 1977, and the first to qualify at more than 210, a mark he reached in 1983, the year he became the only Washington native to win the world's most prestigious auto race.

45. John Olerud. A Bellevue native and a graduate of WSU, where he was a consensus All-America, Olerud went directly to the majors in 1989 and enjoyed a 17-year career with the Blue Jays, Mets, Mariners, Yankees and Red Sox. The AL batting champion in 1993 (.363), Olerud played for the Mariners from 2000–04, winning three Gold Gloves (2000–03), and earning an All-Star appearance in 2001.

44. Mark Brunell. A one-time owner of five Rose Bowl passing records and a member of UW's 1991 national championship team, Brunell threw for 4,008 yards and 28 touchdowns in his career (1989–92) with the Huskies. MVP of Washington's 46-34 win over Iowa in the 1991 Rose Bowl, Brunell threw for more than 31,000 yards and 180 TDs in 13 NFL seasons with Green Bay, Jacksonville and Washington.

43. Mac Wilkins. A product of Clover Park High (Tacoma), Wilkins won Olympic gold in the discus in 1976 and silver in 1984, was an eight-time national champion in the event and the 1977 national champion in the shot put. Upon his induction into the U.S. Track and Field Hall of Fame in 1993, he held the world's top combined results for the discus, shot put, javelin and hammer throw.

42. Ray Allen. Acquired in a February 2003, trade for Gary Payton, Allen proved to be one of the greatest shooters in Sonics history. Between 2003–07, he averaged 24.5 points per game and achieved a single-game high of 54 on January 12, 2007 against the Utah Jazz.

41. Bob Schloredt. He began the 1959 Husky football season as a reserve and finished his career two years later as a two-time All-America quarterback, a two-time Rose Bowl MVP and a *Sports Illustrated* cover boy (October 3, 1960). Schloredt entered the College Football Hall of Fame in 1989 and the Rose Bowl Hall of Fame in 1991.

40. Ted Garhart. Between 1939–42, the stroke of the Washington crew never lost a race, a feat unmatched in the 100-plus-year history of the Husky rowing program. The Garfield High alum stroked the UW to IRA national championships in 1940–41 and made the World Rowing Hall of Fame in 1972.

39. Jamie Moyer. The July 1996 trade that sent OF Darren Bragg to Boston for Moyer proved one of the Mariners' biggest heists. A 22-year MLB veteran, Moyer won more games (145) than any pitcher in franchise history and twice won 20 (20 in 2001, 21 in 2003), making him the only pitcher in club annals to accomplish that feat.

38. Detlef Schrempf. The German-born Schrempf, who went to high school in Centralia, became an All-America at the UW, where he led the Huskies to back-to-back Pac-10 titles in 1984 and 1985, then embarked upon a 16-year pro career with the Mavericks, Pacers, Sonics and Trail Blazers. Schrempf won two Sixth Man of the Year awards and was a three-time All-Star.

37. JoAnne Carner. A Kirkland native, Carner won three different U.S. Golf Association championship events, the USGA Junior Girls (1956), U.S. Women's Amateur (five wins between 1956–68) and U.S. Women's Open (1971, 1976). The LPGA Player of the Year in 1974, 1981 and 1982, Carner was inducted into the World Golf Hall of Fame in 1982.

36. Guyle Fielder. Starting in 1953–54, "Golden Guyle" spent 15 seasons in a Seattle uniform, including 11 with the Totems, whom he led to three Western Hockey League titles and five WHL finals. Fielder led the league in scoring seven times and was an 11-time All-Star and six-time MVP.

35. Corey Dillon. The Franklin High graduate played only one season at the UW (1996), but posted the greatest year of any UW running back—1,555 yards and 22 TDs, including an NCAA record 222 yards and four TDs in the first quarter against San Jose State. Dillon spent seven years with the Cincinnati Bengals and three with New England Patriots, amassing 11,241 yards and 89 TDs.

34. Shawn Kemp. The Reign Man made five All-Star teams during his Sonics tenure (1989–97), and in 1996 averaged 19.6 points and 11.4 rebounds, when the club won 64 games and reached the NBA Finals. The Indiana native averaged at least 15 points per game seven times and double figures in rebounding six times.

33. Brandon Roy. Pac-10 Player of the Year and a first-team All-America in 2005–06, Roy, a Garfield High grad, was second in the conference in scoring (20.2), third in field goal percentage (.508) and fourth in assists, leading UW to the NCAA tournament. After finishing his career as Washington's 10th all-time leading scorer (1,477 points), Roy was named NBA Rookie of the Year following his first season with Portland.

32. Curt Warner. The Seahawks' first-round selection from Penn State in the 1983 NFL draft, Warner topped the AFC in rushing as a rookie (1,449) and went on to amass 6,705 yards, 55 TDs and 23 100-yard rushing games during his six seasons (missed all of 1984 with a knee injury). He made the Pro Bowl three times (1983, 1986, 87).

31. Drew Bledsoe. An All-America quarterback at WSU (1990–92), where he threw for more than 7,000 yards and 33 TDs, Bledsoe was the first pick in the 1993 NFL draft (New England Patriots). During his pro career with the Patriots, Bills and Cowboys, Bledsoe earned four Pro Bowl invitations and threw 251 TD passes.

30. Warren Moon. The 1977 Co-Pac-8 Player of the Year and 1978 Rose Bowl MVP led the Edmonton Eskimos to five consecutive Grey Cup titles after leaving the UW. The Los Angeles product became one of the most accomplished passers in NFL history, throwing for 49,325 yards and 291 TDs in a 17-year career that included nine Pro Bowl appearances. Moon entered the Rose Bowl Hall of Fame in 1997 and the Pro Football Hall of Fame in 2006.

29. Cortez Kennedy. Selected third overall out of Miami by the Seahawks in the 1990 draft, "Tez" played 167 games in his 12-year Seattle career, was All-Pro five times, made seven Pro Bowls and, in 1992, following a 14-sack season, was named NFL Defensive Player of the Year while playing on a last-place team (2–14).

28. Doris Brown (Heritage). The Seattle Pacific middle-distance runner by way of Peninsula High won five world cross country championships between 1967–72, made Olympic teams in 1968 and 1972, set world records at 3,000 meters and two miles (1971) and finished her career with 14 national titles. She is a member of the USA Track and Field Hall of Fame (1990) and Distance Running Hall of Fame (2002).

27. Shaun Alexander. Selected from Alabama with the 19th overall pick in the 2000 NFL draft, Alexander scored 112 regular season and postseason TDs in seven seasons with the Seahawks, including a league-record (since broken) 28 in 2005 when he was MVP.

26. Jack Sikma. Drafted eighth overall by the Sonics in 1977 out of Illinois Wesleyan, the six-foot-eleven Sikma made the NBA's All-Rookie team in 1977–78 and seven consecutive All-Star teams from 1979 through 1985. When the Sonics traded Sikma to Milwaukee in 1986, he ranked as the franchise leader in rebounds (7,729), blocked shots (704) and free throws made (3,044).

25. Fred Couples. The O'Dea High graduate accumulated 15 PGA Tour victories, highlighted by his triumph in the 1992 Masters and two wins in the Players Championship (1984, 1996). Named PGA Tour Player of the Year twice (1991–92), Couples played on five Ryder Cup teams (1989, 1991, 1993, 1995,1997) and won the Skins Game five times, earning more than $4.2 million and the title "King of the Silly Season."

24. Johnny O'Brien. O'Brien burst into prominence in 1952, when he led the Seattle University Chieftains to a stunning 84–81 victory over the then-serious Harlem Globetrotters. SU's upset received such publicity that the Chieftains were invited to play in the NCAA tournament in 1953, a year in which O'Brien and twin brother, Eddie, were selected All-Americans. Despite standing five-foot-nine, O'Brien in 1953 not only became the first NCAA player to score 1,000 points in a season, he also made his major league baseball debut, playing the first of six seasons with the Pirates, Cardinals and Braves.

23. Bob Houbregs. The only consensus All-America choice in UW basketball history, The Queen Anne High grad led the Huskies to their first Final Four appearance in 1953, when he was NCAA Player of the Year. Still the holder of 10 school scoring records, the six-foot-seven Houbregs earned induction into the Basketball Hall of Fame in 1987.

22. Gary Stevens. After winning a string of riding titles at Longacres in the early 1980s, Stevens moved to Southern California, where the Idaho native became one of the greatest jockeys in the world. He won 15 riding titles at Santa Anita, Hollywood Park and Del Mar, eight Triple Crown races (three Kentucky Derbys), eight Breeders Cup races and 15 other races worth more than $1 million. He entered the Thoroughbred Racing Hall of Fame in 1997.

21. Ryne Sandberg. A three-sport standout at North Central High in Spokane, Sandberg was recruited to WSU as a quarterback, but elected to sign with the Chicago Cubs. During a 16-year career, Sandberg appeared in 10 All-Star games, won the 1984 National League MVP award, earned nine Gold Gloves, and finished his career with 277 home runs, most by an NL second baseman.

20. Mel Hein. A 1930 WSU All-America, Hein played 15 seasons for the New York Giants, during which he became the NFL's first-ever MVP (1938)—while playing center. Hein was part of the first class inductees into the Pro Football Hall of Fame in 1963.

19. George Wilson. Wilson led the Huskies to their first two Rose Bowl appearances in 1923 and 1925 and was named by Grantland Rice to the 1925 All-America backfield along with Red Grange of Illinois and Ernie Nevers of Stanford. In 1928, Wilson became the first former UW player to lead an NFL team to a championship (Providence Steamrollers). Elected to the College Football Hall of Fame in 1951 and the Rose Bowl Hall of Fame in 1991.

18. Gus Williams. A two-time NBA All-Star (1982–83), "The Wizard" had a remarkable six-year run with the Sonics, averaging 20.2 points per game. In Seattle's 4–1 championship series victory over the Washington Bullets in 1979, Williams averaged 26.6 points when the Sonics won their only NBA title.

17. Edgar Martinez. Martinez spent his entire 18-year career with the Mariners, retiring in 2004 as the most respected player in franchise history. He won two American League batting titles (1992, 1995), five Silver Slugger awards and made seven AL All-Star teams. On the occasion of his retirement, Major League Baseball renamed the Designated Hitter of the Year award the "Edgar Martinez Award."

16. John Stockton. The Gonzaga Prep/Gonzaga University grad played 18 years for the Utah Jazz, during which he established NBA records for career assists (15,806) and steals (3,265). He appeared in 10 All-Star Games, won Olympic gold medals in 1992 and 1996, and was named one of the 50 Greatest Players in NBA history in 1996.

15. Kenny Easley. A five-time Pro Bowler and the 1984 NFL Defensive Player of the Year, Easley failed to make the Pro Football Hall of Fame only because a failed kidney limited his career to seven seasons. The former UCLA star was this good: In the 1984 Pro Bowl, Easley, normally a strong safety, switched to cornerback in the second quarter. None of the three NFC receivers he covered, James Lofton, Art Monk and Roy Green, caught a pass. "That guy was a stud," Raiders TE Todd Christiansen told reporters after the game.

14. Phil Mahre. Selected international skier of the year three times and U.S. skier of the year five times, the Yakima native won three World Cup overall titles from 1981–83 and capped his career with a gold medal in the slalom at the 1984 Sarajevo Olympic Games. Mahre entered the U.S. Olympic Hall of Fame in 1992.

13. Helene Madison. During a 16-month stretch in 1930–31, the Seattle native broke 16 world swimming records at distances from 100 yards to one mile. At the 1932 Olympics, the 19-year-old Madison won gold medals in the 100 and 400 freestyle and anchored the gold medal 4x100 freestyle relay team. Inducted into the U.S. Olympic Hall of Fame in 1992, "Queen Helene" set 117 U.S. and world records during her career.

12. Elgin Baylor. Baylor played two years at Seattle University (1956–57, 1957–58) and put up numbers that today look like misprints: 29.7 points, 20.3 rebounds in 1956–57 and 32.5 and 19.3 in 1957–58. Although Seattle U. finished the 1958 season ranked 18th in the *Associated Press* poll, the Washington, D.C., product led the Chieftains to the NCAA championship game, where they lost to Kentucky 84–72. In five tournament games, Baylor averaged 27 points and was named Most Outstanding Player of the Final Four.

11. Alex Rodriguez. Rodriguez had an indelible impact on the Mariners despite playing for the club for just six years. The Miami native made the AL All-Star team four times, led the league in batting in 1996 (.358) and hit more than 40 home runs for three consecutive years (1998–00). The youngest position player (18) in club history and the youngest shortstop in All-Star history, Rodriguez ranks in the top five in every major offensive category in Mariners history.

10. Michelle Akers. A three-time All-America at Shorecrest High and a four-time All-America at Central Florida, Akers' major soccer success came at the international level. She played for the first-ever U.S. women's national team in 1985, dominated the 1991 women's World Cup in China (scored 10 goals), and was part of the USA's gold medal-winning team at the 1996 Olympic Games. FIFA named her its Female Player of the Century in 2002, and she entered the National Soccer Hall of Fame in 2004.

9. Spencer Haywood. The five years that Haywood spent with the Sonics—1970–71 through 1974–75—represented the most productive period of his pro basketball career. The Detroit native made four NBA All-Star teams, two All-NBA First Teams and two All-NBA Second Teams while averaging more than 23 points and 13 rebounds per game.

8. Walter Jones. One of Seattle's two first-round draft choices in 1997 (sixth pick overall), the Hall of Famer-in-waiting became the first Seahawks offensive lineman to play in the Pro Bowl (1999), and went on to earn eight additional selections and three All-Pro awards. In his prime he was the best offensive lineman in the game

7. Ichiro Suzuki. The first MLB position player from Japan and an All-Star since his arrival from the Orix Blue Wave in 2001, Ichiro parlayed the simple single into a Hall of Fame-caliber resume: AL MVP and Rookie of the Year in 2001, batting titles in 2001 and 2004, annual Gold Gloves, annual 200-plus hit seasons, All-Star Game MVP (2007), and DVD full of highlight-reel catches.

6. Hugh McElhenny. A college and pro Hall of Famer, "The King" remains the most celebrated running back in UW history. His 233 points are the most by a non-kicker, and his 125 in 1951 stood as a school record for 45 years. His 296 yards and five TDs against Washington State in the 1950 Apple Cup have never been seriously threatened. Named to the Pro Bowl five times during his NFL career, McElhenny, a Los Angeles product, is the only UW player with three 90-yard scoring plays (100-yard punt return against USC in 1951, a 94-yard kickoff return against Minnesota in 1949, and a 91-yard run against Kansas State in 1950).

5. Randy Johnson. The Big Unit came to Seattle as a throw-in a trade that sent staff ace Mark Langston to Montreal, and turned into the best pitcher in Mariners history. He made five All-Star teams, won the 1995 Cy Young Award, threw a no-hitter (June 2, 1990), and led the AL in strikeouts five times. What the Mariners didn't know when they swapped him to Houston in mid-1998 was that he was about to embark upon the best stretch of his career.

4. Steve Emtman. Winner of the Outland Trophy and Lombardi Award as a junior, Emtman was one of only nine players in college football history to win both in the same season. The anchor of a 1991 defense that allowed a myopic 67.1 yards and 9.2 points per game, Emtman finished fourth in Heisman Trophy voting, and is the only player in UW history to be selected No. 1 overall in the NFL draft. Emtman entered the College Football Hall of Fame and Rose Bowl Hall of Fame in 2006.

3. Gary Payton. The best—and most competitive—player in Sonics history spent 12 seasons in Seattle, earning eight All-Star and two first-team All-NBA (1998, 2000) selections. The Glove, from Oakland via Oregon State, made the All-Defensive First Team a record nine times, was Defensive Player of the Year in 1996 and led the Sonics to the 1996 Finals opposite Michael Jordan's Chicago Bulls. Payton also played for the gold-medal winning 1996 and 2000 U.S. Olympic teams.

2. Steve Largent. The only player in Seahawks history inducted into the Pro Football Hall of Fame (1995), Largent retired from the NFL in 1989 holding the pass receiver's triple crown: his 819 receptions ranked No. 1 in pro history, as did his 13,089 yards and 100 TD catches (all since eclipsed). In his 13 years with the Seahawks, the Oklahoma native earned seven Pro Bowl berths.

1. Ken Griffey Jr. 10-time All-Star, 10-time Gold Glove winner and the 1997 unanimous AL MVP, Griffey is the most significant player in Seattle sports history. Not merely because of the 398 home runs or the numerous spectacular catches, Griffey was the Mariners' first big gate attraction, first superstar, first annual All-Star starter, most forceful personality and the biggest reason the franchise was able to escape its dubious history to become a Northwest summer-entertainment fixture and one of the most successful business operations in pro sports. Griffey hit the late August home run that launched the Mariners on their remarkable comeback run in 1995, scored the run that beat the Yankees in the 1995 ALDS and, in 1999, was named one of the 100 greatest players of the 20th century as well as the player of the decade for the 1990s.

Index